A COMPANION TO THE SPIRITUAL EXERCISES OF SAINT IGNATIUS

BY

ALOYSIUS AMBRUZZI, S. J.

WITH A FOREWORD BY
HIS EMINENCE CARDINAL LÉPICIER

IMPRIMI POTEST :

A. Coelho, S. J.,
Sup. Reg. Miss.

Calicut, die 18 Maii, 1928.

IMPRIMATUR :

✠ **Valerianus,**
Episcopus Mangalorensis.

Mangalore, die 19 Maii, 1928.

Reprinted from the First Edition

Printed by J. J. Rego at the Codialbail Press, Mangalore, S. K.—1934.

A COMPANION TO THE SPIRITUAL EXERCISES OF SAINT IGNATIUS

SANCTO PATRI IGNATIO

ANNO QUINQUAGESIMO

AB ADVENTU SOCIETATIS IESU

IN MISSIONEM MANGALORENSEM

FOREWORD

The Spiritual Exercises of St Ignatius have for so long a time held a foremost place in the rich treasure-house of the Catholic Church; they have been for so many generations a source of inspiration and strength to men of good will, that I feel that it is unnecessary for me to offer my words of praise of so great a book.

All I venture to do is to urge every one who has not yet realized the great beauty and the profound importance of *The Exercises,* to study them with care, in the firm conviction that such a study will be rewarded a hundredfold by a clearer understanding of the truths of our holy Faith and a deeper insight into the beauty of the Spiritual Life.

The present book, which contains and fully develops all the Meditations and contemplations of St Ignatius, will prove of great help to those who want to study *The Exercises,* and, most of all, to those who want to make them. Along with the Commentary published by the same author, it forms one of the best works published in English on the subject, and better than many other books of the kind, it places the true Spiritual Exercises of St Ignatius within reach of every soul of good will. Pictures illustrating each of the Contemplations on the Life, Passion and Resurrection of our Lord, and numerous apt quotations add charm to this already delightful *Companion to the Spiritual Exercises of St Ignatius.*

Rome, the Lateran,

Feast of the Sacred Heart, 1928.

Alexis Henry M. Cardinal Lépicier O.S.M.

AUTHOR'S NOTE

The title, *A Companion to the Spiritual Exercises of St Ignatius*, sufficiently indicates the object of the present book. It supplements the author's Commentary on the Exercises by developing the Meditations and Contemplations assigned by St Ignatius to the four Weeks into which they are divided. To these there have been only added a few Meditations in the First Week, as implicity allowed by the Saint, and one on the Glory of Heaven. To make the book self-contained, as far as possible, it was thought desirable to include Exercises on the Foundation, the Kingdom of Christ, and others, which the author had already treated at length in his Commentary. References to this Commentary, whenever made, will be found at the head of the Meditation. The Appendices will prove serviceable, especially in private Retreats.

It is the author's earnest prayer that these pages may imbue souls with the generous spirit of St Ignatius—enthusiastic love for, and whole-hearted devotion to Christ, the Divine King. The pictures illustrating the Mysteries of His Life, Passion and Resurrection will help to it. The idea of such pictures in a Retreat-book is not a new one. St Ignatius himself found out that they could profitably be a substitute for the usual 'Composition of place,' and accordingly ordered Fr Jerome Nadal to have a series of them prepared. The verses and other appropriate passages which have been interspersed, so far as space allowed it, will be appreciated by readers who love to see the useful blended with the agreeable.

The author thanks all those who have helped him to prepare this book and to get it through the Press; and, most of all, His Eminence Cardinal Lépicier for the appreciative Foreword with which in his great kindness, he has deigned to sponsor it.

St Aloysius' College,
Mangalore.
31 July, 1928.

CONTENTS

APPENDICES

CONSIDERATIONS—

Illustrations

A COMPANION TO THE SPIRITUAL EXERCISES

INTRODUCTION

[*The Spiritual Exercises*, pp. 1-10]

1. Importance of the Spiritual Exercises

"All the methods of preparing and disposing one's soul to free itself from all inordinate affections, and after it has freed itself from them to seek and find the Will of God concerning the ordering of one's life with a view to the salvation of one's soul, are called Spiritual Exercises." Thus says St. Ignatius in the first of the twenty Annotations for obtaining some knowledge of the Spiritual Exercises.

We save our soul, i. e., we secure life everlasting, by submitting ourselves in everything to God's Holy Will. The Spiritual Exercises are a school where we learn the best means to remove, or at least to control, those of our affections that are not in harmony with that Will, and by it to rule our life and all its circumstances.

Their importance, then, is evident. The highest interests are involved: the interests of our soul, of God's glory, and of other souls, because our deeds, good or bad, vibrate all around and influence our fellowmen.

2. Their Excellence

Even from a natural point of view, we cannot but set a high value on the Spiritual Exercises. St. Ignatius compares them to bodily exercises, such as walking, travelling on foot, or running, to bring out the fact that, as bodily exercises develop and perfect the organs of our body, Spiritual Exercises drill the faculties of our soul. They may be called an intensified course of spiritual training, and in particular of will-training. They lay open the weak and bad points in our character, and teach us that habit of self-control, which every man must acquire, if he is not to fall a prey to caprice and vice: *Spiritual Exercises to conquer oneself.* In other words, physical training gives us command over our body and its muscles; the Spiritual Exercises make us masters of our faculties, of our senses, and of our inclinations, for the service of God and the help of our fellowmen.

Still more. We live a divine life in Christ our Lord. In Him we are *nova creatura,* endowed with supernatural faculties and habits: the theological virtues whereby we are united to God, the moral virtues by which we are disposed to do what is right, and the gifts of the Holy Ghost by which we are disposed to become amenable to His inspirations. However, our evil inclinations and the influence of the world tend to weaken, if not to kill, the supernatural life in us. External occupations make heavy demands on the energy of our soul and often turn it away from God, at least for a time. We lose our bearings. We get rusty. Our very spiritual life tends to become a lifeless routine. Slowly and gradually, the world with its principles and its points of view asserts itself.

The Retreat, i. e., the time entirely set apart for the Spiritual Exercises, puts us in working order. We live again, for a few days, in an altogether spiritual atmosphere. We orientate ourselves. By frequently repeated acts, we strengthen our supernatural habits and accustom ourselves to do likewise after the Retreat.

3. The Retreat is God's Seed-time

God is the heavenly Husbandman. He is the Sower who plants in our souls divine seeds of virtue. He is the Cultivator that causes the rain to fall upon and vivify our souls, and the sun to shine upon them and to warm them, that they may become like gardens filled with all sweet-smelling and useful plants, with heavenly trees and flowers. He never ceases to work. The Retreat, however, is peculiarly His time: His seed-time. "Behold the sower went forth to sow." Helped by His grace, it is for us to prepare the ground for the seed.

4. The Divine Sower and the Soul's fourfold Attitude

According to our Lord, men offer a fourfold attitude to the activity of the Divine Sower.

"Behold the sower went forth to sow. And it came to pass that, as he sowed, some seed fell by the wayside, and the birds came and ate it up. And some fell upon rocky ground, where it had not much soil, and straightway it shot up because it had no depth of soil; and when the sun rose it was scorched, and because it had no root it withered. And some fell among thorns, and the thorns grew up and choked it, and it yielded no fruit. And other seed fell upon good soil, and it grew up and made increase and yielded fruit, and it bore thirtyfold, and sixtyfold, and a hundredfold."[1]

1. The wayside is the image of worldly souls. The seed of the Kingdom, i. e., the message of Christ, awakes no response in their hearts. It comes to them, as it were, in an unknown language. They hear its sound, but they do not grasp its inner meaning, or if they grasp it at all, they account it sheer foolishness. "As for those by the wayside, where the word is sown—when they have heard it, straightway cometh Satan, and taketh away the word sown in them."[2]

2. The stony ground stands for superficial, sentimental, and easy-going souls. They have neither strength nor character. In moments of fervour and enthusiasm, they seem ready for every great deed and trial, but at sight of the first difficulty they lose courage and like cowards leave the field. "When they have heard the word, straightway they receive it with joy, and they have no root in them, but last only for a time; then, when affliction or persecution cometh because of the word, straightway they are scandalized."[3]

3. The thorny ground typifies those souls who want to make the best of both this and the other world. Though not engaged in evidently sinful pursuits, they are wholly immersed in the things of

1. Mark iv, 3-8. 2. Mark iv, 15. 3. Mark iv, 16, 17.

this world, and are prompted by the desire to succeed at all costs. The divine seed falls in such souls, but it cannot grow. God's calls are unheeded, and His grace and gifts are neglected. "The cares of the world and the deceits of riches and cravings for other such things enter and choke the word, and it is unfruitful."[1]

4. The good soil is the image of those souls that are ready to receive the impression of the Divine Spirit—"they that hear the word and welcome it, and bear fruit, thirtyfold, and sixtyfold, and a hundredfold."[2]

Such souls not only hear and understand the message of Christ, but accept it with all their heart, and count as nothing the sacrifices it demands, like the man who having found a treasure in a field, hides it, and for the joy thereof goes and sells everything he has and buys that field; or like the merchant who, seeking good pearls, finds one of great price, sells all he has, and buys it. They live by Christ's message and bear fruits of eternal life.

5. Dispositions for a good Retreat

How can we prepare ourselves to remove the obstacles to God's work in our souls, and thus receive the seed of eternal life, and make it grow and bear abundant fruit?

We must, first of all, enter on our Retreat with a joyful heart. Some may look upon the Retreat as a sort of mitigated nuisance or, at least, as an unpleasant duty which must be gone through. They begin it with a feeling of sadness and coldness, or perhaps even of despondency. For them the sooner the Retreat is over, the better. Nothing is more unworthy than such a notion of the Retreat; nothing is more harmful to a soul than entertaining such feelings. The Retreat is a time of joy. It is a holiday of the soul. We withdraw from our usual occupations to live wholly with God, whose conversation has no bitterness. Joy, therefore, should be our predominant feeling, when about to begin the Spiritual Exercises: the joy of a boy leaving for a holiday with his dear ones. We are going to be with Jesus. During the year we are with Him, but so many are our distractions that we rarely taste the sweetness

1. Mark iv, 19. 2. Mark iv, 20.

of His presence. But now we shall be able to taste and see how sweet He is. And if sad thoughts arise in our soul, we should cry with the Priest preparing to ascend the Altar of God :—

"Why art thou sad, O my soul, and why dost thou disquiet me?

"Hope in God, for I will still praise Him, the salvation of my countenance, and my God."

Secondly, we must begin our Retreat wholeheartedly. This is what St Ignatius demands of the Exercitant in the fifth annotation :—

"It will much benefit him who is receiving the Exercises to enter upon them with a large heart and with liberality towards his Creator and Lord, offering all his desires and liberty to Him, in order that His Divine Majesty may make use of his person and of all he possesses according to His most Holy will."

We show our generosity and wholeheartedness :—

(*a*) By diligently observing the time-table and all the regulations of the Retreat. Jesus will pass by with His graces: may we always find ourselves on his way!

(*b*) By keeping perfect silence, i. e., silence of the senses, of the imagination, of the heart, and of the whole soul. It is the most essential requisite for a good Retreat. God speaks to the soul in solitude and in silence. "I will lure her into the wilderness and speak to her heart." *Fuge, tace, quiesce:* tear yourself from all distracting work; keep perfect silence; steep yourself in the meditation which is proposed to you.

(*c*) By performing seriously and thoroughly the various Exercises of the Retreat. We must not be content with listening attentively to the points of the meditation, but we must think over the matter, make it our own, and consider its bearing on our whole life.

(*d*) By refusing nothing that our Lord demands of us.

Thirdly, we must pray constantly and fervently. The Retreat is truly a time of prayer. We should come before our Lord with the faith of the blind man: "O Lord that I may see"; with the confidence of the leper; "If thou wilt, Thou canst make me clean"; with the love of Mary and Martha: "Lord, behold, he whom Thou lovest is sick"; with the humility of the Centurion: "Lord, my servant—my soul and body—lieth at home sick of the palsy and grievously tormented." And Jesus will say, as of old: "I will come and heal him." He will come into our soul and repeat: "This day is salvation come to this house . . . for the Son of Man is come to seek that which was lost."

Lord, with Your grace, I begin this holy Retreat in order to conquer myself. I wish to subject my rebellious will. I wish to bring back to order my ill-regulated affections, that my soul may be intent solely on seeking and finding Your Holy Will, and on following it in all the ways of my life.

Grant me a great heart, a heart truly generous which will give itself without reserve to You, my Lord and my Saviour.

O my God, dispose of my life, of my liberty, of whatever is in me and about me as you please. O my Creator, speak to Your creature. Behold my soul before You like unto a balance, which leans not to any side, unless You place on one side the weight of Your most Holy Will.

I promise You faithfulness to my exercises of piety and to the full time of meditation. It will be my task to exercise myself, to examine my soul and search its ways, and to call upon You, to listen to You, to obey You.

I promise You silence. Not only shall my lips be quiet, but my thoughts shall draw away from the care of other affairs, from the turmoil and the vanity of the world. I know that this interior and exterior solitude is highly meritorious before You. It will help me, moreover, to draw nearer to You, and not to lose any of Your sweet words. It will best prepare me to receive the gifts of Your divine and supreme Goodness.

SOLITUDE

There is in stillness oft a magic power
To calm the breast, when struggling passions lower;
Touch'd by its influence, in the soul arise.
Diviner feelings, kindred with the skies . . .
There is a Spirit singing aye in air,
That lifts us high above all mortal care.
No mortal measure swells that mystic sound.
No mortal minstrel breathes such tones around,—
The Angels' hymn,—the sovereign harmony
That guides the rolling orbs along the sky,—
And hence perchance the tales of saints who view'd
And heard Angelic choirs in solitude.

Newman.

PRINCIPLE AND FOUNDATION

GODWARDS, OR THE END OF MAN

[*The Spiritual Exercises*, pp. 34-5]

The first Prelude is to hear God say, on completing the work of material creation, "Let us make man to our image and likeness."[1]

The second Prelude is to ask for light that I may truly know my origin, the object of my life here and my eternal end hereafter, and for grace that I may direct all my thoughts, words, and actions to this end.

1. God our Creator

Life is a journey from sea to sea—from the sea of our nothingness to that of eternity—across the isthmus of this world. We are not playthings whirled about by unknown and unaccountable forces, or tiny lumps of matter crawling here and there in restless anxiety. We are immortal beings going back to God, the spring of our existence. The world is not a *wood, savage and rough and strong,* with no light to dispel the darkness and no path to guide our steps, but a place of probation and preparation, lit up all round by the eternal light of God.

An infinite Love has fashioned us and placed us in this world. The same Love constantly draws us to Himself through the manifold creatures which half reveal and half conceal Him, till, in Heaven, He makes our hearts throb in unison with His heart and thereby renders us wholly and eternally happy.

The Goodness of God is truly inexhaustible. First, He prepares man's dwelling. He creates light. He calls the earth into being and causes it to bring forth grass and fruit-bearing trees. He peoples it with every kind of creature. He gathers together the waters under the heavens into the vast expanse of the ocean. He sets lights in the firmament: the sun, the moon, and all the stars.

"And God saw that it was good." All has come out of His love, a love yearning to communicate itself. The Father has prepared a home for the child that is soon to make its appearance,

1. Gen. 1, 26.

The Bridegroom has built and adorned the bridal chamber against the nuptial morn.

Then, He creates man. He does not create him like the cattle and the beasts of the earth, nor like the mighty stars in the firmament. The whole Trinity seem to deliberate on this important step.

" And God saw that it was good. And He said, Let us make man to our image and likeness : and let him have dominion over the fishes of the sea, and the fowls of the air, and the beasts, and the whole earth, and every creeping creature that moveth upon the earth."[1]

He forms man's body of the slime of the earth, and into his heavenwards directed face He breathes the breath of life, an immortal soul, as truly a spirit as God Himself. Like God the soul is free from the laws of space and of time, and of all that is called matter. Its activity, like God's, is all intellect and will, its power is will-power, and its size is greatness of intellect. Like God it is incorruptible and immortal. The soul then is a strict likeness of God, and man can truly and rightly be said to have been created to the image of his Creator.

2. God our Father

God might have left the work of His hands in that state. Man would have loved God as his Creator and Master and, after death, he would have passed to the enjoyment of the happiness of which he was capable. But God's love knew no bounds. From the first moment He communicated to man a life which is a participation of His very life, and destined him to a state of happiness which he could neither claim nor merit by his efforts : the immediate vision of God. He raised him, and in him, all his descendants, to the level of the Divinity. He made him His son, by implanting in his heart a divine quality, a spark, as it were, of His Divine Nature, which has been called sanctifying grace.

3. The Goal of Man's Life

Eternal life, however, was to be a gift of God, and at the same time a reward and a crown of justice. God willed that man

1. Gen. ii, 25, 26.

should reach his end by his own acts. By making proper use of life and of the gifts which accompany life, he was to direct himself to God and prepare himself for that close union with Him which constitutes perfect happiness.

God gives everything to him: "Behold I have given you every herb bearing seed . . . and all trees . . . to be your meat."[1]

"And the Lord took man, and put him into the paradise of pleasure, to dress it and to keep it."[2]

To rule over the fishes of the sea, the fowls of the air and all living creatures that move upon the earth, and be subject in everything to the Will of his Creator and Father, was man's task in this life and the only way to reach eternal life.

4. Adoration, Praise, and Submission

In the very first pages of Holy Writ, God wants to impress deeply on us the rules and principles that are to direct our whole life.

1. God alone is *the one that is,* the Self-subsistent Being, Who has deigned to be our Creator: we are His creatures, entirely dependent on Him. That we be not like Satan, of whom our Lord said that "he stood not in the truth,"[3] we must constantly adore and revere our Creator and Lord, i. e., we must confess and acknowledge His absolute Being and our essential dependence on Him, interiorly by the sincere abasement of our soul, and exteriorly by the homage of our body.

2. God is our Heavenly Father Who, with infinite love and pity watches over us, His creatures, and never ceases to impart to us His gifts, however ungrateful and rebellious we be.

We owe Him an ever increasing debt of praise and thanksgiving.

"Bless the Lord, O my soul: O Lord, my God, Thou art exceedingly great."[4]

"What shall I render to the Lord, for all the things that He hath rendered to me?"[5]

3. God is the supreme Master and Lord: His will is the rule to which every one of His creatures must conform itself — most of all, intelligent creatures.

1. Gen. i, 29. 2. Gen. ii, 15. 3. John viii, 44. 4. Ps. ciii, 1. 5. Ps. cxv, 12.

"Of every tree of paradise thou shalt eat: but of the tree of knowledge of good and evil, thou shalt not eat. For in what day soever thou shalt eat of it, thou shalt die the death."[1]

"Human nature," says St Thomas Aquinas, "can never be perfected unless it be united to God." Helped by divine grace, it is in our power to achieve such union by submitting our intellect and our will to God's Reason and Law. By acting independently of God we inevitably bring about our own ruin.

Accordingly, absolute dependence on God, grateful acknowledgement of His loving kindness, and perfect submission to His Holy Will sum up the whole of religion and sanctity. Therein lies order, beauty, happiness, and Heaven itself.

E in la sua volontade è nostra pace.[2]

5. My Lord and my Father!

God's creative act is not a thing of the distant past. It is an eternal and ever present act, prompted, in some true sense, by the love God bears me. Every moment, accordingly, is a new creation. *Now* God creates and maintains the world for me. *Now* He creates and conserves me and gives me a share of His creatures for my use and for His service. *Now* He imparts to me His deifying grace. Must I not look upon myself and the whole world as beings that absolutely depend on God, and on myself, in particular, as the constant object of His infinite love and mercy? "Who are carried by my bowels, are borne up by my womb."[3] Should I not make God the object of every aspiration of mine, never, not even for a moment, turning away from Him or departing from His Law.

O my God, I believe that You have created me, that You continually sustain me, and that You unceasingly work in me. I am nothing, absolutely nothing. I have nothing of myself but misery and sins. I can but sin and spoil Your work. You alone are the One that is.

O my God, make me constantly and intimately feel my utter nothingness—my loathsome sinfulness—my absolute dependence on You, my Creator and my All.

1. Gen. ii, 16-17 2. Dante, *Paradise* iii, 85. 3. Is. xlvi, 3.

O my God, give me grace and strength that my every thought, desire and action may be prompted purely by the desire to accomplish Your most Holy Will, to praise and glorify You. Give me light to know more and more that in this lies my perfection and happiness here and in eternity.

O Jesus, my Master and my Saviour, my Guide and my Way, be truly Jesus to me. Open to me Your Sacred Heart. Make me learn of You the annihilation with which I must always stand before God, Your Father and my Creator, and the complete submission I owe to His Holy Will.

Give me, my Jesus, a little of the infinite humility and submission of Your Divine Heart. Give me grace that, as through Your abasement and Your obedience unto the death of the Cross, You attained to Your glory, I may also through humiliations and obedience attain to salvation.

REVERENCE

"Reverence is the secret of all religion and happiness. Without reverence, there is no faith, nor hope, nor love. Reverence is the motive of each of the Commandments of Sinai—reverence of God, reverence of our neighbour, reverence of ourselves. Humility is founded on it; piety is conserved by it; purity finds in it its shield and buckler. Reverence for God, and all that is associated with Him, His ministers, His temple, His services—that is religion. Reverence for our neighbour, his goods, his person, his chattels—that is honesty. Reverence for ourselves—clean bodies and pure souls—that is chastity. Satan is Satan because he is irreverent. There never yet was an infidel but he was irreverent and a mocker. The jester, and the mime, the loud laugher and the scorner, have no part in the Kingdom."

Sheehan, *Luke Delmege.*

PRINCIPLE AND FOUNDATION

SELF-CONTROL, OR THE END OF CREATURES

[*The Spiritual Exercises*, pp. 35-8]

The first Prelude is to see God the Creator showing me the whole universe and saying: Behold I have given thee all.

The second Prelude is to ask for light that I may know the origin of created things and the object for which God gives them to me, and for grace that I may use them according to His Holy Will, for His love and glory.

1. End of Creatures

"Our time is as the passing of a shadow . . . . Come, therefore, and let us enjoy the good things that are present, and let us speedily use the creatures as in youth . . . And let not the flower of the time pass by us. Let us crown ourselves with roses before they be withered: let no meadow escape our riot. Let none of us go without his part in luxury: let us everywhere leave tokens of joy: for this is our portion, this is our lot."[1]

Such was the cry of the worldly and material man for whom "the death of man and of beasts is one, and the condition of them both is equal."[2]

And yet he could not deny his nature. The gross pleasures of the beast could not fill the void of his heart, nor could the other joys and satisfactions which life and the world afford him. In the midst of things unstable and changeable, he longed for something firm and constant. In the midst of agitation and never ceasing anxiety, he hungered for calm and peace. In the midst of cruel and inevitable pain, he felt he was made for happiness. And in the midst of a world which is but a vast cemetery, he had intimations of eternity.

Reason might have enlightened man concerning his high destiny and the proper use of the things which God had placed at his disposal. But reason had been debased and obscured. At any

1. Wisd. ii, 5-9. 2. Eccl. ii, 19.

rate it could never provide that brilliant and steady light which alone would enlighten man's path through the labyrinthine ways of the world, dispel all darkness, and eclipse all false lights. God Himself came to man's help and revealed to him his true value and his real end, and the value and use of created beings.

We have no abiding place here: We are pilgrims going home. Created things, however beautiful and attractive, are not our end: they cannot satisfy the boundless longings of our hearts. They are but faint likenesses of God's infinite beauty, steps of the ladder which unites earth with heaven, and by which we climb to God's throne.

They are our servants. "And the other things on the face of the earth are created for man's sake, in order to aid him in the prosecution of the end for which he is created." They are given to us that we may direct them and ourselves to the common Creator and Lord. We are the mind of those that cannot reason, the eye of those that cannot see, and the heart of those that cannot worship and love. We are the priests of creation, set apart to offer to God the prayer and the incense of the creatures below us. The whole earth is a temple and our heart is an inner shrine. We are the conductors of the universal choir singing the glory of the Creator.

2. Right Use of Creatures

All created things are, first, means to know God, the Creator and Primal Cause, and His infinite perfections.

"For since the creation of the world His invisible attributes—His everlasting power and divinity—are to be discerned and contemplated through His work."[1]

Nature, i. e., the ever recurring spectacle of natural phenomena, and still more, the course of events in the Church, in human society, and in each individual soul, is the book written by the wisdom and the love of God. Each page, each line, bears His imprint.

Every created thing is a means to love God more and more. The whole meaning of life is the desire of God to take possession of man whom He has left free. As mothers invite their children to their arms with sweets and playthings, so does God attract us to

1. Rom. i, 20.

Himself through His creatures, as through so many gifts of His loving Heart. "I will draw them with the cords of Adam, with the bands of love."[1] They are the rays along which we get to the Sun of justice, the river that takes us back to the Spring of life. To love them is not sinful. It is sinful to love them independently of God, to stop at them instead of rising from their love to the love of God. It is only the few and the strong that can renounce the tenderness of secondary loves and fly straight to the very source of love. Most of us can only go on foot, pausing to pick the flowers and taste the fruits on the way, taking care that all should lead us to the Eternal Love.

As for the leaves, that in the garden bloom
My love for them is great, as is the good
Dealt by the Eternal Hand that tends them all.[2]

The good things of this world are given us also to develop our activities as individuals, as members of a family, and as members of society We must, then, take proper care of our body and of its senses, of our soul and its faculties; and see that they reach the perfection which God requires of us. We must work for the spiritual and the material welfare of the family or of the institution to which we belong. We must not forget that we are members of a divinely instituted society, the Church, and of a large human society, the State, and that it is our duty to work for the good of both according to the means which God has placed at our disposal.

Lastly, some creatures are meant, in God's loving providence to afford us matter for the exercise of self-denial and the practice of patience. They are the pleasures and the satisfactions that God forbids to all or to some of us, and the sufferings which are inevitable to our state of life, or which God sends us.

3. Wrong Use of Creatures

To use the good things of this world merely for the pleasure they afford, to embrace them against God's Will, and to shrink from what is hard and painful when duty commands otherwise, is disorder and sin. Sin is nothing else but the *wrong use* of something

1 Osee xi, 4. 2. Dante, *Paradise* xxvi, 64-66.

good in itself. It is to do violence to creation - to make it, in the words of St. Paul, *subject to vanity*, to force it into *the servitude of corruption*, and make it groan and travail in pain. It is to make created things the instruments of our corruption and debasement. We belong to our belongings and become like the things which we love.

4. Ignatian Indifference

The danger of being carried away by the love of created goods, forgetful of God, and of pursuing illusory and fleeting creatures instead of the Eternal is, alas, only too great for such weak and blind creatures as we are. St. Ignatius, therefore, wants that we should always be masters of ourselves in all things, never allowing ourselves to be led in our choice by whims and caprices. Duty, i. e., the Will of God made known to us in His Law, through our lawful superiors, and through the circumstances of our life, must be our only guide, whenever we choose anything or reject it.

"It is, therefore, necessary, that we should make ourselves indifferent to all created things, in so far as it is left to the liberty of our free will to do so and it is not forbidden."

St. Ignatius singles out four classes of creatures against which we should constantly be on our guard, not to be drawn through motives of either love or fear, to act against the voice of duty.

"In such sort that we do not for our part wish for health rather than sickness, for wealth rather than poverty, for honour rather than dishonour, for a long life rather than a short one."

The Saint displays here a deep psychological insight. Every deviation from the path of duty is the result of our inordinate longing for honour and high places, for the good things of this world, for comforts and luxuries, for a long and happy life. Every neglect of duty is an act of cowardice. We shrink from humiliations. We hate the very idea of financial loss and consequent poverty. We dislike hardship and pain, and we dread death. Hence the need of arming ourselves against the inordinate inclinations of our nature and the weakness of the flesh. A man that fears not poverty, nor the obloquy and the neglect of men, nor pain nor even death is a free man—indeed the only free man. All the others are more or less slaves and cowards.

5. God in the Innermost of our Heart

"Desiring and choosing only those things which most lead us to the end for which we are created."

We must constantly choose what, in the circumstances, will help us most to know God, to love Him, to develop our activities, and to offer to our Creator a worthy sacrifice. As far as we can, we must avoid whatever hinders our soul from attaining these ends. For this we have but to throw on every creatures the light of God—His Holy Will. It will light up our path

Amid the blaze of sophistry and doubt
Wherein we mortals wander aimlessly.

If we place God in the innermost depths of our heart and make Him the principle and the aim of all our activity, everything will speak to us of Him and take us to Him.

We often distinguish between secular and religious things, forgetting that there is but one secular and godless thing, and that is sin. Sin—mortal sin—is essentially disorder; it is a break in the universal harmony. Man belongs to God, to mankind, to himself. Whenever he places himself in opposition to God, to mankind, or to himself, he is off the right track, a planet out of its orbit: he sins. Man is essentially and wholly for God. God alone perfects him. God alone is the proper object of his aspirations, his last end and his eternal resting place. By seeking only his pleasure in created things in opposition to God's Holy Will, man makes himself unfit for the Eternal Beauty and the Eternal Good, and the creatures which should have been his ladder of ascent to God, become his ladder of descent into the abyss.

O my God, grant that I may know more and more clearly that every creature, whether pleasing or displeasing, comes to me from You, as the means of loving and serving You, of drawing me nearer to You.

Nothing, absolutely nothing, can be a hindrance to my serving You, if only I make a proper use of it—no place, no occupation, no difficulty, no temptation.

O my God! grant that in all things, I may see You alone, and Your most Holy Will.

O my God! I know that it is the love of created things—of comforts and ease, of honours, of material, social and intellectual wealth—and the fear of hardships, of sufferings, of neglect, and of poverty—that leads me to sin or at least keeps me away from Your perfect service.

I know that I cannot be truly indifferent. That is why I beg of You, my Jesus, to give me a high esteem, love, and desire of those things which You loved, and an utter hatred of those things which You hated. Thus indeed shall I be able to make a proper use of creatures, to accept and reject them as You desire—to choose those which lead me best to my end—to serve and glorify You. Amen.

GOD AND OUR OWN SOUL

The unprofitableness and feebleness of the things of this world are forced upon our minds; they promise but cannot perform, they disappoint us. Or, if they do perform what they promise, still (so it is) they do not satisfy us. We still crave for something, we do not well know what; but we are sure it is something which the world has not given us. And then its changes are so many, so sudden, so silent, so continual. It never leaves changing; it goes on to change, till we are quite sick at heart:—then it is that our reliance on it is broken. It is plain we cannot continue to depend upon it unless we keep pace with it and go on changing too; but this we cannot do. We feel that, while it changes, we are one and the same; and thus, under God's blessing, we come to have some glimpse of the meaning of our independence of things temporal, and our immorality. And should it so happen that misfortunes come upon us (as they often do), then still more are we led to understand the nothingness of this world; then still more are we le l to distrust it, and are weaned from the love of it, till at length it floats before our eyes merely as some idle veil, which, notwithstanding its many tints, cannot hide the view of what is beyond it;—and we begin, by degrees, to perceive that there are but two beings in the whole universe, our own soul, and the God who made it.

Newman.

THE THREE SINS

THE CREATURE'S GREATEST EVIL

[*The Spiritual Exercises*, pp. 47-51]

The first Prelude is to see with the eyes of the imagination and to consider that my soul is imprisoned in this corruptible body, and my whole self in this vale, as if it were in exile amongst brute beasts.

The second Prelude is to ask for shame and confusion at myself, seeing how many have been lost for a single mortal sin, and how many times I have deserved to be condemned eternally for my numerous sins.

* * *

We cannot realize the beauty of a soul in glory—

A light upon the shining sea
The Bridegroom with His bride.

A soul in grace is a soul on its way to Heaven, and it accordingly partakes of the light and beauty of eternity. Hence its ineffable charm, whether it be the soul of a little child, or that of a sinner who has just come back to God.

The happiness of a soul in glory is perfect. A soul in grace has anticipations of it. "Blessed are ye," says our Lord to His followers.

Man's soul is an image and likeness of God. Its perfection and sanctity is obtained through submission to God and harmony with His Holy Will.

The soul is made to love God, first of all, and under God, all creatures.

What can possibly stain the beauty of a soul, deprive it of happiness, make sanctity impossible, and kill love? Neither persecution, nor sufferings, nor death, but sin and sin alone. Sin is the destroyer of beauty, of happiness, of sanctity, of love. Sin is essential ugliness, and misery, and malice, and ingratitude, and hatred. Heaven, Eden, Earth, and Calvary are four theatres vividly portraying the awful ravages of sin.

1. Sin in Heaven or the Sin of the Angels

God created the Angels according to His own image and likeness, and without any merit of theirs He endowed them with the most excellent gifts of nature and of grace. Pure spirits, immortal, free, and powerful above all inferior creatures, they were destined to see and possess God eternally, provided they persevered in His service and stood the trial by which God intended to test their obedience; for they had to work out their salvation by free submission to His Will.

Many of them failed. They sinned by seeking their good through their own free will, independently of the rule of the Divine Will. Their sin was one of pride. They refused subjection to God, where subjection was due. Lucifer desired to be as God. Not that he desired, St. Thomas remarks, to resemble God by being subject to no one else absolutely; but he sought resemblance with God in this respect, that he wished as his supreme beatitude something which he could attain by virtue of his own nature, turning away his appetite from supernatural beatitude which is attained by God's grace. Or, if he desired as his last end that likeness of God which is bestowed by grace, he sought to have it by the power of his own nature, and not from divine assistance according to God's ordering.

An inexorable punishment followed the sin of the demons. They were deprived of all affective knowledge that comes from grace. Their will became obstinate in evil—what death is to us, says St. John Damascene, their fall was to the angels—and they were thrown into the everlasting fire of Hell, which God purposely created for them.

"God spared not angels that sinned, but plunged them into hell's caves, delivering them to be kept there for judgment."[1]

It was to this fearful fall of the sinning angels that our Lord referred when, to remove from the mind of His Apostles any thought of vanity and pride at the sight of the marvels God had worked through them, He said: "I saw Satan like lightning falling from Heaven."[2]

Absolute and eternal ugliness is the effect of the first sin.

2. Sin in Paradise or the Sin of our First Parents

God, out of His pure goodness, created our first parents according to His own image and likeness. He gave them the gift

1. II Pet. ii, 4. 2 Luke, x, 18.

of original justice, subjecting their appetites to reason and their flesh to the spirit. He freed them from mortality and the penalties to which by nature they were subject, and granted them a free and most contented state. Man's body was indissoluble by reason of a preternatural force given to the soul by God, whereby the soul was enabled to preserve the body from all corruption so long as it remained itself subject to God.

God gave all these gifts to Adam as the head of the human family. Adam would transmit them to his descendants, provided he kept God's command.

Our first parents also had to work out their salvation by submission—by making use of creatures according to God's Will. Instead they chose the free enjoyment of them, against the command of their Creator. They aspired to be gods, i.e., masters of their own destiny, and able to fashion it according to their own notions. At the suggestion of Satan—"Why hath God commanded you, that you should not eat of every tree of Paradise?"—they claimed freedom of thought and freedom of action.

Instead, they are deprived of original justice, subjected to death, and to all the miseries of a corruptible body. They are cast out of Paradise to live in suffering and humiliation. With them, all their descendants are condemned, and the earth itself is cursed.

Utter misery and suffering are the result of the second sin.

3. Essence and Ravages of Mortal Sin

A Christian is a child of God and a member of Christ's mystical body. He is raised to a higher level of life, to the very life of God. His actions spring from a supernatural principle of life—from grace. All of them, even the most ordinary, are divine actions, worthy of an eternal reward. Nothing can deprive him of such high dignity.

"For I am confident that neither death, nor life, nor angels, nor principalities, nor things present, nor things to come, nor powers, nor height, nor depth, nor any other creature shall be able to separate us from the love of God in Christ Jesus our Lord."[1]

Nothing, indeed, except mortal sin.

1. Rom. viii, 38, 39.

Man must attain salvation through submission and obedience, but, alas, with the rebel angels and his disobedient first parents, he too claims freedom and independence – freedom and independence of thought, of love, of action, of enjoyment. Though but a creature, a son, a soldier, and a subject, he cries *non serviam* to his Creator, his Father, his Commander, and his King.

Mortal sin is a violation of God's Law. It is a turning unduly to some mutable good and a consequent turning away from God the immutable Good. The sinner disobeys God not because He loves Him not, but because he loves Him *less* than a creature, *less than himself*. Placed between God and a creature forbidden by God, he would not like to be forced to choose, but he does choose and he chooses to please himself. His conscience may yield with a pang of heart, but it yields. Every creature is but a means to serve God and to go to Him. The sinner turns it into an idol and shamefully lowers himself in front of it.

What a horrible thing, then, every mortal sin is! It destroys all good things in man.

It destroys the supernatural life. Man is, by charity, united to God, his last end and the principle of moral order. Sin is the rejection of this order.

Sin causes a stain on the soul.

"Man's soul has a twofold comeliness; one from the refulgence of the natural light of reason, whereby he is directed in his actions; the other, from the refulgence of the Divine Light, i. e., of wisdom and grace, whereby man is also perfected for the purpose of doing good and fitting actions. Now, when the soul cleaves to things by love, there is a kind of contact in the soul: and when a man sins, he cleaves to certain things, against the light of reason and the Divine Law . . . . The loss of comeliness occasioned by this contact is metaphorically called a stain on the soul."[1]

"The stain of sin remains in the soul even when the act of sin is past. The reason for this is that the stain . . . denotes a blemish in the brightness of the soul, on account of its withdrawing from the light of reason and of the Divine Law. And therefore so

1. *Summa*, I. IIae, Q. 86, a. 1.

long as a man remains out of this light, the stain of sin remains on him . . . . For though the act of sin ceases, whereby man withdrew from the light of reason and of the Divine Law, man does not at once return to the state in which he was before, and it is necessary that his will should have a movement contrary to the previous movement. Thus if one man part from another on account of some kind of movement, he is not reunited to him as soon as the movement ceases, but he needs to draw nigh to him and to return by a contrary movement."[1]

Sin deprives the sinner of all supernatural merits he may have gained. By striking at the root of the tree of life, it causes all its branches and leaves to wither.

Sin gives a certain inclination to what is evil, even as human acts produce an inclination to like acts.

Through it reason is obscured especially in practical matters, the will is hardened to evil, good actions become more difficult, and concupiscence more impetuous.

Sin incurs a debt of eternal punishment.

"If a sin destroys the principle of the order whereby man's will is subject to God, the disorder will be such as to be considered in itself irreparable, although it is possible to repair it by the power of God. Now the principle of this order is the last end to which man adheres by charity. Therefore whatever sins turn man away from God, so as to destroy charity, considered in themselves, they incur a debt of eternal punishment.

"Sin comprises two things. First, there is the turning away from the immutable good, which is infinite, wherefore, in this respect, sin is infinite. Secondly, there is the inordinate turning to mutable good. In this respect sin is finite, both because the mutable good itself is finite, and because the movement of turning towards it is finite, since the acts of a creature cannot be infinite. Accordingly, in so far as sin consists in turning away from God, its corresponding punishment is the *pain of loss*, which also is infinite, because it is the loss of the infinite good, i. e., God. But in so far as sin turns inordinately to the mutable good, its corresponding punishment is the *pain of sense*, which also is finite."[2]

1. *Summa*, I. IIae, Q. 86, a 2. 2. *Summa*, I. IIae, Q. 87, aa. 3, 4.

We can, then, understand, how truly Christ would say, when alluding to Judas: "One of you is *a devil;*"[1] and when talking of the sinner in general: "He shall be cast forth as a branch, and shall wither and they shall gather him up, and cast him into the fire, and he burneth."[2]

It is in Hell that one learns what sin is.

4. Sin, the Killing of Love

Sin is the killing of love.

How beautiful, how happy, and how glorious was the Son of God made Man to be, by right! But He took upon Himself to atone for the sins of mankind, and see what sin has done with Him.

Not only is mortal sin the destroyer of man's supernatural life, but by its nature it aims at destroying God Himself. The moment God appeared in a human and passible form, sin actually killed Him.

See our Lord crucified. Behold His head crowned with thorns—His face spat upon—His eyes dimmed—His arms disjointed—His tongue embittered with gall and vinegar—His hands and feet pierced with nails—His back and shoulders torn with lashes—His soul sad unto death—His Heart immersed in an ocean of desolation!

Why is He hanging on the Cross?

For our sins; to avert from us the anger of His Father, and to free us from the punishment due to our sins.

And what have we done to this infinite Lover?

Alas! We have repeatedly pierced His Heart with ever new swords. We have pierced it with the sword of indifference. We professed to believe in Christ's love, and yet that love has had no place in our heart. We have been in constant pursuit of other loves.

We have pierced Jesus' Heart with the sword of ingratitude.

"O my people, what have I done to thee? Or in what have I afflicted thee? Answer Me.

"What more ought I to do for thee, and have not done it? I planted thee, indeed, my most beautiful vineyard: and thou art become to Me exceeding bitter; for thou hast given Me vinegar in

1. John vi, 71. 2. John xv, 6.

My thirst; and with a spear thou hast pierced the side of thy Saviour.

"I went before thee in a pillar of a cloud; and thou hast brought Me to the palace of Pilate.

"I gave thee a royal sceptre: and thou hast given Me a crown of thorns.

"I have exalted thee with great strength; and thou hast hanged Me on the gibbet of the cross."

We have pierced the Divine Heart with the sword of contempt. Urged to choose between Christ and Barabbas, i. e., the satisfaction of our passions, we have cried out: "Not this, but Barabbas."

We have plunged in the Heart of our Creator and Lord the sword of treason. Repeatedly we swore fidelity to Christ, and yet, with Judas, we have gone to His enemies—to Satan, the world, and our passions—and asked of them: What will you give me? What pleasure and what satisfaction are you going to give me, and I will deliver Christ unto your hands to be again tortured and crucified?

And yet He is still our loving Father; He still opens His arms and his very Heart to us. What then can we do but plunge ourselves into that abyss of love and mercy to be there purified and to live, henceforth, only by its life.

O Father! O Jesus mine! Who by Thy Death Divine
With life our souls dost warm,
Thou, in creation's hour, whose plastic power
Made man to Thy own blessed form,
Is it not, O Christ! O King! a cruel, cruel thing,
That naught has been loved by me
Save sins that the soul defile, save all things base and vile,
That are loathsome unto Thee?

OUR OWN SINS

THE SENSE OF OUR OWN SINFULNESS

[*The Spiritual Exercises*, pp. 51-3]

The first Prelude is to see with the eyes of the imagination and to consider that my soul is imprisoned in this corruptible body, and my whole self in this vale, as if it were in exile amongst brute beasts.

The second Prelude is to beg great and intense sorrow and tears for my sins.

1. The Number of our Sins

In the First Book of the Machabees we read that "All the army assembled together, and they went up into Mount Sion. And they saw the sanctuary desolate, and the altar profaned, and the gates burned and the shrubs growing up in the courts as in a forest, or on the mountains, and the chambers joining to the temple thrown down. And they rent their garments, and made great lamentation and put ashes on their heads: and they fell down to the ground on their faces, and they sounded with the trumpets of alarm, and they cried towards heaven."[1]

Having considered the ravages of sin in others, we must enter into our own soul and realize the havoc it has worked therein. A simple glance at our past life—running through its stages, the places where we have dwelt, the offices, occupations and employments that we have had, and our dealings with others—should easily convince us that we are great sinners, loaded with sins without number. We must look at our soul as it truly stands before God, guarding against all hypocrisy and false principles. Alas, often an ugly polypus settles in our heart, and throws its ramifications into the brain. Blinded by it, we say: "I am rich, and have grown wealthy, and have need of nothing." While a voice, unheeded if not despised, keeps whispering "And knowest not that thou art the wretched and pitiable and poor and blind and naked one."[2] Let us then, anoint our eyes with the salve which Christ offers to us, that we may see.

1. I. Mac. iv, 37-40. 2. Apos. iii, 17.

Like the Jews, we shall see the sanctuary desolate – the temple of our soul deprived of sanctity, or, at least of the sacred fire of fervour; the altar profaned – the Divine Sacrifice and the Sacrament of Love treated irreverently and even offered or received sacrilegiously; and the gates burnt – the doors of our senses thrown open that wild beasts may enter into the soul and devour it; and the shrubs growing up in the courts – worldly and evil habits daily asserting themselves; and the chambers adjoining the temple thrown down—the edifice of good resolutions pulled down and its ruins scattered all around.

And if God's powerful hand has preserved us from serious falls our offences and negligences have been truly innumerable.

"Sigh and grieve that thou art yet so carnal and worldly, so unmortified in thy passions, so full of the motions of concupiscence: so unguarded in thy outward senses, so often entangled with many vain imaginations:

"So much inclined to exterior things, so negligent as to the interior:

"So prone to laughter and unbridled mirth, so hard and indisposed to tears and compunction:

"So prompt to relaxation and the pleasures of the flesh, so sluggish to austerity and fervour:

"So curious to hear news and to see fine sights; so slack to embrace things humble and mean:

"So covetous to possess much, so sparing in giving, so close in keeping:

"So inconsiderate in speech, so little able to keep silence:

"So disorderly in thy carriage, so over-eager in thy actions:

"So eager about food, so deaf to the word of God:

"So hasty for rest, so slow to labour:

"So wakeful to hear idle tales, so drowsy to watch in the service of God:

"So hasty to make an end of thy prayers, so wandering as to attention; so negligent in saying thy office; so tepid in celebrating; so dry at the time of Communion:

"So quickly distracted, so seldom quite recollected within thyself:

"So easily moved to anger, so apt to take offence at others;
"So prone to judge, so severe in reprehending:
"So joyful at prosperity, so weak in adversity:
"So often proposing many good things, and effecting little."[1]
O Lord, be merciful to me, a sinner!

2. Intrinsic Ugliness of Sin

Sin is disorder and ugliness itself.

The glory of God is the end of creation. All creatures give glory to God, and at the same time attain to their perfection and happiness, by pursuing their object in life and thus contributing to the perfect harmony of the whole universe.

The aim of man is to direct himself and all creatures to God—to keep his senses and lower appetites under the control of reason, and his reason subject to God, to pursue his welfare as the member of a social body and in unison with all his fellowmen. In this harmonious working lies his happiness and his perfection.

Any sin is an attempt at marring this harmony and subordination. It is an attack on the essential order of things and on the greatness and dignity of human nature. Hence its extreme ugliness and malice, expressed in the saying: "As ugly as sin."

Every disorder is ugly. Sin is the greatest disorder.

And if sin is so ugly in any creature simply endowed with reason, how much more so in a Christian redeemed by the Blood of Christ and made to share in His life, in a religious soul bound to Him by the most sacred ties, and in a Priest charged with the task of continuing His mission of saving souls?

3. The Littleness and Vileness of the Offender

The malice of an offence is measured by the greatness and excellence of the person offended, and the littleness and the vileness of the one that offers it. And what is man in comparison with God? "The whole world before Thee is as the least grain of the balance, and as the drop of the morning dew that falleth down upon the earth."[2] All creatures, however perfect and beautiful, are as

1. *Imit. of Christ*, IV, 7. 2. Wisd. xi, 23.

nothing before God. "All nations are before Him as if they had no being at all, and are counted to Him as nothing and vanity."[1] Then, what can I alone be? The attitude towards God of even the highest of creatures—the Blessed Virgin—is one of absolute humility and subjection. And I have dared to rise against Him and to refuse obedience to His Holy Will!

If only I were mere nothingness! But when I turn to look at myself, what a horrible sight do I behold! My body is a dunghill of corruption and foulness; my soul is an ulcer and abscess whence have issued so many sins and iniquities and such deadly poison. And a thing so vile and contemptible has dared to prefer itself to God, to make of itself a god, to set its pleasure, its will and its little interests before God's Will and Glory!

Have mercy on me, O my God, have mercy on me!

4. The Infinite Greatness of the Offended God

The malice of every mortal sin is, in a true sense, infinite on account of the infinite Majesty of the offended God. God is infinitely wise, omnipotent, just, and good. The sinner insults each of these attributes and, as far as lies in him, seeks to destroy them.

God commands that we "do the truth in charity."[2] The sinner is a liar, "that loveth and maketh a lie;"[3] a fool that condemns by his life the wisdom of God and of His Divine Law. He is a self-constituted god that claims to know good and evil.

The sinner is weakness and powerlessness itself. Without God's help, he could not possibly make the slightest movement or conceive the simplest thought. And yet he rises against the Almighty. He challenges the arrows of God's vengeance. "Who have said: We will magnify our tongue: our lips are our own; who is Lord over us?"[4] "I have sinned and what harm hath befallen me?"[5] Still more, he forces the Almighty to serve with his sins, to aid him to think, to speak and to do what is abomination to God's Sanctity.

God is infinite Justice and Sanctity. The perfection of every one of us lies in reflecting the Sanctity of God in our life, in an ever

1. Is. xl. 17. 2. Eph. iv, 15. 3. Apoc. xxii, 15. 4. Ps. xi, 5. 5. Eccli. v, 4.

increasing degree, by taking His Will as the only rule of our own. The sinner rejects the all-holy Will of God. He embraces what is opposed to God, Who is infinite Beauty and Order and Harmony. With Satan he cries: "Evil, be thou my good." No wonder if his act has been defined as an attempt on the very life of God.

God is infinite Goodness. He is the All-Good: *Summa fons et origo omnium bonorum.* "When Thou openest Thy hand, they (the creatures) shall all be filled with good."[1] He has showered all His gifts on everyone of us—gifts of creation, of loving conservation and care. "Is he not thy Father that hath possessed thee and made thee, and created thee?" And yet, "thou hast forsaken the God that begot thee and hast forgotten the Lord that created thee?"[2]

He has showered on our soul far higher gifts: the gifts of His grace. He has made us partakers of His Divine Nature, brothers of His Son, and the living shrines of His Spirit of Love.

And we have risen against Him. We have rejected His gifts. We have despised His Love. We have trodden under foot the Son of God—and all that for a vile pleasure, for a paltry sum of money, for a mark of vain honour and distinction, or to avoid a transitory sacrifice and humiliation.

O my God, how is it that Your creatures have suffered me to live and have preserved me in life while I was so grievously offending You, their Creator and benefactor? How is it that Your Angels, who are the sword of Your Divine Justice, have born with me and guarded me, and prayed for me? How is it that the Saints have interceded for me? How is it that the heavens, the sun, the moon, the stars and the elements, the fruits of the earth, the birds, the fishes and the animals have served me and helped to sustain me? How is it that the earth has not opened to swallow me up, creating new hells that I might suffer in them for ever?

"The mercies of the Lord that we are not consumed: because His commiserations have not failed."[3] Thanks to You, O my Lord: thanks to Your infinite mercy. It is You that have stopped the avenging hand of Your creatures. It is You that have given me life till now.

O give me grace also to amend myself--to live only for You and for the accomplishment of Your Holy Will!

1. Ps. ciii, 28. 2. Deut. xxxii, 6, 18. 3. Lam. iii, 22.

THE TRIPLE COLLOQUY

THE GRACE OF CONVERSION

[*The Spiritual Exercises*, pp. 53-5]

St Ignatius wishes us to repeat the Exercise on our own sins along with the provious Exercise. The Colloquy that is to end this third meditation, is of the greatest importance as it sums up the main fruits of the First Week.

We are directed to ask three graces, first of all, praying our Lady that she may obtain them from her Son; and then Christ, the Divine Mediator, that He may obtain them from the Father; and lastly, the Father that He may grant them to us.

The three graces are: (1) that we may feel an interior knowledge of our sins and detestation of them; (2) that we may feel the disorder of our actions, in order that abhorring it, we may amend and set in order our life; (3) that we may know the world in order that abhorring it, we may cast away from us whatever is worldly and vain.

FIRST GRACE: *That I may have an intimate knowledge of my sins and may detest them.*

We ask, not for knowledge of sin in general, but for an intimate knowledge of our own sins, and especially of those which we have committed since our last Retreat. Each one in particular must examine in the presence of God and *in amaritudine animae*:—

1) What are his habitual sins;
2) What is his besetting sin;
3) What are the ordinary occasions of his failures.

We must, moreover, conceive a real and heartfelt hatred of our sins. We fall so often into the same sins, because we are but little convinced of their intrinsic malice and how displeasing they are to the Heart of Jesus. It is far better to concentrate our attention on a few more heinous sins and deal with them in a serious and businesslike way, than to keep revolving in our daily Examens and repeatedly confess many venial sins and defects which we do not detest in our heart of hearts.

Lastly, each one must see how he is to use properly the ordinary means to remove or, at least, to diminish his habitual sins. Such means are: the Particular and the General Examen of Conscience and, above all, the Sacrament of Penance.

SECOND GRACE: *That I may feel the disorder of my actions, in order that abhorring it, I may amend and rightly regulate myself.*

We ask here to feel—which is far more than simply to know—the roots or the occasions of our ordinary sins and failures. Such roots and occasions are the lack of a right and pure intention, want of order and forethought, the lack of self-control, the habit of sluggishness, and an easy-going disposition.[1]

THIRD GRACE: *That I may know the world in order that, abhorring it, I may cast away from me whatever is worldly and vain.*

The world is the embodiment of sin and of the three concupiscences that lead to sin. Christianity, the Church, Religious Congregations, direct all their efforts towards implanting and strengthening the life of God in man. The world, with all its branches and its manifold activities, aims directly—more often indirectly—at the destruction of this life. Hence the world is our great enemy. Against the world our Lord has inveighed in the most emphatic terms. The whole life of our Lord, as a matter of fact, is a standing protest against the principles and ways of the world.

The disciples are no less emphatic than the Master. *Mundus totus in maligno positus est.*[2] As the whole race of man is *in Adam*, so all believers are *in Christ*. He is the life they live, the atmosphere they breathe, and the sunshine that illumines their path. On the other hand, as to *the world*, i. e., the unbelievers, those who reject Christ, their vine, their head, the air they breathe, the light that illumines their path, is Satan. They live and move *in the Evil One*, being well content with, and submissive to his rule.

"Love not the world, or the things in the world. If any one love the world, the love of the Father is not in him; for all that is

1. Cf. Meditation on Tepidity, p. 48. 2. I John, v, 19.

in the world—the lust of the flesh, the lust of the eyes, and the pride of life—is not from the Father, but from the world."[1]

All the Saints, in words and still more in deeds, resemble the Master and His first Disciples in their hatred of the world.

The world is not less dangerous today. Rather, it has become more subtle, more refined, more accommodating. No wonder that it often becomes an acceptable visitor—alas, not rarely a permanent guest—in Christian homes and in religious houses too.

If we wish to remain faithful to our Lord, to live in Him and realize His plan concerning us, we must hate the world and be constantly on our guard against it.

But what are the principles of the world and what the three concupiscences which constitute the essence of the world's malice?

1) The first characteristic of the world, says Bishop Hedley, is naturalism, a practical denial of the very idea of Christianity. It is a revival of pagan principles and practices; a love and esteem for only what one sees and touches, for the beauty and glamour of the present life. For some this implies absolute unbelief; for many others, practical indifference to God and to the things of the soul. Such people may externally profess the Christian Faith, but they do not guide their everyday life by it. Their everyday life is influenced by the world's principles and is judged by the world's standard. Religion is for them a cloak which they put on for some time on Sunday, and, may be, for a few minutes daily, and which they soon remove and entirely forget.

Obviously the life of a person consecrated to God prevents him from losing sight of the supernatural world altogether. Everything reminds him of it; it is as it were thrust upon him. All the same, he may easily lose his supernatural point of view. In his manner of thinking and acting, he may be led by mere human reason and human principles. He may learn to admire what the world admires, to crave for what the world craves for, to judge things and persons by the standard of the world, to adopt ways of acting that are popular with the world, to look for worldly success and results. In his dealings with his superiors and companions, in the discharge of his duties, in the treatment of his body, he may take up quite a

1. I John ii, 15, 16. Cf. also Gal. vi, 14, Rom. viii, 3, and Jas. iv, 4.

human and worldly attitude. Such an attitude may not be intrinsically wrong. A pagan, a Greek, a man of the Renaissance might have adopted it. But we are neither pagans, nor followers of any New Paganism. We are Christians: we are the close friends of Christ. And Christ has revealed to us a life far higher than the natural life. He has revealed to us the excellence of obedience, of chastity, of humility, of self-sacrifice, in one word, of the Cross which the men of our time, no less than the Greeks of old, account as foolishness. Not content with this divine illumination, He has given us His grace and he has made us share in His life. We may fall through weakness, but the principles of Christ and of His Gospel must be ours. We must hate the world, its tenets and its glamour, if we want to be Christ's.

2) The second mark of the spirit of the world is pride and rebellion. The impulse to refuse to obey, to scorn dictation, to criticize, and to set ourselves up as our own masters in religious and moral matters may be natural, and even extremely human. But we have to make our own choice. Either we give in to it, and then we range ourselves in the army that is opposing Christ, or we prefer to be Christ's disciples, and as such we must repress it and resist it to the utmost. The spirit of the Gospel is a spirit of humility, of childlike docility, and of obedience.

If this is true of every Christian, what should we say of a Religious, and still more of a Priest of Christ? And yet the spirit of pride and rebellion is all along trying to penetrate the hearts even of persons consecrated to Christ and to the spreading of His Kingdom. Freedom of action, i. e., independence of rule and authority in one's activity, sometimes under pretext of working better for souls, and freedom of speech, i. e., the love of criticizing everything and everybody—are not these the two main privileges that many are tempted to claim in the presence of the great democratic upheaval of our day?

3) The third mark of the world is sensuality.

There is a gross sensuality, every manifestation of which is sinful. Though we must always live in holy fear, the very ugliness of such sensuality is a good safeguard.

But there is a more refined sensuality. It consists in avoiding all that is hard and troublesome, in seeking our own comfort in everything, in setting a limit even to our bodily pleasures to enjoy them all the more.

It is this sensuality that easily finds its way even among us. We often long for amusements and recreations, for comforts and pleasures in food and drink. We dislike to be disturbed; we hate worry.

Nothing could be more contrary to the spirit of the Gospel than this spirit. It stands condemned by every feature of ecclesiastical and still more, of religious life, both of which imply the practice of continual mortification.

The effects of such a tendency, moreover, are fatal.

It leads the soul to laziness. Lay people can afford to indulge in many of the comforts of life and yet work seriously. Not so with a Religious or a Priest. There is a great deal of truth in the saying that a Religious or a Priest who is not a hero is less than a man.

It leads to sins against chastity. At first it will lead us into doing something which is not openly sinful—into indulgence in food and drink, in looking and reading, into taking certain liberties with ourselves. Or it will lead us into forming some sentimental connection, or into dealing freely with others. Then, little by little, something more serious will follow, and with it doubts and pricks of conscience. They will be stifled, and the ruin of our soul will not be far.

How can we keep free from the world and the spirit of the world that causes such havoc in the soul? There is only one way: if Christ and His Cross fill our heart, the world and its three concupiscences will find no admittance therein.

O Mother of my Saviour, my Blessed Queen and Mother, vouchsafe to intercede for me with thy Divine Son, my Lord, and obtain for me these three graces:—

The grace to know and feel the malice of my sins, and to detest and abhor them;

The grace to know and feel the disorder of my actions, to abhor it, and to amend my life and set it in order;

The grace to know the world and abhor it, and to put away from myself all worldly and vain things. *Hail Mary.*

O my Lord Jesus, for the sake of Thy Blessed Mother, obtain for me from Thy Eternal Father these three graces:

The grace to know and feel the malice of my sins, and to detest and abhor them;

The grace to know and feel the disorder of my actions, to abhor it, and to amend my life and set it in order;

The grace to know the world and abhor it, and to put away from myself all worldly and vain things. *Anima Christi.*

O Eternal Father, in the name of Jesus Christ Thy Son, I beseech Thee to grant me these three graces I implore of Thee:

The grace to know and feel the malice of my sins, and to detest and abhor them;

The grace to know and feel the disorder of my actions and abhor it, and to amend my life and set it in order;

The grace to know the world and abhor it, and to put away from myself all worldly and vain things. *Our Father.*

FROM 'PECCAVI, DOMINE'

O Master, all my strength is gone;
  Unto the very earth I bow;
I have no light to lead me on;
  With aching heart and burning brow,
I lie as one that travaileth
  In sorrow more than he can bear;
I sit in darkness as of death,
  And scatter dust upon my hair.

The God within my soul hath slept,
  And I have shamed the nobler rule;
O Master, I have whined and crept;
  O Spirit, I have played the fool.
Like him of old upon whose head
  His follies hung in dark arrears,
I groan and travail in my bed,
  And water it with bitter tears.

Archibald Lampman.

HELL

MISSING FOR EVER THE END

[*The Spiritual Exercises*, pp. 55-7]

The first Prelude is the composition of place which is here to see with the eyes of the imagination the length, and breadth, and depth of Hell.

The second Prelude is to ask for that which I want. It will be here to ask for an interior sense of the pain which the lost suffer, so that if I should, through my repeated faults, forget the love of the Eternal Lord, at least the fear of punishment may help me not to fall into sin.

1. The Thought of Hell

We are created to know, to serve, and to love God in this life, and to enjoy Him for ever hereafter. The love of God, our Creator and our Father, should be the ordinary motive of our actions. However, there are moments in our life when temptations of the most alluring kind assail us, when all ideas of right and wrong, so clear at other times, become vague and uncertain, when even God seems to depart from us, leaving us for a moment exposed to the attack of our bitter enemies. It is the thought of Hell that will prove most helpful at such times.

That is why the Saints were familiar with it; even those who most excelled in the love of God. By thinking of the fire of Hell, many martyrs rejected the blandishments of tyrants, and suffered torments, prison, and death for Christ. By thinking often of Hell many Christians refrain from sin in the midst of dangers and temptations. "It is Hell that peoples Heaven," said Pascal.

Hence our Mother the Church often reminds us of that eternal prison, and prays that we may be delivered from it. At the most solemn moment of Mass, the priest, with his hands spread over the oblation, asks "that we may be delivered from eternal damnation." Again, just before receiving the Body of Christ, he tenderly whispers to his Lord: "Never permit me to be separated from Thee."

Let our whole soul, then, and our very senses be filled with the thought of Hell and of the terrible sufferings which the lost endure there, so that the fire of Hell may quench the fire of our passions and the thought of what is in store for the sinner may make us to turn away in horror from any suggestion to sin.

2. THE EXISTENCE OF HELL

But, does Hell truly exist? Why, the whole Gospel is full of this tremendous fact, the existence of hell. Many a time does the merciful Saviour warn His disciples against it. "And if thy right eye scandalize thee, pluck it out and cast it from thee. For it is expedient for thee that one of thy members should perish, rather than thy whole body be cast into Hell."[1] "The children of the kingdom shall be cast out into the exterior darkness: there shall be weeping and gnashing of teeth."[2] "Depart from me, you cursed, into everlasting fire."[3] "They shall gather him up, and cast him into the fire, and he burneth."[4]

The voice of the Incarnate Son of God rises persistently to warn us against the danger of eternal punishment. He is not satisfied with having done all He could to induce us to submit to His sweet guidance and thus enter the way that leads to life. Seeing our wilful blindness and waywardness, He tenderly begs of us to consider that, though the way along which we gambol is broad and full of flowers, sooner or later it will inevitably end in an abyss of miseries from which there will be no exit.

There is a Hell as truly as there is a God, and as truly as there are men free to choose between good and evil, with souls destined to live for ever. Heaven is the choice of God begun in this life and made irrevocable on passing into eternity; Hell is the final rejection of God.

Our very sense of justice demands a Hell. Sin is an offence of an infinite magnitude. It requires an infinite punishment—an eternal Hell. It is because many think little of God and of His rights that they find it hard to believe in the existence of Hell. They lay hold of God's mercy as their support, and forget that Hell is but the result of a persistent contempt of this very mercy on the part of the obdurate soul.

1. Matt. v, 29. 2. Matt. viii, 12. 3. Matt. xxv, 41 4. John xv, 6.

3. Locus Tormentorum

What is Hell? The most terrifying descriptions have been drawn up by preachers and writers—the consuming fire, the torments of every sense, the agony of the soul, the cries, the despair, the curses and blasphemies—and they have been called by many the work of wild and diseased imaginations. And such, indeed, they are in one sense.

"My dear friend, I must change my life."

"Are you mad to believe all that nonsense?"

"I am not mad. I merely don't want to go to Hell."

Thus spoke two young men who had gone in fun to a sermon on Hell. A few years after, the impenitent one died and appeared in a globe of fire to his former friend, crying:

"There is a Hell, and I am in it."

"Was it merely about a figment of the imagination that the Friar preached to us long ago?"

"Yes, it was a figment of the imagination. What he said was absolutely nothing compared with the reality. The reality is beyond comprehension."

What is Hell? *Locus tormentorum*: a place of torments. We may conjure up the most terrifying scenes, but we shall never conceive a better idea of Hell than that conveyed by these two words of the Son of God. Let us look into that dark prison enlightened only by the fire of God's anger, and see Dives plunged into it and horribly tormented. He lifts up his eyes and cries to Abraham: "Father Abraham, have mercy on me, and send Lazarus that he may dip the tip of his finger in water, to cool my tongue: for I am tormented in this flame."[1] For nigh two thousand years the wretch has been in that flame, for nigh two thousand years he has been asking for that little solace, and he will continue to ask for it for all eternity, and always in vain. "Between us and you there is fixed a great chaos."

4. The Loss of God

But it is not physical torments that make Hell. Even in their midst a soul may be happy and at peace. Hell is the loss of God.

1. Luke xvi, 24.

"Depart from me, you cursed, into everlasting fire."[1]

We are made for God and in Him alone we can find rest and peace. God alone can satisfy our immense craving for happiness. In this world we should go to God through creatures. They are steps to His throne, reflections of His Beauty, windows to look into eternity. But the sinner attaches himself to them: he makes them his idols, forgetful of God and in defiance of His Will. It is a perversion—an anticipated Hell, as a matter of fact, though the distractions, the tumult and the glamour of the world, somehow, conceal it from him.

In death the sinner's soul leaves behind this world of sense and all its illusions. It enters a solitude where nothing is left to make it happy but God alone. Alas! The evil dispositions with which it has entered into eternity remain eternally impressed upon it. It is forever chained to the object of its love—a love in opposition to the eternal Love—and it is fully conscious that this love is but nothing, and that it will never appease its hunger.

The soul was created for beauty, for truth, for holiness, for love, for happiness. God alone is Beauty, Truth, Holiness, Love and inexhaustible Happiness; and the soul hates Him. God alone is its Father, its Lover, its Home; and the soul will be eternally separated from Him.

"Dost thou want Me?" was, up to the very last moment of the sinner's life, the continual pleading of the Divine Lover. And he passed away rejecting Him. His soul landed on the shore of eternity in a state of deformity and of opposition to the Infinite Love, and that is why there is hatred and eternal hatred in it. There is no love in it, because it has lost the Eternal Love.

Between the lost sinner and God there is no more any affinity. In him there is no power to grasp God. He sees God still in every creature, but no longer can he go to Him. He has eyes, but they are sightless. He has a heart, but it is void. He has a mind, but it is empty.

The consciousness that he was made for God, that only in God he can satisfy all his longings, but that now God is absolutely unattainable, drives him to despair. He knows that he is an exile,

1. Matt. xxv, 41.

a disinherited son, a rejected partner, a wreck on the shore of eternity, an outcast from God, a true atheist, i. e., a man with no God.

If the lost sinner could, at least, conceive some feeling of sorrow and contrition! Nothing of the kind. Grief on account of the punishment which he endures for his sins, he will have—but sorrow for his sins, never. He will cling desperately to the sinful objects of his love, though they have now become his executioners. He will be eternally sunk in filthy mire—eternally united most intimately with a horrid corpse, a worse plight than that of Jane the Mad carrying about with her, in all her travels, the dead body of her husband, Philip of Burgundy.

The lost day of my life . . . . . .
I do not see them here, but after death,
God knows, I know the faces I shall see.
Each one a murdered self, with low, last breath;
"*I am thyself—what hast thou done to me?*
"*And I—and I—thyself (lo! each one saith),*
"*And thou thyself to all eternity.*"

5. Eternity of Hell

And this eternally: "Depart from me, you cursed, into the everlasting fire."

"Duration without motion, changeless, uniform—a noontide heat without a breath—a wilderness without a limit—a leaden sea without a ripple—and never any change, never any hope." These are faint ideas of eternity.

In billions and billions of centuries a bird may possibly dry up the boundless ocean—an ant may rub off the mighty Himalayas—a man may count every atom of created matter, but eternity will still be at its beginning. This whole world will pass away, new worlds may possibly be created and in turn pass away, and eternity will remain changeless and unchangeable like God Himself. There will be neither past nor future in it, but an infinite *now*, heavily pressing on the soul, like a tremendous ball of iron whose weight is entirely felt by the underlying surface on one single point.

Truly the eternity of Hell is the most terrible and frightening thing. As long as God will last, the soul of the impenitent sinner will be plunged in that lake of fire, rejected and cursed. Its torments will continue for ever—never will it know any kind of comfort or solace.

Eternity alone can counterbalance the attractions of the flesh and of the world. For eternal beings a temporary pain is little—less than a drop of water compared with the immensity of the sea. The comparative inefficiency of Purgatary is the best proof of this.

Si finis omnium similis erit, praeteritum omne pro nihilo est, quia non quaerimus quid aliquando fuerimus, sed quid semper futuri sumus.[1]

6. Three Momentous Questions

And now each one of us must ask himself three questions.

"Have I deserved Hell?"

What feelings of gratitude, of love, and of desire to atone for the past must burst from my heart! "The mercies of the Lord that we are not consumed: because His commiserations have not failed."[2]

"Do I deserve Hell?" Is there any unrepented for and unforgiven mortal sin in my soul? If so, I stand on the very brink of that bottomless abyss. If death comes upon me I shall fall into it by my sheer weight; and yet I remain unmoved.

Consider, O my soul, that your eternal fate is at stake. Have mercy on you: have pity on Christ Who for you has shed all His Blood. You say that it is difficult to fight against your passions and avoid sin. Difficult, indeed, it is, but will you find it easier to stand the fire of Hell, not for a moment, but for a whole eternity?

"Shall I eventually deserve Hell?" Along which way am I walking? Is it the hard road of self-denial and of submission to God's Will? Is it the royal road of the Cross? It will infallibly lead me to life. Or is it the broad and spacious road of self-indulgence, of compliance with one's caprices and whims of freedom and independence? The end will be eternal misery and despair. "Enter ye in at the narrow gate; for wide is the gate, and broad is the way that leadeth to destruction, and many there are who go in thereat. How narrow is the gate, and straight is the way that leadeth to life: and few there are that find it."[3]

1. St Jerome. 2. Lam. iii, 22. 3. Matt. vii, 13, 14.

Fight and you will be crowned. Give way, and you will be eternally lost. Do God's Will, and in that Will you will find eternal happiness. Refuse submission to it, and you will eternally be a member out of joint. Use all creatures as means to go to God, and they will lead you to Him. Use them for your own pleasure, and they will become your tormentors.

7. 'That Way lies Hell'

How often, climbing a high and difficult mountain, the mountaineer sees bright, alluring paths branching off right and left. They attract him with the attraction of the unknown and of the unexplored. They may be short-cuts or, at most, they may lengthen the way but a little. And it is sometimes so tiresome to follow the beaten track, in company with so many others, and forced to obey the directions of the expert guide. O just for a bit of adventurous romping! Woe to the inexpert and wayward mountaineer if he follows the promptings of his heart and takes to one of these inviting paths. On and on he will go, with less and less desire to return, till he loses himself and falls to the bottom of this or that precipice, over the corpses of others whose ruin he had treated as but a tale to frighten children.

For a good Christian the way to Hell is naturally a horror-inspiring view. No one who has begun climbing God's holy mountain would turn back and plunge into the valley below. But there are other ways apparently harmless and almost innocent—ways that depart here and there from the beaten path, i. e., from the narrow road of the Gospel, on one side of which there rises the safe wall of the Commandments of God and of the Church, and on the other that of our duties and obligations. Woe to the man that forgetting the beaten track, takes to some of these alluring ways! 'That way lies Hell.' Of course, he never means to turn back altogether, into the valley of death. But he is no more on the royal path. He is no more protected by walls and embankments, no more under the guidance of expert guides, no more in the company of trusty fellow travellers who would ever support him, encourage him, animate him with their very presence. He will soon go astray—astray in the midst of luxuriant vegetation, of enchanting views. He will find it difficult to return. Most probably he will not even think of it He is lost.

O my Jesus, how infinitely good and merciful You have been to me. How many souls are suffering unspeakably in Hell! Had I died in sin I also would now be among them. I would be, in that place of torments—to curse You and to be burnt for ever...

Thanks, infinite thanks to You, O my Saviour, Who have had such pity and mercy on me. Truly you have stood between me and Hell with Your mangled Body and with Your pierced Heart, pleading for me with Your Divine Father.

O Jesus, give me grace that I may never offend You. Give me grace never to grow lukewarm in Your service—never to leave the royal road of generosity, to follow the easier way—never to give up fighting against my habitual sins, my evil tendencies, my worldly and natural inclinations. Let the thought that a little yielding may slowly, gradually, and almost insensibly, lead me away from You, to Hell, restrain me and strengthen me to keep straight in the narrow path that leads to eternal happiness.

O Mary, my Mother, help me!

FROM 'E TENEBRIS'

Come down, O Christ, and help me! reach thy hand,
For I am drowning in a stormier sea
Than Simon on thy lake of Galilee:
The wine of life is split upon the sand,
My heart is as some famine-murdered land
Whence all good things have perished utterly,
And well I know my soul in Hell must lie
If I this night before God's throne should stand.

Oscar Wilde.

VENIAL SIN

DEVIATING FROM THE ROAD

The first Prelude is to see myself in the sight of God like the man full of leprosy that approached Christ our Lord crying : "Lord, if Thou wilt, Thou canst make me clean."

The second Prelude is to ask light and grace to know and feel the malice of my sins and to detest and abhor them.

1. Half-Deliberate Venial Sins

There are many venial sins which we can hardly avoid : --

1) Sins of infirmity, committed through weakness;

2) Sins of surprise, committed by sudden and strong temptation ;

3) Sins of impetuosity, when passion carries a man for a moment beyond self-control ;

4) Sins of indeliberation, i.e., done in haste, before conscience and reason have had time to deliberate and weigh what they were about.[1]

We are like soldiers in warfare: we cannot help being wounded and spattered by the blood of conflict. We are labourers out in the fields, and the stains of our toil cleave to us. We are wayfarers on the road, and the dust settles down upon us almost without our knowing it.

Impossible though it be to avoid all such half-deliberate venial sins, we can and we should try to diminish their number.

Vigilate et orate. The spirit of prayer, the habit of serious work and of attention to our own business, the practice of mortification and of generosity, will incredibly diminish the number of such venial sins.

Such failures, moreover, should help us to increase in self-knowledge, in humility, and in humble trust in the Lord. The two daily Examens of Conscience—the General and the Particular—and

1. Cf. Manning, *Sin and its Consequences.*

the practice of frequent Confession will greatly serve to increase the purity of our soul.

2. Malice of deliberate Venial Sin

There are venial sins which we commit deliberately.

We deliberately misjudge our neighbours; we murmur and entertain uncharitable thoughts. We make spiteful remarks and indulge in uncharitable gossip. We are testy, jealous and exacting. We are easily ruffled and say angry words. We tell "white lies." We indulge in vain and proud thoughts.[1]

Against sins such as these we must declare war, *à outrance*, if we truly love God and our soul.

Many persons, though apparently pious, make light of deliberate venial sin—in their manner of acting, if not in their mind. And yet, after mortal sin, there is no evil greater than venial sin.

The least venial sin is a greater evil than any temporal evil: it is a moral evil and an offence against God. "The Church holds that it were better for the sun and moon to drop from Heaven, for the earth to fail, and for all the many millions who are on it to die of starvation, in extremest agony (as far as temporal affliction goes), than that one soul, I will not say should be lost, but should commit one venial sin."[2] To know God's Will and to act against it, is in a true sense, an evil of infinite gravity.

The ingratitude implied in a venial sin is enormous. To grasp that we have but to consider:—

1) What God has done for us;

2) What Christ has done in Bethlehem, on Calvary, on the Altar;

3) What we ought to be in our relations with God our Father and our Spouse. Nothing we do could be enough for Him, and instead we are deliberately mean and niggardly with Him. We are attached to what He denounces, and we persevere in the danger of losing Him altogether. What would happen if a child were to treat his father, a friend, a friend or a bride her bridegroom, as we have treated Christ, our Father, our Friend, and the Bridegroom of our soul?

1 Cf *Venial Sin* by Rt. Rev. J. S. Vaughan. 2. Newman, *Anglican Difficulties*.

3. Lamentable Effects of Venial Sin

1) Venial sin deprives the soul of its beauty.

It does not destroy charity, nor does it diminish it, but it hinders its exercise: the divine fire is smothered.

Mortal sin is the death of the soul: venial sin is the leprosy that disfigures it. It is true that God loves the soul notwithstanding the number of venial sins it commits, "just as a mother loves her child covered with fostering ulcers, but will no longer press it to her bosom, nor smother it with kisses, because its flesh is one mass of filthy scabs, but she will not cast it off from her....Only when absolutely cold and dead, she tearfully submits to be separated from it."[1]

The diminution of fervour might produce such supernatural torpor in the soul that it would be disarmed in the presence of a grave temptation and succumb to it.

2) Venial sin leads the soul into mortal sin:—

a) positively. By committing a venial sin, says St Thomas, *aliquis ordo praetermittitur.* The will becomes accustomed to yield. The judgment grows hazy: the windows of the soul get dark and dusty. Faith is weakened and a fatal indifference spreads about the heart. This is especially true on all occasions when the matter being grievous, one only doubts whether full consent was given. In other words, venial sin blunts the conscience, brings on insensibility, and clouds the presence of God.

b) negatively. Venial sin withdraws the soul from the special influence of God's love. We all stand in need of actnal grace. The soul that habitually commits venial sins will not get such grace, because it will not pray for it.

4. The Punishment of Venial Sin

According to St Thomas, the torments of Purgatory exceed every evil of this life, even the sufferings of Christ Our Lord, just as the glory of the Saints surpasses every good of the present life.[2] St Catherine of Genoa says: "They (the souls) suffer such extreme

1. Vaughan, *Venial Sin,* ch. ii. 2. Cf. *Summa.* III. Q. iii, p. 46, a, 6 *ad* 3.

pain that no tongue can tell it, nor mind conceive the least portion of it, unless by special grace of God."[1] And again: "No tongue can tell nor mind conceive, what Purgatory really imports. I see that, as regards the pain, it is equal to that of Hell, and nevertheless I perceive that the soul which perceives the very least blemish accepts the pain as a mercy and counts the suffering as nothing compared to that bar which sunders it from its Love. And it seems to me that the greatest pain endured by the souls in Purgatory arises from their seeing in themselves something displeasing to God, and committed willingly against such goodness as His."[2]

Truly, then, after mortal sin, venial sin is the greatest evil!

To end with the *Triple Colloquy* to our Lady, to our Lord, and to the Eternal Father.

FROM 'THE DREAM OF GERONTIUS'

Take me away, and in the lowest deep
There let me be,
And there in hope the lone night-watches keep,
Told out for me.
There, motionless and happy in my pain,
Lone, not forlorn,—
There will I sing my sad perpetual strain,
Until the morn.
There will I sing, and soothe my stricken breast,
Which ne'er can cease
To throb, and pine, and languish, till possest
Of its Sole Peace.
There will I sing my absent Lord and Love:—
Take me away,
That sooner I may rise, and go above,
And see Him in the truth of everlasting day.

Newman.

1. *Treatise on Purgatory* by St Catherine of Genoa, Chap. ii.
2. Id Chap. vii.

TEPIDITY

THE HABITUAL DEVIATION FROM THE ROAD

The first Prelude is to see myself in the sight of God like the man who going down from Jerusalem to Jericho, was stripped and wounded by robbers, and left half dead by the roadside.

The second Prelude is to ask light and grace to know and feel the disorder of my actions and to abhor it, that I may amend and set my life in order.

1. Tepidity is a State of the Soul

Tepidity is not to be mixed up with desolation, nor with the mere want of sensible love for the things of God, nor with real weariness and fatigue. Tepidity is a state of the soul. To feel tepid now and then is not to be in the state of tepidity, just as one is not necessarily fervent because he has occasional moments of fervour. Tepid is the soul that commits venial sins habitually, not out of surprise or weakness, but out of sheer carelessness about small offences.

Mortal sin is the profanation of God's temple: deliberate and habitual venial sin is the neglect of it. A tepid soul may be compared to a church where all is untidy and out of order. Of course even the finest and most jealously guarded shrine will be covered with some stain and dust, and needs constant cleaning. We fall very frequently and get specked and stained. We have but to rise, cleanse ourselves in the Sacred Blood of Christ, and walk with greater circumspection. If we continue to do so, without giving way to discouragement, far from being in the state of tepidity, we shall steadily advance along the road that leads to sanctity.

2. Tepidity is Sluggishness

What, then, in practice, is tepidity?

It is to let oneself go, to let loose the rein, to be content with that control over our senses, our faculties, our heart and our passions which excludes grave sins. It is a state of slothfulness and self-indulgence.

The tepid person is sluggish in all he does. First of all he is sluggish in his spiritual exercises. He shortens them. He performs them hastily. His mind is in a state of constant distraction and dissipation. Solitude becomes irksome to him.

He is sluggish in all his other duties. He begins by performing them with a certain carelessness. He soon becomes unpunctual and irregular. He proceeds to leave duties undone as regards God, his soul, and his neighbour. Formerly the Will of God was his rule—at least in theory. Now he lives by the rules of worldly men and thinks with them.

Fervour renders easy whatever we do, and whatever we do easily, we do with pleasure and find a sweetness in it. It is not emotion. It implies regularity, punctuality, and exactness. It is doing our duty by rule, at the right time, and as perfectly as we can. It cancels and drives away sin. It makes sin difficult to commit, if not impossible. Sluggishness, on the contrary, makes the dust of continual venial sins settle on our soul and on the wonderful organism of our senses and faculties. It clogs them. They move with difficulty in the praise and service of God. Soon they will not move at all Tepidity is a kind of sleeping-sickness which, once acquired, produces increased lethargy and insensibility. It is a millstone around the neck.[1]

3. Tepidity is Self-Indulgence

Self-indulgence is another mark of tepidity. The tepid person has lost the habit of severe self-control, of mortification, of self-sacrifice for the good of others. He gives free vent to his passions and his whims, and makes use of his knowledge of the spiritual life and of Moral Theology to go as far as the brink, without falling into the abyss. This habit of self-indulgence is for him the source of numberless sins of commission and omission in his relation to God, to his superiors and companions, and to himself. How often, especially in the matter of purity and chastity, the tepid man crosses

1. Cf. Manning, *Sin and its Consequences.*

the boundary that divides venial sin from mortal, and deliberately remains under the delusion that he does not.

4. Danger for Persons Consecrated to God

Cardinal Bourne knew well what he was talking about when he made the following statement to the Priest at Wonersh on 2nd May 1921:

"After a long experience I am convinced that our greatest danger does not lie in some fierce temptation, nor—at any rate at first—in actual sin. It comes rather with the parting of the ways, when the choice lies between two paths, the one more generous, the higher path, and the other, not sinful, but easier and more self-indulgent, the lower path."

The greatest danger, then, for those of us who are specially consecrated to the service of God is to make the *good enough* and not the *best* our rule; to be contented with doing only *our bit,* instead of trying to do *our utmost.* Speculatively such an attitude is not bad. It may seem quite a reasonable one. But, practically, it will insensibly drag us lower and lower into the state of tepidity. If God does not entirely fill our heart, the world and the flesh will surely do it.

There is something peculiar in the things of God that makes tepidity easy. In the things of the world, barring deceit, efficiency counts for everything. If you do not get on, you go under. If you do not advance ahead of others, you will soon be left behind. Not so in the things of God. We may grow slack, perfunctory, and unbusinesslike, and yet we may not suffer for it in the eyes of men; we may even profit by it. Only the Heart of Jesus will grieve, and souls will be scandalized or left starving.

5. The Fight against Tepidity

We must be on our guard against tepidity.

It is a cruel tyrant.

It implies such disloyalty to God, such meanness and insincerity, that our Lord threatens the severest punishments against it.

"To the angel of the Church in Ephesus write: .... But I have against thee that thou hast left thy first love. Remember, therefore, whence thou hast fallen: and repent and do the former works: but if not, I will come to thee, and I will move thy lamp out of its place, unless thou repent."[1]

"And to the angel of the Church in Laodicea write: .... I know thy works; thou art neither cold nor hot. Would that thou hadst been cold, or hot! As it is, because thou art lukewarm, and neither cold nor hot, I am about to vomit thee out of my mouth."[2] On which Fr. A. Lapide comments: *Licet frigidus sit peior tepido, tamen peior est status tepidi, quia tepidus est in maiori periculo manendi sine spe resurgendi.*

However, what is naturally impossible to man becomes possible with God's grace.

Fidelity and generosity in the performance of our duties—and especially of our spiritual exercises—the determination never to make things easy, but to fight strenuously against sluggishness and to mortify ourselves, will keep up the fervour of our soul or restore it if lost.

Nor should we forget the promise made by our Lord to the clients of His Divine Heart: "Those who are tepid will become fervent, and the fervent will soon reach to a high degree of sanctity."

To end with the *Triple Colloquy* to our Lady, to our Lord, and to the Eternal Father.

1. Apoc. ii, 4, 5. 2. Apoc. iii, 14-16.

DEATH AND JUDGEMENT

IN THE LIGHT OF ETERNITY

The first Prelude is to see myself as if I were at the point of death.

The second Prelude is to ask light and grace to know the world, to abhor it, and put away all worldly and vain things.

*   *   *

"The land of a certain rich man brought forth plenty of fruits. And he thought within himself, saying: What shall I do, because I have no room where to bestow my fruits? And he said: This will I do: I will pull down my barns and will build greater; and into them I will gather all things that are grown to me, and my goods. And I will say to my soul: Soul, thou hast much goods laid up for many years; take thy rest: eat, drink, make good cheer. But God said to him: Thou fool, this night do they require thy soul of thee: and whose shall those things be which thou hast provided?"[1]

"Thou fool," the same voice seems to ring in the ear of each one of us, "you dream of long years of life—of happy, thoughtless life—and you know not how fast death is approaching. Shortly—this year—why not this very day?—they will require thy soul of thee and what will become of thy life, of thy goods, and of all thy castles built on the sands of transitory existence?"

1. Certainty of Death

We must die. "It is appointed to all men once to die."[2] We die every day. Every minute brings us nearer to the boundless sea of eternity. We are travellers, pilgrims, exiles going home. This world is a house of probation, a novitiate. "We have here no abiding city, but we seek for that which is to come."[3] Death is the departure from this world to the eternal. "Man shall go into the house of his eternity."[4]

1. Luke xii, 16-20. 2. Heb. ix, 27. 3. Heb. xiii. 4. Eccl. xii, 5.

We must leave all—our goods, our work, our dear ones, our friends, even our body, the faithful companion of our soul. We shall enter on that awful journey alone. No, not alone: "their works do follow them."[1]

Our good and evil deeds—be they ever so little—will cling to us, to be our salvation or our condemnation. Whatever, during our lifetime, we build on God—every thought of Him and every longing after Him, every deed fulfilled in compliance with His Holy Will, every cross patiently borne and every act of self-denial, every deed of kindness and charity, even a glass of water given in His Name, will be as so many wings that bear our soul higher and higher—to the Throne of God. Every sin will be a millstone dragging it into the abyss. And yet instead of living in the light of eternity, we live as if this world were to be our dwelling place for ever. Instead of gathering gold and precious jewels, we load ourselves with straw that will have to burn out in the fire of Purgatory, or it may be with heavy and unbearable stones, with stinking mud and mire.

2. Shortness of Life

We must die. We know it only too well, though we do our best to drive the thought of death away. We like to dwell on life, its pleasures, its length. All around us is a conspiracy to make us forget how flimsy, how short, how fleeting life is.

Man's life is as a bird that "flies through the air, of the passage of which no mark can be found, but only the sound of the wings beating the light air and parting it by the force of her flight; she moved her wings and hath flown through, and there is no mark found afterwards of her way."[2] It is "as a ship that passeth through the waves: whereof when it is gone by, the trace cannot be found, nor the path of its keel in the water."[3] "As when an arrow is shot at a mark, the divided air presently cometh together, so that the passage thereof is not known: so also we being born, forthwith cease to be."[4] We come forth like flowers in the morning, soon to wither away. Our days upon earth are but a shadow: they vanish like smoke. "Whatsoever thy hand is able to do, do it earnestly:

1. Apoc. xiv, 13. 2. Wisd. v, 11. 3. Wisd. v, 10. 4. Wisd. v, 12, 13.

for neither work, nor reason, nor knowledge shall be in the grave where thou art hastening."[1]

3. Suddenness of Death

Fleeting as every man's life is, inexorable death often pounces upon its victim before it has run its natural course. The suddenness of death is the great truth that our Lord so many times sought to impress on His disciples.

"Be ye then also ready, for at that hour ye think not, the Son of Man will come."[2]

"I will come as a thief, and thou shalt not know at what hour I will come upon thee."[3]

Is not this truth confirmed almost every day by many an unexpected death? Who, then, can assure us that we shall have time to make our peace with God, to turn fervently to Him, and to give Him at least a few days of fervent service before the great day of reckoning?

"O! I shall always have time to cry 'God forgive me,'" an obdurate sinner would say to the priest who used to exhort him to repentance. He was thrown off his horse and died cursing God.

Who will assure us that, even when dangerously ill, we shall realize that death is approaching? How often death proves, though not sudden, yet unforeseen and unprovided!

And who assures us that even in the presence of death we shall have the strength and the courage to break away with our evil habits and turn to God seriously and sincerely? How many have cried, at that moment, "I cannot, I cannot." We must, then, watch, and be always ready. "Let your loins be girt and lamps burning in your hands, and you yourselves like to men who wait for their lord, when he shall return from the wedding: that when he cometh and knocketh, they may open to him immediately. Blessed are those servants, whom the Lord when He cometh shall find watching. Amen I say to you, that He will gird Himself, and make them sit down to meat, and passing will minister unto them. And if He shall come in the second watch, or come in the third watch, and find them so, blessed are these servants."[4]

1. Eccl. ix, 10. 2. Luke xii, 40. 3. Apoc. iii, 3. 4. Luke xii, 35-38.

Our Divine Saviour desires that we keep Him constantly in our hearts, and that we try to accomplish His Will in everything. Whenever we think of death we are to think of it not as something bitter and inexorable, not as the end of all, but as the drawing aside of the veil, the pulling down of the wall and the appearance of the Master Whom we have loved and for Whom we have lived. We see immortality in death. Our cry should be the cry of the Apostle of Love: "Come, O Lord Jesus!" Death is the throwing of ourselves into the arms of Jesus: "And when the evening was come, Jesus said: Let us pass to the other side." Judgement will hold no terrors for the soul that has watched constantly for the coming of the Lord and served Him alone.

4. Before Christ the Judge

But woe to the sinner: woe to the unfaithful soul!

"O Death, how bitter is the remembrance of thee to a man that hath peace in his possessions!"[1]

The past will rise up with all its horrors: sins committed, scandals given, souls lost, graces neglected, favours abused—all will surround the bed of the dying sinner and try to drive him into despair, by crying: "We are thine."

The present will torment the sinner with the thought of the immediate separation from whatever he most cherishes. "Doth bitter death separate in this manner?"[2]

And the future will be a frightening vision.

To have to appear before Christ—before Love slighted, insulted, and crucified.

"I am Joseph." These words by which the ill-treated son of Jacob manifested himself to his brothers, were said with a smile and with tenderness; but "his brethren could not answer him, being struck with exceeding great fear."[3]

What shall we say when Christ will appear, and showing us His hands, His feet, His Heart, will thunder: "I am Jesus, your loving God. What have you done with your hands? with your eyes? with your tongue? with your body? with your mind? with your will? with your heart? What have you done to Me? What have you done to so many souls dear to Me?

1. Eccli. xli, 1. 2. I Kings xv, 32. 3. Gen. xiv, 3.

And in a flash of light our whole life will stand revealed: all our sins in their number, their circumstances, their malice; good deeds neglected, and good deeds badly done.

Shall we bring forward excuses? Impossible. The devil will be our first accuser. Of what avail the fact that we only followed he crowd in sinning? The Gospel, the Commandments of God and of the Church, the obligations of our state of life will be the code according to which we shall be judged.

"And they say to the mountains and to the rocks: Fall upon us, and hide us from the face of Him who sitteth upon the throne, and from the wrath of the Lamb, for the great day of their wrath hath come and who can stand."[1]

What will be the sentence that would be pronounced on me if I were to die and appear before the tribunal of Christ at this very moment?

O King of fearful Majesty,
Thou savest freely, O save me,
Thou art sweet pity's Fountain Head,
With blushes deep and heartfelt moan,
O God, oppressed with guilt I groan,
Spare one who for Thy pardon strives.

May I live from today in the light of eternity! May I live as I shall wish to have lived on the day of my death! May I judge of things as I shall judge of them on the day of judgement! May the Gospel be the guide of my soul, and the Commandments of God and of the Church and my duties, my only rule of life, so that my sentence may be: "Come, you blessed of my Father, possess you the Kingdom prepared for you from the foundation of the world."[2]

To conclude with the usual *Triple Colloquy.*

1. Apoc. vi, 16. 2. Matt. xxv, 34.

THE PRODIGAL*

BACK TO THE ROAD TO GOD

The first Prelude is to see with the eyes of the imagination the house of the Prodigal, the road leading into a far country, and the farm where he is sent to feed swine.

The second Prelude is to ask light to know the infinite goodness of God whom I have offended, and grace to trust in is equally infinite mercy.

PART I

THE PRODIGAL'S INGRATITUDE

1. The Shocking Request

"A certain man had two sons; and the younger of them said to his father: Father, give me the portion of substance that falleth to me. And he divided unto them his substance."

The younger son lacked nothing in his father's house. He was the father's beloved. But, one day, looking round him, it seemed to him that many of his companions were enjoying a freedom which he had not. From that day he longed to shake off his father's yoke, till, forgetful of his father's love, he went up to him and cried out: "Give me the portion of the substance that falleth to me."

With the heart near breaking, the father divided his substance between them.

God is our Heavenly Father and we are His beloved children. In His house alone we experienced true joy and happiness. We were constantly loaded with His favours. We had only to love Him and to use His gifts to love Him more and more.

Unfortunately we stopped to look with regret at the imagined happiness of worldly men, or, at least, at the freedom and success of those who take things easy, and make the best of this world in the house of God. "Why so many bonds and restrictions for us?"

---

* Luke xv, 11-24.

And one day we cried to God: "Take Your gifts, the robe of innocence and grace. Give me back my senses, my imagination, my heart, my intelligence, that I may freely use and enjoy the things and the persons of this world." Or if we did not wholly reject God's gifts, we did what in His eyes is almost worse: we began to neglect them, to make light of them, and to leave them unused. "I would thou wert cold."

God, our Father, our Creator and Lord, could have refused to give back to us what was His by so many titles. He might have instantly put an end to our life. Instead He let us go. But His Heart was bleeding: a new sword had pierced it cruelly.

2. Into a Far Country

"And not many days after, the younger son, gathering all together, went abroad into a far country."

He cannot stand the sight of his father and of his home. He must needs sell his substance, turn it into money, and go far, far away, that nothing may remind him of his father's love and of his past dependence on him.

In long years of patient work we had acquired many good habits and some degree of sanctity. In a moment sin destroyed everything. The distance between the All-Holy and the sinful creature is immeasurable. Still, even after throwing off the sweet yoke of God, we could not leave His home: we can never escape from Him. We were, however, only physically present to Him. In reality, we lived in another world, far away from our Father. The stream of Divine life passed us by, hardly entering into us. Seeing we did not see, and hearing we did not hear. Prayer to God became a heavy burden, and the very remembrance of Him, painful.

3. Living Riotously

"And there he wasted his substance living riotously."

The sinner wastes God's goods. He loses the most precious supernatural virtues. He loses the Divine gifts. Even the good things he does, cease to be meritorious for eternal life.

Impurity, in most cases, causes such ruin. It gradually makes the sinner a wreck; morally, always, often even physically and intellectually.

On the other hand, freedom of the senses, an uncontrolled imagination, and the plunging into external things fix the soul in the state of tepidity. God's gifts, if not wasted, remain idle, and God's graces lie unused. The soul is the idle, wicked, and unprofitable servant against whom the Lord has pronounced a terrible sentence of condemnation.

PART II

THE MISERY OF THE PRODIGAL

1. In Want

"And after he had spent all, there came a mighty famine in that country, and he began to be in want."

What wild dreams of happiness had the sinner dreamt! To realize them he sacrificed God and his soul, and, behold, he finds no satisfaction and no peace. Independence, ambition, pleasures, cannot fill his heart. "To be in want," to be plunged in a bottomless abyss, has become his fate.

God alone can satisfy the thirst and the hunger of our souls. If we leave Him and His sweet service to go in pursuit of other consolations, we soon experience the misery of the Prodigal; and that sad experience will be a real blessing. Woe to us if, as a penalty for our infidelities, we were to find pleasure in things which displease God, and feel no remorse of conscience!

2. In a Tyrant's Clutches

"And he went and cleaved to one of the citizens of that country."

He, the beloved son and a free man, becomes, in his search after false liberty, the slave of a cruel master.

We were the free children of God. We had, it is true, to carry the yoke of His Law, but it was a sweet yoke. Sin delivered us into the hands of our passions. We became the slaves of cruel, low, and insatiable tyrants. They bound us hand and foot as by so many iron chains. And yet, horrible to say, we kept kissing our bonds.

3. Feeding Swine

"And he sent him into his farm to feed swine. And he would fain have filled his belly with the husks the swine did eat; and no one gave unto him."

Such is the state of a soul that has turned away from God.

"They that were brought up in scarlet, have embraced the dung."[1] "They have forsaken Me, the fountain of living water, and have digged to themselves cisterns, that can hold no water."[2]

Away from all good influences, the sinner is wholly engrossed in feeding his lowest passions. Often he would fain be even a swine. "Happy those that know no God, that hear not the voice of conscience," he murmurs to himself. "O! If I were not a Christian! If I were not a Priest, a Religious! If I had never heard His Call!"

Look at him, in that far distant country—naked—starved—in the midst of swine! Look at the change in his senses; at the havoc which sin has worked in his mind and in his heart! What has become of the man in him—of the Christian—of the Priest?

Do I perchance recognise myself in that wretch?

PART III

THE PRODIGAL'S REPENTANCE

1. I perish with Hunger

"And returning to himself, he said: How many hired servants in my father's house abound with bread, and I here perish with hunger."

1. Lam. iv, 5. 2. Jer. ii, 13.

It is in the midst of his utter misery that the memory of home comes to him.

The sinner is one that lives out of himself. He is all abroad. Distractions and excitement are his daily food. What he fears most is solitude. It is so with the tepid and lukewarm man. Recollection, prayer, self-examination, he cannot bear. The very thought of a retreat frightens him.

Something extraordinary may recall the sinner to his senses, and then, face to face with his soul, he sees it like a garden through which a pack of wild animals have passed on a dark night. He thought himself happy and free, and now he sees that he is "wretched, and miserable, and poor, and blind, and naked." He realizes that others, whom he thought bigoted and narrow-minded and dissatisfied, abound in all good things. "Do you remember," a voice whispers in his heart, "the days of your fervour?"

2. I WILL ARISE

"I will arise, and will go to my father, and say to him: Father, I have sinned against heaven and before thee: make me as one of thy hired servants."

Satan suggests to the unhappy Prodigal thoughts of diffidence and even of despair: "My iniquity is greater than that I may deserve pardon,"[1] but the Prodigal remembers that the father whom he has cruelly offended is still his father: that he is blood of his blood.

However much we may have sinned, however great and numerous our infidelities may be, God is still our Father and we the creatures of His hands. Let us, then, rise from our misery and go to Him with confidence and hope. We shall make a simple and straight confession of all our sins, and be ready for any consequence. We only know that we are utterly unworthy of enjoying the sweetness which God keeps for His dear friends.

3. He Came to His Father

"And rising up he came to his father."

1. Gen. iv, 13.

The difficulties and obstacles must have been great. He was weak. His evil habits made constant attempts to reassert themselves. His past friends mocked at him. The shame which he knew he had to face would frighten him. And yet on he went.

PART IV

THE FATHER'S FORGIVENESS

1. THE FATHER'S LOVE

"And when he was yet a great way off, his father saw him, and was moved with compassion."

The ingratitude of the son had wounded the father's love, but had not diminished its strength. The old man had waited for the return of the Prodigal. Daily he would look out for him, though scorned by all, especially by his elder son. The Prodigal felt instinctively how much the father loved him, when he said: "I will arise and go to my father." It was that love that drew him home. One day the father saw a traveller from afar. "It is he," he cried, and his heart beat violently.

Even the greatest sinners are God's children, His images, the princes of His Court, and the sharers of His life. They are created for eternal happiness. He cannot bear to see them rushing towards the abyss. He Himself goes to them and sweetly touches their heart with His grace. He invites them to Him in so many and such wonderful ways. Everywhere, through friends, through His ministers, through His creatures, He cries to the sinner: "Come back to My Heart!"

2. THE FATHER'S FORGIVENESS

"And running to him, fell upon his neck, and kissed him."

The old man, forgetful of his years and of his dignity, runs. He waits for no other advance on his son's part. He kisses him before any confession. He does not allow him to complete it.

This is but a faint idea of the meeting between God and the penitent soul.

3. Let us Eat and Make Merry

"And the son said to him: Father, I have sinned against heaven and before thee, I am not now worthy to be called thy son.

"And the father said to his servants: Bring forth quickly the first robe, and put it on him, and put a ring on his hand, and shoes on his feet: and bring hither the fatted calf, and kill it, and let us eat and make merry."

What a change the return of the Prodigal has worked—the father is rejuvenated and the son sits at table like a king.

Put on him the best robe, i. e., the stole of divine grace. Again will the Angels recognize in the penitent soul the child of God; with his virtues, good habits, and past merits.

Put a ring on his hand: he is again united to God. Again are his hands made beautiful with the ring of the free.

Put shoes on his feet: no more shall he walk in the mud. Henceforth he will run freely on the way of God.

Bring hither the fatted calf: God the Father gives him the object of His own happiness—His Word become Flesh, hidden under the Sacramental Species.

And let us eat and make merry: there is joy in the heart of the repentant sinner, and even greater joy in Heaven before the Angels of God.

To end with a Colloquy of mercy, giving thanks to our Lord that He has given me life until now, and resolving to amend for the future with His grace.

The Call of the Divine King

My will is to conquer the whole world, and all enemies, and thus to enter into the glory of My Father. Whosoever, therefore, desires to come with Me must labour with Me, in order that following Me in suffering, he may likewise follow Me in glory.

THE KINGDOM OF CHRIST

THE CALL OF THE DIVINE KING

[*The Spiritual Exercises*, pp. 66-72]

The first Prelude is to see with the eyes of the imagination the synagogues towns, and villages through which Christ our Lord went preaching.

The second Prelude is to ask of our Lord that I may not be deaf to His call, but prompt and diligent to accomplish His most Holy Will.

The Everlasting King

"The fulness of time is come, and the Kingdom of God is nigh; repent, and believe in the Gospel."[1]

Such is the message which Christ addressed to the Jews nineteen centuries ago, and which He keeps on repeating to every man "that cometh into this world." His Kingdom is as everlasting as Himself. "Jesus Christ is the same yesterday, and today, yea and for ever."[2] "And of His Kingdom there shall be no end."[3] It is the full recognition and acceptance of the Gospel, of the *Good News* which Christ announces, and which is nothing else but Himself as "the Way, the Truth, and the Life."[4]

Christ has willed that His life on earth should not be limited to the thirty-three years which He spent visibly amongst us. The words which He spoke to His own disciples, on ascending to Heaven only assure us of His abiding presence in our midst.

"Behold I am with you, even to the consummation of the world."[5]

In us and through us, He continues the life which He led in Palestine and the work which the Father gave Him to do.

"As the Father hath sent Me, I also send you."[6]

To live a Christian life implies something more than the modelling of our life on that of Christ. It means the constant denial of ourselves in order that Christ may reign in our minds, in our hearts,

1. Mark i, 15. 2. Heb. xiii, 8. 3. Luke i, 33. 4. John xiv, 6.
5. Matt. xxviii, 20. 6. John xx, 21.

and in our bodies. Every Christian must be able to say with the Apostle, in some measure at least: "It is no longer I that live, but Christ that liveth in me."[1]

The whole world, then, has become a vast extended Palestine where every day, in the various members of His mystical Body, Christ is born amidst the poor surroundings of Bethlehem, works in the silence and concealment of Nazareth, goes about doing good and announcing the Gospel of the Kingdom, suffers and even dies for the salvation of men. And that is why, before starting to contemplate the mysteries of our Lord's life, St Ignatius wants us "to see with the eyes of the imagination the synagogues, towns and villages through which Christ our Lord went preaching." We should, in other words, re-create the Holy Land in our hearts. Still more, The light of Faith must transfigure for us the towns, villages, plains, and hills of our land into the land of Christ—the land that Christ wants to hallow through us. Every town will then be Nazareth or Jerusalem; every mountain, a Mountain of the Beatitudes; every hillock, a Calvary; and every tree, a cross. It was in this light that St Ignatius came to regard Rome, Italy, Europe, the whole world itself, as the Holy Land to which he and his companions had at first vowed to go.

Christ walks through the length and breadth of the earth calling men to Him as He called His first disciples, while passing along the shore of the lake of Gennesaret or through the streets of Capharnaum. Not only does He summon many to leave all things—father, mother, brethren, and possessions—and join Him in the immediate work of saving souls, but He constantly invites everyone of us, whatever our state of life may be, to come nearer and nearer to Him. He calls us by the secret whispering of His grace, by the dispositions of His Providence, by the voice of our superiors, of our Rules or of our duties, by the silent example of our companions and their demands on our time, our patience, and our sympathy.

Must we not continually cry out with St Paul: "Lord, what wilt Thou have me to do?"[2]—or, with the Prophet Samuel: "Speak, Lord, for Thy servant heareth;"[3]—or, with St Ignatius, ask grace from our Lord that we may not be deaf to His call, but

1. Gal. ii, 20. 2. Acts. ix, 6. 3. I Kings iii, 10.

prompt and diligent to accomplish His most Holy Will. O that our Divine King and Saviour would indeed remove the veil off our eyes and the crust off our hearts, so that, turning a deaf ear to the cravings of our passions, we may constantly hearken to His calls and answer Him readily and wholeheartedly.

PART ONE

1. The Exercitant's Dispositions

Who is our King? What is his plan and programme? What are the conditions which He offers to His followers? What are their answers and the motives that prompt them? Of what nature is their oblation? Such are the main points of this truly magnificent contemplation of St Ignatius.

The feelings of shame, of confusion and sorrow, of hatred of self on the one hand and of heartfelt gratitude on the other, with which our hearts must be overflowing at the end of the First Week, are the best preparation to grasp and enter fully into the spirit of the *Kingdom of Christ.* We stand before our King and all His court like recreant knights covered with shame and confusion, criminals bound in chains and deserving of death, firebrands plucked out of Hell. At the feet of Christ nailed on the Cross for our sins, each one of us has put to himself that momentous question: *What shall I do for Christ?* And Christ himself suggests the answer, when He invites us to be His dearest friends and companions, to labour and suffer with Him.

2. The Parable of the Temporal King

However, that we may all the better grasp the significance of the call of the Divine King, and be convinced of the whole-hearted generosity with which it must be answered, St Ignatius introduces the parable of *The call of the temporal king.* We are to place before our eyes "a human king elected by God Himself" and, accordingly, endowed with all the qualities that call forth the most enthusiastic devotion, or, as St Ignatius says, "whom all Christians reverence and obey." St Louis of France, the noblest of Christian kings, loved and obeyed even by those of his vassals who thought his crusades hopeless adventures, would be the nearest approach to the ruler of the parable.

"It is my will to conquer the whole country of the infidels," says the king, addressing his subjects. "Wherefore, whoever desires to come with me must be content to eat as I eat, and likewise to drink and be clothed. In like manner he must, as I do, labour by day, and watch by night, in order that afterwards he may share with me in the victory, according as he has shared in the toils."

Obviously, such a proposal is beyond man's power and condescension. But if it were possible, what would good subjects answer a king so genreous and so gracious? As a matter of fact, what answer did men give, in the past, to appeals made by kings and leaders not endowed with the qualities of the king of St Ignatius' parable, for objects far less noble and holy, and in circumstances and conditions that bear no comparison with those of the parable? Without recalling the heroism of times long past, we have before us the example of the millions of men who in the Great War freely offered themselves to extreme hardships. They faced death almost hourly and constantly endured what is even worse—the agony of fear and of expected attack. They suffered excruciating pains in trenches, on battle-fields, and in hospitals, often with joy, and even with a smile on their lips, anxious to distinguish themselves by acts of bravery and self-sacrifice, and repeatedly asking to be sent on the most dangerous and desperate expeditions. Who can forget the contempt that was felt everywhere for those who lagged behind, and refused to join till compelled by force? And to what purpose were such devotion and so many sacrifices? To defend one's country against what seemed an unjust and unwarranted attack. And under what conditions? To die on the battle-field, or to come home a cripple for life, wearing perhaps a military cross, if fortunate enough to have called for recognition.

With good reason, then, does St Ignatius conclude his parable by inviting us to consider that "if anyone were not to accept the call of such a king he would deserve to be reprobated by all the world and held as a wicked knight."

PART TWO

1. Christ, the King of Love

Is the king of the parable merely a fanciful figure, and are the conditions which he offers to his followers quite beyond the realm of reality? On the contrary, though the parable itself is but imagined, it falls infinitely short of the reality which it is meant to set forth.

Christ is the Divine and Supreme King, the "King of Kings, and Lord of Lords."[1]

He is the Creator of all and their Eternal Lord, "the image of the invisible God, the first born of every creature: for in Him were created all things in Heaven and on earth, things seen and things unseen, whether thrones or dominations or principalities or powers – all creation is through Him, and unto Him. And Himself is prior to all, and in Him all things hold together."[2]

Even as Man, He is our King, by reason of His personal union with the Word of God. We are His, and we owe Him adoration and obedience.

But He is our King by another title, even more glorious for us, He has ransomed us from the power of evil and the darkness of Hell.

"Ye are not your own, for ye have been bought at a price."[3]

And he has ransomed us out of love. Love prompted the Son of God to take a human body and redeem us through His sufferings and death. We are the spoils of the Sacred Heart, the slaves bound to it as to a conqueror's chariot. The whole world is subject to Him. His last words to the Apostles: "All power is given to Me in Heaven and on earth,"[4] clearly indicate the greatness of His power and the infinite extent of His Kingdom. And yet it is not by force that He wants to reign over us, but by the charm of His infinite beauty and goodness and by the all-powerful attraction of His love. Truly is He the King of hearts.

1. Apoc. xix, 16. 2. Coloss. i, 15-17. 3. I Cor. vi, 20. 4. Matt xxviii, 18.

2. The Call of Christ

Hence He invites us to Him, when He could have commanded us. He wants free and willing service; and His invitation is made to each one in particular.

What is the plan and programme of the Divine King?

"My will is to conquer the whole world and all enemies, and thus to enter into the glory of My Father."

He wants to destroy the power of evil, to submit all men to His dominion, and thus deliver to God, the Father, an eternal and universal Kingdom—a Kingdom of truth and life, a Kingdom of holiness and grace, a Kingdom of justice, love, and peace. He wants to reign in our minds, which must assent with perfect submission and firm belief to His revealed truths and His doctrine. He wants to reign in our wills, which must obey the laws and precepts of God. He wants to reign in our hearts, which must spurn natural desires and love God above all things, and cleave to Him alone. He wants to reign in our bodies and in our members, which should serve as instruments for the interior sanctification of our souls.[1]

"Then shall be the end, when He shall surrender the Kingdom to God the Father, when He shall have brought to nought all other rule and all other authority and power. For He must reign until the Father hath put all His enemies under His feet.... And when all things shall be subject to Him, then shall the Son Himself be subject to the Father Who subjected all things to Him, that God may be all in all."[2]

3. Self-denial, the Condition to Enter into the Kingdom

"The Kingdom" implies a constant and unrelenting warfare against all its enemies—the world, the devil, and the flesh, with all their confederates. This warfare is a *conditio sine qua non* to enter the Kingdom and become one of its subjects.

"Repent," says our Lord: i. e., change thy mind, convert thyself by a perfect change of feelings, of judgments, of aims, of the ordinary values of life.

1. Cf. The Encyclical Letter on the Kingship of Christ. 2. I Cor. xv, 24-28.

"If any man will come after Me, let him deny himself,"[1] i. e., let him make himself indifferent to his own feelings and interests that he may follow Christ. "Let us first learn what it is to deny another, and then we shall know what it is to deny oneself," says St John Chrysostom. To deny another, he observes, is to disown him, stand aloof from him, let him suffer as though it were no concern of ours. Denial of self implies all this towards ourselves.

4. Solidarity with Christ

It is our Lord Himself, however, Who is to wage war and, through His powerful grace, defeat the enemy in us and through us. We have only to follow Him and do as He does.

What, then, are the terms that Christ offers to those who want to join Him? He does not order them to go and fight, but He invites them to come and live with Him. "Come," He says, "and be with Me. Thou shall encamp under My tent. Thou shalt eat at My table, and drink of the same cup, and be clothed as I am clothed. Be with Me and labour as I do; like Me work by day and watch by night; like Me, and with Me, suffer and endure."

He calls us out of our selfish, vain, and easy-going life, out of our whims and evil inclinations, to be with Him in the poverty of Bethlehem, in the submission of Nazareth, in His fatigues and labours for poor and often ungrateful souls, in His desolation, in His insults, in His agony and crucifixion. "Come and be with Me."

This is the Kingdom which Christ offers us—the Kingdom which the Father gave Him and in which He wants us to share.

"And you are they who have continued with Me in My temptations: and I dispose to you, as My Father hath disposed to Me, a Kingdom; that you may eat and drink at My table, in My Kingdom: and may sit upon thrones, judging the twelve tribes of Israel."[2]

The Kingdom spells solidarity with Christ. It is to live Christ's life, and do Christ's work in Christ's own way. It is to share in His Mission of suffering and of saving souls. It is a companionship, strengthened here on earth by the partaking of His Body and Blood, and perfected in Heaven by the vision of His

1. Matt. xvi, 24 2. Luke xxii, 28-30.

glory and our transformation into Him. It is only when the Kingdom is solidly established in our hearts that we can help Christ to establish it in the hearts of others. Look at our Lord. He first calls the disciples to Himself and shows them the final object of their vocation. "Come ye after Me, and I will make you to be fishers of men."[1] Meanwhile, however, He establishes in them the interior Kingdom and reveals to them the mystery of the Cross. Then only, He sends them to conquer the world through the Cross. Establishing the Kingdom in ourselves is the condition, the means, and the measure of our establishing it in others. That is why St Ignatius so strongly insists on *this*. The goal, however, is not the cross, but to work with Christ for the salvation of the whole world.

5. The Saints and Christ's Kingdom

Thus have the Saints understood the Kingdom of Christ. To mention but a few, St Paul in his epistles, constantly repeats that we are dead to sin and to the passions of the flesh, and live a new life in Christ and with Christ; and he earnestly requests us to put on Christ and have the same mind which was in Him. The life of St Francis of Assisi was but a walking with Christ. His desire to reproduce in his own life every detail of Christ's life on earth was so ardent and so sincere that "while he called himself only the Herald of the Great King, he was justly saluted as *another Christ*, having shown himself before the men of his age and those of future ages as Christ come to life again."[2] To live again the life of our Lord on earth was likewise the mainspring of St Ignatius' life, the central point of his Spiritual Exercises, and the characteristic note of the Society founded by him.

6. The Answer to Christ's Call

What must be our answer to the invitation of the Divine King?

Not to accept it is out of the question for any one of us. By such unworthy conduct we would, indeed, deserve to be accounted

1. Matt. iv, 19. 2. Pius XI.

as the most ignoble and wretched of men and reprobated by all the world, if only the world knew it. We should certainly be accounted as such in the eyes of God and of His Angels!

Two answers are possible. The first is the answer of reason. It is truly proper and reasonable that we offer ourselves to fight God's enemies and our own—Satan, the world, and our passions—and thus establish in our souls the Kingdom of God, that is to say, the supremacy of His rule. This constitutes the following of Christ in the way of the precepts. In the First Week we worked to implant in our souls a deep hatred of sin and of a disorderly life; now we offer ourselves to labour and fight *with Christ.* It is this union and incorporation with Christ, and not the mere avoidance of evil and the doing of one's duty, which turns a man into a Christian and a soldier of the Divine King. This, in fact, is what we vowed at Baptism, when we renounced Satan, the world and its pomps, and professed our allegiance to Christ.

Secondly, there is the answer of love and of generosity, the answer of those "who wish to show greater affection and to distinguish themselves in every kind of service of their Eternal King and Universal Lord;" in other words, the answer of those who want to be the special friends and companions of Christ. Others may content themselves with being simple soldiers in the big army of Christ, stationed sometimes in the fighting line, but more often behind the line. Not so the more generous hearts. As far as it lies with them, they set no limit to their service. They want to follow their King as closely as possible, to be with Him, to labour, to fight, to suffer and even to die with Him. If in His kind condescension, Christ holds out to His friends the prospect of an eternal reward as an inducement to follow Him, it is love for Him and an ever intense desire to prove themselves worthy of Him that prompt His devoted followers.

And what are the offerings of greater worth and moment made by such generous souls?

These offerings from the central point of the *Oblation* with which St Ignatius ends the contemplation of the *Kingdom of Christ* and which may be called an heroic act of consecration to the Divine King.

"Eternal Lord of all things, I make my oblation with Thy grace and help, in the presence of Thine infinite goodness, and in the sight of Thy glorious Mother, and of all the Saints of the Heavenly Court, protesting that I wish and desire, and that it is my deliberate determination, provided only it be to Thy greater service and praise, to imitate Thee in bearing all injuries, and all reproach, and all poverty, as well actual as spiritual, if only Thy Divine Majesty be pleased to choose and receive me to such a life and state."

As far as it lies in its power, the generous soul is ready and willing to imitate Christ "in bearing all injuries and all reproach and all poverty as well actual as spiritual," to follow him in the way of poverty and humiliation, in the difficult path of the Evangelical Counsels. Obviously the King alone has the right to choose His close friends. But He has only to say the word, "Come, after Me," and the soul is at His side.

7. The Inner Meaning of the Oblation

Why is it that, in the wording of the *Oblation*, St Ignatius lays so much stress on poverty and humiliations? The Saint wants to inflame the soul with the desire to follow Christ in the hardest things. Poverty and humiliations are such. They were the inseparable companions of Christ, the two pieces, so to speak, of His Cross. By it He entered into His Kingdom, and by it alone is it given to us to enter the same Kingdom with Him. The esteem and love of poverty and humiliations constitute the quintessence of His message. "Blessed are the poor in spirit." "Blessed are ye when they shall revile you, and persecute you, and speak all that is evil against you, untruly, for my sake."[1] Poverty and humiliations lovingly accepted are the means that most effectively take us out of ourselves to enter into Christ, to live His life and to do His work. The love of the things of this world, on the contrary, and the longing for its praise and glory are the most powerful destroyers of God's work in individuals and in corporate bodies, and the only disqualifications for service in Christ's army.

Poverty, and above all humiliations, make up the uniform of Christ's soldiers. It is not enough to enlist in His army. It is only

1. Matt. v, 3, 11.

when we share in the poverty and humiliations of Christ that we are truly His, and can cry out with St Ignatius of Antioch: "Now I begin to be Christ's disciple." No wonder if *Pati et contemni pro Te* was the ardent prayer of so many Saints. Though it is not given to all actually to observe the Evangelical Counsels or to be with the suffering and despised Master, the *spirit* of the Evangelical Counsels and the *desire* to imitate Christ in privations and humiliations are for every high-souled Christian.

8. HOW TO PREPARE ONESELF TO MAKE THE OBLATION

How shall we be able to make the offerings of greater worth and moment implied in the *Oblation*, to accept lovingly from the hands of our King poverty and humiliations? By fighting constantly against our own sensuality, i. e., the love of ease and comfort and of what pleases our senses, against our carnal love, i. e., human and natural affections not based on God, against our worldly love, i. e., the longing for praise, honour and recognition. But it is not enough to wage war against the world, the flesh, and the devil. That must be done by everyone who wants to be in Christ's army. Those who desire to be Christ's close companions must detest His enemies and their own, pursue them to their very last retreat, and exterminate them. They must not be satisfied acting on the defensive, but often take the offensive. Constant and serious self-denial mortification out of love and reverence for Christ, losing one's life for Him, giving up all things and becoming like little children—these are the essential preliminary steps to enter into the Kingdom, to be numbered among the friends of the Divine King and to act as such.

But how can we seriously make our *Oblation*, and say that "we wish and desire and that this is our deliberate determination to imitate Thee in bearing all injuries and all reproaches and all poverty," when we probably resent even the slightest word of blame, when we cannot stand the least neglect, and when we long so much for comforts? Are we not deceiving ourselves?

Well, if we feel that we cannot with truth say, *Volo et desidero et mea est determinatio deliberata*, we may at least acknowledge that we are far from the way of Saints. At the same time we may ardently desire to make the *Oblation* in full sincerity, and hope that, by constant self-denial in little things, we may, one day, be found worthy of making our oblation *ex toto corde* and of being thus enrolled amongst Christ's chosen ones.

Let the *Oblation of the Kingdom* be the goal of our endeavours. Though we may still be walking in the valley, it is good to keep our eyes wistfully fixed on the heights above.

FROM 'A SONG OF THE LOVE OF JESUS'

A mother He to me has been,
That ere my birth to me took heed;
With baptism washed the nature clean
All sin-defiled with Adam's deed.
With noble meat He fed my kind* *Nature.
For with His flesh He would me feed;
A better food may no man find;
To lasting life it will us lead.

Brother and sister He is because
Himself declared and taught that lore
That whose did his Father's laws
Sisters and brothers to Him they were;
My nature too He took there-till; * *Thereto.
Full verily I trust therefore
That He will never let me spill,
But with His mercy salve my sore.

After His love then I must long
For He has mine full dearly bought;
When I was gone from Him with wrong,
For me from heaven to earth He sought;
My wretched nature took, for me,
And all His noblesse set at nought,
Poverty suffered and penance strong,
Ere He to bliss again me brought.

His sides all bruised and bloody were
That sometime used full bright to be;
His heart was pierced with a spear,
His bloody wounds we ruth* to see. *Pitiful.
He paid, I wis, my ransom there,
And gave His life for guilt of me;
His doleful death should grieve me dear,
And pierce my heart for pure pity.

To heaven He went with highest bliss
When he had vanquished His battail.* *Battle.
His banner broad displayed is,
When so many foe will me assail.
Well ought mine heart then to be His
For He is friend that ne'er will fail;
And nothing He desires, I wis,
Save my true love for His travail.

His lovely lore with works fulfil
Well should I strive, if I were kind,
By night and day to work His will,
And have Him evermore in mind.
But ghostly* enemies grieve me ill, *Spiritual.
And fleshly frailty makes me blind;
Therefore His mercy I take me till,
For better help I can none find.

No better help is there to me
Than to His mercy me to take;
Who with His blood has made me free,
And me, a wretch, His son would make.
I pray that Lord for His pity
For sin me never to forsake,
But give me grace sin for to flee,
That in His love I never slake.* *Slacken.

The Coming of the Divine King

The Angel answering said to her:

"The Holy Ghost shall come upon thee, and the power of the most High shall overshadow thee. And therefore also the Holy which shall be born of thee shall be called the Son of God."

And Mary said:

"Behold the handmaid of the Lord, be it done to me according to thy word."

And the Word was made flesh, and dwelt among us.

THE INCARNATION

THE COMING OF THE DIVINE KING

The first Prelude is to call to mind how the Three Divine Persons, beholding all the surface and circuit of the whole world, full of men, and seeing that so many were going to Hell, determined, in Their eternity, that the Second Person should become Man to save the human race; and thus, when the fulness of time had come, They sent the Angel Gabriel to our Lady. (Luke i, 26-28 ; John i, 24).

The second Prelude is to see the great extent and circuit of the world where so many and such divers nations dwell; then likewise to see in particular, the house and chamber of our Lady, in the city of Nazareth, in the province of Galilee.

The third Prelude is to ask for an interior knowledge of our Lord that I may love Him and follow Him better.

1. Significance of the Incarnation

The Incarnation is the great landmark that divides the history of mankind into two periods. The first period is one of long preparation and expectation. From the gates of Eden, fallen man sets out on a painful journey, through a dark and barren country only now and then illumined by stars, in search of a Saviour. The Incarnation marks the beginning of the second period, one of ever progressing development in Christ. It is the joyful journey of man along with Christ, towards that sublime moment when, God the Father, having put all His enemies under His feet, "the Son Himself shall be subject to the Father who subjected all things to Him, that God may be all in all."[1]

The Incarnation is the central fact of the whole universe. Everything finds its reason in the Word Incarnate. Everything converges towards Him.

St Paul states this truth in the clearest terms. "He (Christ) is the image of the unseen God, first-born before every creature. For in Him were created all things in Heaven and on earth, things seen and things unseen, whether thrones or dominations or principalities or powers, all creation is through Him and unto Him. And Himself is prior to all, and in Him all things hold together."[2]

---

1. Cor. xv, 28. 2. Coloss. i, 15-17.

For each man, to believe in the Incarnation is to begin an altogether new life; to penetrate more deeply into that abysmal mystery is to rise nearer to God: incorporation with Christ is his all in all.

2. Mercy and Love in the Incarnation

The malice of Satan had defaced the beauty of man, the marvel of God's creative power. Deprived of original justice, man could no longer render to God the love that He owed Him. Then it was that the Son of God, Who had taken part in man's creation, offered Himself to atone for man's sin and to repair his misfortune. The end of the Incarnation is to reinstate man in his former condition, i. e., in that supernatural sonship which he lost by sin. It was fitting that this gratuitous adoption as sons should be restored to us by Him Who is naturally and of necessity the Son, for thus we become heirs by grace with Him Who is the heir by nature, and we have Him for our elder Brother Who is the Son of the Eternal Father.[1]

The mystery of God's Holy Will, according to St Paul, is "to bring all things to a head in Christ, both the things in the heavens, and the things upon the earth;"[2] or, as our Lord says: "As Moses lifted up the serpent in the desert, so must the Son of Man be lifted up; that whosoever believeth in Him, may not perish, but may have life everlasting. For God so loved the world, as to give His only begotten Son."[3]

3. Mankind before the Incarnation

At the very moment that He cast out our first parents from the garden of Eden, God opened to them a vista full of hope. Addressing the serpent, He said: "I will put enmities between thee and the woman, and thy seed and her seed; she shall crush thy head and thou shalt lie in wait for her heel."[4]

Thousands of years had to pass before the Great Event, here foretold, would be accomplished. Man had first to learn by experience that salvation is only from the Lord and that, far from becoming a god, of himself he could only sink lower and lower.

1. E. Hugon, *The Mystery of the Incarnation*. 2. Eph. I, 10. 3. John iii, 14-16. 4. Gen. iii, 15.

It is the sight of the horrible state of moral depravity in which the world had sunk just before the coming of Christ that St Ignatius wants us to contemplate minutely when he says: "to see the persons ... on the face of the earth, so varied in dress and bearing, some white and others black; some weeping, and others laughing ; some in health, others sick; some being born, and others crying, etc.... to hear how they converse with each other, how they swear and blaspheme, etc... to consider what they are doing, viz., smiting, killing, and going down into Hell, etc."

None can deny or even belittle the high stage of civilization reached by many ancient peoples before Christ. Egypt, India, Greece, and Rome surpassed in material wealth and outward show, in philosophy and literature, in architecture and the fine arts, in law and the art of government, anything our modern times have achieved. However, we have only to read the first chapter of St Paul's Epistle to the Romans to realize the spiritual misery of one of the most advanced peoples of the world before the coming of Christ.

"Being filled with all wickedness, villainy, covetousness, malice ; replete with envy, murder, strife, guile, spite ; backbiters, slanderers, God-haters, insolent, arrogant, braggarts, devisers of evil, rebellious to parents, without understanding, without honour, without affection, without pity."[1]

God looked down with eyes of pity on these poor creatures of His hands, and proceeded to fulfil the Promise which He had made in the garden of Eden and which He had often renewed, in the course of the ages, to the Patriarchs and the Prophets. "When the fulness of time came, God sent forth His Son, born of a woman."[2]

4. The Fact of the Incarnation

"The Angel Gabriel was sent from God into a city of Galilee, called Nazareth, to a virgin espoused to a man whose name was Joseph, of the house of David, and the Virgin's name was Mary."

The Divine message is not sent to the great ones of the world, but to a poor and unknown maiden, living in an obscure village of a small and insignificant country. And yet this maiden is so noble

1. Rom. i, 29-31. 2. Gal. iv, 4.

and high that she draws the Son of God into her womb. How greatly do God's judgments differ from those of men!

"Hail, full of grace, the Lord is with thee: blessed art thou among women."

Far from being elated by such a greeting and by the announcement it implied, the pure and humble Virgin "was troubled at his saying and thought within herself what manner of salutation this should be. And the Angel said to her: Fear not, Mary, for thou hast found grace with God. Behold thou shalt conceive in thy womb, and shall bring forth a Son, and thou shalt call His name Jesus. He shall be great, and shall be called the Son of the Most High, and the Lord God shall give unto Him the throne of David His father, and He shall reign in the house of Jacob for ever. And of His Kingdom there shall be no end."

The Son is the long-expected Messiah.

Either to make sure of the reality of the Divine message, or to show that she esteemed her spotless virginity above all other gifts of God, Mary said to the Angel: "How shall this be done, because I know not man? And the Angel, answering, said to her: The Holy Ghost shall come upon thee, and the power of the Most High shall overshadow thee. And therefore, also, the Holy which shall be born of thee shall be called the Son of God .... And Mary said: Behold the handmaid of the Lord, be it done to me according to thy word."

To celebrate the espousals of the Divine with our human nature, God waits for the consent of Mary, the only unspotted flower of the seed of Adam. Mary's answer to the undreamt-of offer is one of the deepest humility—"Behold the slave of the Lord"—and of the most perfect submission—"Be it done unto me according to thy word." Among all creatures, she stands out as the most perfect model of that deep humility and submission which behoves the creature in the presence of the Almighty Creator. Those simple words embody the programme of her whole life. They are the key to the greatness of her soul. At the first *fiat*, in the beginning, light was made. At Mary's *fiat*, in the fulness of time, "the Word was made flesh and dwelt amongst us," i. e., a most perfect human nature, created by God in Mary's womb and out of her purest blood, began to exist through the Personality of the Word that is from all eternity.

To the humble and whole-hearted *fiat* of the Mother of God there answers an act of infinite humiliation and submission on the part of her Son, the Incarnate Word: "For He, though He was by nature God, yet did not set great store on His equality with God: rather, He emptied Himself by taking the nature of a slave and becoming like unto men. And after He had appeared in outward form as man, He humbled Himself by obedience unto death, yea, unto death upon a cross."[1] Truly humility and submission sum up the whole life of Mary and of Jesus.

5. The Fruits of the Incarnation

The Word Incarnate works the restoration of mankind. The Church expresses this fact beautifully in one of the prayers at Mass: "O God, Who in creating human nature didst marvellously ennoble it, and hast still more marvellously renewed it, grant that, by the mystery of this water and wine, we may be made partakers of His divinity Who vouchsafed to become partaker of our humanity, Jesus Christ, Thy Son, our Lord."

First, by His Incarnation, Christ saved us from sin: "Thou shalt call His name Jesus; for He shall save His people from their sins."[2]

Secondly, He gave testimony to the truth. He brought to us the knowledge of God and the knowledge of ourselves—of our misery and of our greatness. He revealed God as a loving and watchful Father, and taught us to see in every man not a rival nor an enemy nor a slave, but a brother.

Thirdly, in Himself He has made us one with His Father and one with all our fellowmen. "I in them and Thou in Me," is the double filling up: St Paul's pleroma, constituted by the mystery of the Incarnation.

The Incarnation, then, is not only the nuptial feast of humanity indissolubly united in Christ to the Word of God, but our bridal feast too. By the strength of the God Incarnate, we are lifted up to God,

1. Phil. ii, 6-8. 2. Matt. i, 21.

even to the participation of His Divine Nature: *divinae consortes naturae.* It is the feast of our union with all God's children, the lost only excepted—the feast of our oneness with them as brothers in Christ.

To live in Christ, in union with our fellowmen, is the whole secret of the New and Eternal Alliance. Sanctity is the constant effort to find Christ and to possess him more and more. The Church is nothing else but the internal and external union of men in Christ. All God's works which have any relation to the end of the Incarnation — to restore all things — will be done through Christ's Humanity. Truly, then, the Word Incarnate is all in all to everyone of us.

At the end of the Contemplation let a Colloquy be made with the three Divine Persons or with the Eternal Word Incarnate or with our Lady, His Mother, begging grace that I may the more closely follow and imitate our Lord become Incarnate for me.

'AVE MARIA'

It was the springtime, and it was the end of the day. And she sat in her garden. And God sent His Angel to announce the 'great thing' to her. But she must not be frightened. She, so dear to God, the little maid of fifteen, all wonder and shyness and innocence, she must not be frightened. She sat in her garden, among her lilies. Birds were singing round her; the breeze was whispering lightly in the palm trees; near by a brook was plashing; from the village came the rumour of many voices. All the pleasant, familiar sounds of nature and of life were in the air. She sat there, thinking her white thoughts, dreaming her holy day-dreams. And, half as if it were a day-dream, she saw an Angel come and kneel before her. But she was not frightened—for it was like a day-dream—and the Angel's face was so beautiful and so tender and so reverent, she could not have been frightened even if it had seemed wholly real. He knelt before her, and his lips moved, but, as in a dream, silently. All the familiar music of the world went on—the bird-songs, the whisper of the wind, the babble of the brook, the rumour of the village. They all went on—there was no pause, no hush, no change—nothing to startle her—only, somehow, they seemed all to draw together, to become a single sound. All the sounds of earth and heaven, the homely, familiar sounds of earth, but the choiring of the stars too, all the sounds of the universe, at that moment, as the Angel knelt before her, drew together into a single sound. And 'Hail,' it said, 'hail Mary, full of grace!'"

Henry Harland.

GOD'S MOTHER

A garden bower in bower
Grew waiting for God's hour:
Where no man ever trod,
This was the Gate of God.
The first bower was red—
Her lips which 'welcome' said.
The second bower was blue—
Her eyes that let God through.
The third bower was white—
Her soul in God's sight.
Three bowers of love
Won Christ from Heaven above.

Laurence Housman.

The First Appearance of the Divine King

And Joseph also went up from Galilee, out of the city of Nazareth into Judea, to the city of David, which is called Bethlehem; because he was of the house and family of David, to be enrolled with Mary his espoused wife, who was with child.

And it came to pass, that when they were there, her days were accomplished, that she should be delivered.

And she brought forth her first-born son, and wrapped Him up in swaddling clothes, and laid Him in a manger: because there was no room for them in the inn.

THE NATIVITY

THE FIRST APPEARANCE OF THE DIVINE KING

The first Prelude is to call to mind how our Lady and St Joseph set forth from Nazareth in order to go to Bethlehem to be enrolled, and how, while there, Mary gave birth to the Son of God (Luke ii, 1-7).

The second Prelude is to see, with the eyes of the imagination, the road from Nazareth to Bethlehem and the place of the Nativity.

The third Prelude is to ask light to know intimately my Divine King Who has become a little Child for me, and grace to love Him and follow Him in poverty, suffering, and humiliations.

1. The Nativity of our Lord

Though it must needs have been hard in their circumstances, Joseph and Mary prepared to obey Caesar's command, seeing in it, in their spirit of humble submission, not the exaction of a harsh and grasping master, but a disposition of their ever watchful and ever loving Father.

Bethlehem is some eighty miles distant from Nazareth. Riding on an ass, as, with St Ignatius, we may piously conjecture, Mary covered the distance with much suffering and with many privations, sweetened by the thought of Jesus dwelling in her, and the companionship of Joseph. At last, having left behind them the plain of Esdraelon, Sichem, and Jerusalem, they reached Bethlehem, and immediately went to the place where they had to be enrolled and had to pay the tribute. This done, Joseph went in search of some shelter in the public inn. But Mary and Joseph were too poor to find a welcome in that place, when there were so many important persons to be attended to.

"There was no room for them in the inn." Bethlehem could offer hospitality to thousands of its children. Every house rang with the cheering voices of relatives and friends, happy to sit at the common board, after years of absence. The prophet Micheas had foretold that Bethlehem would gain immortal glory from its being the birthplace of Christ. "Out of thee shall He come forth unto me that is to be the ruler in Israel."[1] And yet no door opens to welcome the Divine King. Not even the public inn can spare a corner for Him.

"He came unto His own, and His own received Him not."[2]

It is a presage of the great rejection that was to come after—"Not this man, but Barabbas"—and of the numberless rejections that would follow it along the centuries, even at the hands of many who call themselves Christians and who receive Him not, or, at most, give him the coldest and most neglected corner in their hearts.

Mary and Joseph, the greatest beings our race has produced, are forced to take shelter in a cave, used as stable by the people in the neighbourhood of Bethlehem. In this wretched place, in the cold of the night, deprived of all things, and crying out once more: "Behold the handmaid of the Lord, be it done unto me according to thy word," Mary, with her virginal purity unsullied, brought forth the Son of God Whom she had miraculously conceived.

2. Looking on the Child Jesus

"As many as received Him, to them He gave power to be made the sons of God, to them that believe in His name."[3]

In company with Mary and Joseph, let us gather with lively faith around our newly-born King to do Him homage, and to look lovingly on Him, that we may, as we promised in *The Kingdom*, in all things feel as He feels, and do as He does.

"For He, though He was by nature God, yet did not set great store on His equality with God: rather, He emptied Himself by taking the nature of a slave and becoming like unto men."[4]

The contrast between the Eternal Son of God in the bosom of His Father, and the Incarnate Son of God in a manger, more than any other consideration, is apt to bring out, "what is the breadth and length, and height and depth" of the charity of Christ.

In Heaven, He is the God of majesty: "great and terrible above all them that are about him."[5] In the manger, He has made Himself a little Child, exceedingly lovable.

1. Mich. v, 2. 2. John i, 11. 3. John i, 12. 4. Phil. ii, 6-7. 5. Ps. lxxxviii, 8.

There, the Cherubim form His throne: "Thou that sittest upon the Cherubim . . . stir up Thy might and come to save us."[1] Here He is laid on straw, between two beasts:

He shrank not from the oxen's stall,
He lay within the manger bed.

In Heaven, His garment is the infinite light of the Godhead: "being the flashing forth of His (the Father's) glory."[2] In the manger, He is wrapped up in poor swaddling clothes.

There, He is the Word of the Father, by Whom everything has been created and is sustained. Here He lies helpless and must be fed with His Mother's milk.

Let us look lovingly on that Divine Babe. Why has He thus humbled Himself? "I live in the faith of the Son of God Who *loved me,*"[3] answered St Paul long ago, for each one of us. Christ lies in the manger out of love for me, to make Himself like me, and to draw my cold heart to His. Truly is the Infant Jesus born to me: a child is given to me, that with Him so little I may become little, that with Him so poor I may become poor, with Him so humble I may become humble, with Him so patient and meek I may become patient and meek.

3. Listening to the Child Jesus

The manger is the first pulpit of our Divine Master. His tongue utters no word, but His Heart speaks and His limbs are eloquent. The very walls of the cave are loud with appeals and with reproaches.

The Child Jesus speaks to His Father. He lovingly accepts from Him the manger, the cold, and the straw, and offers Himself as a Victim to atone for the sins of His brethren. "Behold, I am come to do Thy Will."[4]

He speaks to men. From the manger He cries, in deed: "Learn of Me because I am meek and humble of heart."[5] "Unless you be converted, and become like little children, you shall not enter into the Kingdom of Heaven."[6]

1. Ps. lxxix, 2-3. 2. Heb. i, 3. 3. Galat. ii, 20. 4. Heb. x, 9
5. Matt. xi, 29. 6. Matt. xviii, 3.

He whispers to the heart of each one of us the invitation He gave in *The Kingdom:* "Come and stay with Me. Come and live under this tent of Mine. Be contented with the food that I take, with the drink and the clothing that I have."

Who can resist the charming appeals of the Divine King, made a little helpless Babe for the love of us? Shall we not affectionately embrace His manger, and kiss it repeatedly and then, casting ourselves at His feet, beg of Him never to suffer us to be separated from Him?

4. Sufferings of the Child Jesus

"The whole life of Christ was a cross and martyrdom."

As soon as He is born, He begins to suffer poverty, pain, and contempt. Nay, of His own free will, He so arranges the course of events as to be born at the worst time of the year, at the coldest hour of the night, in the vilest place in the town, in the greatest poverty, ignored and despised by His very people. In Bethlehem the Son of God makes His first entry into this world of ours. He has, therefore, to show at the outset the nature of His Kingdom, of His throne, of His instruments of warfare, and of His insignia, and how diametrically opposed they are to those of the world.

Let us approach with trust and love the new-born Child as He lies in Mary's arms. Surely He will not cast us off nor drive us away, as each one of us cries in his heart:—

"Thou art my Saviour and my Redeemer, O Lord my God. For the sake of Thy boundless love blot out all my iniquities. I am sick and covered with sores; heal my soul. I am blind and naked; enlighten my darkness and clothe me with Thy virtues. I am withered and crippled; water me with Thy tears."

It is through Mary that Jesus has come to us. Only through her may we hope to go to Him and be gradually transformed into His likeness.

I will, then, conclude this contemplation by wholeheartedly welcoming our Lord as the Way, the Truth, and the Life, and by taking, at the feet of the Divine Mother, my oath of allegiance to Him poor and humble.

THE BURNING BABE

As I in hoary winter's night
Stood shivering in the snow,
Surprised I was with sudden heat
Which made my heart to glow;
And lifting up a fearful eye
To view what fire was near,
A pretty babe all burning bright
Did in the air appear;
Who, scorchèd with excessive heat,
Such floods of tears did shed,
As though His floods should quench His flames,
Which with His tears were bred:
'Alas!' quoth He, 'but newly born
In fiery heats I fry,
Yet none approach to warm their hearts
Or feel my fire but I!'

'My faultless breast the furnace is;
The fuel, wounding thorns;
Love is the fire, and sighs the smoke;
The ashes, shames and scorns;
The fuel Justice layeth on,
And mercy blows the coals,
The metal in this furnace wrought
Are men's defilèd souls:
For which, as now on fire I am
To work them to their good,
So will I melt into a bath,
To wash them in my blood.'
With this He vanish'd out of sight
And swiftly shrunk away,
And straight I callèd unto mind
That it was Christmas Day.

Venerable Robert Southwell.

The Oblation of the Divine King

"Now Thou dost dismiss Thy servant, O Lord, according to Thy word in peace; because my eyes have seen Thy salvation, which Thou hast prepared before the face of all peoples: a light to the revelation of the Gentiles, and the glory of Thy people Israel."

And Simeon blessed them, and said to Mary:

"Behold this Child is set for the fall, and for the resurrection of many in Israel, and for a sign which shall be contradicted; and thy own soul a sword shall pierce."

THE PRESENTATION IN THE TEMPLE

THE OBLATION OF THE DIVINE KING

The first Prelude is to call to mind how, forty days after the birth of Jesus, Mary went to the Temple of Jerusalem to fulfil the twofold precept of the Law of Moses—that of her own Purification and of her Son's Presentation to the Lord; and how Simeon and Anna recognized Him as the long promised Messiah (Luke ii, 22-38).

The second Prelude is to see the road from Bethlehem to the Temple of Jerusalem, and in the Temple, the Women's Court where, it is believed, the mystery took place.

The third Prelude is to ask light to know intimately my Divine King Who offers Himself to the Father for me, and grace to love Him and be with Him a victim on the altar of God's Will, for my salvation and the salvation of others.

1. The Sacrifice of Jesus and Mary

The Temple was the centre of the religious and national life of the Jews. It was the great external sign of the indwelling of God in the midst of His people, and the place where the various victims were offered to Him throughout the year. Though at the time of Jesus the Temple could rival neither the splendour nor the sanctity of the one built by Solomon, it was destined to be far more glorious. It was to witness the coming of God, not, as of old, in the shape of a passing cloud enveloping the Tabernacle, but in the form of Man pitching His tent in the midst of men, like one of them. "And presently the Lord Whom you seek, and the Angel of the Testament, Whom you desire, shall come to His Temple. Behold He cometh, sayeth the Lord of Hosts."[1]

Christ enters the Temple to fulfil whatever the Temple stood for. He is the true Emmanuel, God with us, throwing open to all, by His sacrifice, the way to the true Holy of Holies.

The mystery of the Presentation brings out the sacrificial character of the Divine King. So far He had been slain in the many victims that were constantly offered in the Temple to appease and propitiate God. Now He comes to renew the oblation He made at the moment of His Incarnation.

1. Mal. iii, 1.

He is the Priest and the Victim, "the first-born among many brethren," offering Himself to the Father for all of us. That is why Mary need not bring an ordinary lamb with her as an offering. She offers on the altar of God's Will the "Lamb of God Who taketh away the sin of the world." Now as later, at the foot of the Cross, she is the heavenly Mediatrix and the *Virgo Sacerdos*. Jesus is indeed given back to her, but as a devoted Victim. For long years, she must prepare Him for the blood-stained sacrifice of Calvary. He will be a "sign which shall be contradicted," and finally, He will be nailed to the Cross.

"And thine own soul a sword shall pierce"—the sword forged by men's indifference to the infinite love of Christ, and by their rejection of His claims. It is the sword that even now pierces the heart of every disciple of Christ, and specially of every Priest.

2. Obedience of Jesus and Mary

Humility and obedience are the main traits of our Lord from the very first days of His life on earth. "He humbled Himself, by obedience unto death."[1] In Bethlehem His humility strikes us most; here His obedience.

"Though not subject to the law, He wished nevertheless to submit to the Circumcision and to other burdens of the Law in order to give an example of humility and obedience, and to show His approval of the Law....For the same reasons, He wished His Mother also to fulfil the prescriptions of the Law, to which nevertheless, she was not subject."[2]

3. The First Followers of the Divine King

Who are the first followers of the Divine King? The Shepherds, the Magi, and in this mystery, Simeon and Anna—all simple and straightforward souls, conscious of their lowliness and spiritual poverty, seeking their salvation only in God and ready to welcome Him in whatever form He chose to appear to them. They may have had their own views and even their own prejudices, but these vanish in the presence of the Divine Child, their King and Saviour.

1. Phil. ii, 8. 2. *Summa* P. III, Q. 27, a. 3.

"And they (the shepherds) came with haste; and they found Mary and Joseph, and the Infant lying in the manger. And seeing, they understood of the word that had been spoken to them concerning this Child."[1]

"Where is He that is born King of the Jews? ... And entering into the house, they found the Child with Mary His Mother, and falling down they adored Him."[2]

"He also (Simeon) took Him into his arms, and blessed God, and said: Now thou dost dismiss Thy servant, O Lord, according to Thy word in peace; because my eyes have seen Thy salvation, which Thou hast prepared before the face of all peoples: a light to the revelation of the Gentiles, and the glory of Thy people Israel."[3]

And Anna "spoke of Him to all that looked for the redemption of Israel."[4]

4. For the Fall and for the Resurrection of Many

"Behold this Child is set for the fall and for the resurrection of many in Israel and for a sign which shall be contradicted ... that, out of many hearts, thoughts may be revealed."

The coming of Christ is, even now, a sign of division between those who dream of success, of riches, and of temporal happiness, and those who, seeking Him alone, welcome Him in poverty and suffering. Even now Christ is a principle of division between those who are instinctively and by a kind of secret affinity, drawn to Him, and those who draw themselves apart or remain, at best, indifferent to Him, having no eyes to perceive the Light, nor ears to listen to the truth. The greatest test of men – God's test—is how they react to Christ. That is why Christ is set for the fall and for the resurrection of many.

Let the contemplation be concluded with a fervent act of faith and of wholehearted homage to the Divine King, in the spirit of the just and devout Simeon.

1. Luke ii, 16-17. 2. Matt. ii, 2, 11. 3. Luke ii, 28-32. 4. Luke ii, 38.

The King in Exile

Behold an Angel of the Lord appeared in sleep to Joseph, saying:

"Arise, and take the Child and His mother, and fly into Egypt: and be there until I shall tell thee. For it will come to pass that Herod will seek the Child to destroy Him."

Who arose, and took the Child and His mother, by night, and retired into Egypt.

THE FLIGHT INTO EGYPT

THE KING IN EXILE

The first Prelude is to call to mind how, to escape Herod's fury, an Angel of the Lord appeared to St Joseph in sleep and ordered him to take the Child and His mother and fly to the land of Egypt (Matt. if, 13-18).

The second Prelude is to see the little house where the Holy Family dwells in Bethlehem, and the road to Egypt, lying for a few miles across the mountains of Juda, and then along the shore of the Mediterranean.

The third Prelude is to ask light to know intimately our Divine King Who is forced to fly into Egypt as to a place of exile, and grace to love Him more and follow Him ever more closely wherever He leads me.

1. The Enemies of the Divine King

No sooner is Christ born than the powers of evil rise against Him. Herod—mean, cruel, and treacherous—personifies them. He can have no peace so long as Christ breathes. He must destroy Him, no matter what crimes this might entail. Fear overpowers him, and drags him along a desperate and foolish course of action.

Herod continues to live and to plot against the Child Jesus in everyone of us. Fear is still Christ's greatest enemy. I am afraid

lest, having Him, I must have naught besides.

And though such fear does not always lead me to drive Christ away, it often silences His voice, drives Him into a corner of my soul, and prevents the expansion and development of His life in me.

2. The Apparent Weakness of the Divine King

What a strange King does our Lord show Himself in this mystery!

"Arise, and take the Child and His mother, and *fly* into Egypt: and be there until I shall tell thee .... Who arose, and took the Child and His Mother *by night*, and retired into Egypt."

Brought face to face with the powers of this world, the Divine King offers no resistance, and seeks safety in prompt and secret flight. Such apparent weakness and powerlessness will be one of the characteristic features of His public life too, till *His hour* comes and He delivers Himself into the hands of His enemies. He recommends the same attitude to His disciples: "And when they shall persecute you in this city, flee into another."[1] The history of the Church is but a long series of apparent defeats and failures, which, however, always end in new achievements and conquests. Like Christ, she is to succeed through apparent failures, and to show strength in weakness.

3. The First Martyrs of the Divine King

No less mysterious is our Lord's dispensation concerning the Holy Innocents. He allows them to be massacred and their mothers to endure the cruellest martyrdom. And yet it is just such a death, encountered for the sake of Christ, that has given these little children of Bethlehem such an important place in the Gospel narrative and in the Liturgy of the Church and, still more, the high thrones of glory which they occupy in Heaven, around the Lamb. Had their lives been spared, they would have passed away unnoticed like so many other children of Palestine. They might have even joined those who, on Good Friday, cried out that Christ should be crucified. And though nothing is known of the fate of their mothers, we may rest assured that their sufferings have been amply rewarded by the Divine Child. Truly, if for a soul to meet the Saviour means to partake of His cross, it means likewise to share His crown of glory, with the difference that while the tribulation is light and momentary, the glory is exceedingly great and eternal.

4. Trustful Confidence of the Holy Family

How sweet it is to look on Jesus, Mary and Joseph, sleeping peacefully in the house of Bethlehem, with no thought of the storm which is about to burst on them, still less with any anxiety weighing on their hearts. "The Lord ruleth me: and I shall want nothing.... For though I should walk in the midst of the shadow of death, I will fear no evils, for Thou art with me."[2]

1. Matt. x, 23. 2. Ps. xxii.

See how readily Joseph and Mary obey the voice of the Angel. The order is hard, but it comes from God, and Mary humbly repeats: "Behold the handmaid of the Lord: be it done unto me according to thy word."

Notice how serenely they dwell in Egypt, though in the midst of hardships and sufferings and uncertainties.

"And be there until I shall tell thee," the Angel had said. So long as he does not speak again, they know what is God's Will, and that is all they wish to know. To do God's Will moment after moment, ready to start, at the voice of God, on any new and perilous journey, with neither regret nor anxiety, and praying for light when doubts arise, is the quintessence of sanctity.

To end with a Colloquy with the Child Jesus. How inspiring is the sight of Him lying in the arms of Mary. He is the model of what everyone of us must become to enter into the Kingdom of Heaven – a trustful loving child that through Mary, rests peacefully in the arms of the heavenly Father and only desires to love Him and obey His voice blindly.

HAIL, BRIGHTEST STAR!

Hail, brightest Star! that o'er life's troubled sea
    Shin'st pity down from heaven's elysian blue,
Mother and Maid! we fondly look to thee,
    Fair Gate of bliss! where Heaven beams brightly through.
Star of the Morning! guide our youthful days,
    Shine on our infant steps in life's long race;
Star of the Evening! with thy tranquil rays
    Gladden the agèd eyes that seek thy face.

Denis Fl. Mac Carthy.

The First Message of the King

from a Woodcut by Gabriel Pippet

And His mother said to Him :

"Son, why hast Thou done so to us? Behold Thy father and I have sought Thee sorrowing."

And He said to them : "How is it that you sought Me? Did you not know that I must be about My Father's business?"

THE FINDING IN THE TEMPLE

THE FIRST MESSAGE OF THE KING

The first Prelude is to call to mind how our Lord, being twelve years of age, went up to Jerusalem and remained there, after His parents had departed; and how, when they found Him in the Temple, He said to them: How is it that you sought Me? Did you not know that I must be about My Father's business? (Luke ii, 41-50).

The second Prelude is to see the road from Nazareth to Jerusalem and the Temple.

The third Prelude is to ask light to know intimately my Divine King and His message, and grace to love Him more and follow Him more closely, cost what it may.

1. Jesus goes to the Temple

Just for a moment the Evangelist lifts the veil that enshrouds the long silent years of Nazareth to record faithfully and graphically, as he must have heard it from the lips of the Blessed Virgin, an important episode in our Lord's life. At twelve the Jewish boy entered upon a new period of his life. He became a "son of the Law," subject to its prescriptions, and, to some extent, exempt from family government. Even nowadays, it is the time when the boy begins to orientate himself, to plan and live his own spiritual and mental life, and to take that shape which succeeding years will only improve or harden. How does our Lord enter upon this period of His life?

Since the day when, in His Mother's arms, He had been offered to the Eternal Father, Jesus had never gone up to the Temple. He must have anxiously waited for this visit, to pour out His Heart to the Father in that most hallowed place, and to renew the oblation of that sacrifice which, He, the true Lamb of God, would, later, offer on Mount Calvary.

Really He needed no temple to commune with God. His Heart was the true temple of God: "the Sacred Temple of God: the Tabernacle of the Most High: the House of God and Gate of

Heaven." Later on He will say: "Woman, believe Me that the hour cometh, when you shall, neither on this mountain, nor in Jerusalem, adore the Father .... when the true adorers shall adore the Father in spirit and in truth."[1]

And yet He wanted to teach us, by His example, that there were places where, even then, God's presence was more easily felt. As for us, our churches are not mere places of prayer: they are "the tabernacle of God with men;" they are Bethlehem, Calvary and the Supper Room extended throughout the centuries, all over the earth. They enshrine the Body of the Lord dwelling with us.

2. Jesus remains in the Temple

"And the Child Jesus remained in the Temple." Just at this turning point of one's life, the passage from childhood into adolescence, Christ shows in Himself what the service of God may imply for some of us. It is not a question of a few days spent in the house of God and in the company of our friends, to return afterwards to our ordinary avocations. Some of us feel called to higher things: to leave all and remain for ever in the companionship of Jesus. To obey the call is hard, but, then, it is only at the cost of many sacrifices that great things are achieved. And Christ shows us the way. He well knew the suffering which His Mother would endure while seeking for Him, and yet He leaves her without a word. "And His parents knew it not." And when after two nights and two days of a martyrdom which only mothers can somewhat understand, she finds Him and reveals the greatness of her grief in that tender reproach: "Son, why hast Thou done so to us? Behold Thy father and I sought Thee sorrowing," Jesus merely remarks: "How is it that you sought Me?"

To be detached from one's parents, and if need be, to leave them, is the first step that a soul, anxious to embrace the state of Evangelical perfection, must take. Only thus is one able to live one's life, and realize in it God's plan. To be inordinately attached to things and persons of this world, to love them, but not in God and for God, is to shut oneself out from great things, to see through

1. John iv, 21-23.

coloured spectacles, and render oneself deaf to the voice of Heaven. "If any man come to Me, and hate not his father, and mother, and wife, and children, and brethren, and sisters, yea, and his own life also, he cannot be My disciple."[1] "He that loveth father or mother more than Me, is not worthy of Me."[2]

3. "I MUST BE ABOUT MY FATHER'S BUSINESS"

"Did you not know, that I must be about My Father's business?" It is the first sentence from the Saviour's lips which has come down to us, and it reveals His relations with God and the programme of His whole life. His relations with God are those of a child with his father. To do His Father's Will and to accomplish the work which he had given Him to do is the *raison d' être* of His life.

To do God's Will is man's only duty. In His love and providence, God has planned out the life of each one of us in all its details, with the one object of showing His love for us and drawing us to His Heart. Sometimes the course of life fixed for us by God is an ordinary one. We must do His Will, glorify Him, and sanctify ourselves, in the performance of the simple duties of life, as members or heads of a family, in the class or office-room, or behind the counter. At other times He calls us to apply ourselves exclusively to the service of God and the saving of souls. It is for us to find out God's Will concerning us in particular, and then work to realize it, cost what it may. God's grace flows like a river in its bed, and the bed of God's grace is the state of life appointed for everyone of us by Divine Providence.

Let the contemplation be ended by fervently renewing the oblation of *The Kingdom*.

1. Luke xiv, 26. 2. Matt. x. 37.

The Hidden King

They returned into Galilee, to their city Nazareth. And the Child grew, and waxed strong, full of wisdom; and the grace of God was in Him.

NAZARETH

THE HIDDEN KING

The first Prelude is to call to mind how our Lord went down with His parents and came to Nazareth; and was subject to them; and how He advanced in wisdom, and age, and grace with God and men (Luke ii, 51-52).

The second Prelude is to see the house of Nazareth in detail: the place where Jesus and Mary and Joseph dwell; where they gather together; where they work.

The third Prelude is to knock reverently at the door of the home of the Word Incarnate, and ask Mary, our Mother, to allow me to step in and spend some time with Jesus, her Son and our Lord, with her, and with her beloved Spouse St Joseph.

* * *

Christ is our Model. Every act of His is a lesson to be treasured up and lovingly reproduced in our life so far as circumstances allow. As of Mary so of every Christian it should be said that he keeps all the words of Jesus, and still more His deeds, pondering them in his heart. But of all the lessons of our Saviour it is the lessons which He gives in the House of Nazareth that must be most deeply impressed on our hearts. They are the lessons of thirty long years, by far the greatest part of the Saviour's life. They are meant for all Christians, whatever their condition or state of life may be—for all Christian families and all Christian homes. They lay open the secret of the interior life, i. e., the life of the soul and the life of the heart: "Ye are dead and your life is hidden with Christ in God."[1]

PART ONE

INTERIOR LIFE

1. Importance of the Interior Life

"This is no other but the house of God, and the gate of Heaven."[2] In the sweet and holy house of Nazareth we breathe a

1. Coloss, iii, 3. 2. Gen xxviii, 17.

divine atmosphere—an atmosphere of joy, of peace, of tranquility and order.

But it is to Jesus that our eyes are immediately directed. *Inspice et fac secundum exemplar.* A simple look on the Saviour is life-giving. The companionship and conversation of great and holy men elevate and ennoble our souls. The companionship and conversation of Jesus deify them. By looking constantly on Him, the mist is lifted off our eyes and the ice around our heart is melted away. We begin to see things eye to eye with Jesus. Our heart throbs along with His Divine Heart, and at last we cry out with St Paul: "It is no longer I that live, but Christ that liveth in me."[1] Then alone are we counted among His true disciples.

There is nothing in this holy house of Nazareth to strike the eyes accustomed to the marvels of the world—nothing of what the world calls great and heroic. All is interior.

And really, true nobility is nobility of the soul. It is only the life of the heart that matters—what we are, not what we do. And we are what we love. The life of the heart of Jesus, especially in Nazareth, is, then, the infallible criterion of true greatness and nobility—of life, in one word, for it is life and a greater life that He has come to give us: "I am come, that they may have life, and may have it more abundantly."[2]

Let us, then, look on Jesus and enter, as much as possible, into His Heart, the Sacred Temple of God. What is it that constitutes the life of the Sacred Heart? It is a life of perfect conformity with the Will of His Father. It is a life of perfect and uninterrupted prayer. It is a life of burning zeal for the salvation of souls.

2. Christ's Conformity with the Will of the Father

Doing willingly the Will of His Father, in everything and at every moment—this is the life of the Divine Heart. At the first instant of His existence He cried out: "I delight to do Thy Will, O My God: Yea Thy law is within My heart." And now: "I do always the things that please Him."[3]

He lives in a secluded spot, in a lowly village, engaged in humble occupations. But such is the Will of His Father. Christ loves

1. Gal. ii, 20. 2. John x, 10. 3. John viii, 29.

it and far from desiring that it might be otherwise, He finds it infinitely lovely. And the humble duties of daily life, the humdrum tasks which Mary and Joseph enjoin on Him, the simple furniture His hands turn out, are as beautiful as the stars that came out of the hands of the Word that was in the beginning. They are the colours with which Christ paints things of eternal beauty, the instruments on which He plays a heavenly melody, and the words that form poems of unsurpassing excellence.

In Mary and Joseph He sees the representatives of His Divine Father—their will and their desires are the Will and the Desires of His Father. See how promptly and attentively He listens to their voice. How readily He complies with their commands. How perfectly and how lovingly He conforms His Will to theirs. "And He came to Nazareth, and was subject to them." That is all that the Evangelist, inspired by God, has recorded for us of those long thirty years. Now, as later, Christ can say: "My meat is to do the Will of Him that sent Me."[1]

Nor is Mary's life different from that of her Son. In the temple, in her home, and here in Nazareth, she is always the handmaid, the slave of the Lord. Her life is the accomplishment of the Divine Will: "Behold the handmaid of the Lord. Be it done unto me according to thy word."

And St Joseph's life is the same. He lives to obey the Divine Voice, whether it tells him to fear not to take Mary as his wife or to fly into Egypt, or to return to the land of Israel, or to dwell in Nazareth and be the master of the Son of God and then die just when Christ was about to open the Messianic era.

3. Christ's Perfect and Uninterrupted Prayer

The life of Jesus in Nazareth is a life of perfect and uninterrupted prayer.

To pray is to raise one's mind to God, and to commingle our hearts humbly and confidently with the Heart of our Creator and Father.

1. John iv, 34.

Prayer is natural to Christ—every throb of His Heart is a prayer of the most perfect kind. His prayer is continuous. It is fervent and calm, not something artificial and constrained. It is humble. It is full of gratitude and confidence.

His prayer is the prayer of the Saviour of men. From the first moment of His Incarnation He has gathered in His Heart all our aspirations, our needs and miseries. On our behalf He adores the Father; He offers Himself to Him, and with Himself He offers everyone of us; He gives to Him the tribute of thanks; He pleads for our sins; He asks of the Divine Goodness the graces and favours which we need.

The prayer of Jesus knows no cessation, nor does that of Mary or of St Joseph. Mary's heart is one with the Heart of her Son, and St Joseph's heart stands between the two.

Along with this interior prayer, they love to meet, at stated times during the course of the day, to pray in common.

Look at them pouring out their souls to God in the fervent aspirations of the Psalter at dawn, at midday before and after their simple meal, and at evening. See with what devotion they attend Divine Service in the Synagogue, and join in the singing of the Psalms, or listen attentively to the Prophecies which, they know, have begun to be fulfilled.

Truly this house is the Temple of God and the Gate of Heaven.

4. Christ's Burning Zeal

The life of Jesus in Nazareth is a life of burning zeal for the salvation of souls.

To save His people and give His life as a ransom for many, is the work which the Father has given Him to do. And even now, in the solitude of Nazareth, He is wholly in it. Not only does He teach us the most important lessons of life, and obtain for us the grace to sanctify our humble duties, but He is the Victim for the remission of sin, the Lamb of God that takes away the sins of the world. Calvary will only see the consummation of the Sacrifice begun at the Incarnation.

And with Jesus, Mary and Joseph work also at the salvation of souls, offering the Divine Victim to the Father, and with Him offering themselves as victims of propitiation.

Sanctity is not something saddled on our ordinary life. It is an orientation, an atmosphere, a life—it is living with Christ, through Christ, and in Christ. Jesus, Mary and Joseph teach us how independent it is of every external circumstance—nay, how a poor, humble, hidden state of life forms the best background to the highest sanctity.

It is the fulfilment of, and conformity with, the Will of God, out of love; it is prayer, the communing of our hearts with the Heart of God; it is zeal and love of souls. Nazareth is the school of sanctity, and the Heart of Jesus is its source.

Let us dwell in that Divine Heart, with Mary and Joseph. His conformity with the Will of the Father, His prayer and His zeal are ours.

PART TWO

LIFE OF LOVE

1. THE COMMANDMENT OF LOVE

Christ our Lord is the Love of God made visible to men. All His words and deeds are but the expression of this love. All His commands are summed up in one, the commandment of love. "This is my commandment, that you love one another as I have loved you."[1] "These things I command you, that you love one another."[2] One thing does He fervently desire for His disciples—perfect union of love. "And not for them (the Apostles) only do I pray, but for them also who through their word shall believe in Me; that they all may be one, as Thou Father in Me, and I in Thee, that they also may be one in Us."[3]

If all the disciples of Christ, however widely they differ in race, language, economic and social conditions, must be bound together by such a love, how much more, those who, after freeing themselves of

1. John xv, 12. 2. John xv, 17 3. John xvii, 20, 21.

all earthly ties, have joined together to reproduce more easily in themselves the traits of the Divine Saviour and make earth the antechamber of Heaven.

"That they may be one as We also are one." The union of the Blessed Trinity, however, on which our union is to be modelled, is unfathomable to our minds. God, therefore, has willed that there should be a visible counterpart of it in the loving union of the Holy Family. Nazareth is Heaven on earth, and Jesus, Mary and Joseph are the earthly embodiment of the Heavenly Trinity. If every religious house is an attempt to continue throughout the centuries the life of Nazareth, all its members must be bound together by the love that unites Jesus, Mary and Joseph.

2. The Love of the Holy Family

The love of Jesus, Mary and Joseph is kind. It is sympathetic. It is helpful.

Let us look attentively on them and study with reverence their very feelings. Virtue will even now go out of them to heal our miseries.

Listen to their words—how sweet and kind. Look on their faces—how serene and smiling. Consider their conversation—how joyful and yet how heavenly.

See how they help one another in the performance of their daily tasks. There is not the least trace of self-love in this holy house; each one lives and sacrifices himself for the others, and vies with the others in taking upon himself what is most humiliating and hard. "Christ did not please Himself"—His only pleasure is to do His Father's Will and sacrifice Himself in the service of Mary and Joseph: "The Son of man also is not come to be ministered unto, but to minister, and give His life a redemption for many."[1]

Let us enter into their hearts and see, if we can, how sympathetically they feel for one another, how each one rejoices in the joys of the others and grieves in their sufferings. "Rejoice with them that rejoice; weep with them that weep."[2] How tenderly is this feeling of common suffering conveyed in those words of Mary: "Behold Thy father and I have sought Thee sorrowing."

1. Matt. xx, 28. 2. Rom. xii, 15.

Truly this is "the House of God and the Gate of Heaven," where peace is supreme—the peace of the children of God who repose trustfully in the arms of their heavenly Father, and have but one object in life—to fulfil His Will and to love one another.

3. The Neighbourliness of the Holy Family

Happy those who can approach this holy house and experience the kindness, the helpfulness, the sympathy of the love of Jesus, Mary and Joseph!

See the sweet smile with which Mary welcomes the poor women of Nazareth that come to her! How ready she is to please and to help them! What words of comfort and of encouragement come from her lips! How they leave the place happier, stronger, and brought nearer to God!

Look on Joseph transacting business with the men of Nazareth. See his constant calm, his straightforwardness, his sense of the presence of God even in the most material actions of life!

But above all keep your eyes constantly on Jesus. How sweet and kind He is to all, even to those who are rude to Him, who refuse to pay what they owe Him. "He shall not contend, nor cry out, neither shall any man hear his voice in the streets."[1] He passes along the streets of Nazareth doing good and healing those tormented by the devil, not by means of miracles, but by the sweet odour of His virtues. Already He conquers hearts by the meekness of His own Heart and the charm of His ways.

May the sight of Jesus, Mary and Joseph cause the ice of our heart to melt away! May they fill it with their kind, helpful and sympathetic love, so that whether with the dear circle in our home, which should be the home of Jesus, or with outsiders, our feelings, our words, and our actions may, however faintly, reproduce the feelings, the words, and the actions of the Holy Family of Nazareth!

---

1. Matt. xii, 19.

PART THREE

LIFE OF HARDSHIP

1. Poverty of the Holy Family

"I am poor and in labours from my youth."[1]

The life of the Holy Family in Nazareth is a life of hardships, of privations, of toil, and of neglect on the part of men. It must be so. To be in want, to work hard, and to live unknown to men, if not actually despised by them, is the lot of most of us. Our Divine Teacher and Saviour has, then, to show us how to make these painful circumstances and trials the means of our salvation and sanctification. He has to gain for us the grace to embrace them lovingly for His love and in union with Him.

First of all, see how poorly the Holy Family lives. The house is that of a poor artisan. The furniture is what is strictly necessary, and even that is of the simplest kind. Their clothes, clean though they be, bear the marks of long years. Their fare is simple and often scanty. Alas! Sometimes Jesus goes to His Mother for bread, and she has none to give Him.

They feel the bitter effects of poverty—the necessity to work for their daily bread, the knowledge that there is no more food in the cupboard, the need to sell the work of their hands, to deal with hard and cruel men, to beg and be sent away with harsh words, and, what is still worse to tender hearts, the inability to relieve the misery they see around them.

And yet no complaint crosses their lips. They are happy in their poverty, in the feeling that a Father watches over them, and in the knowledge that their trials are golden chains that bind them close to His loving Heart.

O that we may copy in our lives the poverty of the Holy Family—that we abhor the comforts and the luxuries of the world, and rejoice in the want even of necessary things, with Jesus and like Jesus!

1. Ps. lxxxvii, 16.

2. Work

"In the sweat of thy face shalt thou eat bread."[1]

Labour, manual labour above all, which, since the Fall has been a punishment, is turned by Jesus into a means of expiation.

All work hard in the house of Nazareth.

We have contemplated the spiritual activities of the Holy Family—the continued elevation of the Heart of Jesus, of Mary, of Joseph. Let us see now their external activity also.

Let us follow our Blessed Mother as she goes about her work from early morning till late at night. Truly she is the valiant woman of the Proverbs. "She has girded her loins with strength and hath strengthened her arm .... She has put out her hands to strong things, and her fingers have taken hold of the spindle .... She hath looked well to the paths of her house, and hath not eaten her bread idle."[2] She is busy, either in cleaning the house, or in preparing the meals for Jesus and Joseph, or in mending their poor clothes, yet always finding time to help others poorer and more needy than herself.

Let us enter the workshop of Joseph. It is early morning and we already hear the sound of the hammer. It is hot midday: big drops of sweat stare on the Saint's forehead, but he continues to work. It is night, but the light within tells us that the Saint is still at work.

Jesus is no less active. Let us see Him, first of all, helping His Mother to go through the humble tasks of a poor housewife. There He is, carrying water and firewood, lighting the fire, laying the table, washing the plates. Then, let us look at Him at work with St Joseph. The hands of Him Who has created the universe handle the hammer, the plane, the saw. The first thing He fashions is a cross. His Mother sees it, and the sword predicted by Simeon pierces her heart.

This is really the house of work—of painful and unceasing work. If we want to be in the company of Jesus, Mary and Joseph, we must work like them. We must work seriously; we must work constantly; we must declare war on any kind of idleness.

1. Gen. ii, 19. 2. Prov. xxxi

How can we possibly remain idle in the presence of these holy Persons who know no rest? The house of Nazareth is not for idle people. But woe to us if we do not live there!

3. Concealment

"Love to be unknown and to be accounted as nothing."

This is the last lesson which the Holy Family teaches us, and it is the most difficult of all. We can endure every trial if only it brings our little self to prominence. On the other hand, nothing is harder than self-concealment, and nothing embitters one so much as neglect.

And yet this is the lot of the Holy Family.

There is no one on earth, and there never will be anyone, that comes near their high dignity. God Almighty looks down on them with infinite complacency. The Angels come down from Heaven to sing the Divine Praises around this blessed abode; and yet their concealment and the neglect which they suffer could not be greater. Their relations are all poor, and so are their acquaintances. Even these seem to make very little account of the Holy Family. Later on they will be offended with Jesus and will say: "Whence hath this man this wisdom, and these mighty works? Is not this the carpenter's Son? Is not His mother called Mary?" .... "Is not this the carpenter, the Son of Mary?" His very cousins will, for long, refuse to believe in Him. "For neither did His brethren believe in Him."

Not only is the splendour and the glory of the world completely absent from this place—even sanctity seems to hide itself. We hear but one voice: "Learn of Me, because I am meek and humble of heart."[1]

"This is my rest for ever and ever: here will I dwell, for I have chosen it."[2] Here shall I often come to look upon Jesus and Mary and Joseph, and learn from them the lessons of life.

Meanwhile I shall ask leave to retire and having prostrated myself to receive the blessing first of Jesus, then of Mary, and then of St Joseph, I shall take leave of them with humility, with tenderness, with love.

---

1. Matt. xi, 29. 2. Ps. cxxxi, 14.

THE TWO PATHS

Two paths I see before me now,
And my spirit hears a voice,
Which bids me look along them both
And freely take my choice.
Both paths are good; on each the Cross
Its hallowing shadow throws,
And both upon the mountain height
Are lost in glory close.

The first leads on through battlefields
Where souls for God are won,
And in the sight of heaven and earth
Horoic deeds are done.
Where toil and sweat and tears and blood
For the good cause are given,
And many a glorious trophy gained
To grace the courts of Heaven.

The other way scarce seen by men
Through lowly vales doth wind,
And Nazareth-like the shady nooks
That travellers here may find.
Here also souls are won for God,
But 'tis by silent prayer,
By many a secret sacrifice
And many a lonely tear.

No praise of men doth here beguile
The roughness of the road,
For all ignored or all despised
Are those who here have trod.
Lord, if I needs must take my choice,
This second way is mine,
For there lie all Thy Mother's years
And all but three of Thine,
My soul thirsts for those hidden springs,
Those ways to men unknown,
To be forgotten by all else
And live to Thee alone.

Emily Patmore.

THE TWO STANDARDS

THE STRATEGY OF THE DIVINE KING

[*The Spiritual Exercises*, pp. 77-85]

In this meditation we are not asked to deliberate whether we should serve under Christ or under Satan. The very idea would be revolting to any Christian; most of all at this stage of the Exercises. In the *Kingdom*, we have sworn fidelity to Christ, and offered ourselves wholeheartedly to embrace for His love humiliations and poverty—poverty of spirit in all cases, and even actual poverty, if only His Divine Majesty be pleased to choose and to receive us for such a life. Whether we have yet to find out the state of life in which God wishes to make use of us, or have embraced it long ago, we are animated by one desire only: to model our whole life on that of Christ. Christ is the Way that leads us to God, the Truth that enlightens our path, the Life that throbs in our whole being. However, it is not enough to have enlisted in His army; we must study His strategy that we may bravely and effectively fight with Him and like Him; and we must study also the strategy of Satan that we may beware of his traitorous snares and ambuscades. The meditation on *Two Standards* is an abstract of the most important lessons of our Lord's public life, the three years' campaigning of the Divine King. It is the handbook of every soldier of Christ.

* * *

The first Prelude is to call to mind how Christ invites and desires all men to serve under His Standard, while Lucifer, on the contrary wants to enlist them all under his.

The eternal fight between Christ and Satan, between Good and Evil, is the central point of history; before it every other fact pales into insignificance. The two leaders stand apart, each with his standard raised aloft and his liegemen about him. Around Christ there are gathered thousands and thousands of faithful souls—

Priests, Religious, lay apostles. Around Satan there prowl hordes of demons. They alone are his true liegemen, as no man would willingly become a vassal of Satan, the natural enemy of the human race.

* * *

The second Prelude is to see a vast plain embracing the whole region around Jerusalem, where stands the supreme Captain General of the good, Christ our Lord; and another plain, in the region of Babylon, where the chief of the enemy, Lucifer, is found.

A truly magnificent vision is this—the vision of the world divided into two big cities, Jerusalem and Babylon, the city of God and the city of Satan, the city of peace and the city of confusion, the city of obedience and the city of rebellion.

It was the vision that haunted the great mind of St Augustine. "These two cities are made by two loves: the earthly city by the love of oneself even to the contempt of God; the heavenly city by the love of God even to the contempt of oneself. The one glories in itself, the other in God; while the one seeks glory from men, to the other God, the witness of conscience, is its greatest glory. The one lifts up its head in its own glory, the other says to its God, 'my glory and the lifter up of my head.'"

However, St Ignatius does not conceive, as St Augustine does, the whole of mankind as divided into two distinct camps—the camp of the good and that of the bad—with a great gulf fixed between them. First of all, in his eyes Satan and the devils constitute the horde of the bad, and not properly, or at least not chiefly, wicked men. And, then, between St Ignatius' two vast plains there lies a vast intermediate ground where men who have sworn fidelity to Christ, move about freely, constantly laying themselves open to Satan's attacks. It is for such that the contemplation on *Two Standards* is chiefly meant.

Jesusalem and Babylon are no figments of the imagination. They find a local habitation in men's hearts and in human institutions, according as God's Will is obeyed or is resisted.

* * *

The third Prelude is to ask for knowledge of the deceits of the wicked chieftain and for help to guard myself against them; for knowledge of the true life which the supreme and true Captain points out, and for grace to imitate Him.

We must see the whole world as the field where Christ wages a ceaseless battle against Satan, with the aim of conquering and reigning supreme in our hearts; and while renewing our oath of allegiance to Him, we should often humbly pray: *Ab insidiis diaboli, libera nos Domine.*

We do not ask to know, and still less to be delivered from the *open attacks* of Satan, i. e., from temptations to do what is evil or to neglect a clear duty; but that we may know his *tricks and snares*, and may be on our guard against them.

Christ shows us the *true life*. Though His teaching is at first a teaching of death, and His hand points to a scaffold, it is a death that alone has in itself the germ of life, and a scaffold that is the pedestal of a throne.

Lose, that the lost thou may'st receive;
Die, for none other way canst live.

PART ONE

THE MORTAL ENEMY OF MANKIND

1. Satan in his Real Garb

Satan appears beautiful and attractive to men. Whatever delights the senses, tickles the imagination and satisfies the longing of the natural man, of his passions and of his caprices, is found, at least apparently, in Satan alone. He even knows how to transform himself into an angel of light and to deceive the very servants of God, on the specious pretext of promoting God's greater glory, the good of souls, and the prestige of the Church.

But, in reality, how abominably ugly and filthy he is. See him as St Ignatius portrays him, in that great plain of Babylon, seated as on a lofty throne of fire and smoke, horrible to behold. You notice his characteristic marks: the love of comfort, the hatred of every restraint, the love of pre-eminence and power, the spirit of rebellion and of criticism, agitation, darkness and confusion, fear and terror. Splendid and charming though he may look at times, some of these traits are always there to reveal infallibly his true nature. Often he tries to enter into our souls slowly and subtly; he just introduces his *cauda serpentina*—a feeling, a thought, a longing for something apparently harmless; and yet if we give way to it we soon experience in ourselves the traits of Satan. "By their fruits you shall know them." "Begone Satan," should be our resolute cry at the first approach of the enemy.

2. The Gathering of God's Enemies

Satan summons together innumerable devils and spurs them to go, some to one city, some to another, throughout the world, omitting no province, place or state of life, nor any person in particular.

His attack is universal. St Ignatius is the last man to attribute all temptations to the devil. Still the fact remains, and the Saint strongly emphasizes it, that Satan is constantly at our side, as the embodiment of evil, bent on organizing the attacks of the world and the flesh against us, and on undoing God's work in our souls. St John affirms it in unmistakable terms:

"He that doth sin is of the devil, because the devil sinneth from the beginning. To this end was the Son of God manifested, that He might undo the works of the devil."[1]

St Peter is no less emphatic:

"Your adversary the devil goeth about like a roaring lion, seeking to devour."[2]

St Paul is even more definite on this matter, throughout his Epistles.

It is Satan who raises all kinds of obstacles to the preachers of the Faith, who encourages idolatry, sows the seeds of doubt, and fans the spirit of revolt. He contends with Christ for the empire of this world. He is Christ's great enemy: "he that tempteth." That is why the Apostle writes to the Ephesians as follows:

"Put ye on the full armour of God, that ye may be able to stand against the wiles of the devil. For our wrestling is not against

1 I John iii, 8. 2 I Peter v, 8.

flesh and blood, but against the principalities, against the powers, against the world-rulers of this darkness, against the spirits of wickedness in the regions above. Wherefore take ye up the full armour of God, that ye may be able to resist in the evil day, to do your whole duty and to stand your ground. Stand, then, 'with your loins girt in truth,' and having on the breastplate of justness,' and with 'your feet' shod 'in readiness to carry the gospel of peace,' taking up withal the shield of faith, wherewith ye shall be able to quench all the fiery darts of the evil one. And take 'the helmet of salvation' and 'the sword of the spirit,' which is 'the word of God.'"[1]

Vigilance, prompt and strong resistance, are the infallible means to triumph over all infernal attacks.

3. Satan's Plan

Satan admonishes his satellites to lay snares to entrap men, and prepare chains to bind them fast once they are taken. He instructs them to direct their attacks not against sinners, but against those who profess to follow Christ, though from afar, and who would reject any temptation to what is openly sinful. The fact that such people are not resolved to fight *à outrance*, that they want the eternal and yet would keep the temporal, that they accept Christ's teaching, but act mostly on the principles of the world, makes them an easy prey to the snares of the Evil One.

As a rule, the devils are directed to tempt such men, in the first place, with the lust of riches, so that they may more easily come to the vain honour of the world, and then to unbounded pride, the root of all evil.

Riches include, besides money, all showy gifts; and honours include power, influence, prestige, and glory. Riches and honours are the *ordinary steps* by which Satan leads men to unbounded pride. In themselves they are indifferent creatures, i. e., they may help or hinder us in the attainment of the end for which we are created. However, to love and to desire them is always dangerous and has often proved fatal to many souls. That accounts for the terrible woes pronounced by Christ:

---

1. Eph. vi, 11-17.

"Woe to you that are rich: for you have your consolation. Woe to you that are filled: for you shall hunger. Woe to you that now laugh: for you shall mourn and weep. Woe to you when men shall bless you: for according to these things did their fathers to the false prophets."[1]

With fervent Christians, and even more, with persons consecrated to the service of God, as are all Priests and Religious, the tactics of Satan obviously vary. In some he fosters the love of bodily comforts and ease, or an inordinate attachment to a particular person, place, or work. In others he stirs up a craving for praise, external success and power, under the pretext of better promoting God's glory. In others still, he rouses the spirit of independence and criticism. Thus slowly and gradually, Satan makes such souls discontented with their lot—they do not get what they want, or at least, not as much as they want; and, what is even worse, he keeps them constantly busy with their miserable self. In their blindness, they may not be fully aware of it. Under the cloak of working for God's glory, they seek self and their own exaltation. However, sooner or later "the fire shall try every man's work, of what sort it is:" a deep humiliation or some such heavy trial shows what he really is.

Each one, therefore, must, seriously and in the presence of God, consider, first, the particular trick which Satan uses to lead him to ruin, and, then, steadfastly keeping it before him, drive, if need be, the opposite way. We should not say that this attitude is good for Saints, or that it is but a counsel of perfection. There is no other sure way to guard oneself against the treachery of the Evil One and to stave off eternal ruin.

PART TWO

OUR SUPREME CAPTAIN AND LORD

1. The Loveliness of our King

Our true and supreme Captain, Christ our Lord in aspect beautiful and lovable, takes His stand on a lowly spot, in a great plain near Jerusalem.

---

1 Luke vi, 24-26.

With these few touches does St Ignatius delineate the characteristic notes of our Divine Leader -- readiness to work for God's glory, true liberty and large-heartedness, peace and order, humility and submission. The contemplation of the mysteries of our Lord's public life will abundantly show how correct is the portrait here drawn.

By such traits are His disciples known, and likewise by such traits it is always possible to make out whether desires and inspirations which purport to be good, really proceed from God.

2. THE KING'S VASSALS

The Divine King is constantly on the look-out for generous souls whom He may call to Himself, instruct in His sacred doctrine, and then send into the world to spread this doctrine among all states and conditions of persons. He has been doing it since the day when He called Peter and Andrew, James and John: "Come after me and I will make you to become fishers of men."[1] His call is a personal one. To every man to whom He whispers it, He says: Thou hast not chosen Me, but I have chosen thee; and I have appointed thee, that thou shouldst go, and should bring forth fruit, and thy fruit should remain. As the Father hath sent Me, I also send thee. Going, therefore, teach thou My sacred doctrine—the doctrine which I have entrusted to My Church. As far as it lies in thee, leave no place, no state, no condition of persons untaught. Fear not: all power is given to Me in heaven and on earth; and behold I am always with thee. It is I Myself that will abide with thee, and through thee, continue My saving mission.

THE MESSAGE OF THE DIVINE KING

What is the quintessence of the doctrine which Christ desires to teach His servants and friends that they may spread it throughout the world? It is the love of poverty — poverty of spirit and actual poverty if one feels called to it—and the love and desire of reproaches and contempt, for the love of Christ and in imitation of Him Who was *pauper et humilis.*

1. Mark i, 17.

"Every one of you that doth not renounce all that he possesses cannot be My disciple."[1]

"Amen, amen, I say to you, unless the grain of wheat falling into the ground die, itself remaineth alone. But if it die, it bringeth forth much fruit."[2]

In other words, give up everything, deny thyself and divest thyself of thy self-love, thy self-will, thy self-interest.

"Sit down in the lowest place."[3]

"If any man desires to be first, he shall be the last of all, and the minister of all."[4]

In other words, desire to be unknown and little esteemed by men. Seek no praise for thyself, but ever rejoice when others are praised. Thank God when thou art neglected, reprimanded, snubbed or thwarted. Love the humble and hard work which God or thy superiors have entrusted to thee, and be always at the beck of every one.

The twofold love of privations and self-effacement will establish our souls in humility and perfect submission to God's Holy Will, and with it all good things will come to us.

We must fervently beg our Lady to obtain for us this twofold love from her Son; we must ask Christ, our Divine Mediator, to intercede for us with His Father; and we must pray the Father Himself to grant it to us.

O Mary, my sweet Mother, obtain for me grace from your Son and my King that I may follow Him under the Standard of the Cross, in privations and hardships, in concealment and neglect, in humble submission and obedience. *Hail Mary.*

O Jesus, my Divine King and Saviour, obtain for me from Your Eternal Father, that I may follow You under the Standard of the Cross, in privations and hardships, in concealment and neglect, in humble submission and obedience, for Your love, and to be like You in all things. *Anima Christi.*

O Eternal Father, You Who have said of Christ: "This is My beloved Son, hear Him," give me grace that I may follow Him under the Standard of the Cross, in privations and hardships, in concealment and neglect, in humble submission and obedience, that I may be made in all things conformable to His image. *Our Father.*

1. Luke xiv, 33. 2. John xii, 24, 25. 3. Luke xii, 10 4. Mark ix, 34.

HORA AMANTIS

Thine hour, my Lord I hear Thee say—
Desirable that hour must be
Which straitens by its short delay
The Ruler of Eternity:
O let me see Thee then rejoice,
And grant me such an hour to know:
  I hear Thy Voice
Reply in accents grave and low:
 "Hora Amantis illa est
  Qua pro amico patitur."

Then that was not some tender hour
Of converse with Thy Mother sweet,
Nor when the wonders of Thy power
Brought new disciples to Thy feet:
Thine Hour was that drear April noon
When to the Cross they nailed Thee down;
  Death is the boon
For joy of which Thou wear'st a crown:
 "Hora Amantis illa est
  Qua pro amico patitur."

Then my hour shall not be the hour
When creatures praise and favour pay,
Nor even when Thy love and power
Lead me rejoicing on my way;
My hour like Thine, My Lord and Love,
Shall be the hour of pain and loss;
  Darkness above,
Beneath, the thorns, the nails, the cross:
 "Hora Amantis illa est
  Qua pro amico patitur."

Emily Patmore.

THE THREE CLASSES

THE TEST OF SINCERITY

[*The Spiritual Exercises*, pp. 86-90]

Every lover of Christ longs to follow Him in the hardest things—even in actual poverty and humiliations, if He so wills—that he may truly resemble Him. *Amor aut pares invenit aut facit.* How is it, then, that only a few realize in themselves perfect similarity with Christ? Alas, we are tied down to some creature or other, and never manage to break away from it and find God in peace. The meditation on *Three Classes* is meant to enlighten our minds as to the danger of such an attachment and to give us strength and generosity to break away from it.

* * *

The first Prelude is the history concerning three Classes of men, each of which has acquired ten thousand ducats, honestly, though not purely and duly for the love of God. They all desire to save their souls and to find God our Lord in peace, by ridding themselves to this end of the burden and impediment which they find in their affection for the thing acquired.

Each one must probe the depths of his heart to feel what it is that prevents him from finding God in peace—that is from going straight to Him and cleaving wholly to Him. He may be attached to some pleasing creature—money, comforts, a particular way of thinking or acting, a person, a place, or office which he holds or desires to have. He may fear that something hard and unpleasant may befall him—a failure or a repulse, sickness or removal from some place or office, some difficult work, or some extra claim on his time and energy. In none of these cases is there question of a sinful attachment. Implying as this would do an attitude of mind directly opposed to God's Holy Will, it is not even to be thought of at this stage of the Exercises. The weight and the impediment which the Exercitant experiences in finding peace of soul, is not due to the fact that the creature which he likes, or the means by which

He has attained to it, is sinful, but solely to His *inordinate* attachment to it.

We must sincerely desire to know what prevents us from finding God in peace. How often we even refuse to think about it. How often it hides itself in some dark corner of our soul, and mockingly defies all perfunctory investigation.

St Sebastian, the martyr, had assured Cromatius, Prefect of Rome, that he would be cured of gout if he believed in Christ and destroyed all his idols. Cromatius broke to pieces more than two hundred of them and yet he grew worse. On enquiry, St Sebastian found out that he had spared some instruments which he was wont to use for astrological superstitions and which he thought he could now look upon as mere curios. No sooner were these destroyed than Cromatius was healed.

We all have some such idol, which we want not indeed to set up as ultimate in our life, but to keep, to purify, and to consecrate to God. There is no use proceeding further till it is ferreted out and destroyed.

* * *

The second Prelude is to see myself how I stand in the presence of God our Lord and of all His Saints, that I may desire and know that which is most pleasing to His Divine Goodness.

The third Prelude is to beg for grace to choose that which is more for the glory of His Divine Majesty, and for the salvation of my soul.

These two preludes bring out the attitude of a Christian that seeks the Lord and seeks Him constantly. He walks in the sight of God and of His Saints, anxious to know what is most pleasing to God, and begging for grace to do it unhesitatingly.

1. The First Class

All the three Classes desire, somehow, to get rid of the affection they have for the thing acquired, in order to find our Lord in peace and thus save their souls. The first Class make procrastination the rule of their conduct. Though they do not positively refuse to employ the means necessary for their reform, they indefinitely put off employing them.

Do I belong to this Class? Many a time has God urged me to break to pieces the idol in my heart, and yet in spite of my repeated promises to do it, it still lies undisturbed. It would have been far better if I had refused point-blank to make the sacrifice. I might then have had the chance of realizing, sometime or other, how by disobeying the voice of God I was endangering my very salvation. Instead, by constantly putting off redeeming my pledge I have been fatally deceiving myself and acting in a manner unworthy of a man of serious purpose.

Let me then throw myself at the feet of my Saviour, and cry with the blind man, "Lord, that I may see."

2. The Second Class

The second Class too desire to get rid of the inordinate affection. They expect, however, that God should suit Himself to their desire to let them keep what they have gained; they are not determined to give it up in order to go to Him, even though this would be the best state for them.

Imaginary detachment and real attachment, want of straightforwardness and a policy of compromise, are the distinguishing marks of the second Class. Like the first Class they wish to get rid of their inordinate affection for the thing acquired. Unlike the first Class, however, they are sincerely willing to do a deal for this purpose, always provided they are not required to sacrifice what they have gained.

The attitude of the second Class is the bane of the spiritual life and the ruin of souls without number. If the first Class is swelled by idlers and pious wishers, the second is full of weaklings and self-seekers.

Do I find myself in this second Class? The idol of my heart has, perhaps, been cleaned, sprinkled with holy water, and placed as an offering before our Lord. It is understood, of course, that I only love it in the Lord, and keep it solely for His honour and glory. And I take care to be constantly on my guard, to purify my intention, and to control my feelings in its regard. But why, I say to myself, should I sacrifice it? Are not creatures given us that we may use them, and are not opportunities offered to us that we may seize upon them?

Plausible though such an attitude may seem, the effects of it are truly disastrous: I attain to no sanctity; I achieve next to nothing for God and for souls; and I endanger the very salvation of my own soul. My whole energy, may, indeed, be absorbed in enthusiastic work, but I seek self in it, and not God: and self-seeking is poison that corrupts everything. It is a form of idolatry, the setting up and worshipping of my own purpose and pleasure instead of God's.

The tragedy of it is that we are often tied down to the creature not by a heavy chain, but by a slender silken cord which we could easily snap, if only we would.

What can I do but throw myself at the feet of the Divine Saviour and beg for light and strength. "Lord, behold, he whom Thou lovest is sick."

3. The Third Class

Straightforwardness and earnestness are the characteristic traits of the third Class. They really want to get rid of their inordinate affection and to find God in peace, cost what it may. Possibly, God may not demand of them actually to sacrifice the ten thousand ducats, but merely to purify their attachment to it. But how can they be sure that God's love alone moves them to keep the money, and not rather the love of self, under the disguise of God's honour and glory? As far as lies in their power, they first give up the money, and then, proceed to consider, whether, for the sole reason of serving Him better, it is God's Will that they should take it back.

Such souls are firmly and solidly established in God and His Holy Will, and enjoy complete freedom and peace. They are fit instruments in God's hands. They generously follow Christ wherever He calls them, even in poverty and humiliations, and choose in everything that which is more for the glory of his Divine Majesty and for the salvation of their souls. Far from being sad, their life is one of constant joy – no matter whether it is the joy of possessing things for God, or the even greater joy of sacrificing them for His love. In giving up all things, they soon realize they have found the All-Good.

I must then strain every nerve to implant in my soul the generous disposition of this third Class. I must make a complete donation to God of whatever hinders the peace of my soul. Do I not desire to do in all things God's Holy Will and to promote His greater glory? Why, then, should I fear to leave in God's keeping everything to which my heart is attached? I must offer myself generously to anything unpleasant and humiliating which God may have in store for me. "Yea, the very hairs of your head are numbered." Though my whole nature rebels at the thought of such a sacrifice, in my colloquies to God, I should offer myself for it; I should even desire it, beg and supplicate for it, if it be for the service and praise of His Divine Goodness.

To end the meditation by making the same *Triple Colloquy*, as was made in the preceding meditation on *Two Standards*.

'ME'

My angered soul is dark, yea, dark as night,
When shadows fold a ruined, dismal shrine,
But, Oh, horror grips me at the sight,
For still an idol holds this heart of mine!

What is this fetich in the dismal cell,
This craven image, shrunk with misery?
Ah, ask not, soul, for thou dost know too well,
'Tis but the god proud men enshrine, named "Me."

G. A. MacCabe, S. J.

THREE MODES OF HUMILITY

RANKS IN CHRIST'S ARMY

[*The Spiritual Exercises*, pp. 92-95]

Before entering on the work of the Election, or, as is more often the case, on the work of self-reform, St Ignatius wants us, in order that we may be well affected towards the true doctrine of Christ our Lord, to consider three Modes of Humility, i. e., three attitudes concerning the service of God and the use of created things, one more perfect than the other. Though the Saint assigns no definite time to their consideration, but simply desires that we keep revolving them in our minds during the day, we may make them the subject of some sort of meditation.

* * *

At first Prelude we may see Christ our Lord climbing to Calvary carrying His Cross, followed by Mary and John, the Beloved Disciple.

In the second Prelude, we implore our Lord to be pleased to elect us to the third Mode of greater and more perfect humility, the better to imitate and serve Him. We must repeat this petition as often as possible during the day.

1. First Mode

The first Mode of Humility consists in submitting myself to the Will of God in such a way as not to deliberate about breaking any commandment, whether Divine or human, which binds under mortal sin, even though its transgression might lead me to wealth, honours, health, and long life; or its observance entail poverty, dishonour, sickness, and death itself.

Such a determination is absolutely necessary to anyone who wants to be saved. Not to have it, would imply that he is in a state of opposition to God, or at least of apathy towards, and disregard for Him. On the other hand this *habitual* disposition not to *deliberate* about offending God grievously is not inconsistent with an *actual* fall at times. As a matter of fact there are moments and circumstances in life when nothing short of grim courage and true heroism will enable one to remain true to God. Apart from the thousands and thousands of canonized Saints, who endured the loss of goods, imprisonment, and death itself to be faithful to God, there are the uncanonized millions who often undergo a hidden martyrdom to keep themselves chaste in or out of wedlock, and to be truthful, just, and charitable in their dealings with others. Fear of God, humble prayer, and control of one's passions will maintain a soul in the disposition of the first Mode of Humility.

The first Mode requires in one the substantial indifference that makes him look upon God as his ultimate and supreme End, and upon all creatures as means to reach Him. Hewever, that being presupposed, one who has but the disposition of the first Mode, loves and pursues the good things of the world, and avoids what is hard and humiliating. Such is, after all, the disposition of so many average Christians.

2. Second Mode

The second Mode of Humility consists in submitting myself to the Will of God, in such a way as not to deliberate about breaking any commandment, whether Divine or human, though it binds only under venial sin, and even when its transgression might lead me to wealth, honours, health, and long life; or its observance entail poverty, dishonour, sickness and death itself.

Such a disposition is far nobler than the previous one. However, we are still within the limits of reasonableness and justice. As a matter of fact, is it not just and reasonable that we avoid everything that offends His Divine Majesty? And is not the smallest venial sin, even in the light of reason, an incomparably greater evil than all the so-called evils of this world, greater than poverty, dishonour, sickness, and death itself?

To act faithfully and constantly according to such a disposition requires greater energy and strength. One must be perfectly indifferent to all created things, i. e., he must have complete control of himself, of his passions, his whims and caprices, not only in serious matters, as in the first Mode, but in light matters as well. In the first Mode, while keeping his eyes and his steps towards God, his final goal, he allows himself many a digression off the straight road : in the second Mode he walks straight on along it.

If the holy fear of God, humble prayer, and self-denial are necessary to any one who wants to be faithful to the disposition of the first Mode, how much more essential are they to one who desires to maintain himself in the disposition of the second ?

3. Third Mode

The disposition required by the first and second Mode of Humility is a positive disposition of the will. It consists, directly, not in avoiding mortal and venial sin, but in submitting one's will more and more perfectly to the Will of God, and in an ever greater control of self in using the good things of this world and in enduring its hardships and humiliations.

We are created to serve God, i. e., to do His Holy Will, and all other creatures are given us to attain this end.

In the first Mode we obey God's Holy Will commanding under penalty of mortal sin, and make free use of creatures as long as they do not take us entirely away from God.

In the second Mode we obey all the commands of God, even those binding under venial sin only. Towards creatures we keep an attitude of perfect indifference so long as God's Will is not known.

In the third Mode we submit to God's Holy Will not only when He commands under penalty of sin, mortal or venial, but even when He merely expresses a desire ; in other words, we are determined to do everything that pleases Him, to avoid every imperfection, to follow all counsels and obey all inspirations. As regards the use of creatures, knowing well that Christ has chosen what pleases God most, and anxious to be like Him, our Eldest Brother, we choose, as far as lies in us, to be poor with Him poor, to be insulted with Him covered with insults, and to be esteemed as worthless and fools for Him who was first held to be such. The indifference of the second Mode, becomes positive acceptance of, and longing for privations, humiliations, and sufferings, i. e., *for the higher and harder path*, out of pure love for Christ and to be truly like Him in everything.

Only such a disposition can make it possible for one to do God's well-pleasing Will in all circumstances. The love of the Cross cuts at the very root of even the slightest opposition to it and prepares one to face great trials bravely.

The third Mode of Humility—perfect obedience to God's Will, with and like Christ poor, humble, and crucified—is the central point of the Exercises. It is the folly of the Cross: "He humbled Himself by obedience unto death, yea, unto death upon a cross."

To conclude with a fervent Colloquy, first to our Lady, then to our Lord and then to God the Father asking that my will be solidly established in the disposition of the third Mode of Humility. *Pati et contemni pro Te.*

FROM 'THE MISTRESS OF VISION'

"Pierce thy heart to find the key;
With thee take
Only what none else would keep;
Learn to dream when thou dost wake,
Learn to wake when thou dost sleep.
Learn to water joy with tears,
Learn from fears to vanquish fears;
To hope, for thou dar'st not despair,
Exult, for that thou dar'st not grieve;
Plough thou the rock until it bear;
Know, for thou else couldst not believe;
Lose, that the lost thou may'st receive;
Die, for none other way canst live.
When earth and heaven lay down their veil,
And that apocalypse turns thee pale;
When thy seeing blindeth thee
To what thy fellow-mortals see;
When their sight to thee is sightless;
Their living, death; their light, most lightless;
Search no more—
Pass the gates of Luthany, tread the region Elenore."

Francis Thompson.

REFORM

[*The Spiritual Exercises* p. 101]

I

The object of the Spiritual Exercises is to free oneself from inordinate affections, and then to seek and find the Will of God concerning the ordering of one's life. Accordingly, they are primarily meant to help the Exercitant to choose a state of life in accordance with God's Holy Will. However, when such choice has been made, and no change is either possible or advisable, St Ignatius wants that the Exercitant should carefully examine what changes in his manner of living he should adopt, to serve and praise God better. In other words, he should try to amend and reform his present life and state. *To amend* refers to the negative side: the correction of sins and evil habits; while *to reform* refers to the positive: the giving of a new form or cast to one's whole life.

Before the Exercitant begins the work of reform, St Ignatius wants that he should free himself from illusions and self-deceptions and be resolved to serve God with the greatest courage and liberality. Hence the Exercises on *Two Standards* and on the *Three Classes*, the consideration of the *Three Modes of Humility*, and the frequent repetition of the Colloquy of the Two Standards throughout the contemplation of our Lord's public life.

II

In drawing up our reform, we are apt to be vague and lay down general resolutions, which while satisfying our feeling that something must be done, leave our course of life practically unchanged. It is not enough to be resolved, in general, to fight under the flag of the Divine King, but we must frame definite resolutions that meet our present needs and circumstances.

How can we effect a proper reform of our whole life?

1. We must place before us our end as Christians, as Priests, as Religious.

2. In all the particular things of our life we must choose, in the presence of God, and solely prompted by the dictates of reason and Faith, the best means to reach our end, just as we should like to have chosen, were we now at the point of death, or in the presence of the Divine Judge.

III

The following might be the main points of our Reform.

I. The Past.

" What have I done for Christ?

We may write down our chief sins and defects, the illusions and dangers to which we are exposed.

II. The Future.

" What must I do for Christ?

We may write down

1. What we must avoid:
   Our habitual sins as apparent from our Confessions.
2. The points against which we must be constantly on our guard.
3. What we must do:
   i) Concerning our exercises of piety;
   ii) Concerning our work;
   iii) Concerning our relations with
      a) superiors,
      b) companions,
      c) charges,
      d) inferiors;
   iv) Concerning our own self: care of health, practice of self-control and self-denial.

III. Means to put our resolutions into practice and renew our fervour.

1. Devotions: the Holy Eucharist, the Sacred Heart, our Lady, St Joseph, our Guardian Angel, the Holy Souls,

2. Daily Examination of Conscience and frequent Confession.

3. The monthly Recollection, and spiritual direction.

Our Reform will be the more thorough the more we keep in mind the principal with which St Ignatius ends the second Week of the Spiritual Exercises:

" Let each one reflect that he will make progress in all spiritual matters, in proportion as he shall have divested himself of his self-love, self-will, and self-interest."

SELF-DENIAL

It is right then almost to *find out* for yourself daily self-denials; and this because our Lord bids you take up your cross daily, and because it proves your earnestness, and because by doing so you strengthen your general power of self-mastery, and come to have such an habitual command of yourself, as will be a defence ready prepared when the season of temptation comes. Rise up then in the morning with the purpose that (please God) the day shall not pass without its self-denial, with a self-denial in innocent pleasures and tastes, if none occurs to mortify sin. Let your very rising from your bed be a self-denial; let your meals be self-denials. Determine to yield to others in things indifferent, to go out of your way in small matters, to inconvenience yourself (so that no direct duty suffers by it), rather than you should not meet with your daily discipline. This was the Psalmist's method, who was, as it were, "punished all day long, and chastened every morning."[1] It was St Paul's method, who "kept under," or bruised "his body, and brought it into subjection."[2] This is one great end of fasting. A man says to himself, "How am I to know I am in earnest?" I would suggest to him, Make some sacrifice, do some distasteful thing, which you are not actually obliged to do (so that it be lawful), to bring home to your mind that in fact you do love your Saviour, that you do hate sin, that you do hate your sinful nature, that you have put aside the present world. Thus you will have an evidence (to a certain point) that

1. Ps. lxxiii, 14. 2. I Cor. ix, 27.

you are not using mere words. It is easy to make professions, easy to say fine things in speech or in writing, easy to astonish men with truths which they do not know, and sentiments which rise above human nature. "But thou, O servant of God, flee these things, and follow after righteousness, godliness, faith, love, patience, meekness." Let not your words run on, force every one of them into action as it goes, and thus, cleansing yourself from all pollution of the flesh and spirit, perfect holiness in the fear of God. In dreams we sometimes move our arms to see if we are awake or not, and so we are awakened. This is the way to keep your heart awake also. Try yourself daily in little deeds, to prove that your faith is more than a deceit.

I am aware all this is a hard doctrine; hard to those even who assent to it, and can describe it most accurately. There are such imperfections, such inconsistencies in the heart and life of even the better sort of men, that continual repentance must ever go hand in hand with our endeavours to obey. Much we need the grace of Christ's Blood to wash us from the guilt we daily incur; much need we the aid of His promised Spirit! And surely He will grant all the riches of His mercy to His true servants; but as surely He will vouchsafe to none of us the power to believe in Him, and the blessedness of being one with Him, who are not as earnest in obeying Him as if salvation depended on themselves.

The Divine King starts His Campaign

Now it came to pass, when all the people were baptized, that Jesus also being baptized and praying, Heaven was opened; and the Holy Ghost descended in a bodily shape, as a dove upon Him; and a voice came from Heaven:

"Thou art My beloved Son, in Thee I am well pleased."

THE BAPTISM OF CHRIST

THE DIVINE KING STARTS HIS CAMPAIGN

The first Prelude is to call to mind how Christ went from Galilee to the Jordan to be baptized by John, and how on His coming out of the water, the Heavens opened and the Spirit of God, in the shape of a dove, descended upon Him, while a Voice from Heaven said: "This is my beloved Son, in Whom I am well pleased." (Matt. iii, 13-17; Mark i, 9-11; Luke iii, 21-22.)

The second Prelude is to see with the eyes of the imagination the little house of Nazareth and the road that led southwards to Bethabara, beyond the Jordan—a spot located, by tradition, opposite to Jericho—where John was baptizing.

The third Prelude is to ask light to know intimately the Divine King and the feelings with which He starts His campaign, that I may love Him more and follow Him more closely beneath His holy Standard.

1. Significance of our Lord's Public Life

The whole of Christ's life is the pattern on which our own life is to be modelled. His hidden life—especially that portion of it spent in Nazareth—brings vividly before us the virtues we need to practise in our homes. His Passion and Death convey lessons of patience and courage, in the hour of grief and agony. His Resurrection raises our souls to Him and to the glory which He has prepared for us.

But we often overlook His public life. And yet the Gospels are mostly concerned with it: two of them begin relating the Baptism of the Son of God, entirely passing over all previous events. St Ignatius himself in the Contemplation of the *Kingdom of Christ*, which opens the Second Week of the Exercises, wants us "to see with the eyes of the imagination the synagogues, towns and villages, through which Christ our Lord went preaching."[1]

Nowadays, nowhere is Christianity truly the Religion of the land. The principles that practically rule public and social life are often diametrically opposed to the principles of Christ. Even good people

1. Animated by this thought, St Ignatius and his companions wanted to go and work in Palestine, copying the Divine King in everything. It was only later that they found that the Holy Land was to be every country in Christendom. However, the copying of Christ's life continued to be the key-note of the Society which the Saint founded.

sometimes lead a double life, or a life that is but a contradiction in terms. They believe one thing and do just the opposite; they act one way in private and in quite a different way in public.

Christ's teaching and example will show us what to think of the various problems of life and how to act in all social occurrences.

Christ's public life is a life of zeal, of service, and of sacrifice. The Divine Master lives to do good and to help the needy, to teach and enlighten those that grope in the dark, to suffer and to die for their salvation. And he calls us to follow Him: *Si quis vult post Me venire*, or, in the words of St Ignatius: "My Will is to conquer the whole world, and all enemies, and thus to enter into the glory of My Father. Whoever, therefore, desires to come with Me, must labour with Me, in order that following Me in pain, he may likewise follow Me in glory."

With His Baptism, the Divine King starts His campaign.

2. Our Lord takes Leave of His Mother

(i) THE SAD NEWS

First, he takes leave of His Blessed Mother.

Since the day of Simeon's prophecy, and still more, since the day she heard those words: "I must be about My Father's business," Mary was always dreading this sad farewell. But so many years had passed since the finding of her Boy in the Temple, that, we may well imagine, she had come to think that she might be spared that grief. Fond mothers often cherish in their hearts the most unrealizable hopes, and what mother has been fonder of her children than Mary was of her Divine Son. She probably hoped that Jesus would close her eyes in the sleep of death, as He had done Joseph's. That was to be the sword foretold by Simeon.

One evening, however, Jesus accosted His Mother, and, calm and serene, broke the sad news to her. What grief for the heart of Mary! Think of a mother's grief in bidding farewell to her only child that goes far away, to war, to death! Mary well knew that her Son's journey would end on the Cross. But she does not say: "Why hast Thou done so?" She only bows to the Divine Will and repeats: "Behold the handmaid of the Lord: be it done unto me according to Thy word."

(ii) MARY'S GRIEF

They passed the night together, mostly in silence and in prayer. There was no need for talk. In such moments the soul tries to remember all the past—even the most insignificant details, the very features of the beloved, that it might treasure them passionately all through the endless hours of separation. This it is that makes those moments so infinitely precious.

Mary goes over the thirty years she has passed with Jesus—the great Message of the Angel, the miraculous birth in the stable of Bethlehem, her trials and her joys, the sweet and intimate companionship with Jesus—and on the morrow all would be over. She would meet her Son from time to time, but she knew she would no more be the happy Mother of Nazareth. Henceforth Jesus would belong to others: "Who are My Mother and My brothers?"

No wonder that her heart endured and would continue to endure

The pang of all partings gone,
And partings yet to be.

(iii) THE GRIEF OF JESUS

No less intense was the grief of the Divine Saviour. He loved Mary with a most passionate love. He knew that she would be left all alone, with relations that could not understand her. His Heart bled for her, but He had heard the call of His Father, and cost what it may, He had to be about His Father's business. The hearts of Jesus and Mary were just like our own hearts, except that they were sinless. They felt the parting as we have felt many a parting in our lives—and infinitely more. It was only their submission to God's Will and their love for souls that conquered their grief.

(iv) THE PARTING

And now it was dawn. Jesus knelt for His Mother's blessing, and took the road southward. Mary stood on the threshold—her heart a veritable ocean of grief—till Jesus reached the corner of the road. He stopped to wave His last farewell. The next moment Jesus had disappeared, and the tears, which the Mother had so far kept back, began to flow freely. Of her, even more than of Jerusalem, the prophet could say: "Weeping she hath wept in the night and her tears are on the cheeks: there is none to comfort among all them that were dear to her." [1]

Meanwhile Jesus pursues His way to the Jordan whither the voice of His Father calls Him. Step by step, He will follow that voice wherever it leads Him—entirely trusting in the Father's love and care, with one object in view: the accomplishment of God's Will and the salvation of souls.

Let us obey the Divine call with childlike confidence. Let us do God's Will even if that implies the sacrifice of all that is dearest to us—of our family affections, our comforts, our bonour, our plans and schemes. Only then shall we deserve to be numbered among the disciples of Christ.

3. Baptism of Our Lord

(i) MISSION OF THE BAPTIST

"It came to pass in those days that Jesus came from Nazareth of Galilee and was baptized of John in Jordan."[2]

The journey of our Lord from Nazareth to the Jordan is second only to the Incarnation. Then, He left His Father and His eternal home to come down to the earth. Now he leaves His Mother and even the little comforts of His temporal home to do His Father's work, to open the Messianic era.

His entry into public life was being prepared for and heralded abroad.

Thirty years before, Zacharias had foretold of his son: "And thou, child, shalt be called the prophet of the Most High, for thou shall go before the face of the Lord to prepare His ways."[3] The task of John was thus fixed. While preparing for his mission "the child grew, and waxed strong in spirit, and was in the desert till the day of his showing unto Israel." [4]

1. Lam. i, 2. 2. Mark i, 9. 3. Luke i, 76. 4. Luke i, 80.

At last that day rose. "In the fifteenth year of the reign of Tiberius Caesar.... Annas and Caiphas being the high priests, the word of God came unto John the son of Zacharias in the wilderness. And he came into all the country about the Jordan, preaching the baptism of repentance for the remission of sins."[1]

John's preaching is summed up in those words: "Do penance," i. e., change your wills, turning them to God, "for the Kingdom of Heaven is nigh unto you." And people came from Jerusalem, from Judea, and from the countries lying round the Jordan, to hear that voice crying in the wilderness, which spared none, and talked of the hope of Israel to the poor and to the humble.

(ii) SIGNIFICANCE OF CHRIST'S BAPTISM

Might he not be the expected Messiah? "No," he had answered to the Priest and Levites sent from Jerusalem to ask him, Who art thou? "I am not the Christ, nor Elias, nor that prophet. I am the voice of one crying in the wilderness. Make straight the way of the Lord."

"I baptise with water, but there standeth One among you Whom ye know not. He it is Who coming after me is preferred before me, the latchet of whose shoe I am not worthy to unloose."[2]

It was Jesus on the bank of the Jordan, waiting, along with the publicans and sinners, to be baptized by John.

But why such a public humiliation? Does He not seem thereby to disown His innocence and His Divine origin?

Having taken upon Himself the form of a servant and made Himself similar in all things to us His brethren, Christ willed to obey in everything the laws of natural and intellectual growth. Like every child of Israel, He was circumcised and offered in the Temple, and like them He passed many years in solitude and silence.

But, at last, the time is accomplished: the Messianic era, the era of Christ, is about to begin. John opens it by calling the people to repentance: "Make straight the way of the Lord: Do penance for the Kingdom of Heaven is at hand." And Christ, too, comes to seek baptism of John. Not only does He mix with

1. Luke iii, 2, 3. 2. John i, 26-27.

sinners to show that He loves them and has come mainly for them, but He is the Great Penitent. The Baptism of Christ is His public and solemn consecration to the office of Saviour of the world. He was such from the moment of His Incarnation. Henceforth His office assumes a public character.

"Behold the Lamb of God, behold Him Who taketh away the sin of the world."[1]

He is the Victim for sin: for the sins of the whole world.

There are two elements in the expiation of sin: first, the humiliation of the heart, i. e., shame and contrition; and, secondly, the satisfaction. In Baptism, Christ takes on Himself the humiliation and shame due to the sins of men, and on the Cross, He makes satisfaction for them.

His Baptism, then, is not a mere external rite. It is the formal acceptance of His Messianic rôle and the vow of His future immolation.

(iii) "IT BEHOVES US TO FULFIL ALL JUSTICE"

John had surely good reasons to wonder when he saw Christ descend into the waters of the streams along with the penitents, and ask for baptism at his hands: "I ought to be baptized by Thee, and comest Thou to me?" he exclaimed in words that recalls those of St Elizabeth, his mother. "And he withstood Him."

"Suffer Me to do this now, thus it behoves us to fulfil all justice," was the Christ's answer: His second word recorded by the Gospel.

It was Heaven's decree that Christ should begin to redeem mankind by the deepest humiliation.

Humility, particularly the sense of sin, the feeling of shame and the hatred of self, is the fundamental virtue of Christianity, out of which there arises the true love of God and of men. Pride and self-conceit mark one off as the child of Satan.

All the more then is the sense of sin, shame and hatred of self, proper to those souls who work for the salvation of others and who want to be victims for sin. At Mass, especially, and whenever they

1. John i, 29.

appear before God to plead for themselves and for others, should they be imbued with a sense of their lowliness and unworthiness.

4. "THOU ART MY BELOVED SON"

"And straightway, as He came out of the water, He saw the heavens rent asunder, and the Spirit coming down upon Him as a dove; and there came a voice from the Heavens, Thou art My beloved Son, in Thee I am well pleased."[1]

Over the Incarnate Son of God lying in a manger the Angels had sung: "Glory to God in the highest, and on earth peace to men of good will." Laden with all the sins of men, He stands now on the bank of the Jordan as a sinner in need of purification, as much as the harlot and the publican; and above Him the Heavens are again thrown open. The Father Himself comes to glorify Him, and the Holy Spirit descends in bodily shape upon Him, in the form of a dove, as a sign of the boundless grace shed on His soul: "For God giveth not the Spirit by measure: the Father loveth the Son, and He hath given all things into His hand."[2]

The effusion is a permanent one. Truly could the Baptist say: "I saw the Spirit coming down as a dove from Heaven and It remained upon Him."[3] At the same time the voice of the Father is heard, declaring Christ to be His own beloved Son, and expressing an absolute and eternal complacency in Him. "Thou art My beloved Son, in Thee I am well pleased."

The Messianic era is thus opened. Christ is the Son that will lead men back to God, block the descent to Hell, and open the way to Heaven. He Himself will be the Way. In Him and through Him men will become children of God, well-pleasing to their Heavenly Father.

At the same time the way to this Divine Sonship is shown. The Father manifests Christ as His Son and as the Messiah after the Humiliation of His Baptism. The same had happened at His Birth and at His Presentation in the Temple. Still more, His Resurrection and His Glorification by the Father, as Messiah and Saviour of men, will follow the sufferings and the humiliations of His Passion.

1. Mark i, 10, 11. 2. John iii, 35. 3. John i, 32.

"Ought not Christ to have suffered these things, and thus to enter into His glory?"[1]

It is in sufferings and humiliations that we are truly born children of God and that we achieve the salvation of men.

To end the contemplation by making a Colloquy to our Lady asking her to obtain for me grace from her Son and Lord to follow Him beneath the Standard of His holy Cross, with the deepest feelings of humility and shame, and with readiness to bear all insults for His love. *Hail Mary.*

To ask the same of our Lord that He may obtain it for me from the Father. *Anima Christi.*

To ask the same of the Father that He may grant it to me. *Our Father.*

SEMETIPSUM EXINANIVIT

"He made Himself void or empty," as the earth had been "void and empty" at the beginning; He seemed to be unbinding and letting loose the assemblage of attributes which made Him God, and to be destroying the idea which He Himself had implanted in our minds. The God of miracles did the most awful of signs and wonders, by revoking and contradicting, as it were, all His perfections, though He remained the while one and the same. Omnipotence became an abject; the Life became a leper; the first and only Fair came down to us with an "inglorious visage," and an "unsightly form," bleeding and (I may say) ghastly, lifted up in nakedness and stretched out in dislocation before the eyes of sinners. Not content with this, He perpetuates the history of His humiliation; men of this world, when they fall into trouble, and then recover themselves, hide the memorials of it. They conceal their misfortunes in prospect, as long as they can; bear them perforce, when they fall into them; and, when they have overcome them, affect to make light of them. Kings of the earth, when they have rid themselves of their temporary conquerors, and are reinstated on their thrones, put all things back into their former state, and remove

1. Luke xxiv, 26.

from their palaces, council-rooms, and cities, whether statue or picture or inscription or edict, all of which bear witness to the suspension of their power. Soldiers indeed boast of their scars, but it is because their foes were well-matched with them, and their conflicts were necessary, and the marks of what they have suffered is a proof of what they have done; but He, who *oblatus est, quia voluit*, who "was offered, for He willed it," who exposed Himself to the powers of evil, yet could have saved us without that exposure, who was neither weak in that He was overcome, nor strong in that He overcame, proclaims to the whole world what He has gone through, without the tyrant's shame, without the soldier's pride—He (wonderful it is) has raised up on high, He has planted over the earth, the memorial, that that Evil One whom He cast out of Heaven in the beginning, has in the hour of darkness inflicted agony upon Him. For in truth, by consequence of the infinitude of His glory, He is more beautiful in His weakness than in His strength; His wounds shine like stars of light; His very Cross becomes an object of worship; the instruments of His Passion, the nails and the thorny crown, are replete with miraculous power. And so He bids the commemoration of His Bloody Sacrifice to be made day by day all over the earth, and He Himself is there in Person to quicken and sanctify it; He rears His bitter but saving Cross in every Church and over every Altar; He shows Himself torn and bleeding upon the wood at the corners of each street and in every village market-place; He makes it the symbol of His religion; He seals our foreheads, our lips, and our breast with this triumphant sign; with it He begins and ends our days, and with it He consigns us to the tomb. And when He comes again, that Sign of the Son of Man will be seen in Heaven; and when He takes His seat in judgement, the same glorious marks will be seen by all the world in His Hands, Feet, and Side, which were dug into them at the season of His degradation.

Newman.

The Features of Christ's Kingdom

Again the devil took Him up into a very high mountain, and shewed Him all the kingdoms of the world, and the glory of them, and said to Him:

"All these will I give Thee, if falling down Thou wilt adore me."

Then Jesus saith to him:

"Begone, Satan: for it is written: 'The Lord thy God shalt thou adore, and Him only shalt thou serve.'"

OUR LORD IN THE DESERT

THE FEATURES OF CHRIST'S KINGDOM

The first Prelude is to call to mind how, after His Baptism our Lord was led by the Holy Spirit into the wilderness where, having fasted forty days and forty nights, He was tempted by Satan (Matt. iv, 1-11; Mark i, 12, 13; Luke iv, 1-13).

The second Prelude is to see with the eyes of the imagination the wild and dreary desert waste—a hill to the west of Jericho—where Christ was led by the Holy Spirit.

The third Prelude is to ask light to know how the Divine King prepares Himself for His mission and lays bare the deceits and snares of Satan, the great enemy of His Kingdom; and grace to love Him more and more and to do as He does.

* * *

"And straightway the Spirit casteth Him out into the wilderness."[1]

This retreat of the Saviour is usually called the Messianic preparation. Jesus is led into the desert to show in Himself the characteristic traits of His fellow-labourers, and to find out and defeat for them the ruses of the enemy, bent on marring the work which he cannot prevent. From the outset Christ wants us to understand what His Kingdom is *not*, to banish illusions, and to dispel false hopes.

1. The Life of our Lord in the Desert

"And He was in the wilderness forty days, being tempted the while by Satan and He was with the wild beasts."[2]

"And in those days He did eat nothing."[3]

In the forty days spent in the desert, Christ strikingly teaches us some virtues, which, though practiced by Him throughout His life, might otherwise be overlooked by many of us in contemplating the mysteries of His public life.

First of all, He shows in His own person how an apostle must prepare himself for work in the Kingdom of God. Humility of heart is, certainly, most required, but it is not enough. Preaching

1. Mark i, 13. 2. Mark i, 12, 13. 3. Luke iv, 2.

and teaching are effective when thereby, one delivers to others the fruits of one's contemplation. In order not to become a sounding brass or a tinkling cymbal, the apostle must constantly cultivate the spirit of self-recollectedness, and to secure this he must, besides severely controlling his senses and imagination, from time to time withdraw entirely from the crowd and from the ordinary duties of life. This he does every year during his Retreat; every month at the time of his monthly recollection; and if he is careful, everyday also from the moment he retires at night, to the moment his spiritual duties are over in the morning.

Recollection leads to prayer. The apostle must be essentially a man of prayer, if he is to be a fit instrument in the hands of God for the conversion and sanctification of souls. He must be filled with what St Ignatius calls *familiaritas cum Deo in spiritualibus devotionis exercitiis.*

Bona est oratio cum jejunio. If every Christian must carry the cross of self-abnegation and self-mortification, how much more should an apostle do it, whose only object in life is to witness to a Crucified God against a world that craves for pleasures, to rescue souls from the abyss, and to atone to the Divine Justice for his own sins and for the sins of others. Sincere contempt for the comforts of life and love for whatever is hard and painful, for sufferings and privations, mark out the true man of God from him who is but a weakling or a hypocrite.

2. Our Lord is Tempted

The Spirit of God leads Christ into the desert, not, properly speaking, that He may there give Himself entirely to prayer and mortification, but that He may be tempted by the devil. St Matthew says: "Jesus was led by the Spirit into the desert to be tempted by the devil." At first, we are almost shocked at hearing this of our Divine Master. For us temptations are the effects of our evil passions and of our corrupt nature, adroitly used by our enemy. To some extent, they are connected with something evil, though they are not always evil in themselves. We must discard these ideas when talking of the temptations of Christ. However difficult it may be to explain them, let it be understood that Christ's interior faculties were not affected by the suggestions of the enemy. These came from outside, and not for a moment did they trouble the inner peace and purity of the Saviour.

The fact, however, remains that Christ was tempted. How could He, just a moment before proclaimed the Son of God, allow the enemy to approach Him with evil insinuations? Besides the three Synoptics, St Paul is the only sacred writer that speaks of these temptations of Christ. The words which he uses may serve to explain to us the object which Christ had in view in allowing them.

"And though He was Son, He learned obedience from that which He suffered."[1] "For we have not a High Priest who is unable to realize in Himself our weaknesses, but rather one who hath been tried in every way like ourselves short of sin."[2] "Whence it behoved Him to be made like unto His brethren in all respects, that He might become a merciful and faithful High Priest in things pertaining to God, so as to atone for the sins of the people. For because He hath suffered, being tried Himself thereby, He can give help to those who are under trial."[3]

Christ, our Divine Leader, has started His campaign against the chieftain of all the enemy. Accordingly He first shows in Himself that His soldiers should never fear Satan's attacks, however painful and humiliating. To be attacked by Satan is a sign that we belong to Christ. He wants, moreover, to teach us in a practical way, how to find out and how to baffle the ruses of the Evil One.

Christ was to be our Saviour. But such He could never perfectly be if He contented Himself with redeeming us from sin, and heeded little the causes of sin, i. e., our passions, and the occasions of sin, i. e., our temptations. To understand our dangers, as far as He could, having taken upon Himself our human nature with all its infirmities, He further allowed Himself to be tempted by His enemy and the enemy of us all, His brothers.

This episode of our Lord's life must inspire us with the greatest confidence.

Christ is the second Adam, the Head of the regenerated human family. In the earthly paradise Adam had yielded to Satan's

1. Heb. v, 8. 2. Heb. iv, 15. 3. Heb. ii, 17, 18.

temptation and had thus made all his descendants prone to follow in his footsteps. In this new kind of Eden, Christ faces the enemy and puts him to an ignominious flight, thus securing for us the courage and the strength to conquer all our temptations. We have but to imitate His promptitude in resisting the suggestions of the Evil One. Against the claims of the flesh and of vanity we must oppose, as Christ did, the rights of God and our duty to Him.

3. The Temptations

(i) THEIR NATURE

The temptations of our Lord are not ordinary temptations.

They may be called Messianic temptations. Their object is not so much to induce Christ to do evil as to make Him deviate from the straight path. Satan tries to get Jesus to choose an easier and pleasanter path than the hard one which God had marked out for Him. He tries to lead Him to follow His own way instead of God's, to make God His servant, rather than Himself the servant of God. In other words, the temptations are not directly against the Kingdom of God; they aim at perverting its nature. Hence their importance for every minister of Christ.

Christ is first of all attacked in His faith in His Divine Origin and Mission and in His confidence in the Father. Is He really the Son of God? The temptation is occasioned by His sufferings—"He afterwards felt hungry"—and by the apparent abandonment on the part of His Father. The temptation will again recur in the Garden and on the Cross: "He trusted in God, let Him deliver Him now, if He will have Him: for He said: I am the Son of God."

Presumption follows: God ought to intervene and manifest His Son to the world by some extraordinary sign, which should spare Him the many sufferings and humiliations of His public life and of His Passion.

Lastly, the material kingdom is offered instead of the spiritual, human and political action, instead of self abnegation and personal sacrifice. In one word the choice between the vulgar Messianism of the Jews and the Divine plan of Redemption is proposed to Christ at this moment of His manifestation as Messiah.

Everyone that tries to continue Christ's work is exposed to similar temptations, and they are the most subtle temptations of all: discouragement, love of whatever is showy, striking and marvellous, and the perverse use of religion and of the things of God to pursue temporal and material gains.

(ii) HOW CHRIST WITHSTANDS SATAN'S ATTACK

It is good to watch the manner in which Christ withstands the temptations: all His future steps will be inspired by it.

To the Evil One suggesting thoughts of diffidence and discouragement, Christ opposes now, even as He will continue to oppose to His agonizing end, the boundless confidence of a child. Though humbled, despised and having no place whereon to lay His head, He will never doubt the love and the Providence of His Father, nor His transcendent origin.

To Satan prompting spectacular effects, and, later on, to the Jews asking for them, He persistently answers with humble and patient work.

And, lastly, to Satan offering Him all the kingdoms of the earth, Christ answers indignantly, just as He will answer the Jews, anxious to make Him their king, by hiding Himself and by even concealing the title of Messiah, that He might the better maintain the spiritual and interior character of His Kingdom, though He knows that such an attitude will bring about His final rejection at the hands of the people. His Kingdom will be based on the will to suffer for men and to love them to the very end, in spite of all.

Satan is discomfited. The Angels who had expelled the old Adam from the garden of Eden, come to serve the new Adam in the Desert.

To end the contemplation with the usual *Triple Colloquy* to our Lady, to Christ, and to the Eternal Father, of the exercise on *Two Standards*, asking grace to guard myself against the deceits and the illusions of Satan and to follow the Divine King under the Standard of the Cross in poverty, in concealment and humiliations, fully trusting in His infinite love and wholly submissive to His Divine Will.

The First Citizens of the Kingdom

" Come, follow Me, and I will make you fishers of men."
And straightway they left the nets and followed Him.

THE VOCATION OF THE APOSTLES

THE FIRST CITIZENS OF THE KINGDOM

The first Prelude is to remember how our Lord gradually called His Apostle to follow Him and be one with Him.

The second Prelude is to see with the eyes of imagination the places where our Lord successively calls His Apostles to Himself – the bank of the Jordan, the shore of the Lake of Genesaret, and the Mountain of the Beatitudes.

The third Prelude is to ask grace from our Lord that I may not be deaf to His call or irresponsive to His desire to see me enrolled under His Standard, but prompt and diligent to accomplish His most Holy Will.

1. The First Whisper

Having graphically shown what the Kingdom of God is not and how the attacks of the Evil One are directed against its very foundations, Christ proceeds to enrol its first citizens.

Of all vocations to follow Christ, those of Peter, of Andrew, and of John are typical of Christ's ways in dealing with souls. The three were called by degrees to an ever closer companionship with Christ. At first they were only admitted to a certain intimacy with the Divine Master, retaining their liberty to return to their former calling.

Leaving the Desert, the Master wended His way towards the place where John was baptizing and where He had heard the voice of the Father. On seeing Him, John cried out: "Behold the Lamb of God! Behold Him Who taketh away the sin of the world!"[1]

And describing the vision he had witnessed on that very bank, the Baptist ended by saying: "And I saw; and I gave testimony, that this is the Son of God. The next day again John stood, and two of his disciples. And beholding Jesus walking, he saith: Behold the Lamb of God. And the two disciples heard him speak and they followed Jesus. And Jesus turning, and seeing them following Him, said to them: What seek you? Who said to Him: Rabbi (which is to say, being interpreted, Master), where dwellest Thou? He saith to them: Come and see. They came, and saw

1. John I, 29.

where He abode, and they stayed with Him that day; now it was about the tenth hour. And Andrew the brother of Simon Peter was one of the two who had heard of John, and followed him. He findeth first his brother Simon, and saith to him: We have found the Messiah, which being interpreted, the Christ. And he brought him to Jesus. And Jesus looking upon him said: Thou art Simon the Son of Jona: thou shalt be called Cephas, which is interpreted Peter."[1]

2. The Call

Jesus has already cast a spell on them: they will never be the same men again. Yielding to that spell, they follow the Divine Master through Samaria and Galilee. Then, for some time, we lose sight of them, till we find them on the lake of Genesaret, where, the Master Himself calls them to His service.

"And Jesus walking by the Sea of Galilee saw two brethren, Simon who is called Peter, and Andrew his brother, casting a net into the sea (for they were fishers). And He saith to them: Come ye after Me, and I will make you to be fishers of men. And they immediately leaving their nets, followed Him. And going on from thence, He saw other two brethren, James the son of Zebedee, and John his brother, in a ship with Zebedee their father, mending their nets: and He called them. And they forthwith left their nets and father, and followed Him."[2]

As yet, however, they are only numbered amongst the many disciples that every day attach themselves to the new Prophet. It is only some time after that our Lord chooses them as His own Apostles, destined to be always with Him, and to share His joys and tribulations, His shame and glory.

"And it came to pass in those days, that He went out into a mountain to pray, and He passed the whole night in the prayer of God, and when day was come He called unto Him His disciples; and He chose twelve of them (whom also He called Apostles)."[3] "He calleth whom He would, and they went to Him. And He appointed twelve, whom moreover He named Apostles, to be with Him."[4]

1. John i, 34-42. 2. Matt. iv, 18-22. 3. Luke vi, 12, 13. 4. Mark iii, 13, 14.

What were the feelings of the Divine Saviour that night preceding the day on which He was to lay the foundation of the great work for which He had been sent by the Father? How instinctively we feel, especially from St Luke's narrative, the importance and solemnity of such a moment, and of such a choice.

Henceforth the Apostles are truly one with Christ, Christ's friends and ambassadors, His ministers and the instruments of His grace and infinite power. They are to be always with Him, to be taught by Him in a peculiar way, and invested, eventually, with all His power: "As the Father hath sent Me, so do I send you," to spread the Church all over the world and be the twelve pillars of the City of God. They are to be *other Christs*, to continue Christ's life and mission, to be the echoes of His Voice and the channels of His Grace.

It is however, only on Pentecost Day that the Apostles fully realize the meaning of their vocation. Truly from that day Christ becomes their life, and the spreading of His Kingdom, their supreme task.

3. Our Vocation

At Baptism we were all enrolled in the army of Christ, though most of us were not conscious of it. We publicly ratified our oath of allegiance at our Confirmation. We became far more attached to our Lord when we answered His call to higher things—to the Priesthood, or to the Religious Life, or to both. It is to this special call that we refer whenever we speak of our vocation, and, indeed, it deserves such a name in a peculiar way. It is, however, incorrect to think of our vocation as something definitely settled with God; as if having answered His call to a higher state of life, and trying now to fulfil its obligations, we have done all we were expected to do. Our vocation is not a thing settled for ever. Christ is constantly calling us. He stands in our midst; He is walking amongst us; He abides in us, and by His hand, His eye, His secret inspiration, He invites us to follow Him. Besides the ordinary inspirations to the accomplishment of single acts, from time to time, and specially during the Retreat, Jesus calls us, as He called His Apostles, to follow Him in a more perfect manner, to give to our life a new and more perfect orientation.

Woe to us if we do not answer such a call. The Apostles did follow it and it was the ultimate cause of all their glory. The rich young man declined to listen to it. He might have been one of the pillars of the Church; instead he preferred a common-place life, and many have serious doubts about his eternal salvation.

Our weaknesses, our deficiencies and miseries should not deter us from following Christ's noble and arduous way, or from following it more perfectly day by day, in the footsteps of the Saints. The Apostles were not great or learned in the eyes of the world; still less in their own eyes. They were poor and ignorant men. And yet it is through such men that Christ has willed to convert the world. If we think that there is some good in us, we must be all the more humble, if we would be the instruments of the Almighty, Who chooses the foolish things of the world that He may confound the wise, and the weak things of the world that He may confound the strong.

The Apostles were simple and generous souls, anxious to follow the Divine Call wherever it led them, and ready to sacrifice all they had for it. They were patient and enduring. Such must be the builders of the Kingdom of God.

To end the Contemplation by offering myself wholeheartedly to the Divine King and by fervently renewing the *Triple Colloquy* of the contemplation on *Two Standards*.

DIVINE CALLS

We are not called once only, but many times; all through our life Christ is calling us. He called us first in Baptism; but afterwards also; whether we obey His voice or not, he graciously calls us still. If we fall from our Baptism, He calls us to repent; if we are striving to fulfil our calling, He calls us on from grace to grace, and from holiness to holiness, while life is given us. Abraham was called from his home, Peter from his nets, Mathew from his office, Elisha from his farm, Nathanael from his retreat;

we are all in course of calling, on and on, from one thing to another, having no resting-place, but mounting towards our eternal rest, and obeying one command only to have another put upon us. He calls us again and again, in order to justify us again and again, — and again and again, and more and more, to sanctify and glorify us.

It were well if we understood this; but we are slow to master the great truth, that Christ is, as it were, walking among us, and by His hand, or eye, or voice, bidding us follow Him. We do not understand that His call is a thing which takes place now. We think it took place in the Apostle's days; but we do not believe in it, we do not look out for it in our own case. We have not eyes to see the Lord; far different from the beloved Apostle, who knew Christ even when the rest of the disciples knew Him not. When He stood on the shore after His Resurrection, and bade them cast the net into the sea, "that disciple whom Jesus loved saith unto Peter, It is the Lord."[1]

Now what I mean is this: that they who are living religiously, have from time to time truths they did not know before, or had no need to consider, brought before them forcibly; truths which involve duties, which are in fact precepts, and claim obedience. In this and such like ways Christ calls us now. There is nothing miraculous or extraordinary in His dealings with us. He works through our natural faculties and circumstances of life. Still what happens to us in providence is in all essential respects what His voice was to those whom He addressed when on earth: whether He commands by a visible presence, or by a voice, or by our consciences, it matters not, so that we feel it to be a command. If it is a command, it may be obeyed or disobeyed; it may be accepted as Samuel or St Paul accepted it, or put aside after the manner of the young man who had great possessions.

Newman.

1. John xxi, 7.

The Code of Christ's Kingdom

And seeing the multitudes, He went up into a mountain, and when He was set down, His disciples came unto Him.

And opening His mouth He taught them saying:

"Blessed are the poor in spirit; for theirs is the Kingdom of Heaven."

THE SERMON ON THE MOUNT

THE CODE OF CHRIST'S KINGDOM

The first Prelude is to remember how our Lord, after choosing His twelve Apostles, delivered to them and to the great multitude that had gathered from the surrounding towns and villages the sublime discourse known as the Sermon on the Mount.

The second Prelude is to see with the eyes of the imagination the Mountain of the Beatitudes—a somewhat strangely shaped mountain, crowned by two peaks, separated from each other by a stretch of green level plain.

The third Prelude is to ask for light to know the true life which the supreme and true King, Christ our Lord, points out, and for grace to imitate Him.

1. Christ on the Mount

Having enrolled His soldiers, Christ raises His standard and issues His proclamation—the programme and the code of the new Kingdom.

St Luke lays stress on the time and the place of this important event in our Lord's life.

"And it came to pass in those days that He went out into a mountain to pray and He passed the whole night in the prayer of God. And when the day was come, He called unto Him His disciples and He chose twelve of them (whom He named Apostles) .... And coming down with them He stood in a plain place, and the company of His disciples and a very great multitude of people .... And lifting up His eyes on His disciples, said: Blessed are the poor."[1]

The Saviour has come down from the peak where He has spent the whole night in fervent prayer, and where, from amongst His followers, He has chosen the pillars of His Church. He stands now with the Twelve around Him, like a Commander-in-Chief, a King, surrounded by His Staff. A little lower are the other disciples; and further down, a large multitude of people.

The Sermon which He is going to deliver is *the* Gospel—Christ's Good News.

1. Luke vi, 12-20.

2. The Beatitudes

First of all, Christ marks off the citizens of the new Kingdom, lays down the titles to its possession, and at the same time gives a new philosophy of life. It was the custom with moral teachers of the time to discuss the nature of true happiness. Christ also opens His lips and there flow from them the words that will be spiritual food for millions of souls throughout the ages.

(i) "BLESSED ARE THE POOR"

"Blessed are the poor in spirit, for theirs is the Kingdom of Heaven."

Poverty, spiritual and material, is the preliminary step towards the Kingdom. Whoever does not feel his misery cannot dream of rising higher in Christ; whoever is not detached from the things of earth, cannot think of those of Heaven.

Christ, first of all, declares blessed, i. e., infinitely more than happy, the lowly, the hungry, those that fear the Lord, the humble and contrite of heart, the little children—all those that feel their misery and their utter insufficiency. Only these can enter the Kingdom of Heaven, for they alone feel how far they are from it. On the contrary, nothing excludes one from it more surely than intellectual pride, self-approval, and self-complacency.

Christ likewise declares blessed those who are poor in the things of this world.

"Woe to you that are rich," i. e., that seek in your riches your end and your whole comfort, "for you have your consolation." It is not riches or poverty in themselves that bring us to misery or to happiness. A rich man may be poor in spirit, as a poor man may be discontented and envious. Poverty leads to blessedness if borne in the true Christian spirit; wealth begets misery if used in the spirit of the world. Only, "how hardly shall they that have riches enter into the Kingdom of God."

(ii) "BLESSED ARE THE MEEK"

"Blessed are the meek, for they shall possess the land."

The first beatitude gives the soul's attitude to God and to the things of this world; the second, its attitude to men.

The meek are those that suffer and endure everything without complaint, men of a retiring, submissive, and chastened spirit. They seem to be naturally excluded from the spoils of victory. Our Lord promises them, instead, a secure and peaceful possession of the land whereby, as St Thomas says, is denoted the solid reality of eternal goods. In other words, they will really conquer. The disciples of Christ, then, will promote the interests of Christ and of His Church not by wrangling and fighting, nor by self-assertion, but by a meek, yielding, and conciliatory spirit.

(iii) "BLESSED ARE THEY THAT MOURN, HUNGER AND THIRST"

"Blessed are they that mourn, for they shall be comforted."

"Blessed are ye that weep now, for you shall laugh."

"Blessed are they that hunger and thirst after justice, for they shall be filled."

"Blessed are ye that hunger now, for you shall be filled."

Mental sorrow, chiefly for one's sins and for the delay of glory and bodily sufferings, provided they are borne meekly and for Christ's sake, will bring ineffable happiness to the soul. If we can say to God with the Prophet Jeremias: "I have not desired the day of man," [1] He will surely come to wipe away all our tears. And if we desire to live only according to God's Will, His joy will fill our hearts.

Instead, "woe to you that are filled, for you shall hunger," and "woe to you that laugh now, for you shall mourn and weep;" i. e., woe to you that are so satisfied with the things of the world as not to think of eternal life.

(iv) "BLESSED ARE THE MERCIFUL"

"Blessed are the merciful, for they shall obtain mercy."

The mercy which our Lord praises is, first of all, that which induces us to look with pity and sympathy on the miseries of others, whether of body or of soul—"With what measure you mete, it shall be measured to you again." Secondly, our Lord extols the mercy that leads us to give of the things we have, and to lend a

1. Jer. xvii, 16.

helping hand to those that stand in need, irrespective of their position or merit, and unmindful of the trouble we may have to face. People usually recede from works of mercy lest they be burdened with other people's misery. Our Lord promises the merciful that they will obtain mercy and be delivered from all misery.

(v) "BLESSED ARE THE PURE OF HEART"

"Blessed are the pure of heart, for they shall see God."

The disciples of Christ must be clean not only of legal impurities or of sins which are outward and shock public opinion, but of all sin. They must be pure of body and pure in intention, having only God in view, and seeking His glory in everything. To such souls God will reveal Himself even in this life.

(vi) "BLESSED ARE THE PEACEMAKERS"

"Blessed are the peacemakers, for they shall be called the children of God."

Peacemakers are those who make peace, first, in themselves, by subjecting all their faculties to God, and then amongst others, between men and men, between men and God.

They are promised the glory of the Divine sonship consisting in perfect union with God through consummate wisdom. They become "children of God" in the likeness of Christ, the great Peacemaker, through whose Blood peace has been made between the things of earth and the things of Heaven.

(vii) "BLESSED ARE THEY THAT SUFFER PERSECUTION"

"Blessed shall you be when men shall hate you, and when they shall separate you, and shall reproach you, and cast out your name as evil, for the Son of Man's sake. Be glad in that day and rejoice; for behold your reward is great in Heaven." [1]

Persecution is the hardest thing to bear: hence it is placed the last. The various ways in which it can show itself are arranged in climax—as much as to say, the fiercer the presecution, the greater the blessedness. On the other hand, "woe to you when men shall

1. Luke vi, 22, 23.

bless you," i. e., when the world applauds you, for it is a strong indication that you are living according to its maxims. It was thus that, of old, men praised false prophets.

3. The Law of Love

Christ lays down as the main, distinctive characteristic of His disciples, what pagans thought mean and cowardly, and what is surely above man's strength and only possible with God's grace, i. e., to love our enemies, to forgive the injuries they inflict on us, and be almost blind to their faults.

"But I say to you: Love your enemies: do good to them that hate you. Bless them that curse you, and pray for them that spitefully use and persecute you. And to him that striketh thee on one cheek, offer also the other. And him that taketh away from thee thy cloak, hinder not to take thy coat also. That you may be the children of your Father Who is in Heaven—for He is kind to the unthankful and to the evil—Who maketh His sun rise upon the good and upon the bad, and raineth upon the just and the unjust.

"Be ye, therefore, merciful as your Father also is merciful. Judge not and you shall not be judged: condemn not and you shall not be condemned. Forgive and you shall be forgiven. And why seest thou the mote in thy brother's eye: but the beam that is in thy own eye thou considerest not?"[1]

"Up to the present moment," says Giovanni Papini in the *Story of Christ*, "man has loved himself alone, he has returned hatred for hatred; the future man, who shall inhabit the Kingdom, must hate himself and love his enemy. To love one's neighbour as oneself is but an inadequate formula, a mere concession to universal egotism. For he who loves himself cannot love others with a perfect love, and finds himself, of necessity, opposed to others. The one solution of the problem is to hate oneself. We are all overfond of self, we admire and flatter ourselves too much. In order to overcome this blind love we must bring ourselves to see our own baseness, our nothingness and iniquity. Self-contempt is humility, and consequently the beginning of repentance and ultimate perfection."

1. Cf. Matt. v; Luke vi.

The Father's Love

"Behold the birds of the air, for they neither sow, nor do they reap, nor gather into barns: and your heavenly Father feedeth them. Are not you of much more value than they?"

4. THE FATHER'S LOVE

Absolute trust in the Father's love and care must also be the characteristic of the children of the Kingdom. They must rest in His Divine arms and fear nothing.

"Be not solicitous"—i. e., do not even begin to be anxious—"for your life, what you shall eat, nor for your body what you shall put on . . . . Behold the birds of the air, for they neither sow, nor do they reap, nor gather into barns; and your Heavenly Father feedeth them . . . . Consider the lilies of the field, how they grow . . . . Be not solicitous . . . . For your Father knoweth that you have need of all these things. But seek ye first the Kingdom of God and His justice: and all these things shall be added unto you."[1]

"Be not afraid of them who kill the body and after that have no more that they can do . . . . Are not five sparrows sold for two farthings and not one of them is forgotten before God? But even the very hairs of your head are all numbered. Fear not, therefore: you are of more value than many sparrows."[2]

5. THE LORD'S PRAYER

The prayer which our Lord teaches to His disciples sums up all His doctrine.

"Our Father Who art in Heaven."

"Hallowed be Thy Name." The Name of God is His Essence as manifested. May Thou be sanctified and glorified by men! Man is created to give glory to God, to revere, praise and serve Him. That is his supreme end; and that is why it is placed here as the petition that should ever be first and foremost in his mind. "Father, glorify Thy Name."[3]

"Thy Kingdom come." First, Thy internal Kingdom in the heart of every man: the Kingdom of Thy Christ. And, then, Thy external Kingdom, i. e., Thy Church. May Thy Church spread all over the world, that Thou mayest be known and loved by all men. And, lastly, may Thy eternal Kingdom come, when Thou shalt be all in all!

1. Cf. Matt. vi; Luke vi. 2. Luke xii, 4, 6, 7. 3. John xii, 28.

"Thy Will be done on earth, as it is in Heaven." Therein lies our peace and happiness.

"Give us this day our daily bread." Give us all the things we need today for the support of our life. Tomorrow we shall again turn to Thee for help and sustenance.

"And forgive us our trespasses as we forgive them that trespass against us."

"And lead us not into temptation." Do not allow us to fall. Give us not up to the desires of our hearts by withdrawing Thy grace, Thy face and countenance from us, leaving us a prey to our appetites and passions.

"But deliver us from evil." Deliver us, O Father, from the Evil One and from all evil, past, present, and future.

The principles which our Lord has proclaimed on the Mountain are diametrically opposed to the principles of the world and to many instincts of our nature. He alone, however, is the Way, the Truth, and the Life. We must often climb to this Mountain in spirit, sit near the Divine Master, listen to His words, and beg of Him that they may sink deep in our minds and hearts. They will lift the mist which continually grows before our eyes in our contact with the world and in the very performance of our duties, and which makes us see things so differently from the way Christ and His friends saw them.

To end the contemplation with a Colloquy with Christ, the Incarnate Truth, crying with St Peter: "To whom shall we go? Thou alone hast the words of eternal life," and asking grace that my whole life may be in harmony with His teaching.

THE SERMON ON THE MOUNT

> The Sermon on the Mount is man's greatest title to existence; it is the adequate justification of his presence in the universe; it is the patent of our dignity as beings with a soul; the proof that we may rise above ourselves and become more than men; the pledge of this supreme possibility, of this hope, of our ascension.

Should an Angel come down to us from a higher sphere and ask to see our best and most precious possession, the best proof of our certainty, the master-piece of mind at its highest power, we would not show him our great greasy machines, those mechanical marvels of which we are so foolishly proud, although, indeed, they have shortened our lives and rendered them more difficult and slavish, and are nought but matter at the service of material needs and superfluities. We would show the Angel the Sermon on the Mount, and after that, perhaps, but only after it, some few pages taken from the poets of all peoples. The *Sermon,* however, will always remain the diamond of unique magnificence, shining in all the splendour of its white purity amidst emeralds and sapphires that are splendid in colour only.

And should man be summoned to appear before a superhuman tribunal to render an account of his fatal errors, of the long-standing atrocities that every day are renewed, of the massacres that have been going on for thousands of years, of all the blood that has flowed from the veins of our brothers, of the tears shed by the children of men, of our stony-heartedness and perfidy which is equalled perhaps only by our imbecility, he would not seek to justify himself by means of philosophical arguments, no matter how learnedly and cleverly turned, nor by the sciences, which are but ephemeral systems of symbols and formulæ, nor by adducing our laws, which are but disgraceful compromises between cruelty and fear. To place in the balance against so much evil, in part payment of our debt, in extenuation of sixty centuries of revolting history, we would only have the few verses of which the Sermon on the Mount consists.

He who has read them without once experiencing (at least while his eyes still rested on the page) a throb of grateful tenderness, a tightening in his throat, an impulse of love and remorse, a vague but pressing need to do his part that these words may not remain mere words, that this Sermon may not remain a mere sign and echo, but become an immediate hope, a source of vitality to all the living, and actual, ever-enduring truth for all; he, I say, who has not experienced all this is more deserving of our loving pity than any one else, for not all the love of mankind can suffice to compensate him for what he has lost.

Giovanni Papini.

Our Companion in Labours

When Peter began to sink, he cried out, saying: "Lord save me."

And immediately Jesus stretching forth His hand took hold of him, and said to him:

"O thou of little faith, why didst thou doubt?"

CHRIST UPON THE WATERS

OUR COMPANION IN LABOURS

The first Prelude is to call to mind how Christ our Lord, seeing His Apostles, whom He had ordered to embark for Capharnaum, toiling at the oar came to them walking on the sea, and at Peter's request, bade him come to Him (Matt. xiv, 22-33.)

The second Prelude is to see with the eyes of the imagination the Sea of Galilee and, in the distance, the mountain-peak where our Lord retired to pray.

The third Prelude is to ask light to know the loving and watchful Providence of our Divine King and grace blindly to trust in Him in the midst of labours, of sufferings, and of apparent failures.

* * *

Having enrolled and initiated His soldiers in His Divine strategy. our Lord proceeds to establish in their hearts that virtue without which even the best resolutions to follow Him and to work and suffer with Him, would prove but the vain longings of momentary enthusiasm. That virtue is an unshakable confidence in His loving and watchful Providence in the midst of all difficulties, of failures, and even of spiritual anguish.

1. On the Stormy Sea

The storm on the Lake followed one of the greatest of our Lord's miracles, the multiplication of loaves. The enthusiasm of the crowd rose high:

"Then those men, when they had seen the miracle that Jesus did, said: This is of a truth, that prophet that should come into this world."[1]

Having given to the Apostles a startling sign of His loving power, Jesus wanted to test their confidence and faith. He forced them to set sail at once and go before Him to the other side of the Lake. How hard it must have been for the Apostles to obey such a command! A moment ago they had seemed so near the realization of their dreams. They had fully shared the enthusiasm of the crowd:

1. John vi, 14.

their Master was going to be made a King. Instead they must leave Him, and cross to Bethsaida when a storm was clearly preparing.

That is Christ's ordinary way of dealing with souls. He calls them to Himself, He instructs them, He shows them His love and His power, and, then sends them to face the stormy sea, to work and suffer in the dark night—apparently, away from Him.

2. "I WILL FEAR NO EVIL, FOR THOU ART WITH ME"

"And having dismissed the multitude, He went up into the mountain alone to pray. And when it was evening, He was there alone: but the boat in the midst of the sea was tossed with the waves; for the wind was contrary."[1]

Our Lord dismissed the crowd and retired to pray on the summit of the mountain. He is our Divine Mediator, always interceding for us His brothers, in Heaven, in the Tabernacle, in our very hearts, as He did, that night, for His beloved Apostles. The most violent storms may arise on the sea of life, and our frail boat be, every moment, on the point of foundering or of striking against the rocks. And yet if we know, that, in committing ourselves to the waves, we have but obeyed His commands, that our work and circumstances are not of our own choosing but His, we need fear nothing. The Apostles did neither despair, nor give up their toil in the midst of the stormy darkness, but they rowed strenuously, though with heavy hearts, trying to make for Capharnaum. Likewise, the thought that Jesus is praying for us must fill our hearts with great confidence and give us strength to pursue our course, to be faithful to His voice and message, and to work untiringly for the spread of His Kingdom, though the storm rage furiously around us. In time of desolation we must remain firm and constant in the resolutions already taken, insist more on prayer and self-denial, and keep a stout, patient and confident heart.

"The Lord ruleth me: and I shall want nothing . . . For though I should walk in the midst of the shadow of death, I will fear no evils for Thou art with me."[2]

1. Matt. xiv, 23-24. 2. Ps. xxii.

"The nearness of God," says a famous American writer, "is a constant security against terror and anxiety, a source of absolute repose and confident calmness. It is not that we are at all assured of physical safety, or deem ourselves protected by a love, which is denied to others, but that we are in a state of mind equally ready to be safe or to meet with injury. If injury befalls us, we are content to bear it because the Lord is our keeper and nothing can happen to us without His permission. If it be His Will, then, injury will be for us a blessing and no calamity at all. Thus, and thus only, is the trustful man protected from harm. Though sensitive to pain as the most highly strung organism, the worst of it is conquered, and the sting taken out of it altogether, by the thought that God is our loving and sleepless keeper, and that nothing can hurt us without His Will . . . . And, indeed, how can it possibly fail to steady the nerves to cool the fever, and appease the fret, if one be sensibly conscious that no matter what one's difficulties for the moment appear to be, one's life as a whole, is in the keeping of a Power Whom we can completely trust? Whoever not only says, but feels 'Thy Will be done,' is nailed against every weakness."

3. "It is I, fear not"

Jesus had been invisibly helping His Apostles all through the night. It was through Him and the infinite efficacy of His prayer that the Apostles had not been overcome either by the violence of the storm, or by feelings of discouragement and diffidence in the loving Providence of their Master. From the top of the mountain He had constantly watched over them and as St Mark tells us, "seeing them labouring in rowing," He interrupted His sweet intercourse with the Father, and came down to them, walking on the waves. He might have stilled the violence of the storm from afar as well, but He must do something more: He wants to console His Apostles with His Divine Presence. He comes to them walking upon the waters, and while they cry out in terror, thinking it is a spirit, He speaks out clearly those words which have been a source of strength to millions of souls: "Be of good heart. It is I, fear not."

To us also the Lord will come just when the night is darkest, the anguish bitterest, and the difficulties quite insurmountable. One thing is demanded of us: never to grow weary of the fight. If the Lord's coming "make any delay, wait for it: for it shall surely come and it shall not slack."[1]

4. Peter upon the waters

"And Peter making answer, said: Lord, if it be Thou, bid me come to Thee upon the waters. And He said: come. And Peter going down out of the boat, walked upon the water to come to Jesus. But seeing the wind strong, he was afraid; and when he began to sink, he cried out, saying: Lord, save me. And immediately Jesus stretching forth His hand took hold of him, and said to him; O thou of little faith, why didst thou doubt? And when they were come up into the boat, the wind ceased."[2]

How vividly does this episode bring out all the traits of Peter's character—his love for the Divine Master and his faith in His almighty power, his desire to distinguish himself, his fearlessness and generosity in facing even the greatest dangers, and in strange contrast, his faint-heartedness in the presence of a comparatively small obstacle. Obviously one who felt that at Christ's command, he could walk upon the waves as though on dry land, should not have been frightened by a sudden gust of wind.

St Peter typifies many souls, as generous and earnest as the third class of men in resolving and setting to work, but easily dismayed by unforeseen difficulties. Like Peter, they trust too much in themselves and forget to gaze fixedly on Christ, across the obstacles that ever rise to block their path. The Saviour mercifully allows them to realize their utter helplessness that they may intimately feel that it is not in their power to acquire or retain great devotion, ardent love, tears, or any other spiritual consolation, and that they must place their confidence in God alone.

"Lord, save me," Peter cries out, in an agony of fear. No sooner have the words passed his lips than Jesus stretching forth His hand, takes hold of him. The tender, loving pressure of that hand restores confidence and courage to the Apostle. "O thou of

1. Hab. ii, 3. 2. Matt. xiv, 28-32.

little faith, why didst thou doubt?" Thus does the Master lovingly reproach Peter. Why didst thou doubt My love and My power?

The cry of the Apostle must be our cry when difficulties, temptations, and discouragement, like so many pitiless waves, assail the frail boat of our soul. The Master surely will come to us, and once more, stretching forth His hand, He Himself will take hold of His helpless little children.

To conclude the contemplation by renewing the *Triple Colloquy* of the contemplation on *Two Banners*, and protesting my readiness to throw away at the command of Jesus, even the last plank to which I firmly cling, and walk to Him on the stormy sea supportless, with my gaze steadily fixed on His Heart, and trusting solely on His infinite love and His almighty power.

'IT IS I; BE NOT AFRAID'

When I sink down in gloom or fear,
    Hope blighted or delay'd,
Thy whisper, Lord, my heart shall cheer,
    "'Tis I; be not afraid!"

Or, startled at some sudden blow,
    If fretful thoughts I feel,
"Fear not, it is But I!" shall flow,
    As balm my wound to heal.

Nor will I quit Thy way, though foes
    Some onward pass defend;
From each rough voice the watchward goes,
    "Be not afraid!... a friend!"

And oh! when judgement's trumpet clear
    Awakes me from the grave,
Still in its echo may I hear,
    "'Tis Christ; He comes to save."

Newman.

Our Divine Friend

"I am the Resurrection and the Life: He that believeth in Me, although he be dead, shall live: and everyone that liveth and believeth in Me shall not die for ever."

THE RAISING OF LAZARUS

OUR DIVINE FRIEND

The first Prelude is to call to mind how our Lord, two days after hearing that His friend, Lazarus, was dangerously ill, went to Bethany and rewarded the faith of Martha and Mary, the dead man's sisters, by raising him to life (John xi, 1-45).

The second Prelude is to see with the eyes of the imagination the road from Perea to Bethany and Lazarus' tomb—a cavern chiselled out of the rock and sealed with a stone.

The third Prelude is to ask light to know the infinite love of our Divine King and grace to put all my trust in Him.

1. King and Friend

Contemplating the apparition of our Lord to His Disciples on the lake of Genesaret we have been encouraged to follow the course He has lovingly planned out for us, by the sure knowledge that He constantly watches over us and is ready to come to our help in the darkest moment of despair. Now St Ignatius wants us to realize that though our work is hard, thankless and apparently fruitless, we are not alone. Jesus is not only the King that watches the progress of the battle and runs to the rescue of His faithful soldiers, but He is our loving Friend also, the tenderest of friends. "I will not now call you servants .... But I have called you friends."[1] "As the Father hath loved Me, I also have loved you. Abide in My love."[2]

The present contemplation is meant to bring out the tender love of our Divine Friend and the infinite power which is His and which He places so to speak at the disposal of those whom He loves.

2. The Love of Jesus

"Now there was a certain man sick, named Lazarus, of Bethania of the town of Mary and Martha her sister.... His sisters therefore sent to Him, saying: Lord, behold, he whom Thou lovest is sick.

1. John xv, 15. 2. John xv, 9.

And Jesus hearing it, said to them: This sickness is not unto death but for the glory of God: that the Son of God may be glorified by it.

"Now Jesus loved Martha, and her sister Mary, and Lazarus. When He had heard therefore that he was sick, He still remained in the same place two days: then after that He said to the disciples: Let us go unto Judea again....

"Martha therefore, as soon as she heard that Jesus was come, went to meet Him: but Mary sat at home. Martha therefore said to Jesus: Lord, if Thou hadst been here, my brother had not died. But now also I know that whatsoever Thou wilt ask of God, God will give it Thee."[1]

The whole episode of the raising of Lazarus is brimful of a love as tender and ardent as any that has ever burnt in the heart of man. The message of Mary and Martha is love pleading to Love: "Behold he whom Thou lovest is sick." John, the Apostle of love, hastens to remark that "Jesus loved Martha, and her sister Mary, and Lazarus." Christ Himself speaks of Lazarus as a friend: "Lazarus our friend;" and at the sight of Mary's tearful sorrow He "groaned in spirit and troubled Himself" and wept, so that the Jews could not help saying: "Behold, how He loved him."

It is usually imagined that our Lord did not grant the loving request of the two sisters, but stayed in Perea two days more to give Lazarus, so to speak, time to die, and to Himself, the occasion to work a miracle. In reality when the messenger sent by the two sisters reached Jesus, Lazarus had just died. Neither of them, as a matter of fact, reproaches the Master for not having come to the bedside of their dying brother. One after the other merely says: "Lord, if Thou hadst been here, my brother had not died."

Their faith in Christ's power, however, is still unshaken and their confidence in His loving care, boundless. "But now also I know that whatsoever Thou shalt ask of God, God will give it Thee." Martha does not openly ask Christ to raise her brother to life, sure that He sees the wish of her heart and would not fail to grant it.

Loving recourse to our Divine Friend in our needs and boundless confidence in His love and infinite power even when all seems to rise

1. John xi, 1-22.

against us, and He Himself, to have forgotten us, must be the breath of our life.

" Who shall separate us from the love of Christ? Shall affliction or anguish or persecution or hunger or nakedness or danger or the sword?.., Yet amidst all this we more than conquer through Him Who hath loved us."[1]

3. "THOU ART THE CHRIST THE SON OF THE LIVING GOD"

"Jesus saith to her: Thy brother shall rise again. Martha saith to Him: I know that he shall rise again in the resurrection at the last day. Jesus said to her; I am the Resurrection and the Life; he that believeth in Me, although he be dead, shall live: and everyone that liveth and believeth in Me shall not die forever. Believest thou this?

" She saith to Him: Yea, Lord I have believed that Thou art Christ the Son of the Living God Who art come into this world."[2]

Christ is the Resurrection and the Life. Through Him we rise from the worst of deaths—the death of sin – to live of the very life of God. Through Him we live eternally of His life, and though our body shall have to undergo the penalty of death, it will one day rise by the power of Christ and share in the happiness and glory of the soul.

" He that believeth in Me hath life everlasting."[3]

" He that eateth My Flesh and drinketh My Blood, hath everlasting life: and I will raise him up in the last day."[4]

To believe that Christ is the principle of resurrection and life is to believe in His Divinity. That is why Martha answers the question of the Saviour: "Believest thou this?" with St Peter's cry, "Thou art Christ the Son of the Living God." To reveal Himself to the crowd and to His enemies as the Son of God, our Lord raises Lazarus to Life.

"And Jesus lifting up His eyes said: Father, I give Thee thanks that Thou hast heard Me. And I knew that Thou hearest Me always, but because of the people who stand about have I said it: that they may believe that Thou hast sent me."[5]

1. Rom. viii, 35-37. 2. John xi, 23-27. 3. John vi, 47. 4. John vi, 55. 5. John xi, 41-42.

The message of the Church during the last nineteen centuries, the aim of her activities and of her never ending martyrdom is "that you may believe that Jesus is the Christ the Son of God: and that believing you may have life in His name."[1]

The cry of Peter and of Martha must be the constant cry of our souls—the rock on which the edifice of our spiritual life stands unshaken and ever rises towards the throne of God.

To conclude the contemplation with a Colloquy with Christ my God and my Friend, begging of Him the grace of an unshaken confidence in His loving Heart and of a life of intimate union with Him under the standard of the Cross because He alone is the Resurrection and the Life.

"AND JESUS WEPT"

He wept from very sympathy with the grief of others. "When Jesus saw Mary weeping, and the Jews also weeping which came with her, He groaned in the spirit, and was troubled." It is the very nature of compassion or sympathy, as the word implies, to "rejoice with those who rejoice, and weep with those who weep." We know it is so with men; and God tells us He also is compassionate, and full of tender mercy. Yet we do not well know what this means, for how can God rejoice or grieve? By the very perfection of His nature Almighty God cannot show sympathy, at least to the comprehension of beings of such limited minds as ours. He, indeed, is hid from us; but if we were allowed to see Him, how could we discern in the Eternal and Unchangeable signs of sympathy? Words and works of sympathy He does display to us; but it is the very sight of sympathy in another that affects and comforts the sufferer more even than the fruits of it. Now we cannot see God's sympathy; and the Son of God, though feeling for us as great compassion as His Father, did not show it to us while He remained in His Father's bosom. But when He took flesh and appeared on earth, He showed

1. John xx, 31.

us the Godhead in a new manifestation. He invested Himself with a new set of attributes, those of our flesh, taking into Him a human soul and body, in order that thoughts, feelings, affections, might be His, which could respond to ours and certify to us his tender mercy. When, then, our Saviour weeps from sympathy at Mary's tears, let us not say it is the love of a man overcome by natural feeling. It is the love of God, the bowels of compassion of the Almighty and Eternal, condescending to appear as we are capable of receiving it, in the form of human nature.

Jesus wept, therefore, not merely from the deep thoughts of His understanding, but from spontaneous tenderness; from the gentleness and mercy, the encompassing loving-kindness and exuberant fostering affection of the Son of God for His own work, the race of man. Their tears touched Him at once, as their miseries had brought Him down from Heaven. His ear was open to them, and the sound of weeping went at once to His heart.

Newman.

The King Meek and Humble of Heart

A very great multitude spread their garments in the way: and others cut boughs from the trees, and strewed them in the way. And the multitudes that went before and followed, cried, saying:

"Hosanna to the Son of David: Blessed is He that cometh in the name of the Lord: Hosanna in the Highest."

PALM SUNDAY

THE KING MEEK AND HUMBLE OF HEART

The first Prelude is to call to mind how our Lord started from Bethany, mounted on the colt of an ass, amidst the enthusiastic acclamation of the people, and how as He drew near Jerusalem, He wept over it (Matt. xxi, 1-11).

The second Prelude is to see the road from Bethany to Jerusalem.

The third Prelude is to ask light to know our Divine King and the nature of His Kingdom, and grace to love and follow Him more and more.

* * *

On the tenth day of Nisan the paschal Lamb was set apart. It is the day which Christ, the true Passover to be slain for us, chooses for making His public entry into Jerusalem and the Temple, and for declaring solemnly the nature of the Messianic Kingdom which He will open in a few days.

1. Our Lord's Triumph

"And it came to pass, when He was come nigh to Bethphage and Bethania unto the mount called Olivet, He sent two of His disciples, saying: Go into the town which is over against you, at your entering into which, you shall find the colt of an ass tied, on which no man ever hath sitten: loose him, and bring him hither. . . .

"And they brought him to Jesus. And casting their garments on the colt, they set Jesus thereon. And as He went, they spread their clothes underneath in the way."[1]

The Saviour had always rebuked those friends of His who had urged Him to show Himself to the world. He had often forbidden those whom He healed, to publish His miracles abroad. He had silenced the devils that would proclaim Him the Son of God. He had run away from the crowd bent on making Him King. He wanted wholly to dispel the vain dreams of a temporal Messiah, so common amongst the Jews of His time.

---

1. Luke xix, 29-30; 35-36.

And yet He is truly the King of the Jews, the Messiah foretold by the prophets and expected by all men of good will. A few months ago He had elicited from his Apostles the confession of His Divinity. Today He triumphantly enters Jerusalem and receives, without the least opposition, the acclamations of the crowd saluting Him as the Messiah of Israel. In a few days He Himself will proclaim His mission before the two greatest tribunals: that of Israel and that of the Romans.

He does not set out however, as the deliverer of His people from the oppression of the foreigner.

"Tell ye the daughter of Sion, behold Thy King cometh unto thee, meek and sitting upon an ass, and a colt, the foal of an ass."

Such was God's plan. The Messiah was to be a true King—*Rex regum et Dominus dominantium*—and yet a King Who would conquer through meekness and humility, and whose throne would be a cross.

The whole of our Lord's life, and the three years of uninterrupted preaching had been directed to exemplify and bring home that hard lesson to His Apostles and to the people. The object of today's triumph is to repeat it once more in the capital of Israel, during the Paschal time, in the midst of millions of pilgrims.

2. "Seeing the City, He Wept over it"

"And when He drew near, seeing the City He wept over it, saying:

"If thou also hadst known, and that in this thy day, the things that are to thy peace; but now they are hidden from thy eyes. For the days shall come upon thee: and thy enemies shall cast a trench about thee, and compass thee round, and straiten thee on every side, and beat thee flat to the ground, and thy children who are in thee: and they shall not leave in thee stone upon a stone; because thou hast not known the time of thy visitation."[1]

It was our Lord's final appeal to the ungrateful City. But alas, He knew it would be rejected. Already He has heard the murmurings of His enemies irritated by the enthusiasm of the crowd. Shortly they will be bold enough to nail Him to the Cross.

1. Luke xix, 41-44.

"And seeing the City, he wept." It was not on account of His coming Passion that Christ shed tears; His Heart was too brave and generous for that. For His people He would have endured not one, but a thousand deaths. It was their blindness, their ingratitude, and alas, the punishment that would inevitably fall on them, that made Jesus cry in the midst of the universal rejoicing. Another would have called God's vengeance on the City, but the Saviour wept over her fate.

The mercy and patience of our Lord are everywhere admirably manifested. He repeatedly knocks at the heart of the sinner, and if the sinner refuses the proffered mercy, He weeps over him and his impending ruin. If human freedom is to be respected even by God, sin committed cannot escape punishment.

On the other hand, we are here shown what hinders the soul from seeing and accepting God's plan and dispensation. Any self-seeking and wilful blindness is an impenetrable wall that stands between the soul and God.

Only the poor of heart, the humble and the pure will see God and joyfully enter into His Kingdom. The lovers of this world, the proud, and the hypocrites can see but themselves and work only to establish or strengthen the kingdom of Satan.

3. The Acclamations

"And when He was now coming near the descent of Mount Olivet, the whole multitude of His disciples began with joy to praise God with a loud voice, for all the mighty works they had seen, saying:

"Blessed be the King Who cometh in the name of the Lord, peace in heaven, and glory on high!

"And some of the Pharisees from amongst the multitude said to him: Master, rebuke Thy disciples.

"To whom He said: I say to you, that if these shall hold their peace, the stones will cry out."[1]

It is simple souls and little children that enthusiastically acclaim the Divine King: "and the children crying in the temple, and saying: Hosanna to the Son of David."[2]

1. Luke xix, 37-40. 2. Matt. xxi, 15.

Only to such the vision of the Kingdom is vouchsafed: "I confess to thee, O Father, Lord of Heaven and earth. because Thou hast hid these things from the wise and prudent, and hast revealed them to the little ones."[1]

And even they must guard it most carefully against the false lights that may distort it, or make it appear as a mere illusion of an enthusiastic mind. Alas, how many, who today have cried out: "Hosanna," will, on Good Friday, ask for the Crucifixion of Jesus. And likewise how many who, in their prayer, fall in love with the meek and humble King, deny Him their homage in almost every incident of their life and every aspiration of their hearts.

To end by renewing to our Divine King the oblation of *The Kingdom.*

TOWARDS THE MOUNTAIN CITY

The life of Jesus went as swift and straight as a thunderbolt. It was above all things dramatic; it did above all things consist in doing something that had to be done. It emphatically would not have been done if Jesus had walked about the world for ever doing nothing except tell the truth. And even the external movement of it must not be described as a wandering in the sense of forgetting that it was a journey. This is where it was a fulfilment of the myths rather than of the philosophies; it is a journey with a goal and an object, like Jason going to find the Golden Fleece, or Hercules the golden apples of the Hesperides. The gold that He was seeking was death. The primary thing that He was going to do was to die. He was going to do other things equally definite and objective; we might almost say equally external and material. But from first to last the most definite fact is that He is going to die. No two things could possibly be more different than the death of Socrates and the death of Christ. We are meant to feel that the

1. Matt. xi, 25.

death of Socrates was, from the point of view of his friends at least, a stupid muddle and miscarriage of justice interfering with the flow of a humane and lucid, I had almost said a light philosophy. We are meant to feel that Death was the bride of Christ as Poverty was the bride of St Francis. We are meant to feel that His life was in that sense a sort of love-affair with death, a romance of the pursuit of the ultimate sacrifice. From the moment when the star goes up like a birthday rocket to the moment when the sun is extinguished like a funeral torch, the whole story moves on wings with the speed and direction of a drama, ending in an act beyond words.

Therefore the story of Christ is the story of a journey, almost in the manner of a military march; certainly in the manner of the quest of a hero moving to his achievement or his doom. It is a story that begins in the paradise of Galilee, a pastoral and peaceful land having really some hint of Eden, and gradually climbs the rising country into the mountains that are nearer to the storm-clouds and the stars, as to a Mountain of Purgatory. He may be met as if straying in strange places, or stopped on the way for discussion or dispute; but His face is set towards the mountain city. That is the meaning of that great culmination when He crested the ridge and stood at the turning of the road and suddenly cried aloud, lamenting over Jerusalem.

Chesterton.

The Labours of the Divine King

They say to Him:

"By what authority dost Thou these things? Or who gave Thee this authority to do these things?"

But Jesus said to them:

"I will ask you one question; answer Me, and I will tell you by what authority I do these things."

THE PREACHING IN THE TEMPLE

THE LABOURS OF THE DIVINE KING

The first Prelude is to call to mind how our Lord was teaching daily in the Temple; and the chief priests and the scribes and the rulers of the people sought to destroy Him (Luke xix, 47).

The second Prelude is to see the courts and galleries of the Temple of Jerusalem where Christ gave His last instructions to the people.

The third Prelude is to ask for light to know how the Divine King labours for souls, and grace to do likewise.

* * *

Our Lord, says St Ignatius, sends His servants and friends throughout the whole world to diffuse His sacred doctrines among all states and all conditions of persons. Accordingly, the main duty of those who have answered the special call of the sovereign and true leader, Christ our Lord, is to announce the Gospel. And that is why St Ignatius wants us to consider the example He gives us in this matter, so that, having listened to His Divine Message, and filled our hearts with confidence and courage, we may now clearly see the path along which we have to walk in spite of difficulties, of failures, of discouragement and desolation, always, however, in His company.

1. Our Lord's Preaching

St Ignatius does not invite us to consider the Galilean ministry of our Lord. It had been a glorious one. The Master had been almost constantly surrounded by an enthusiastic crowd, attentive to every word of His, eager to follow Him even in the desert, and ever ready to acclaim in Him the King of Israel. The Saint carries us to Jerusalem, the stronghold of the enemies of Christ and those who only dreamt of a temporal Messiah. He there places, before our eyes, the Saviour announcing to such people, not the gospel which even many of the best amongst them were awaiting—"We hoped that it was He that should have redeemed Israel"[1]—but one which

1. Luke xxiv, 21.

ran counter to all their ideas and which was to shatter the very basis of their material and worldly greatness. While choosing this phase of our Lord's apostolic life, had not St Ignatius in view many missionaries sent to announce the Faith in centres of incredulity and unbelief, to peoples imbued with pride, errors and prejudices, and engrossed in the things of this world, no less than the Jews of our Lord's time? Christ's conduct must be theirs also.

Christ preaches with vigour and zeal, from morning to night, without losing a single moment of the little time that is still at His disposal.

He preaches with fearlessness. He knows that His enemies are plotting His death and trying in all ways to ensnare Him in His speech, and yet He delivers His message in clear and unmistakable terms. He purifies the Temple, casting out them that sold and bought, and overthrowing the tables of the money-changers, and the chairs of those that sold doves. In the parables of the wicked husbandmen, He announces the destruction of Jerusalem and of the Temple itself: "He will come and destroy the husbandmen, and will give the vineyard to others."[1]

He is not put out by the malice and the tricks of His enemies. He continues the work of His Father though all around Him spells complete failure, and His preaching seems but to increase the hatred of His enemies. He perseveres in doing good—"And the blind and the lame came to Him in the temple, and He healed them"[2]—though He knows that in a few days many of them will ask for His death.

2. Men's Neglect

The second of the two points of this contemplation runs as follows: When He had finished preaching, as He had no one to receive Him in Jerusalem, He returned to Bethany. The Evangelist St Mark says: "When now the eventide was come, He went out unto Bethany with the twelve."[3]

It is an important trait in our Lord's life. Not one of His admirers or of those benefited by Him thinks of offering Him food and shelter, or is willing to face the danger that such an act might

1. Mark xii, 9. 2. Matt. xxi, 14. 3. Mark xi, 11.

possibly imply. How sad and heartrending it must have been for the Divine king to look around and see no welcome on any face—sad for Himself, and sadder still for the sake of His dear Apostles!

Such is, sometimes, the fate of many a man of God. After a long day of tireless work there is no one that will meet him with a smiling face, that will say the word that cheers and offers something to soothe the fatigue—none, not even amongst His friends. On these occasions the vision of Jesus going out to Bethany will bring comfort to the sorrowing heart. We may always turn to our dear Friend, in the Blessed Sacrament, and listen again and again to those consoling words: "Come to Me, all you that labour and are burdened and I will refresh you."

To conclude with the Triple Colloquy of the contemplation on *Two Standards.*

ZEAL AND PATIENCE

O Comrade* bold of toil and pain!
Thy trial how severe,
When sever'd first by prisoner's chain
From thy loved labour-sphere!

Say, did impatience first impel
The heaven-sent bond to break?
Or, couldst thou bear its hindrance well,
Loitering for Jesus' sake?

Oh, might we know! for sore we feel
The languor of delay,
When sickness lets our fainter zeal,
Or foes block up our way.

Lord! Who thy thousand years dost wait
To work the thousandth part
Of Thy vast plan, for us create
With zeal a patient heart.

Newman.

* St Paul.

THE PASSION OF OUR LORD

INTRODUCTION

1. The Passion of Our Lord is the Food of the Soul

The Passion of our Lord has always been the main spiritual food of Christian souls a source of strength to them, and an ever flowing fountain of consolation. In the Middle Ages, in particular, those great centuries of Christian Faith, "souls of prayer loved to follow the suffering Lord with tears and " still mourning ' and ' love-longing,' step by step along the Way of Sorrow ; to finger gently each running wound to plunge their whole-hands into His side, and there to ' feel Christ's Heart so hot loving ' them."[1] "For myself, dear brothers," said St Bernard in an address to the monks of Clairvaux, "from the first beginning, of my conversion, seeing myself to be wanting in all virtues, I took to myself this bundle of myrrh made up of all my Saviour's bitter sufferings, of the privations He endured in His infancy, the toils He underwent in His ministry, the weariness He suffered in His journeyings, His watchings in prayer, His fasting and temptation, His tears of compassion, the snares laid to catch Him in His words, His perils among false brethren, the insults, the blows, the mockeries, the nails, in short the sorrows of all kinds which He endured for the salvation of men. I have found wisdom to consist in meditating upon these things, and I have discovered that here alone is the perfection of justice, the fulness of wisdom, the riches of salvation, and the abundance of merit. Here is that which raises me in depression, moderates me in success and makes me walk safely along the royal road between the good and the evil of this life, removing the perils in the way. This is why I have these things always on my lips, as you know, and why I have them always in my heart, as God knows. They are ever on my pen, as all men see, and the most sublime philosophy which I have in this world is to know Jesus and Jesus crucified."

---

1. *A Book of the Love of Jesus*, xxiii.

2. Vide Amorem Dei!

The Passion of our Lord, is a Divine book where we read the infinite love of the Father Who "so loved the world as to give His only begotten Son,"[1] and of the Son Who "delivered Himself up for us, an offering and sacrifice of sweet savour to God."[2] From the Cenacle to Calvary Christ utters a long cry of love, that has pierced the centuries and has reached the uttermost ends of the earth.

3. Vide Severitatem Dei!

In the sufferings of our Lord we see the immeasurable awfulness of sin. The story of our own life is carefully and accurately written all over His Body and in the innermost recesses of His Sacred Heart and Soul. His head is crowned with thorns, His mouth is parched with intolerable thirst, His hands and feet are pierced with nails, His Body is one wound, His Heart and Soul are sunk in an unspeakable agony, because we have sinned with every member of our body and with every faculty of our soul. He is betrayed by one of His Apostles, denied by the chief of them and abandoned by all the others; He is calumniated, insulted and cursed by His own people, because, alas too often, we have betrayed, denied, and rejected God, our Creator and Lord.

4. Vide Bonitatem Dei!

Christ on the Cross opens for us His Heart with all its infinite treasures of mercy and of grace: "Who of God is made unto us wisdom, and justice, and sanctification, and redemption."[3]

"Behold the Lamb of God, behold Him Who taketh away the sin of the world."[4]

Through His Passion, Christ removes the sentence of death that was against us and restores to us the grace of adoption. He pulls down the barrier that stood between Heaven and earth and reunites them in the kiss of peace.

"Moses, therefore, made a brazen serpent, and set it up for a sign: which when they that were bitten looked upon, they were healed."[5]

1. John iii, 16. 2. Eph. v, 2. 3. I Cor. i, 30. 4. John i, 29. 5. Num. xxi, 6.

We are tormented by evil desires, sinful inclinations, and degrading passions. Hellish serpents have stung us and their poison has infected the very springs of our life: our hearts and minds. However, by looking on Christ Crucified we are healed. A Divine influence comes out from Him, that purifies, elevates and transforms even the most sinful hearts.

We are starving beggars. We lack all that is worth having and at the same time, we feel that all we deserve is to be beaten with many stripes. Looking on the suffering Saviour we hope and trust.

5. Vide Viam Dei!

"Christ also suffered for your sake, leaving you an example that ye might follow in his footsteps.... Who, when He was reviled, reviled not again, Who suffered, and threatened not, but committed Himself to Him that judgeth Him justly; Who Himself bore our sins in His Body on the wood, that having died to our sins, we might live unto justness, by whose bruising ye were healed."[1]

Nothing so powerfully removes the mist off the eyes of our soul, and encourages us to the practice of virtue as the sight of what Christ does and suffers for us. *Christus Crucifixus solutio omnium difficultatum.* The Cross is our light "amidst the encircling gloom;" the tree that will turn all bitter things into sweetness;[2] the plank that we must clutch, to weather the storms of life and reach the haven of salvation.

"Let this mind be in you which was also in Christ Jesus!" By devoutly considering the sufferings of our Divine King we are led into the feelings that prompted every movement of His Heart—His love for His Father and for men, His patience, His meekness, and His boundless generosity—and we are helped to make them our own.

6. Christ Crucified before our eyes

We must not, however, think of Christ's Passion as some historical event that occurred far away in the remote past, but rather as something that takes place at the present moment before

1. I Pet. ii, 21-24. 2. Cf. Ex. xv, 25.

our very eyes. It is in this spirit that we must look upon each of the many sufferings of our Lord, listen to every word of His, and enter into His agonizing Heart.

While engaged in the Exercises of the Third Week and during Passiontide the suffering Lord must be constantly before our minds. Our first waking thought must be the mystery we are going to contemplate. We must not lose sight of it altogether in the course of the day, but frequently recall it to mind, lest the feelings and sentiments conceived during meditation should grow cold by mere lapse of time or by the distracting occupations of the day.

7. Compassion, the main fruit

Though we may, according to the needs of our soul, draw various kinds of fruit from the contemplation of the Passion, the feeling of compassion is doubtless one of the most important of all, being the foundation of the rest. Compassion is, for St Ignatius, the peculiar grace which we must insistently ask for, throughout the Third Week of the Spiritual Exercises. In every contemplation, we are told to ask "sorrow with Christ Who is full of sorrow, a broken heart with Christ heart-broken, tears and interior pain for the great pain that Christ has suffered for me." Knowing by experience how cold and insensible our hearts are, St Ignatius would have us, from the moment we are up, make great efforts to shake off our sluggishness and excite ourselves to grief and sorrow on account of the sufferings so willingly borne for our sake by our Saviour. He also recommends to us to undertake some voluntary penance to obtain the precious gift of tears.

And yet, it is not so difficult a thing to shed tears. Which of us has not wept over the imaginary griefs of the imaginary persons we read of in novels? Is it only for Christ, then, that we cannot weep? The human and tender Heart of Jesus must have felt our lack of sympathy very keenly since He broke forth into the following bitter complaint: "O all ye that pass by the way, attend and see, if there be any sorrow like to My sorrow: for He hath made a vintage of Me, as the Lord spoke in the day of His fierce anger."[1] Oh! if we really loved Him, our grief for

1. Lam. i, 12.

His sufferings would be more intense than for the death of a friend, or of a loving parent. Not that we should feel it as tenderly or that it should burst forth as vehemently, but that it should be really present in our hearts and minds and as effectually move us to action. Did not the very people who came together to witness the Crucifixion smite their breasts? And if such were their feelings, what must have been the sentiments of St John, or of Mary Magdalene, or of our Lady? If we desire to be of their company, we must share in their sorrow.

8. How to grieve for Christ and with Christ

But are not all the sufferings of our Lord a thing of the past? Is He not, at present, in the full possession of joy, happiness and glory? How then can we now grieve for Him and with Him? The answer is clear. Suppose a dear friend of mine had suffered and suffered much for my sake, i. e., to free me from punishment richly deserved by me. Suppose he had even died for me to save me from threatened death. Nay, suppose he had died in torments to rescue me from atrocious sufferings. Even if he were now quite beyond their reach, what would, what should, be my feelings towards him? If I had a human heart, if but a spark of love and gratitude still glowed in that heart, would I not think of his love for me, and of the torments willingly borne for me, and of the sacrifice of his life so generously offered for my sake? Should I deem it too much to shed a few tears for one who had shed his life-blood for me? If I refused my friend such a poor return of gratitude, should I not condemn myself as a heartless brute of a man?

There are, however, two points of difference between my human friend and Jesus. My friend may or may not know how much I now sympathize with him and how seriously I try to repay the great debt of gratitude I owe him. This uncertainty has a chilling effect on the warmth of my feelings. Not so with my Divine Friend, Jesus. He knows to a certainty all that His friends did or are doing to assuage His grief and to afford Him some consolation in His sorrow

The second point of difference is of even greater practical importance. When my earthly friend suffered, he certainly did not know, nor could he know, what I would do for him afterwards. But when Jesus underwent His bitter Passion, He knew exactly all that my love for Him would urge me to do, and what penances I should voluntarily undertake for His sake.

"It came about on a horribly dark night on the Mount of Olives some nineteen hundred years ago. There, of His own free Will, our Redeemer, out of love for us, opened all the sluices of time, so that in one single hour all the waves of suffering surged, streamed in, and burst upon His Sacred Heart. God's omniscience and God's eternity unrolled before the most hallowed soul of Christ the whole history of man's salvation, fashioning thereof an actually present picture full of overwhelming tragedy and truth.

"And in this world-tragedy, the rôle of hero was played by Himself, at once innocent Victim and incarnate God. From the first act, the Fall in Paradise, to the last act of the General Judgement, there appeared before Him all mankind in active participation, all poor sinners, with all their sins for which He was to suffer and die, stood out there against Him and bound and mocked Him and scourged Him to blood and crowned Him with a crown of thorns, and nailed Him to the cross; all—even we—were there present with *our* weight of sin! There the Divine Heart of Jesus, amid torture unspeakable, willed to taste from first to last all the ingratitude of the whole sinful race, till that Heart became contracted and convulsed from terror, loathing and sorrow, and till the blood as if in the sweat of death, oozed out from all the pores of the body. That was Christ's agony in the Garden of Gethsemane, for us and through us.

"But then there came the Angel of God, sent by the Father, to minister consolation. And what does he show Him? He pointed out, how, participating in the bloody drama of His bitter Passion, there are not only His tormentors and enemies, but others also, countless others, friends and lovers, and those happily redeemed by Him. There, too, He saw *our* repentance for sin, all *our* love for Him, whereby we manifest our ingratitude for His bitter Passion. There before His very eyes, we were transformed from executioners to compassionate onlookers. And it was this that ministered consolation to the adorable Heart of Jesus on the Mount of Olives. And this consolation we can offer to His Sacred Heart even today. For whatever we are doing and shall do, He then saw actually present, through God's omniscience and eternity, even as it is actually present, to Him today. And thus it depends upon me, whether, by my perfidy, I shall add to my Saviour's agony, or whether by my loyalty, I shall comfort Him in His agony. It depends upon me, even at this very instant . . . . What then, shall I do?"[1]

9. St Francis on Mount Alvernia

We read that St Francis of Assisi retired once to the mountain of Alvernia to meditate day and night on the Passion of our Lord. His constant prayer was that he might feel the love of Christ in his heart and His sufferings in his body. Let this also be our constant prayer. And may God work in us a little of that wonderful transformation which He worked in the Saint of Assisi when He made him a living copy of the Crucified.

"O most beloved and faithful Jesus, pallid and hanging on the Cross, only hope of the desolate soul, grant me worthily to celebrate the memory of Thy Holy Passion, and by loving compassion to pass into Thy open wounds, where forgetful of myself and mindful only of Thy sorrow, I may no longer faint in any tribulation.

"It is profitable and of great help for me to be mindful of Thy Sacred Passion, to look on Thee as if still possible in the flesh, namely taken prisoner and bound, spat upon, struck, whipped with scourges, crowned with thorns, nailed to the cross, given vinegar and gall to drink, pierced with the lance, condemned with robbers, insulted, blasphemed, despised, abandoned, rejected by all, and finally put to death upon the cross and tearfully buried. I must not pass over even a single point.

"Weeping therefore, I'll weep day and night, and my tears shall be on my cheeks for the sorrow and bitter Passion of my Lord.

"Deeply affected by pity, may the hardness of my heart be broken. Let no man speak to me this day, let no one trouble Me with solace. I'll receive no comfort lest I be hindered from mourning the most bitter Passion of my Lord. Weep with me, sun and moon, and lament with me all ye creatures for our Lord is slain today.

"Go forth, go forth, most abundant tears, and gush out even to exhaustion."[2]

1. E. Wasmann, S. J., *Christian Monism.* 2. From Thomas a Kempis.

CANTUS COMPASSIONIS CHRISTI

Unkind man, give heed to Me,
And look what pain I bear for thee!
Sinful man, on thee I cry,
'Tis only for thy love I die.
Behold the blood from Me down runs
Not for My guilt, but for thy sins.
My hands, My feet with nails are fast,
Sinews and veins are wholly burst.
The blood that flows from My heart-root,
Look! it falls down to My foot.
Of all the pain I suffer sore,
Within My Heart there grieves Me more
The unkindness I find in thee,
Who for thy love thus hanged on tree.
Alas! why lovest thou Me not?
And I thy love so dear have bought!
Save thou love Me, thou dost Me wrong,
Since I have lovèd thee so long:
Two and thirty year and more
I was for thee in travail sore,
With hunger, thirst, in heat and cold,
For thy love both bought and sold,
Painêd, nailed and done on tree,
All, man, for the love of thee!
Love thou Me, as well thou may,
And from sin withdraw away.
I give My body with wounds sore;
And thereto I shall give thee more,
Besides all this, also, I wis,
In earth My grace, in Heaven My bliss.

Jesus. Amen.

The King of Love

Jesus knowing that His hour was come, that He should pass out of this world to the Father, having loved His own who were in the world, He loved them unto the end. And when supper was done, (the devil having now put into the heart of Judas Iscariot the son of Simon, to betray Him) knowing that the Father had given Him all things into His hands, and that He came from God, and goeth to God, He riseth from supper, and layeth aside His garments, and having taken a towel, girded Himself. After that, He putteth water into a basin, and began to wash the feet of His disciples, and to wipe them with the towel, wherewith He was girded.

IN THE CENACLE

THE KING OF LOVE

The first Prelude is to call to mind how Christ our Lord sent two of His disciples from Bethany to Jerusalem to prepare the Supper and then Himself went thither with the others; and how, having eaten the Paschal Lamb, He washed the feet of the disciples, gave them His most Holy Body and Precious Blood, and made His farewell discourse to them (Matt. xxvi, 17-29; John xiii-xvii).

The second Prelude is to see the road from Bethany to Jerusalem and likewise the place of the Supper.

The third Prelude is to ask to feel sorrow, affliction, and confusion because for my sins our Lord is going to His Passion.

PART ONE

THE PASCHAL SUPPER

1. The Preparation for the Supper

On the first day of the unleavened bread the Apostles asked our Lord where they had to prepare for Him to eat the Pasch. The Saviour singled out Peter and John for the task, and told them:

" Behold as you go into the city there shall meet you a man carrying a pitcher of water: follow him into the house where he entereth in: and you shall say to the good man of the house: The Master sayeth to thee: where is the guest-chamber where I may eat my Pasch with My disciples? And he will show you a large dining-room furnished and there prepare. And they going found as He said to them and made ready the Pasch."[1]

In the afternoon, having bidden farewell to His friends at Bethany, Jesus, along with the Apostles, directs His steps towards Jerusalem. If, going up to the City, not long ago, the mere thought of His impending Passion was enough to make Him walk ahead of His Apostles, how much more does He hasten now that the longed for moment has arrived. The Apostles are amazed. Their hearts

1. Luke xxii, 10-13.

are filled with dread forebodings, but they dare not question the Master, always calm and sad. Judas alone is all aglow over his recent bargain. He has sold his Lord to the Jews for thirty pieces of silver and is now thinking how best to keep his shameful promise: "I will deliver Him unto you."

2. The Strife among the Apostles

What a wonderful look light up our Lord's face when, on entering the Cenacle, He bursts forth into that cry of passionate love:

"With desire I have desired to eat this Pasch with you before I suffer."[1]

This is His Pasch. Tonight all figures will cease. He will offer to the Father and eat with His own, the true Paschal Lamb which is none other than Himself, and thereby begin the new and eternal Alliance.

"For I say to you that from this time I will not eat it till it be fulfilled in the Kingdom of God."

They are just taking their places around the table when this allusion to the Kingdom reminds the Apostles of the request of James and John to sit the one on Christ's right hand, the other on His left in His Kingdom, and the remembrance arouses in their hearts feelings of jealousy and of ambition. All want the highest seats for themselves. What a sad sight for the Master at this hour of His sublime sacrifice of love and of His deep humiliation!

"And He said to them: The kings of the Gentiles lord it over them; and they that have power over them, are called beneficent. But you not so: but he that is the greater among you, let him become the younger: and he that is the leader, as he that serveth. For which is the greater, he that sitteth at table or he that serveth? Is not he that sitteth at table? But I am in the midst of you as he that serveth.

"And you are they who continued with Me in My temptations. And I dispose to you as My Father hath disposed to Me a Kingdom that you may eat and drink at My table in My Kingdom: and you may sit upon thrones judging the twelve tribes of Israel."[2]

1. Luke xxii, 15. 2. Luke xxii, 25-30.

They will, indeed, reign with Him, but meanwhile they must partake of His sufferings and of His humiliations, and sacrifice themselves unsparingly on behalf of others.

And He proceeds to give them a sublime lesson of humility and charity.

3. The Washing of the Apostles' Feet

Anxious as each one of the Apostles was to take the first seat and too proud to take the servant's place and bathe his comrade's feet, they have all reclined at table unwashed. None has offered himself to wash at least the feet of the Master after His long weary walk in the dust. But He "knowing that the Father had given Him all things unto His hands, and that He came from God, and goeth to God, He riseth from supper, and having taken a towel, girded Himself. After that, He putteth water into a basin, and began to wash the feet of His disciples, and to wipe them with the towel, wherewith He was girded."[1]

It is with a full consciousness of His infinite dignity and power and of the utter worthlessness of the poor Galileans who stand before Him that Christ our Lord, taking off His upper garment, washes their dirty feet—even the feet of the traitor.

Peter is horrified, when he sees the Master at his feet:

"Lord, dost thou wash my feet? Jesus answered, and said to him: What I do, thou knowest not now, but thou shalt know hereafter. Peter saith to him: Thou shalt never wash my feet. Jesus answered him: If I wash thee not, thou shalt have no part with Me. Simon Peter saith to him: Lord not only my feet, but also my hands and my head. Jesus saith to him: He that is washed, needeth not but to wash his feet, but is clean wholly. And you are clean, but not all."[2]

"Lord, dost thou wash my feet?" The Apostle has caught a glimpse of three infinite abysses: the greatness of Christ, his own littleness and misery, and the lowliness of the office which Christ performs.

"Then after He has washed their feet, and taken His garments being set down again, He said to them: Know you what I have done to

1. John xiii, 3-5. 2. John xiii, 6-10.

you? You call Me Master and Lord: and you say well, for so I am. If then I, being your Lord and Master, have washed your feet; you also ought to wash one another's feet. For I have given you an example, that as I have done to you, so you do also."[1]

Before laying down in words the distinctive mark of His disciples, Christ, their Lord and Master, wants to show those marks in Himself. They are humility and love—humble service for the love of Christ and with the vision of Him girded about with a towel and washing the feet of His proud and jealous Apostles.

4. The Traitor

Christ is happy to be in the midst of His own. Outside there blows an infernal hurricane—His enemies are making their last preparations—but here there are men who, in spite of their petty jealousies and quarrels, love Him tenderly. Alas, not all of them: Judas is amongst them. Jesus sees him and His Heart is filled with unspeakable sadness.

"And when they were at table eating Jesus said: Amen I say to you, one of you will betray Me even he that eateth with Me. They began to be sad and to say to Him one by one: Is it I? He said to them: One of the twelve, he that dippeth with Me into the bowl."[2]

To be betrayed into the hands of one's enemies, for a paltry sum of money, by a friend and comrade who has constantly received special marks of love, and who for months has dissimulated his real feelings, and who now even dares to sit down at a banquet of love—what a wound for any man, however hard and unfeeling. But for Christ? . . . . Leonardo da Vinci tried many times to catch a glimpse of that infinite sadness of Christ and fix it on the canvas of his immortal *Last Supper*, but always in vain.

Oh! if we could recall that sad look of the Saviour announcing the betrayal at least when we are in danger of repeating Judas' crime! If only we would remember His patience, His forgiveness and love towards the traitor when we must share a little in the sufferings of His Divine Heart; when we are disowned and betrayed by those on whom we have lavished our love and our favours!

1. John xiii, 12-15. 2. Mark xiv, 18-20.

"*HE LOVED THEM UNTO THE END*"

Me Lord? can'st Thou mispend
One word, misplace one look on me?
Call'st me Thy Love, Thy Friend?
Can this poor soul the object be
Of these love-glances those life-kindling eyes?
What? I the Centre of Thy arms embraces?
Of all Thy labour I the prize?
Love never mocks, Truth never lies.
Oh how I quake; Hope fear, fear hope displaces:
I would, but cannot hope: such wondrous love amazes.

See, I am black as night,
See I am darkness: dark as Hell.
Lord thou more fair than light;
Heav'ns Sun Thy Shadow; can Sunns dwell
With Shades? 'twixt light, and darkness what commerce?
True: thou art darkness, I thy Light: My ray
Thy mists, and hellish foggs shall pierce.
With Me, black soul, with Me converse.
I make the foul *December* flowry *May*,
Turn thou thy night to Me: I'le turn thy night to day.

See Lord, see I am dead:
Tomb'd in my self: my self my grave
A drudge: so born, so bred:
My self even to my self a slave.
Thou Freedome, Life: can Life, and Liberty
Love bondage, death? Thy Freedom I: I tyed
To loose thy bonds: be bound to Me:
My Yoke shall ease, My bonds shall free.
Dead soul, thy Spring of life, My dying side:
There dye with Me to live: to live in thee I dyed.

Phineas Fletcher.

The Victim of the New Alliance

And taking bread, He gave thanks, and brake; and gave to them, saying: This is My Body which is given for you: do this for a commemoration of Me. In like manner the chalice also, after He had supped saying: This is the chalice, the new testament in My Blood, which shall be shed for you.

PART TWO

THE VICTIM OF THE NEW ALLIANCE

1. The Institution of the Blessed Sacrament

"Jesus knowing that His hour was come, that He should pass out of this world to the Father, having loved His own who were in the world, He loved them unto the end."[1]

Christ has just celebrated the old Pasch which the multitude of the children of Israel have so long immolated in memory of their flight from Egypt. But now the old order is over.

He is the true Lamb of God: "Behold the Lamb of God, behold Him Who taketh away the sin of the world."[2] He is about to pass out of this world to the Father, through the pouring out of even the last drop of His sacred Blood on the Altar of the Cross, and by this bloodstained passage to deliver us from the power of darkness and translate us into His Kingdom.

"He was offered because it was His own will."[3] His is a free oblation but, to all appearances, it will not be so. In the Garden of Gethsemane, He Himself will seem to shrink from the Passion. On Calvary, everything will take the appearance of inevitableness. It will seem as if the Father Himself were deaf to the prayers of His Son, and His enemies had the upper hand. They will even challenge Him to come down from the Cross. Accordingly, at this moment, fully aware of the betrayal of Judas and of the plots of His enemies, and with the clear vision of Calvary and its attending horrors, Christ our Lord stands forth as a free Victim destined for the Sacrifice. He makes over to His father His whole Self, His Soul, His Body and His Blood, and generously accepts the death of the Cross with all that it implies.

Looking down through the centuries, He sees that Calvary will grow dimmer and dimmer: too many will soon forget that the Son of God has died for them. He wants, therefore, that the bloody sacrifice which is on the point of being accomplished on the Cross, should be represented, and that its memory should remain to the end of the world.

1. John xiii, 1. 2. John i, 29. 3. Is. liii, 7.

Tomorrow He, the Head of regenerated mankind, will hang on the Cross, as a Victim to the Father, to bring about man's eternal redemption and be the source of grace and the ever-springing fountain of life. He will give back to God all that God lost through man's transgression, and will restore mankind to the Divine friendship. However, the saving power of the Cross must be applied also to the remission of those sins which are committed by us daily and for other necessities of ours.

Accordingly, in memory of His own passage to the Father and to make us partake of its fruits, He institutes the new Pasch, that is, Himself, to be immolated by the Church, under visible signs.

He takes bread with His holy and venerable hands, and with His eyes lifted up towards Heaven, giving thanks to Almighty God, His Father, He blesses it, and breaks it, and gives it to His disciples, saying: Take and eat ye all of this, for this is My Body that is broken for you. Do this for a commemoration of Me. In like manner, after He had supped, taking the Chalice, He gave thanks and gave to them, saying: Take and drink ye all of this, for this is my Blood of the new and eternal testament, which shall be shed for you and for many to the remission of sins. And as often as you do these things, ye shall do in remembrance of Me. For as often as you shall eat this Bread, and drink this Chalice, you shall show the death of the Lord until He come.

He gives to His Apostles and in their name to their successors in the priesthood a precept to offer up in sacrifice His Body and His Blood, i. e., to do just what He has done.

2. The Mass and Calvary

The Sacrifice of the Mass, which is offered daily in the Church, is not something different from the Sacrifice which Christ Himself offered on Calvary. The Body which is offered up, is one and the same, whether on the Cross or on the Altar, the difference being that while on the Cross it was offered in its natural condition, on the Altar it is offered sacramentally. Ths Priest is one and the same—Christ our Lord, offering the Sacrifice, on the Cross in His own person, and on the Altar, through his representatives. As the

Church says in one of her prayers, the Mass makes us partake of the fruits of Calvary: "As often as the commemoration of this Victim is celebrated, the work of our Redemption is accomplished." It keeps the Sacrifice of Calvary constantly before our eyes. The double consecration of the bread into the Body of Christ, and of the wine into His Blood is a perfect image of Christ's Death and of the real separation that took place between His Body and His Blood.

Christ our Lord did not want that His Priesthood should come to an end through His Death, but gave to His Beloved Bride, the Church, a visible Sacrifice in keeping with the exigencies of the nature of men.

Truly "having loved His own who were in the world, He loved them to the end."

"IT IS THE LORD"

Speak low, kneel softly, for lo! . . . He is here,
Close in a sweet and a mystical guise,
Visible only to innocent eyes,
A love without speech, and a power without fear.

Far over the sunlit peaks and the hills
Of Heaven He speeds. . . . through the arch of the sky,
Yet Love, ere a heart-beat has fluttered, is nigh,
And Love, like a harp, all Infinitely fills.

O, blessed is He who cometh unshod
From Infinity's gates, from a city of light,
To the hearts of His loved ones, a sanctuary white,
To a Chalice made rose with the Blood of a God.

The Revelation of the Sacred Heart

And lifting up His eyes to Heaven, He said:

"Father, the hour is come, glorify Thy Son, that Thy Son may glorify Thee. As thou hast given Him power over all flesh, that He may give eternal life to all Whom Thou hast given Him. Now this is eternal life, that they may know Thee, the only true God, and Jesus Christ, Whom Thou hast sent."

PART THREE

THE REVELATION OF THE SACRED HEART

1. UNION WITH CHRIST

The one great desire of Christ and the object for which He became man is to give us "power to be made the sons of God." Union with Him effects this wonderful transformation.

"Abide in Me, and I in you. As the branch cannot bear fruit of itself, unless it abide in the vine, so neither can you, unless you abide in Me. I am the vine; you the branches: he that abideth in Me, and I in him, the same beareth fruit: for without Me you can do nothing."[1]

(i) BASED ON FAITH

Such union must have as its basis a strong Faith, full of confidence and trust in Christ, true God, consubstantial with the Father and, at the same time, our Eldest Brother:

"He that seeth Me, seeth the Father also....[2] Do you not believe that I am in the Father, and the Father in me?"[3]

"I am the Way, and the Truth, and the Life. No man cometh to the Father but by Me."[4]

"Amen, amen, I say to you, he that believeth in Me, the works I do, he also shall do, and greater than these shall he do."[5]

(ii) SUPPORTED BY PRAYER

It must be supported and strengthened by prayer.

"Whatsoever you shall ask the Father in My name, that will I do: that the Father may be glorified in the Son."[6]

"If you ask the Father anything in My name, He will give you."[7]

"Hitherto you have not asked anything in My name. Ask, and you shall receive: that your joy may be full."[8]

1. John xv, 4-5. 2. John xiv, 9. 3. John xiv, 9-10. 4. John xiv, 6.
5. John xiv, 12. 6. John xiv, 13. 7. John xvi, 23. 8. John xvi, 23-24.

(iii) PERFECTED BY THE HOLY SPIRIT

It will be perfected by the Holy Ghost Who will come to replace Christ.

"And I will ask the Father, and He shall give you another Paraclete, that He may abide with you for ever."[1]

The Holy Ghost will perfect our knowledge of Christ. He will strengthen our hope in Him and our union with Him.

"But the Paraclete, the Holy Ghost, Whom the Father will send in My name, He will teach you all things, and bring all things to your mind, whatsoever I shall have said to you."[2]

"He shall glorify Me, because He shall receive of Mine, and shall show it to you."[3]

"And when He is come, He will convince the world of sin, and of justice, and of judgement."[4]

(iv) CONSISTING IN KEEPING CHRIST'S COMMANDMENTS

Our union with Christ must consist in lovingly doing His Will

"If you love Me, keep My commandments."[5]

"He that hath My commandments and keepeth them, he it is that loveth Me."[6]

"If any one love Me, he will keep My word, and My Father will love him, and We will come to him, and We will make Our abode with him."[7]

"If you keep My commandments, you shall abide in My love: as I also have kept My Father's commandments, and do abide in His love."[8]

"You are My friends, if you do the things that I command you."[9]

2. LOVE OF OUR BROTHERS

After giving the sublimest example of charity by washing the feet of His Apostles, Christ lays down the great law of His Kingdom and the distinctive note of His soldiers.

1. John xiv, 16. 2. John xiv, 26. 3. John xvi, 14. 4 John xvi, 8.
5. John xiv, 15. 6. John xiv, 21. 7. John xiv, 23. 8. John xv, 10.
9. John xv, 14.

He has loved us without any merit of our own. He has sought only our own good, and for our love He has hesitated at no sacrifice, however hard and lowly. We must do likewise to the least of our brethren.

"A new commandment I give unto you: that you love one another, as I have loved you, that you also love one another. By this shall all men know that you are My disciples, if you have love one for another."[1]

"This is my commandment that you love one another, as I have loved you."[2]

"These things I command you, that you love one another."[3]

3. Suffering and Persecution

The disciples must suffer like their Master.

"In the world you shall have distress."[4]

"Amen, amen, I say to you, that you shall lament and weep, but the world shall rejoice."[5]

"They will put you out of the synagogues: yea, the hour cometh, that whosoever killeth you, will think that he doth a service to God."[6]

"Remember the word that I said to you: The servant is not greater than his master. If they have persecuted Me, they will also persecute you."[7]

Suffering then and persecution must be our lot, if we are Christ's. However, in the midst of them our confidence in Him must be unshakable, and our heart must peacefully rest in His.

"Have confidence, I have overcome the world."[8]

"Let not your heart be troubled."[9]

"These things I have spoken to you, that in Me you may have peace."[10]

4. The Prayer of our High Priest

(i) For Himself

This prayer more than anything else, lays open the infinite treasures of love contained in the Heart of Jesus.

1. John xiii, 34-35. 2. John xv, 12. 3. John xv, 17. 4. John xvi, 33. 5. John xvi, 20. 6. John xvi, 2. 7. John xv, 20. 8. John xvi, 33. 9. John xiv, 1. 10. John xvi, 33.

First, Christ prays for Himself or better for His Sacred Humanity, and asks the reward that is due to it.

"Father, the hour is come, glorify Thy Son, that Thy Son may glorify Thee. As Thou hast given Him power over all flesh, that He may give eternal life to all whom Thou hast given Him. Now this is eternal life, that they may know Thee, the only true God, and Jesus Christ, Whom Thou hast sent. I have glorified Thee on the earth: I have finished the work which Thou gavest Me to do: and now glorify Thou Me, O Father, with Thyself, with the glory which I had, before the world was, with Thee."[1]

(ii) FOR HIS APOSTLES

Secondly, He prays for His Apostles.

He asks the Father to keep them under His protection.

"Holy Father keep them in Thy name, whom Thou hast given Me."[2]

He asks Him to shield them against the attacks and frauds of the Evil One.

"I pray not that Thou should take them out of this world, but that Thou shouldst keep them from evil."[3]

He asks Him to set them apart, and consecrate them to announce the world of Truth.

"Sanctify them in truth: Thy word is truth. As Thou hast sent Me unto the world, I also have sent them into the world."[4]

He asks Him to grant that they may be one in love and in faith.

"That they may be one as We also are."[5]

(iii) FOR HIS DISCIPLES

Thirdly, Christ prays for all those that would believe in Him, i. e., for all His disciples till the end of time. He asks for them the most perfect union of mind and heart.

"That they all may be one as Thou Father in Me and I in Thee: that they also may be one in Us: that the world may believe that Thou hast sent Me."[6]

1. John xvii, 1-5.
2. John xvii, 11.
3. John xvi, 15.
4. John xvii, 17-18.
5. John xvii, 11.
6. John xvii, 21.

Christ Himself is to be the bond of union of the disciples with one another and of all of them with God.

"I in them, and Thou in Me: that they may be made perfect in one; and the world may know that Thou hast sent Me, and hast loved them, as Thou hast loved Me."[1]

(iv) FOR HIS APOSTLES AND DISCIPLES

Lastly, our Lord emphatically demands that His Apostles and all His disciples may share His glory.

"Father, I will that where I am, they also whom Thou hast given Me may be with Me: that they may see My glory which Thou hast given Me."[2]

To conclude with a fervent Colloquy to our Lord asking Him to fill my heart with the feelings of humility, love, confidence, and absolute self-surrender with which His Heart overflows; and to be allowed humbly to join Him in His Prayer to the Father.

THE LAMB OF GOD

When Thee (O holy sacrificed Lambe)
In severed sygnes I whyte and liquide see,
As on Thy body slayne I thynke on Thee,
Which pale by sheddyng of Thy bloode became.

And when agayne I doe behold the same
Vayled in whyte to be receav'd of mee,
Thou seemest in Thy syndon wrapt to bee
Lyke to a corse, whose monument I am.

1. John xvii, 23. 2. John xvii, 24.

The lonely Struggle of the King

And kneeling down He prayed, saying:

"Father, if Thou wilt, remove this chalice from Me: But yet not My Will, but Thine be done."

And there appeared to Him an Angel from Heaven, strengthening Him. And being in an agony, He prayed the longer: and His sweat became as drops of blood trickling down upon the ground.

IN THE GARDEN OF GETHSEMANE

THE LONELY STRUGGLE OF THE KING

The first Prelude is to call to mind how Christ our Lord, having manifested to Peter and the two sons of Zebedee the immense sadness of His soul, prayed to the Father that, if possible, the chalice might pass from Him: and how there appeared to Him an Angel from Heaven strengthening Him, and, an agony of distress having come upon Him, He prayed the longer, and His sweat became as drops of blood trickling down upon the ground (Matt. xxvi, 36-39; Mark xiv, 2-36; Luke xxii, 39-44).

The second Prelude is to see the road from the Supper Room to the Garden of Gethsemane, and likewise the Garden and, particularly, the place of the Agony.

The third Prelude is to ask sorrow with Christ in His sorrow, a broken heart with Christ heart-broken, tears and interior pain for the great pain which Christ has suffered for me.

* * *

Christ has come to undo Adam's work, to destroy sin and death and restore us to the dignity of children of God. Adam, yielding to pride and pleasure, had sinned in a garden of delight: the Son of God begins His work of Reparation and of Restoration in a garden of suffering.

He is our Head and our Heart. In Him there is summed up the whole of regenerated mankind. He is, then, the Universal Victim and the Model of us all—not only the King that goes before us and shows us the way, but also the Saviour Who gains for us the grace we need to follow in His footsteps.

It is only by grasping such truths that we gain a glimpse of what Christ suffers in the Garden of Gethsemane.

1. The First Painful Vision of Christ

HIS SUFFERINGS

Christ was to redeem mankind through suffering and shame, through the Cross.

The first man rebelled against the Law of God through the love of pleasure and through pride: "You shall be as gods."[1] It is the love of pleasure, riches and honour that keeps so many of us in the bondage of Satan. And that is why Christ, Who came to teach us the true way of salvation, from the first moment of His Incarnation, planted the Cross in His Heart and chose as His constant companions Poverty, Sufferings and Humiliations. They stood by His cradle; they followed Him all through His life; they were present on Calvary to receive His last sigh as He expired on the Cross. But as we might have thought that, perchance, pleasures and sufferings, glory and shame were but one and the same thing for Him—that, most unlike ourselves, He neither feared sufferings, nor was drawn to pleasures, He allows three of His Apostles, the very three who have already seen His glory, to witness the Agony that begins His sorrowful Passion.

So far the day of His Passion has appeared to Him as the day of His Espousals. He has seen only the speedy end and the glory that would follow, the joy and the fruits thereof. So far He has controlled His imagination. He has allowed His Divinity to exert its influence. He has had Mary as His companion and confidante.

But now it is so no longer. He wants to suffer all that He can. He uses His Omnipotence to increase, not to alleviate, His sufferings. He shuts off from Himself any vision of glory and gives instead free play to His imagination, so that it portrays the minutest details of His Passion in all their naked horror. He suffers in His Heart cumulatively what He will afterwards suffer successively and in detail. He sees Himself betrayed, bound, dragged along, led from tribunal to tribunal, calumniated, denied, spat upon, cried down as a malefactor, as a fool, as worse than the worst of men, scourged, crowned with thorns, nailed to the Cross, and finally dying in an agony of torment.

Moreover, He suffers now whatever each member of His mystical body will suffer down the centuries, even to the end of the world. "Saul, Saul, why persecutest thou Me?" He is put to death with His martyrs, persecuted with His disciples, reviled with His ministers.

1. Gen. iii, 5.

We know how terrible is the apprehension of a future calamity and still more of a certain calamity—how it oppresses and weighs one down. The Heart of Jesus was infinitely more sensitive than ours, His knowledge was more penetrating, and His sufferings were consequently more acute. What wonder if He begins to be sorrowful, and very heavy, and full of terror.

How cruel and humiliating is the feeling of fear! It is the thing great men dread most, yet it is just what Christ deliberately chose to suffer in order to win for us courage to vanquish our fear. We should not think that the Saints were clods of earth. They also shrank from suffering and shame. But it was the fear that Christ underwent, which strengthened them to conquer their natural repugnance.

2. The Second Painful Vision of Christ

THE SINS OF MEN

But it is not only the sight of His Passion and of the sufferings of His future followers that weighs down the Heart of Jesus and makes Him cry: "My soul is sorrowful even unto death." Far more than that it is the weight of sin.

He has come to atone for sin and to destroy its empire: "He shall save His people from their sins."[1] He is "to give His life a redemption for many."[2] "Behold the Lamb of God, behold Him Who taketh away the sin of the world."[3] "This is My Blood of the New Testament, which shall be shed for many unto the remission of sins."[4]

From the first moment of His Incarnation He felt Himself loaded with the sins of all mankind. He knew, all along, that He must fully satisfy for each and every one of them: "All we like sheep have gone astray, everyone hath turned aside into his own way: and the Lord hath laid on Him the iniquity of us all."[5]

However, so far He was supported by the sense of His inward sanctity and sinlessness, and by the thought of His final triumph. Now He is brought face to face with God's inexorable Justice and

1. Matt. i, 21. 2. Matt. xx, 28. 3. John i, 29. 4. Matt. xxvi, 28.
5. Is. liii, 6.

unapproachable Sanctity. His face is crushed to the ground beneath the awful weight of the almost infinite number of the sins of men.

We make light of sin. We do not understand how the Creator can make so much of it.

But consider what sin is in itself—the mortal enemy of the All-Holy. Saints were, sometimes, allowed only a passing glimpse of the ugliness of a single venial sin as it is before God, and they have left it on record that the sight of it would have killed them, had not the vision been instantly withdrawn.

Who can imagine, then, the extreme disgust of Christ when He sees Himself covered all over with the hideous leprosy of sin? Who can imagine His horror when He finds His eyes and hands and feet, His Heart and soul, as if they were the eyes, hands, feet, heart and soul not of God, but of the Evil One.[1]

All the sins of the living and of the dead, of the lost and of the saved, and of the yet unborn gather round the Lord, in troops more numerous than the locusts or the plagues of hail and flies and frogs sent against Pharao, and they all shout out: "We are thine; we are the work of Thy hands!"

They are all before Him now. They are all upon Him and in Him. They are all let loose to wreak their vengeance and fury on the Son of God. And we too were present to Him there. We were there, with every sin committed, as if it were a stone in our uplifted hand to fling at the defenceless head of our Saviour. No wonder He moans: "My soul is sorrowful even unto death!"

3. The third Painful Vision of Christ

THE INGRATITUDE OF MEN

And yet He would willingly have endured even more than the inexorable Justice of the Father demanded, if only He knew that there would be some poor return of love and gratitude from those for whose sake He was suffering, and was to suffer so very much. But alas! He looks round: the eight Apostles, left at the entrance of the Garden, have forgotten Him; His three special friends, to whom He

1. Cf. Newman, *The Interior Sufferings of Christ.*

appealed for support, are asleep; one and all will soon abandon Him and take to flight. Judas is plotting against Him. His own people are preparing to crucify Him.

He looks down the ages, and He sees nothing but ingratitude and indifference from an overwhelming majority of mankind. Millions will not even know Him; others will reject Him; many, even among His friends, will prove ungrateful.

He sees each one of us—our sins, our infidelities, our ingratitude. But ingratitude, alas! is sharper than the serpent's tooth. Hence the touching complaint of Jesus: "I looked about, and there was no one to help. I sought, and there was none to give aid."[1] "What profit is there in My blood?"[2]

Three years ago, Satan had appeared to Him in the Desert and had tempted Him with the allurement of honour and power. Now he comes to tempt Him with feelings of despair and despondency. There he had tried to induce Him to choose other ways to save mankind. Here he works to make Him shrink from the Cross.

4. The Agony

These are three visions that oppress the Saviour to death.

Look at Him prostrate on His face. He has longed for this hour. He has called it the Baptism with which He has to be baptized. He said that He was terribly straitened till it was accomplished. And now He prays to His Father that the chalice of suffering may pass from Him: "Abba! My Father! All things are possible for Thee: if it be Thy Will, take this cup away from Me."

An Angel descends from Heaven to strengthen Him, and indicates to Him once more the Will of His Father. He is to die; He must atone for sin, yea, and that in spite of men's ingratitude.

Our Lord repeats the oblation which He made of Himself in the Supper Room: "Not what I will, but what Thou willest."

A fierce encounter of wills now ensues, i. e., between the superior will of our Lord, determined to suffer and die in obedience to His Father, and His inferior will, seeking to flee from what is so repugnant to nature. In the midst of this conflict, the tormented

1. Is. lxiii, 5. 2. Ps. xxix, 10.

Heart of Christ, the seat of tenderness and love, begins to labour and to beat with unwonted vehemence. "The foundations of the great deep are broken up:" the red streams rush forth, and bursting through the pores, they stand in a thick dew all over his body. Then forming into drops, they roll down, full and heavy, and drench the ground. If that Heart does not break, it is because of the omnipotent Will of Christ to drink the chalice to the dregs.

He has begun to shed His Blood. No soldier's scourge has yet touched His shoulders, nor have the hangman's nails marked His hands and feet. It is His agonizing Heart and Soul which have broken up His framework of flesh and poured it forth. "Behold that Heart!" It is the Passion of the Divine Heart to which we must specially direct our attention in our contemplation of the Agony in the Garden. *Vide amorem: vide dolorem!* Behold the height of love: contemplate the depth of sorrow: "O all ye that pass by the way, attend and see if there be any sorrow like to my sorrow: for he hath made a vintage of Me as the Lord spoke in the day of His fierce anger."[1]

Let me conclude the contemplation by praying, prostrate by the side of my agonizing King, that a drop of His Sacred Blood may reach my sinful and cold heart, purify, and inflame it; and by resolving to come often to this most hallowed place that I may learn from the Sacred Heart how to conquer my fears, how to feel true shame and contrition for my sins and the sins of others, and how to work and suffer in spite of men's ingratitude.

THE ONE VICTIM

There, then, in that most awful hour, knelt the Saviour of the world, putting off the defences of His divinity, dismissing His reluctant Angels, who in myriads were ready at His call, and opening His arms, baring His breast, sinless as He was, to the assault of His foe,—of a foe whose breath was a pestilence, and whose embrace was an agony. There he knelt, motionless and still, while the vile and horrible fiend clad His spirit in a robe steeped

1. Lam. i, 12.

in all that is hateful and heinous in human crime, which clung close round His Heart, and filled His conscience, and found its way into every sense and pore of His mind, and spread over Him a moral leprosy, till He almost felt himself to be that which He never could be, and which His foe would fain have made Him. Oh, the horror, when He looked, and did not know Himself, and felt as a foul and loathsome sinner, from His vivid perception of that mass of corruption which poured over His head and ran down even to the skirts of His garments! Oh, the distraction, when He found His eyes, and hands, and feet, and lips, and heart, as if the members of the Evil One, and not of God! Are these the hands of the Immaculate Lamb of God, once innocent, but now red with ten thousand barbarous deeds of blood? are these His lips, not uttering prayer, and praise, and holy blessings, but as if defiled with oaths, and blasphemies, and doctrines of devils? or His eyes, profaned as they are by all the evil visions and idolatrous fascinations for which men have abandoned their adorable Creator? And His ears, they ring with sounds of revelry and of strife; and His heart is frozen with avarice, and cruelty, and unbelief; and His very memory is laden with every sin which has been committed since the fall, in all regions of the earth, with the pride of the old giants, and the lusts of the five cities, and the obduracy of Egypt, and the ambition of Babel, and the unthankfulness and scorn of Israel . . . . Of the living and of the dead and of the as yet unborn, of the lost and of the saved, of Thy people and of strangers, of sinners and of saints, all sins are there. Thy dearest are there; Thy saints and Thy chosen are upon Thee; Thy three Apostles, Peter, James and John; but not as comforters, but as accusers, like the friends of Job, "sprinkling dust towards heaven," and heaping curses on Thy head. All are there but one; one only is not there, one only; for she who had no part in sin, she only could console Thee, and therefore she is not nigh. She will be near Thee on the Cross, she is separated from Thee in the garden. She has been Thy companion and Thy confidant through Thy life, she interchanged with Thee the pure thoughts and holy meditations of thirty years; but her virgin ear may not take in, nor may her Immaculate heart conceive, what now is in vision before Thee. None was equal to the weight but God.

Newman.

The King betrayed and deserted

As He was yet speaking, behold a multitude: and he that was called Judas, one of the Twelve, went before them and drew near to Jesus for to kiss Him.

And Jesus said to him :

"Judas, dost thou betray the Son of man with a kiss?"

IN THE GARDEN AND BEFORE ANNAS

THE KING BETRAYED AND DESERTED

The first Prelude is to call to mind how our Lord on coming three times to Peter, James and John, for some comfort in His desolation, found them always asleep; how He was betrayed by Judas in the hands of His enemies and abandoned by the other Apostles; and how He was dragged before Annas, insulted and tormented during the whole night, and thrice denied by Peter.

The second Prelude is to see the Garden of Gethsemane, the way leading to the palace of the high priest, and in the palace the judgement-hall, the atrium, and the room where our Lord is mocked and maltreated.

The third Prelude is to ask sorrow with Christ in His sorrow, a broken heart with Christ heart-broken, tears, confusion and pain for the great sufferings which Christ endures for me.

* * *

The death of Christ and that of Socrates have been often compared. The great philosopher also suffered at the hands of his countrymen for justice' sake. But he died surrounded by friends who vied with one another in paying him all the attentions they could, while he leisurely discussed with them the chances which the soul has of living for ever. The Son of God is, from the first moment of His Passion, immersed in a sea of sadness. He begins it with an awful agony of blood. He is left helpless and without any comfort. He is abandoned by all His dearest friends in His hour of need; He is betrayed by one of them, and denied by another.

1. The Loneliness

Judge from His own words how much He feels His loneliness. He has asked His three beloved Apostles to watch with Him; and when, after His terrible agony, He goes to them for some comfort, He finds them asleep. He knew it would be so, but when He is actually confronted with the reality how much more vividly His loneliness comes home to Him! How much more bitter is the chalice which He has to drink alone: "What? Could you not watch one hour with Me?"

It is decreed in Heaven that the Lamb of God shall drink the chalice without a single drop of human consolation to sweeten its bitterness. And the Apostles continue to sleep, notwithstanding the Master's repeated entreaties: "for their eyes were heavy."

It is now as of old. Through His devoted servant, St Margaret Mary, our Lord has repeated the request made to the three Apostles. He has asked His faithful friends to watch with Him, in the silence of His churches, in memory of what passed on that terrible night. How many have answered the invitation? Only a few; and it is just those few souls who keep watching with Jesus that encourage Him to remain with us, till the last of the Elect has entered into eternal glory.

2. THE BETRAYAL

Not only is He left alone by His friends, but one of them is, at this very moment, plotting His death.

The silence of the night is broken by the tramp of hurrying feet. One outstrips the rest. There is a smile on his lips. Surely he is a friend. A friend? Just two days ago, he went to the high priests and asked them: "What will ye give me?" He put no price upon Christ; he was ready to accept anything. And when they offered him thirty pieces of silver, he thought it was a great deal; far more than Jesus was worth. And now he has come to fulfil his part of the contract. He advances, and salutes Him with the words, "Hail, Rabbi," and he kisses Him.

Christ does not shrink from the embrace. He looks upon the traitor with eyes of mercy, and the words that cross His lips are words of love: "Friend, whereunto art thou come?" And then, to show the enormity of the crime, He says: "Judas, dost thou betray the Son of Man with a kiss?"[1] But nothing can melt that obdurate soul. The crime is consummated. One sin more—an act of despair—and Judas will plunge into the eternal darkness of Hell.

Alas, how many have followed in his footsteps! How many have reclined at the Holy Table with sin in their hearts, and after receiving the Mystery of Faith and Love, have gone to sell their God

1. Luke xxii, 48.

for less than thirty pieces of silver! How many, beginning with little sins, have gradually hardened their hearts to the committing of the deadliest of crimes!

And yet the loving embrace which Jesus gives to His traitor is the surest proof that there is hope for all. It gives us the assurance that while there is life there is no hour in which Jesus is not ready to welcome the sinner to His Heart.

3. The Abandonment

If only it had been possible for our Lord to turn to the other Apostles for comfort. Alas! "All leaving Him, they fled."

He knew that it would happen. He Himself had warned them against it, just a few hours before. But when it did come, the wound that it inflicted on the Heart of Jesus was by no means less cruel.

They had seen his miracles. They had confessed His Divinity. They had eaten His Body and drunk His Blood, and yet what cowards! At the very sight of danger, leaving Him, they all ran away. They had promised, and even repeatedly sworn, to be faithful to Him unto death. They heard His voice ordering His enemies not to touch anyone of them. In spite of it, fear overcame them and everything else was forgotten under the impression that self was in danger and must be saved.

And cowards we too are—each one of us. We make no effort to watch with Christ. We do not pray for strength, and temptation overcomes us. The fear—often an imaginary one—of losing honour, the approval of men, or the things of this world, overpowers us. And we give way and run—we do not even know where.

Let us be soldiers with Christ and for Christ: courage counts as two-thirds, at least, of the necessary outfit for any undertaking, supernatural or natural. Let us fight against fear and its shadowy army—against the terrors of the imagination and the greater terrors of reality. We shall do so if we pray unceasingly, even though our soul be in an agony. It is thus that true heroes are tested.

4. The Shame

After the abandonment follows the shame.

To appear in public and to be treated like a criminal is something from which our whole being instinctively shrinks. To be dealt with as one of the worst robbers—to be imprisoned and subjected to the cruellest injuries and torments, and just then to be publicly dishonoured by our dearest friends, is the height of suffering.

Oscar Wilde, in his *De Profundis,* says that the greatest torment in his whole life was to remain for two hours, handcuffed, at Clapham Junction, waiting for the train. What must have been the feelings of our Lord when He saw Himself confronted by the infuriated crowd of the Jews?

"Are ye come out, as against a robber, with swords and clubs to arrest Me? Day after day I was with you in the Temple teaching, and ye seized Me not."[1]

Have you ever seen the wild excitement of villagers on finally catching a man-eater that has worked havoc and ruin? How they all shout for joy! How everyone is eager to give vent to his anger and inflict an additional wound on the already mangled body of the animal! How they congratulate one another!

A far more terrible scene takes place at this moment when the Omnipotence of the Son of God, conceals Itself, so to speak, leaving the human Nature a defenceless and yet a voluntary Victim in the hands of His enemies, who like as many monsters of Hell, instantly rush upon Him.

For nearly three years they have been waiting for this moment. How often they were forced to dissimulate their deep hatred for fear of the people. They stooped so low as to plot with the Herodians. They sent guards to capture Christ. But in vain: His hour had not yet come. Now, at last, He is in their hands. They bind Him fast, that He may not escape as He did in Nazareth. They beat Him. They drag Him to Jerusalem, all the way heaping insults of every kind on Him.

And they bring Him before Annas for the preliminary trial.

What a confusion for the Divine Saviour and Judge of the living

1. Mark xiv, 48, 49.

and of the dead, to appear alone, bound hand and foot, before this contemptible old priest, and to be questioned about His disciples and His doctrine as if He were a visionary, or still worse, a revolutionary tending to upset the security of the State. And because He meets the charge with a calm that disconcerts His judge, He is insulted in a way that would not be tolerated with the vilest of criminals, in the court of even the most uncivilized country of the world.

"One of the servants standing gave Jesus a blow, saying, Answerest Thou the high priest thus?"[1]

There is none to raise his voice on behalf of Christ; and for once Christ Himself expresses a solemn protest against the injustice of the procedure to remind us that, if, later on, no word of complaint crosses His lips, it will not be for lack of sensibility.

"If I have spoken evil, give testimony of the evil: but if well, why strikest thou Me?"[2]

Before such greatness and such majestic calm, Annas has only one course open: to hand Him over to the guards, while waiting for the gathering of the Sanhedrim.

5. The Cruelty

"And the men that held Him, mocked Him, and struck Him. And they blindfolded Him, and smote His face. And they asked Him, saying: Prophesy, who is it that struck Thee? And blaspheming, many other things they said against Him."[3]

Look at the way the Divine Prisoner is treated.

The ruffians spit upon Him, make fun of Him and give Him blows. And as Jesus looks on them with tenderness and love, they cover His Divine face so as to torment Him without any restraint.

We cannot stand the sight of a beast thus treated, and yet we read and even meditate on the account of such horrible sufferings endured by the Divine Saviour without being touched. We firmly believe that He suffered them out of love for us, and yet we do not shed a tear of compassion. We easily weep over our own little sufferings, but the Passion of our Lord makes no impression on us. And yet each one of us was there to insult Christ on that terrible night

1. John xviii, 22. 2. John xviii, 23. 3. Luke xxiii, 63-65.

to spit on Him, to strike Him on the face! It was on each one of us that Christ looked with eyes of infinite love and mercy—just as He looked on His unfaithful Apostle Peter.

"On that face," says St John Chrysostom, "which the sea saw and reverenced, which on the Cross the sun beheld and withheld its rays, they spat and dealt blows.... These are the solemn and august memories of our Religion. On these I pride myself, not merely on the countless dead whom He raised to life, but on the sufferings of His Passion."

6. The Denial

The Apostles have abandoned their Master in the hour of trial. But a greater suffering is in store for the Heart of Jesus. At the voice of a handmaid and of a few guards Peter denies Him. What a wound for our Lord when, from the place of His torments. He hears the Apostle shouting that he does not know Him, that He does not know *this man.* Why, the Apostle whom Jesus has loved so much, and by whom only a few months before He was proclaimed the Christ, the Son of God—the very Apostle on whom He has promised to build His Church, now protests that he has never known Him. And he does it not once or twice, but three times; not in a passing way, but in a stream of curses and of oaths.

Forgetting all His sufferings the merciful Lord turns and looks upon Peter. It is a look full of infinite love and compassion—a look that in a moment reveals the Heart of Jesus to the erring Apostle. Peter sees it—and it truly seems to him that he has not known Christ till now—that he has known Him only in that glance.

"And Peter went out and began to cry." Henceforth his life will be an uninterrupted act of sorrowing love.

To conclude the contemplation by throwing myself at the feet of my suffering Saviour begging with the Apostle Peter, forgiveness for my coldness, my cowardice—perhaps, my repeated denials and betrayals.

THE DIVINE SIMPLICITY OF THE GOSPELS

Every attempt to amplify that story has diminished it. The task has been attempted by many men of real genius and eloquence as well as by only too many vulgar sentimentalists and self-conscious rhetoricians. The tale has been retold with patronizing pathos by elegant sceptics and with fluent enthusiasm by boisterous best-sellers.... The grinding power of the plain words of the Gospel story is like the power of mill-stones; and those who can read them simply enough will feel as if rocks had been rolled upon them. Criticism is only words about words; and of what use are words about such words as these? What is the use of word-painting about the dark garden filled suddenly with torchlight and furious faces? "Are you come out with swords and staves as against a robber? All day I sat in your temple teaching, and you took me not." Can anything be added to the massive and gathered restraint of that irony; like a great wave lifted to the sky and refusing to fall? "Daughters of Jerusalem, weep not for Me, but weep for yourselves and for your children." As the High Priest asked what further need he had of witnesses, we might well ask what further need we have of words. Peter in a panic repudiated Him: "and immediately the cock crew; and Jesus looked upon Peter, and Peter went out and wept bitterly." Has any one any further remark to offer? Just before the murder He prayed for all the murderous race of men, saying, "They know not, what they do"; is there anything to say to that, except that we know as little what we say? Is there any need to repeat and spin out the story of how the tragedy trailed up the Via Dolorosa and how they threw Him in haphazard with two thieves in one of the ordinary batches of execution; and how in all that horror and howling wilderness of desertion one voice spoke in homage, a startling voice from the very last place where it was looked for, the gibbet of the criminal; and He said to that nameless ruffian, "This night shalt thou be with Me in Paradise"? Is there anything to put after that but a full-stop? Or is any one prepared to answer adequately that farewell gesture to all flesh which created for His Mother a new Son?

Chesterton.

The True and Eternal Judge

And the high priest rising up, said to Him: "Answerest Thou nothing to the things which these witness against Thee?" But Jesus held His peace.

And the high priest said to Him: "I adjure Thee by the living God, that Thou tell us if Thou be the Christ the Son of God."

Jesus saith to him: "Thou hast said it."

BEFORE CAIPHAS, HEROD AND PILATE

THE TRUE AND ETERNAL JUDGE

The first Prelude is to call to mind how our Lord was dragged before the tribunal of Caiphas where he was condemned as guilty of death, before the tribunal of Herod where He was set at nought and mocked, and before the tribunal of Pilate by whom He was delivered to the Jews to be crucified.

The second Prelude is to see the judgement-hall in the high priest's palace, that in King Herod's palace, and the Lithostrotos and the hall in the fortress Antonia.

The third Prelude is to ask light to know how utterly false and foolish are the judgements which the world passes on Christ, and grace to glory only in the Cross of our Lord Jesus Christ, by Whom the world must be crucified to me and I to the world.

* * *

The innocent Son of God is dragged from tribunal to tribunal, bound hand and foot like the meanest of criminals, to be charged with crimes which are not His, and to pay the full penalty due to them. And yet, despicable and abject in the eyes of men and without a friend who rises to say a word in His defence, Christ is the true and eternal Judge. The sentence which Caiphas, Herod, Pilate pass on Him is but the sentence of eternal condemnation which they unconsciously pronounce against themselves.

1. Christ before the worldly Ecclesiastic

First, let us enter the palace of Caiphas, the hall where the Sanhedrim is gathered on that early morning of the first Good Friday. Look at the high priest.

He is the incarnation of that awful thing which we call a worldly priest—a priest who has subordinated the eternal to the temporal, the spiritual to the material, who does not live for the Faith but makes his livelihood out of it, and who tries to do what Christ has pronounced to be an impossible thing, i. e., to serve God and the world.

And he is surrounded by men of the same type.

There can be but hatred and irreconcilable enmity between these men and the Man that, at last, stands a prisoner before them.

He has taught that the supreme law of religion is to love everybody, even one's enemies, and that the sacrifice that pleases God most is the sacrifice of a pure heart. He has preferred little children and poor fishermen to the proud doctors of the Law, and instead of the temporal and powerful Messiah they expect, He has announced a Messiah poor, humble, despised, whose diadem would be a crown of thorns, and whose throne would be a cross prepared by them.

What wonder if Priests, Pharisees and Ancients have combined to kill Him, crying, "It is expedient that one man should die for the people," and having taken Him, they are only anxious to square their murderous deed with the principles of the law.

Witnesses follow witnesses but to contradict one another. The Divine Prisoner need say no word to confound them. The diabolical agitation of Caiphas who, while bent on compassing Christ's death wants to keep up appearances, knows no bounds. "And the high priest rising up, said to Him: Answerest Thou nothing to the things which these witness against Thee? But Jesus held His peace."[1]

As a last resort Caiphas puts the last and tremendous question: "I adjure Thee by the living God, that Thou tell us if Thou be the Christ the Son of God?"[2]

This solemn question and the no less solemn answer of Christ form the culminating point in the life of our Lord and in the life of the Chosen People. Israel was set apart and miraculously preserved for this solemn moment. The whole life of Christ was directed towards this great revelation. A few months ago the Father had vouchsafed it to Peter: "Thou art the Christ, the Son of the living God." But it had still to remain a secret.

It is at this moment, when, abandoned even by those who professed to believe in Him, He stands before the highest authority of Israel, that our Lord reveals His nature.

"Thou hast said it. Nevertheless I say to you, hereafter you shall see the Son of Man sitting on the right hand of the power of God, and coming in the clouds of Heaven."[3]

1. Matt. xxvi, 62, 63. 2. Matt. xxvi, 63. 3. Matt. xxvi, 64.

He has delivered His great message. Now He has only to write it with His Blood in the heart of every man, and to open the long series of Martyrs that will, with Him, lay down their lives to confess the truth of it.

But the Pharisees and Sadducees have no place for such a Messiah. "Then the high priest rent his garments saying: He hath blasphemed. What further need have we of witnesses? Behold now you have heard the blasphemy."

And as they seem to waver before the tremendous decision which they were asked to take, he adds:

"What think you?"

"They answered and said: He is guilty of death."[1]

Yes, "He is guilty of death." He has affirmed the rights of God to men who have made God an instrument for satisfying their passions, and He is condemned as a blasphemer. Human hypocrisy has never been so great.

2. Before the licentious and frivolous King

After the worldly churchman there comes the sensual and frivolous king.

Herod typifies the man who has but one object in life — to laugh and amuse himself. Religion for him is but a source or a means of enjoyment. At best, it is only the exterior side of religion — what may be called its sensuous aspect — that appeals to him.

But let religion appear before such a man in its true aspect and he will shrink from it; he will laugh it to scorn.

Christ comes before the murderer of St John, the adulterer, the frivolous Herod.

Herod welcomes Him. He has long been anxious to see Him. He treats Him kindly, and seems to pay little attention to His accusers.

But what can Christ say to this man who tried of ordinary and gross pleasures seeks new amusements from the Incarnate Sanctity of God? "And Jesus held His peace."

1. Matt. xxvi, 65, 66.

The punishment follows swiftly: He is treated as an idiot and a fool. "And Herod with his army set Him at nought, and mocked Him, putting on Him a white garment."[1]

3. Before the wily Politician

After the licentious and frivolous king, the wily politician.

Pilate typifies the man for whom religion has no existence whatever. He neither looks upon it as a source of wealth nor as a means of amusement. He lives for the things of the world, just because in his eyes there is nothing else to live for.

At the same time he is a gentleman. He would do nothing against his innate sense of justice, nothing that would lower him in his own eyes.

And before this man there appears Christ, brought by the people whom he hates as well as fears.

He loathes the whole business and tries his best to get rid of it. "What accusation bring you against this man?" he asks of the Jews; and on getting no satisfactory answer, "Take Him," he says, "and judge Him according to your Law." And, on hearing that Christ is a Galilean, he promptly sends Him to Herod.

Christ comes before Pilate, crosses his path, and disturbs his peace and his security. Pilate cannot dismiss Him. In vain does his wife tell him: "Have thou nothing to do with that Just Man." In vain does he wash his hands. Though cruel enough to spill the blood of hundreds of men, he feels there must be some ground for the condemnation of Jesus, and he finds none. He can neither be as hypocritical as the Pharisees, nor as frivolous as Herod.

But he does not know that there are no half-measures with iniquity. He wants to save Christ, but he wants also to keep away from trouble. His half-measures only mean new and additional sufferings and humiliations for Christ.

He tried all possible means, except the one that, even if unsuccessful, would at least have freed him from all responsibility for the death of Christ. He should have defiled the people to denounce Him to Caesar. He might have been disgraced. What then? His name would have come down as that of the man who,

1. Luke xxiii, 11.

after acknowledging Christ's innocence, had laid down his life for it—the first Martyr of Christianity.

4. Christ still on His Trial

Christ is still on His trial.

Even today He appears in the secret tribunal of our conscience proclaiming His Divine origin and the character of His Kingship, founded on poverty, sufferings and humiliations, as announced on the Mountain of the Beatitudes, and established on Calvary. Alas, as on His first Good Friday, He finds Christians who seek first and foremost the things of this world, who silence His voice, and even put Him to death in their hearts to worship Mammon and Honour.

Even now He appears, in all his sublime austerity, before sensual and frivolous men and sees Himself, once more, laughed by them to scorn, accounted as a fool and as an idiot. And not only by them, but, not rarely, also by Christians, apparently good and pious, but for whom His true Gospel, the love of the Cross, is as great a foolishness as it was to the Greeks, in the days of St Paul.

Even now Christ stands before the tribunal of politicians to suffer, in His members, ignominies of all sorts and to be nailed again to the Cross. Even now there are Christians of half-measures, men who almost wish Christ had never crossed their path.

Let us kneel at the feet of our Divine King and Supreme Judge, insulted and covered with ignominy, and ask ourselves how we have treated Him and what kind of judgements we have passed on Him. Was it that of complete submission to Him and to His teaching, or that of Caiphas, of Herod, or of Pilate? By that judgement we stand or fall: "And this is the judgement: because the Light is come into the world, and men loved darkness rather than the light, for their works were evil."

King and Victim

Then, therefore, Pilate took Jesus, and scourged Him.

KING AND VICTIM

The first Prelude is to call to mind how the people asked that Barabbas should be released and not Christ, and how Christ our Lord was scourged, crowned with thorns and insulted, and then brought forth in the presence of all, bearing the crown of thorns and the purple garment (Matt. xxvii, 15-30; Mark xv, 6-19; Luke xxiii, 17-25; John xviii, 39-40; xix, 1-16).

The second Prelude is to see the Lithostrotos and the hall in the fortress Antonia.

The third Prelude is to ask sorrow with Christ in sorrow, a broken heart with Christ heart-broken, tears, confusion and pain for the great sufferings which Christ endures for me.

PART ONE

THE HUMILIATION

1. "The most abject of Men"

Every mortal sin is an insult to the infinite Goodness of God: In committing it the sinner prefers, at least implicitly, his will to God's Will, the satisfaction of his passions to God's glory and honour. Sin is the love of self reaching out to the contempt of the Creator *Amor sui usque ad contemptum Dei.*

The Son of God, then, having taken upon Himself to atone for our sins and lead us to salvation must needs be subjected to all sorts of outrage. Thus alone can He ever hope to detach our hearts and minds from proud thoughts and give us a leaning towards humility and self-contempt—the surest way to Heaven.

It is not enough, therefore, for Christ to have felt sad even unto death, to have been deserted, betrayed, insulted, and judged worthy of death. It is not enough for Him to appear in chains like a despicable and fearful criminal in broad day-light, in the crowded streets of Jerusalem. He must be looked upon as the worst of men, unworthy of treading upon this earth of ours, of enjoying the light of the sun that rises on the evil and on the good, and of being refreshed by the rain that falls on the just and on the unjust. Such, indeed, would be the fate that awaits every sinner. Against him there would rise all the creatures of the inanimate world and the Angels and Saints of God, were it not for the infinite abasement of the Son of God.

We feel deeply wounded if we are classed with persons of inferior rank. We even resent any preference shown to others, as implying a slight upon our gifts and qualifications. We want equal treatment, at least in so far that no one should be preferred to us. If we have hearts that feel, let us not forget that the Heart of Christ felt infinitely more than any of us.

2. "Away with this Man and release unto us Barabbas"

"Now at the feast he (Pilate) was wont to release to them one prisoner, whomsoever they asked. And there was the man called Barabbas, imprisoned with certain rioters, men who in the riot had committed murder. And when the multitude came up, they began to ask him to do to them as he was wont."[1]

What a fine opportunity for Pilate! He has tried all along to get rid of the whole affair. Forced to take up the case, he loudly proclaims the innocence of Jesus: "Having examined Him before you I have found no fault in this Man, touching those things whereof ye accuse Him." He is eager to release Jesus, though not without first giving some satisfaction to the diabolical fury of the blood-thirsty crowd: "I will, therefore, chastise Him and release Him."

However, now he is sure of success. He will act according to his sense of justice, without rousing the anger of the people to a higher pitch. They are asking the release of a criminal. Let them be forced to choose between Christ and the worst of criminals locked up in the tower, and the fate of Christ will be favourably settled.

And immediately He sets about to produce the man before them—one guilty of murder and rebellion, a man hated by all and hating all, whose life and freedom meant danger and insecurity for everyone.

Pilate said unto them: "Whom will ye that I release unto you? Barabbas or Jesus, Who is called Christ?"[2]

The Son of God is placed side by side with the worst of the children of men; the one who is innocence itself, with the man whose

1. Mark xv, 6-8. 2. Matt. xxvii, 17.

life has been an uninterrupted crime; the Saviour of men with the assassin of men. What a humiliation for Christ our Lord to hear Pilate crying: "Whom will ye that I release unto you? Barabbas or Jesus Which is called Christ?"

And the name of Barabbas is mentioned first as the more reputable!

The people themselves are put out by the proposal – such is the horror which the very name of Barabbas inspires in everyone. And there is a moment's hesitation. But a more bitter humiliation is in store for Christ. "The chief priests and elders persuaded the multitude that they should ask Barabbas and destroy Jesus." And when the Governor asks them again, "Whether will you of the two to be released unto you?" they cried all at once saying, "Away with this Man and release unto us Barabbas."

How deeply does the Heart of Jesus grieve at the sight of His infinite Majesty thus scorned, and of the misery of His people that, rejecting the Author of life, ask instead for the life of a robber and an assassin!

3. The Infamous Proposal

"Whom will you that I release to you, Barabbas, or Jesus?"

How often has such an infamous proposal been made, since that day, to nations, to societies, and especially to individuals! Yes, to individuals especially. How often, in the secret of our consciences, Christ is made to endure the humiliation which He suffered on the first Good Friday! How often we are solicited to choose between Christ and pleasure, between obedience to His Law and the satisfaction of our caprices!

We should have shuddered at the very thought of being invited to deliberate between Christ and Satan, and yet many a time we have cried out with the Jews: "Not this man, but Barabbas. Away with this man, and release Barabbas unto us:" away with Christ and His Law; we want the free use of our senses, of our hearts, of our wills, of our minds, and of every pleasing thing.

O! that we may weep over our monstrous ingratitude! that we may constantly wage war on Barabbas in order that Christ may live for ever in us!

16

PART TWO

THE SUFFERING

1. Victim for Sin

Sin—the repudiation of God in favour of self—is most often the result of sensuality.

The worship of the body has always been a favourite form of worship since "the woman saw that the tree was good to eat, and fair to the eyes, and delightful to behold."[1] In ancient times, and even now in many a pagan country, the flesh was openly adored in the most hideous forms. And if today people are generally careful not to mix up religion with immorality, we are not to conclude hastily that immorality is less rampant than in the past. Not only gross immorality continues to pervade more or less the strata of society, but the worship of the body has become more refined, the love of comforts more intense, and the avoidance of everything hard and annoying more studied.

And it is for this that Christ must suffer unspeakable torments in His Body—to atone for so many sins and to give us grace to fight against sensuality, if need be to the shedding of blood.

He has come into the world to be our Victim, our Teacher, and our Guide. He has assumed a Body that He might suffer. Our body is an instrument of the soul, the source of knowledge and of many innocent pleasures. Not so with Christ. "When He cometh into the world He saith: Sacrifice and oblation Thou wouldst not: but a body Thou hast fitted to Me."[2] Not only, then, is His Body perfect on account of the great perfection of His soul, but it has been made most delicate so that it might suffer more, it has received a kind of infinite capacity for suffering so that it may fully satisfy for the abominations that millions of men perpetrate on their own bodies.

His whole life has been a patient endurance of every kind of bodily suffering. He was born in a stable, deprived of every kind of comfort. Soon after He had to fly to Egypt. The long years at

1. Gen. iii, 6. 2. Heb, x, 5.

Nazareth were years of privations. "I am poor, and in labours from My youth."[1] And during His public life He endured hunger and thirst and fatigue and want. But that is little indeed compared with what He has now to suffer.

2. The Scourging

"Then Pilate, therefore, took Jesus and scourged Him."[2] We read these words and pass on. We do not even shed a tear on the torments of the Saviour and on our sins. Truly "there is none that considereth in the heart."[3]

"And scourged Him;" not according to the Jewish custom, barbarous though it was—the stripes had not to exceed forty "lest thy brother should depart shamefully torn from thy eyes"—nor with the lictor's rods, but with the lash or flagellum reserved for slaves. The severity of cat-o'-nine-tails is well-known. Offenders, writes Fr Gallway, dreaded it more than anything else, death included. Accordingly, the proposal to inflict it on husbands that maltreated their wives was not accepted, because it was said that a husband, once flogged through his wife's evidence, would never forgive her in after years.

One who witnessed in the last century the public flogging of a prisoner at the cart-tail, used to describe how the cart was violently shaken by the convulsion of the howling sufferer, each time the lash fell, and how the skin of the victim was seen sticking to the cords as the executioner passed them through his fingers, after each lash. The Romans were so little inferior to modern executioners that it was not rare for the victim to die under their blows.

The soldiers deputed to scourge the Saviour are only too eager to wreak their fury on Him. They are sure there will be no objection on the part of Pilate, who wishes to satisfy somewhat the blood-thirsty feeling of the crowd. The soldiers have been kept under restraint these days for fear of exciting the Jews. At last they can show what kind of love they bear to the Jews, to this man, who, a few days ago, triumphantly entered the City.

1. Ps. lxxxvii, 16. 2. John xix, 1. 3. Jer. xii, 11.

The Saviour is stripped and tied to a short pillar. The strokes of Divine Justice which would have hurled us into Hell fall inexorably on His innocent Body.

Look, for a moment, at the gentle Jesus under the savage fury of His tormentors. The flesh becomes livid—wounds appear here and there—the blood streams forth.

The executioners are as hard as stones. They are urged on by the entreaties and the bribes of the Pharisees who are afraid lest Pilate should yield. They are instigated by the unseen powers of evil.

The silent patience and the meekness of the Divine Victim only increase their savage cruelty. They want to hear at least a groan from Him. Men succeed each other, to begin in turn the cruel work with redoubled cruelty, till there is no part of that Sacred Body which the lash has not reached, and the Saviour falls to the ground which is all stained with His Blood and strewn with innumerable pieces of His Flesh.

Isaias saw Him and was horrified: "He shall grow up as a tender plant before him, and as a root out of thirsty ground: there is no beauty in Him nor comeliness: and we have seen Him, and there was no sightliness, that we should be desirous of Him. Despised and the most abject of men, a man of sorrows, and acquainted with infirmity: and His look was as it were hidden and despised, whereupon we esteemed Him not. Surely He hath borne our infirmities and carried our sorrows: and we have thought Him as it were a leper, and as one struck by God and afflicted. But He was wounded for our iniquities, He was bruised for our sins: the chastisement of our peace was upon Him, and by His bruises we are healed."[1]

3. At the Feet of Jesus

Let us throw ourselves at His Feet to adore Him and to protect Him from the blows of His enemies. It is our sins—our sins of impurity above all—that are the cause of so much suffering. It is our sins that daily renew His Passion.

1. Is. liii, 2-5.

Shall we again scourge Christ's Sacred Body? Shall we in the presence of this mangled Body indulge in any unlawful pleasure? Shall we say that it is hard to fight against the allurements of the flesh? "Have confidence: I have conquered the flesh," the suffering Saviour tells us. And truly the sight of Christ scourged and the graces He has gained for us, have enabled thousands and thousands of Christians to live pure even in the midst of the greatest corruption.

This is the difference between pagan and Christian times, between pagan and Christian peoples, in spite of so much apparent similarity. While pagan Rome could hardly find ten young women willing to remain chaste, for a time, in honour of the goddess Vesta, millions of angels in the flesh now follow the Lamb without spot throughout their life.

CHRIST'S PALADIN

A man said to his Angel,
"My spirits are fallen thro',
And I cannot carry this battle;
O brother, what shall I do?"...
Then said to the man his Angel,
"Thou wavering foolish soul,
Back to the ranks! What matter
To win or lose the whole,
As judged by the little judges
Who harken not well, nor see?
Not thus by the outer issue
The wise shall interpret thee!"...
Thy part is with broken sabre
To rise on the last redoubt;
To fear not sensible failure
Nor covet the game at all,
But fighting, fighting, fighting,
Die, driven against the wall.

Louise Imogen Guiney.

The Insignia of our King

Then the soldiers of the Governor taking Jesus into the hall, gathered together unto Him the whole band: and stripping Him, they put a scarlet cloak about Him. And platting a crown of thorns they put it upon His head and a reed in His right hand. And bowing the knee before Him, they mocked Him, saying: "Hail, king of the Jews." And spitting upon Him, they took the reed, and struck His head.

PART THREE

THE INSIGNIA OF OUR KING

1. The Crowning of the King

Pride is the other root of sin. Through pride fell the angels in Heaven, and our first parents, in the garden of Eden. To appear greater and superior to others in our state of life, in our qualifications, in dress, if not in anything else, is the longing of sinful man. And Christ is to atone for it.

He has proclaimed Himself a King before Pilate: the soldiers of the Governor must, then, proceed to His solemn coronation.

They take the Saviour into the common hall. They gather unto Him the whole band. They strip Him. They put a scarlet cloak about Him to make fun of Him and scoff at Him. They put on His head a crown, not of gold or of silver, but of most sharp and pricking thorns to show that He is a petty king and a counterfeit God, and at the same time to torment that part of His sacred Body which alone has been left intact by the scourges. They place a reed in His right hand instead of a sceptre, out of derision, and they make Him sit down on a rough stone.

After the coronation comes the act of homage. "They bow the knee before Him, and they mock Him saying: 'Hail, King of the Jews!' And they spit upon Him, and take the reed and they smite Him with their hands."

"Go forth, ye daughters of Sion, and see your king in the diadem wherewith his mother crowned him in the day of his espousals and in the day of the joy of his heart."[1]

See Him with His crown on His head—His royal robe on His shoulders—His sceptre in His hand. He is indeed a Victim, but at the same time a Conqueror and a King, a Teacher who shows us how to conquer and how to reign.

1. Cant. iii, 11.

"Behold the Man"

Pilate, therefore, went forth again, and saith to them: "Behold I bring Him forth unto you, that you may know that I find no cause in Him." Jesus therefore came forth bearing the crown of thorns, and the purple garment.

And he saith to them: "Behold the Man."

When the chief priests therefore and the servants had seen Him, they cried out, saying: "Crucify Him, crucify Him."

2. "BEHOLD THE MAN"

"Behold the man," cries Pilate! "Behold Him wounded with whips, covered over with spittle, all swollen with buffets: behold Him clothed in mockery, and crowned with a crown of sorrow and contempt. He claimed to be a King; He is hardly a man.

And Jesus, in the innermost depth of His Heart, re-echoes the voice of the Governor: "I am a worm and not a man: the reproach of men and the outcast of the people."[1] Wild beasts would be moved to compassion at the sight of our Saviour's sufferings. Pilate is deeply touched, but if he thought he would appease the fury of the people with his new move, he is surely deceived.

"Crucify, crucify Him,' they all cry.

"Shall I crucify your King?"

"We have no King but Caesar." "His blood be upon us and upon our children."

3. AVE REX NOSTER!

But He is *our* King. Let us bow down before Him and worship Him, our Saviour and King, the Way, the Life, and the Truth. Let us promise Him that we shall henceforth be His faithful subjects, that we shall glory to be clothed, for His love, with His insignia—privations, sufferings, and above all insults and reproaches—and that we shall march and fight with Him under the Standard of His Cross.

"One day," writes St Teresa, "entering a chapel, I saw a statue of our Lord there exposed for a special occasion. It represented our Lord covered with wounds and with such an expression that I was deeply moved. I understood better what our Lord has suffered for us, and at the same time I so realised my ingratitude that my heart was nearly broken. I fell on my knees at the feet of the Saviour, asking Him fervently and in the midst of abundant tears to give me grace never more to offend Him. I asked the help of St Mary Magdalene whom I had always loved and whose conversion I often honoured.... She came to my help. Without trusting my good resolutions I put all my confidence in God. I told Him, if I remember rightly, that I would not get up unless I was granted what I had asked, and I am certain that He heard my prayer, because that day was for me the beginning of a new life and never did I cease to make true progress in the way of perfection."

Let us throw ourselves at the feet of our Lord, and beg Him to grant to us a similar favour.

1. Ps. xxvii, 7.

The King on His Throne

And they took Jesus, and led Him forth. And bearing His own Cross He went forth to that place which is called Calvary, but in Hebrew Golgotha.

THE CRUCIFIXION

THE KING ON HIS THRONE

The first Prelude is to call to mind how Jesus went forth, bearing His own Cross, to that place which is Calvary, and was crucified.

The second Prelude is to see the road that leads to Calvary—the *via dolorosa*—and the place of the Crucifixion.

The third Prelude is to ask sorrow with Christ in sorrow, a broken heart with Christ heart-broken, tears, confusion and pain for the sufferings which Christ endures for me.

* * *

The Passion of our Lord must be a frequent theme of meditation for every Christian. "I judged not myself to know any thing .... but Jesus Christ and Him crucified."[1]

Christ Himself, throughout His life, had the thought of His Passion constantly before Him:

"And my sorrow is continually before Me."[2]

"Can you drink of the cup whereof I am to drink; or be baptized with the baptism wherewith I am to be baptized?"[3]

He ardently desired that we should likewise keep constantly before our eyes the price which He has paid for our salvation. For this end, the day before He suffered, the night in which He was betrayed, He instituted the Blessed Sacrament:

"Take ye and eat. This is My Body."

"Drink ye all of this. For this is My Blood of the New Testament, which shall be shed for many unto remission of sins."

"This do ye in remembrance of Me .... For as often as ye eat this bread, and drink of the cup, ye proclaim the death of the Lord until He come."[5]

But even apart from such a sweet command, we cannot truly love Christ without often thinking of His sufferings and without longing to grieve and suffer with Him. To approach Him has always meant to partake of His Cross. The water of grace and the

1. I Cor. ii, 2. 2. Ps. xxxvii, 18. 3. Mark x, 38. 4. Matt. xxvi, 26-28.
5. I Cor. xi, 24-26.

blood of tribulation have always flowed together from the pierced Side of the Saviour.

On the other hand the desire to sympathize and to suffer with our Lord gives strength and nobility to our souls in the midst of sufferings and trials. These naturally tend to concentrate our thoughts on our poor self and to make us selfish and querulous. The thought of our Lord's Passion, on the contrary, gets hold of us and takes us out of ourselves and our petty interests. We fix our attention on the sufferings of the Lord. We measure our sorrows with His sorrows, and we find that they are but a tiny drop before an ocean.

During the famine in Ireland, the famous Fr Burke, entering a Catholic Church with a Protestant friend found a poor woman and her little son, both clad in rags and looking starved, making the Way of the Cross and crying aloud.

"Do they suffer so much?" asked the Protestant.

"They don't cry for their own sufferings, great though they be," answered the Father, "but for the sufferings of Christ."

"Why," added the Protestant, "did it not happen long ago?"

"No, not long ago; for that poor woman and her little boy Christ is now going to Calvary, now He is nailed to the Cross; and that is why, forgetful of themselves and of everything else, they cry so bitterly."

PART ONE

THE WAY TO CALVARY

1. "JESUS WAS DELIVERED UP TO THEIR WILL"

Life is a daily ascent to Calvary—a daily crucifixion. Since the coming of Christ, Calvary is the only height from which the soul may take its flight to Heaven.

We must, then, follow Christ with Mary, John, and Magdalene. We must make our way of the Cross as Mary made it, day after day, till the day of her death.

"Jesus was delivered up to their will."[1]

1. Luke xxiii, 25.

He is condemned to death. Why? The Innocent for the guilty. "He has done no evil," has Pilate said.

No evil? Nay, He has been doing good, He has loved men, His brothers. And now these very men condemn Him to a cruel and ignominious death, between two thieves. This is His reward, and the reward which He promises to His own. To Mary His Mother He has given the sword, to John and James the chalice of bitterness, and to Peter the cross.

2. "Bearing His own Cross"

"And bearing His own Cross He went forth to that place which is called Calvary."[1]

Later on St Andrew will touchingly welcome the wood on which he is to be crucified like His Master. "Hail precious cross, that hast been adorned by the precious limbs of my Lord. Long have I desired thee, ardently have I sought thee, uninterruptedly have I loved thee, and now I find thee ready to receive my longing soul. Secure and full of joy I come to thee; do thou receive me into thy embrace, for I am the disciple of Christ my Lord, Who redeemed me by hanging upon thee." If such were the feelings of the disciple, what must have been the feelings of the Master at this moment?

At the first instant of His Incarnation the Cross was planted in His Heart. In the workshop of Nazareth it always stood before Him. During His public life every tree on the plains and hills of Palestine brought the memory of it forcibly to His mind. And at last the great moment has arrived.

Christ embraces the Cross, and that embrace works the most wonderful transformation. From this moment that terrible instrument of torture changes its nature: it becomes beautiful and beneficent; it soothes all grief and is worthy of all honour.

Christ embraces the Cross and that embrace puts its due value upon everything which we see—upon the lust of the flesh, and the lust of the eyes, and the pride of life. It sets a price upon the excitements, the rivalries, the hopes, the fears, the desires, the efforts,

1. John xix, 17.

the trials, the temptations, and the sufferings of this earthly state. It brings together and makes consistent all that otherwise would be discordant and aimless. It teaches us how to live and how to use this world. It shows what we should desire and what we should detest. At the sight of Christ tenderly embracing the Cross not only are our sufferings and tribulations accepted cheerfully, but they become the most blessed, the most fitting attendants of Christ's followers. That is why the Martyrs and the Saints and all true Christians sought affliction when it did not come to them. They were anxious to bear in their body the marks of the Lord Jesus.

3. Under the Cross

He sets off on His painful journey with His whole Heart, but His limbs fail Him and He falls on the ground once, twice, three times. The agony in the Garden, the scourging, the crowing with thorns have deprived our Lord of all physical strength. The Cross is heavy and His executioners are always at His side, goading Him onwards.

Let us contemplate the Divine Saviour with His face pressed to the ground, surrounded by the brutal soldiery. Let us stoop down to Him and console Him. Alas, it is our relapses into sin that make Jesus fall!

Jesus rises again and toils up the hill. Let us rise with Him and in spite of our repeated falls, let us never give up the determination to follow Him up to Calvary.

4. The saddest of Meetings

And lo! at the turning of the road Mary meets Jesus.

The parting, three years ago, was sad enough ; could the meeting now be sadder? The eyes of the Mother meet those of the Son, and the sword foretold by Simeon pierces her Heart. She sees Jesus bent under the heavy weight of the Cross, His Head crowned with thorns, His face covered with blood, and at that sight not only does she feel the pity and compassion which we experience towards the suffering, not only does she ardently desire to take upon herself the torments of her Son, but she actually suffers in her heart all that

He endures in His body and soul. With Mary, let us accompany Jesus to Calvary. Let us ask her, the Mother of Jesus and our Mother, to put into our hard and insensible hearts a little of the sorrow she felt on the first Good Friday, and ever after whenever she remembered the sufferings of her Son.

Eia, Mater, fons amoris,
Me sentire vim doloris
Fac ut tecum lugeam.

5. Simon of Cyrene

"And they forced one Simon, a Cyrenean .... to take up His Cross."[1]

Happy soul that has the courage and the good fortune to carry the Cross of Jesus! Had this opportunity been given to us how eagerly we would have embraced the Cross in spite of the ignominy attached to it!

And yet from time to time Jesus offers us chips of His Cross: acts of humiliation, of obedience and of self-denial that make us shudder. Let us embrace them eagerly in spite of the repugnance we feel. They are splinters of Christ's holy Cross. Their touch will transform our being into the likeness of our Master.

6. Veronica and the Women of Jerusalem

"And there followed Him .... women who bewailed and lamented Him."[2]

It is the first mark of human feeling from that infuriated horde. It is like the sudden opening of the clouds revealing for a moment a bit of the beautiful sky, while everywhere the storm rages furiously. The Master seems to be taken by surprise by this token of love. To Veronica He leaves the imprint of His suffering face that she may always remember this moment and the sufferings of Christ for her. To the other women, whose compassion was more of a natural kind, He says: "Daughters of Jerusalem weep not over Me, but weep for yourselves and for your children. For behold, the days shall come,

1. Mark xv, 21. 2. Luke xxiii, 27.

wherein they will say: Blessed are the barren, and the wombs that have not borne, and the paps that have not given suck .... For if in the green wood they do these things, what shall be done in the dry?"[1]

As Simon was the first to be united with Christ through sharing in the ignominy and pain of His Cross, so these women are the first to be united with Christ through compassion for His grief and sorrow. And thus, it seems, has our Lord divided the part Christians must take in His Passion. For man, the shame and the burden; for woman, the tears and the sorrow of the heart.

7. And they crucified Him

The sacred writers are very laconic on the supreme moment of our Lord's Passion. They shrink from giving any detail. They show no anxiety to magnify the courage of the Divine Victim. But what a series of unspeakable torments is implied in those words: "And they crucified Him!"

They strip Him of His garments—how painful, now that they all stick to His mangled body, and how ignominious!

They stretch Him on the Cross and nail Him to it. If we feel so much the prick of a needle, what must our Lord have felt when the cruel soldiers with heavy hammers drove a sharp nail through each of His sacred hands and feet!

The soldiers lift up the Cross on high and they drop it into the hole prepared for it, shaking the whole body with intolerable pain.

PART TWO

CHRIST ON THE CROSS

1. "He delivered Himself"

There He is hanging between heaven and earth, eternally appealing to God, constantly appealing to men.

1. Luke xxiii, 28-31.

One long cry resounds down through the centuries: "O ye that pass along the way stop and see if there is any grief like unto My grief!"

He has sacrificed for us whatever this world could give Him. His whole life has been spent in poverty. But now He gives away even His few garments and the seamless robe made for Him by His Mother. He gives away His own Mother—nay even the consolations of His Heavenly Father.

During His life-time the crowds proclaimed Him a prophet, the Son of David, the wonder-worker. A few days ago, they acclaimed Him their King. And now He dies as a blasphemer, as one cursed by God, and as the crowned king of malefactors. His power is laughed at. His miracles are attributed to Satan. His very confidence in God is challenged and mocked.

His body is one wound: "From the sole of the foot unto the top of the head there is no soundness therein." His head, crowned with thorns, can find no repose; His shoulders are bruised by the carrying of the Cross; His back is rent and gashed with scourges: His hands and feet are pierced through with nails: His mouth is parched with intolerable thirst. The weight of His body increases the wounds. The blood gathers together in the head and the heart. Hunger, thirst, fever, violent pain, succeed to momentary faints. For hours He feels at every instant the excruciating agonies of death.

2. Christ Still on the Cross

Who has done it? Who still keeps Christ nailed to the Cross?

Alas, whenever we offend God, we hold the bitter chalice to the lips of Christ, we kiss Him with the treacherous kiss of Judas, we prefer Barabbas to Him, we ply the cruel scourge and press the crown of thorns upon His aching brow, we nail Him to the Cross, and keep Him there in an agony of torments and anguish.

Has He not died on the Cross to give us grace to conquer our love of this world by His poverty, our sensuality by His sufferings, our pride by His humiliations? By refusing to free ourselves from the bondage of sin, we keep Him fixed to the Cross.

And yet "His whole form breathes out love and calls forth love in return: His head bowed down, His hands outstretched, His heart laid bare."

Reflecting on myself to ask what have I done for Christ, what am I doing for Christ, what ought I to do for Christ. Then, beholding Him in such a condition, and thus hanging upon the Cross, to make the reflections which may suggest themselves.

Truly "If any man love not our Lord Jesus Christ, let him be anathema."

May every throb of my heart go up to God laden with two acts: an act of sorrow and an act of love.

QUIA AMORE LANGUEO

In a valley of this restles mind
I sought in mountain and in mead,
Trusting a true love for to find.
Upon an hill then took I heed;
A voice I heard (and near I yede*) *went.
In great dolour complaining tho:* *then
'See, dear soul, how my sides bleed
Quia amore langueo.'

Upon this mount I found a tree,
Under a tree a man sitting;
From head to foot wounded was he;
His hearte blood I saw bleeding:
A seemly man to be a king,
A gracious face to look unto,
I asked why he had paining;
He said, '*Quia amore langueo.*'

I am true love that false was never;
My sister, man's soul, I loved her thus.
Because we would in no wise dissever* *separate
I left my kingdom glorious.
I purveyed her a palace full precious;
She fled, I followed, I loved her so
That I suffered this pain piteous
Quia amore langueo.

My fair love and my spouse bright!
I saved her from beating, and she hath me bet,
I clothed her in grace and heavenly light;
This bloody shirt she hath on me set;
For longing love yet would I not let;* *hinder.
Sweete strokes are these: lo!
I have loved her ever as I her het* *promised.
Quia amore langueo.

I crowned her with bliss and she me with thorn;
I led her to chamber and she me to die;
I brought her to worship and she me to scorn;
I did her reverence and she me villany.
To love that loveth is no maistry;
Her hate made never my love her foe:
Ask then no moo* question why, *more.
But *Quia amore langueo.*

Look unto mine handes, man!
These gloves were given me when I her sought;
They be not white, but red and wan;
Embroidred with blood my spouse them bought.
They will not off; I loose them nought;* *not.
I woo her with them wherever she go.
These hands for her full friendly fought,
Quia amore langueo.

Marvel not, man, though I sit still.
My love hath shod me wonder* strait: *wonderfully.
She buckled my feet, as was her will,
With sharpe nails well thou mayest wait!* *know.
In my love was never desait;* *deceit.
All my membres I have opened her to;
My body I made her herte's bait* *nourishment.
Quia amore langueo.

The Message from the Throne

from a Woodcut by Gabriel Pippet

Now there stood by the Cross of Jesus, His Mother, and His Mother's sister, Mary of Cleophas, and Mary Magdalene. When Jesus therefore had seen His Mother and the disciple standing, whom He loved, He saith to His Mother:

"Woman, behold thy son."

THE LAST SEVEN WORDS

THE MESSAGE FROM THE THRONE

The first Prelude is to call to mind how Christ spoke seven words on the Cross: He prayed for those who were crucifying Him; He forgave the Good Thief; He commended St John to His Mother and His Mother to St John; He complained: "I thirst"; He groaned that He was forsaken; He said: "It is finished"; and finally He cried out: "Father, into Thy hands I commend My spirit."

The second Prelude is to see the place of the Crucifixion.

The third Prelude is to ask of my dying Master, through the intercession of Mary, His Mother and my Mother, of John and Mary Magdalene, light to understand His parting message, and grace to treasure it in my heart and make it the mainspring of my whole life.

* * *

"And seeing the multitudes, He went up into a mountain and when He had sat down, His disciples came to Him, and opening His mouth He taught them."[1]

Calvary is the counterpart of the Mountain of the Beatitudes. There the Master raised His standard and issued the Code of His Kingdom. Here He seals it with His Blood. There He opened His mouth and uttered the words of Eternal Life, in the presence of His ecstatic disciples and the astonished multitude. Here but a few words break forth from His lips, but they come from the innermost depth of His agonizing Heart, and re-echoed by every wound of His body and every drop of His sacred Blood. They sum up and fix the teaching of His life. They are His last message delivered to a few chosen friends, in the presence of an angry, hostile, and scoffing crowd.

The three hours of darkness and of agonizing silence divide the Sermon of Christ into two parts. The first three words refer to the persons around Jesus: His cruel and impenitent enemies: His companion in suffering, the penitent thief; His dear ones, Mary and John. In the midst of His sufferings Christ does not forget to forgive, to console, to help and to succour. The last four words refer to Jesus Himself: the fourth and the fifth reveal the intensity

1. Matt. vi, 1, 2.

of His interior and exterior sufferings; the sixth and the seventh are a cry of triumph and a cry of confidence, and constitute the Saviour's immediate preparation for death.

FIRST WORD

And when they were come to the place, which is called Calvary, they crucified Him there.... And Jesus said: Father, forgive them, for they know not what they do.[1]

1. The Infinite Mercy of Christ

Many a time had Jesus shown His pity for sinners. He had declared that He had come into this world not to judge it, "but that the world may be saved by Him,"[2] "not to call the just, but sinners to penance."[3] The inhabitants of a town once refused to receive Him. Indignant at this insult, James and John said to Him: "Lord, wilt thou that we command fire to come down from Heaven and consume them? And turning, He rebuked them, saying: You know not of what spirit you are. The Son of man came not to destroy souls but to save."

No one, then, could possibly doubt the merciful goodness of the Saviour. However, well knowing how liable we are, after repeated sins, to fall into despondency and despair, He desired to make such a revelation of the infinite mercy of His Divine Heart as to drive out the last shred of diffidence from the heart of even the greatest sinner.

Throughout His Passion our Lord has hardly opened His mouth except to remind His persecutors of that awful day when He will appear to judge them, and to explain to Pilate the object of His mission and the crime the Roman Governor was perpetrating. No feeling of rancour can dwell for an instant in the Heart of Christ—of that we are quite certain. But when for the first time, after a long silence, He opens His lips, will He not call down the Divine vengeance on His ungrateful and cruel executioners and pronounce the final condemnation of His enemies? Instead He only says: "Father, forgive them,"—forgive the soldiers, the priests, the whole people.

1. Luke xxiii, 33, 34. 2. John iii, 17. 3. Luke v, 32.

Let us consider for a moment, on one side the gravity of the crime committed on Mount Calvary, and on the other, the sufferings of our Lord; and then let us measure, if we can, the love and the mercy of His Heart, when, tenderly addressing His Father, He says: "Father, forgive them." "Truly, "many waters cannot quench charity, neither can the floods drown it."[1]

2. The Quintessence of the Law of Love

It is always difficult to forgive in true sincerity, and not merely out of cowardice and laziness. It is difficult even when the wrong done to us, or the sufferings inflicted on us, are things of the past. But to forgive in the very act of being wronged and tormented by the men on whom we have lavished our love and favours, to intercede and pray for them, is surely above man's strength. Christ has obtained for us the grace to do it. He wholly forgets His offended dignity and His outraged love to remember only His infinite mercy and the almost infinite weakness of His creatures.

To love our enemies, to do good to them that hate us, and to pray for them that persecute and calumniate us, is the quintessence of the law of love and the characteristic note of Christianity. We must obey that law and make that characteristic note our own, if we want to be the children of the Heavenly Father, "Who maketh the sun to rise upon the good and the bad, and raineth upon the just and the unjust;" if truly we desire that the Crucified Saviour be our hope in life and at the moment of death. If we look on Him and trust in His all-powerful grace, surely we shall be able, even in the midst of persecution and torments, to repeat with St Stephen: "Lord, lay not this sin to their charge."

3. "They know not what they do"

They have heaped on Him torments and insults of every kind. They breathe freely only when they see Him nailed to the Cross. But not yet is their hatred appeased. They blaspheme Him, they mock Him, they challenge Him to come down from the Cross: "He saved others; Himself He cannot save. If He be the King of Israel,

1. Cant. viii, 7.

let Him now come down from the Cross, and we will believe Him. He trusted in God, let Him deliver Him now, if He will have Him; for He said: I am the Son of God."

Where He the worst of malefactors there would be no justification for all this, and they know it. The only thing they do not know, and that because they did not care to know, is that He is the Son of God. His Heart clings to this slight excuse and cries out: "They know not what they do."

4. The Memento of our High Priest

We have crucified Jesus many a time. Our sins were the executioners of the Incarnate Son of God: "crucifying again to themselves the Son of God and making Him a mockery."[1] For us, then, is that prayer: "Father, forgive them, for they know not what they do." It is the *Memento* of our High Priest offering His eternal Sacrifice for us.

Truly we do not know what we are doing when we sin. We are fools that in a fit of frenzy stab the most loving of fathers. And that Father turns to us with eyes of tenderness and opens to us His Heart—the Heart which in the midst of sufferings, of ingratitude and ignominy, throbs only with love for us His erring children.

If the sight of Jesus, crucified by us and imploring His Father's forgiveness for us, does not pierce our heart; if we do not restrain ourselves with a kind of horror from wounding again the Divine Heart, we may well ask ourselves whether the last shred of human feeling has not perchance disappeared from us.

SECOND WORD

And one of those robbers who were hanged blasphemed Him saying: If Thou be Christ, save Thyself and us. But the other, answering, rebuked him, saying: Neither dost thou fear God, seeing thou art under the same condemnation. And we indeed justly, for we receive the due reward of our deeds; but this man

1. Heb. vi, 6.

hath done no evil. And he said to Jesus: Lord, remember me when Thou shalt come into Thy Kingdom.

And Jesus said to him: Amen I say to thee, this day thou shall be with Me in Paradise.[1]

1. "Remember Me"

Jesus is crucified between two thieves, as if He were one of them—the worst of them. "If He were not a malefactor we would not have delivered Him up to thee." Not even the companions of His torments have pity on Him. In the midst of excruciating pains, one of them finds strength to curse Him and to taunt Him for His want of power to save them; angry, perhaps, at the thought that the execution of Christ has hastened his own.

But while this crucified criminal is preparing to plunge from his cross into the infernal abyss, a miracle of grace is worked in his companion. He has been watching the Divine Saviour. He has heard Him pray for His executioners; and his heart, hardened by years of sin, of cruelty and hatred, opens to the sweet influence of grace. He rebukes his neighbour, and then, turning to Christ, says: "O Lord, remember me when Thou shalt come into Thy Kingdom,"

What a wonderful profession of faith! He sees to his left a man dying, condemned by the leaders of His people as a blasphemer, despised and insulted by the multitude, abandoned by His disciples, and seemingly even by God—and he sees and openly acknowledges in Him the King of a Kingdom that is not from hence, and recognizes in the Cross the means to enter into it.

And what a confiding humility! He solicits no special favour. He only prays, "Remember me," as though he would say: "All that I desire, O Lord, is that you would deign to remember me and turn Your benignant eyes upon me."

2. "This day thou shalt be with Me in Paradise"

A moment ago the Saviour asked the Father's forgiveness for every one. That prayer has obtained for the Good Thief the Grace of repentance, and Christ's patient and sweet attitude has encouraged

1. Luke xxiii, 39-43.

him to make an advance. And now that the repentant sinner turns to Him and begs just for a remembrance, Christ gives to him what alone is worth having—not a few years of mortal life, but Heaven itself, i. e., perfect and eternal happiness.

"Amen, I say to thee this day thou shalt be with Me in Paradise."

Truly, blessed are the meek, because they shall conquer and possess the land. Christ's meekness has conquered one more heart, and the conquest means for the Good Thief the transference from a cross to a kingdom.

Nowadays also the Crucified is despised and rejected by the greatest part of mankind—even by many who exteriorly profess to be His adherents. In spite of this and of the many perplexities that may harass our poor souls, let us constantly acknowledge Him as the King of the Kingdom of God—the King of our souls. Sinners as we all are, let us repeat the humble and the confidant prayer of the Penitent Thief "O Lord, remember me, now that Thou art come into Thy Kingdom."

THIRD WORD

Now there stood by the Cross of Jesus, His Mother.... When Jesus therefore, had seen His Mother, and the disciple standing, whom He loved, He saith to His Mother: Woman, behold thy son. After that, He saith to the disciple: Behold thy Mother. And from that hour the disciple took her to his own.[1]

1. Christ's Co-Redeemer

Christ is about to offer Himself as a perfect holocaust to the Father and thus to restore Adam's sinful descendants to the high dignity of children of God.

"If He shall lay down His life for sin He shall see a longlived seed."[2]

It is the hour when, through His martyrdom on the Cross, He will become "the First-Born among many brethren," the Head of the

1. John xix, 25-27. 2. Is. liii, 10.

Church, i. e., of all those who have been chosen in Him by God before the foundation of the world, to be holy and unspotted in His sight.

"Now there stood by the Cross of Jesus, His Mother."

She was not seen in the hour of triumph, a few days ago, when her Son entered Jerusalem as the acclaimed King of Israel. But now she stands by His Cross that out of the sufferings of both we may be given to partake of the life of God. *Illa spiritu Mater est membrorum Salvatoris: quia cooperata est charitate ut fideles in Ecclesia nascerentur.*[1]

In Bethlehem she gave birth to the Child Jesus in the midst of ecstatic joy. On Calvary she, the *Virgo Sacerdos,* offers Him to the Father as the Victim she has long prepared for the Sacrifice, and is with Him nailed, in spirit, to the Cross. It is the moment when Christ proclaims her *the Woman* that would crush the head of Satan—the new Eve and Mother of the regenerated family of God: "Woman, behold thy son."

St John represented on Calvary all the disciples of Christ. Pointing out everyone of us to Mary, the dying Saviour, says with a lovely glance: "Woman, behold thy son!"

We are not only placed under the protection of Mary, but we are her children—the children born of her travail and just for that reason passionately loved! To her as Christ's co-Redeemer, we owe our salvation and all that salvation implies. *Its cum Filio patiente et moriente passa est et paene commortua, sic materna in Filium iura pro salute hominum abdicavit. Placandaeque Dei justitiae, quantum ad se pertinebat, Filium immolavit, ut dici merito queat ipsam cum Christo humanum genus redemisse.*[2]

2. Christ's Parting Gift

"Behold thy Mother!"

Mary is our Mother in the spiritual order. Through her was Jesus given to us, and through her alone we become brothers of Jesus and children of God.

"Behold thy Mother!"

1. St Augustine. 2. Benedict xv, 22 March 1918.

It is the last gift of our dying Saviour — the last and the best of His gifts: the gift of a Mother and of His Mother. It sums up all other gifts. Whoever finds Mary finds every good thing; whoever keeps his eyes fixed on Mary will never perish.

"O thou, whoever thou art, that knowest thou art exposed to the dangers of the stormy sea of this world more than thou enjoyest the security of dry land, do not turn away thy eyes from the splendour of this Star, from Mary the Star of the sea, unless thou wishest to be swallowed up in the tempest. If the winds of temptation arise, if thou art thrown upon the rocks of tribulation, look towards the Star, call on Mary. If thou art tossed hither and thither on the billows of pride, of ambition, of detraction, of envy, look towards the Star, call on Mary. Should anger, or avarice, or fleshly enticement strike against the bark of thy soul, look on Mary. If thou art terrified at the enormity of thy sins, or confused by the unclean state of thy conscience, or if stricken with awe for thy Judge, thou beginnest to feel thyself sinking in the abyss of sadness or the pit of despair, think of Mary. In danger, in difficulty, or doubt, think of Mary, call on Mary. Thou will not go astray if thou followest her, thou will not despair if thou prayest to her, thou will not err if thou thinkest of her."[1]

FOURTH WORD

My God, my God, why hast Thou forsaken Me?[2]

THE DEEPEST DEPTH OF CHRIST'S SUFFERINGS

It is the supreme moment in our Lord's Passion — the deepest depth of all His sufferings.

In the Garden, God is still a Father. Though He does not hear the prayer of His Son, He does not abandon Him, but sends an Angel to strengthen Him. On the Cross, God is the God of Justice and Sanctity. He suspends the union of protection in Christ — not the substantial union of grace and will, nor the union of glory which gives to Christ's soul the beatific vision — to allow for the oblation of the blood-stained sacrifice for the redemption of mankind.

1. St Bernard. 2. Matt. xxvii, 46.

Now, more than in the Garden, does Christ feel the infinite load of the sins for which He must atone: "being made a curse for us."[1] His bodily sufferings intensify the agony of His soul a thousandfold. He seems Himself, as it were, cast out by God, swimming alone in a limitless sea of grief and of misery, with no star shining on high and no compass to steer His soul through.

Satan is there to deliver his last blow to the defenceless Victim. "Where is the God that cares for thee?" he cries. "If Thou be the Son of God, come down from the Cross."[2]

2. THE INEFFABLE CANON OF THE SAVIOUR'S MASS

And yet it is at this very moment that Chirst mostly works out our salvation.

In the Cenacle, He prayed for His Apostles and for all those who, through them, would believe in Him.

In the Garden, He prayed "with a strong cry and tears," for strength to drink to the last dregs the bitter chalice of His Passion.

On the Cross, our High Priest enters alone the *Sancta Sanctorum*, laden with all our sins, past, present and future, to offer the Eternal Sacrifice to God's infinite Justice and Sanctity, and to intercede for us.

The three hours of Agony constitute the ineffable Canon of our Saviour's Mass.

FIFTH WORD

Afterwards Jesus knowing that all things were now accomplished, that the Scripture might be fulfilled, said: I thirst. Now there was a vessel set there full of vinegar. And they putt in a sponge full of vinegar about hyssop, put it to His mouth.[3]

1. THE PANG OF THIRST

Having mainifested the desolation of His soul, our Lord desires that we should catch a glimpse of one particular torment by which

1. Gal. iii, 13. 2. Matt. xxvii, 40. 3. John xix, 28, 29.

His whole body is racked, and cries out: "I thirst." Most of the sufferings of His sacred body were plainly visible. The pang of thirst, however, might have escaped our notice, though to one crucified it was the most unbearable. And how much more for our Lord! From the previous night He has endured every possible torment of body and soul. He has repeatedly shed His sacred Blood: the last drops of it are now trickling down from His torn hands and feet. The pores of His body are closed. His veins and tongue, His palate and throat are all parched up. A burning fever consumes Him. The Prophet had already cried out in the name of Christ: "My strength is withered as a potsherd, and my tongue hath cleaved to my jaws, and thou hast brought me down into the dust of death."[1] Christ pronounces but one word: "I thirst." The howling of a dying dog moves even the hardest of men to pity. The pitiful cry of the Son of God merely whets the cruelty even of those who are not His enemies. Instead of a cool and refreshing draught they offer Him what can only increase His torment. "And in My thirst they gave Me for drink vinegar."[2] It is what many have been doing throughout the ages. Some have actually heaped new sufferings and insults on the Lord that was dying for them, and was but asking for a word or a look of pity. Others have done all they could to keep Christ still athirst on the Cross by their intemperance and self-indulgence. Generous souls, however, have heard that cry of Christ, "I thirst." and have had no more heart to indulge freely in drink. The thirst of Christ quenched their thirst. Temperance became for them not a health-giving device, still less a means to secure greater productive efficiency or increased savings, but a sacrifice of love offered to their dying Saviour.

2. The Thirst of the Sacred Heart

But besides the physical thirst, there is another thirst, and a more consuming one, that torments the Divine Saviour. It is the thirst of His Divine Heart, the thirst to which He referred when He asked the Samaritan woman to give Him to drink. *Sitit sitiri Deus*, says St Gregory Nazianzen. "God thirsts to be thirsted for." He

1. Ps. xxi, 16. 2. Ps. lxviii, 22.

thirsts for our salvation: *Sitis Mea, salus vestra.* "Do quench My thirst," He constantly cries from the Cross, by giving Me thy soul—by giving Me souls."

"And I, if I be lifted up from the earth, will draw all things to Myself."

It is to appease this thirst of Christ that men draw ever nearer to the Cross, and climb it generously to be nailed with Him on it. *Christo confixus sum Cruci.* It is the cry of Christ that has called millions of men and women away from home, from comforts and worldly success, and has fired them with a like thirst for souls. It is to appease that thirst that they work and suffer unceasingly "in much patience, in tribulation, in necessities, in distresses, in stripes, in prisons, in seditions, in labours, in watchings, in fastings, in chastity, in knowledge, in long sufferings," happy if they can bring even one soul to their Master and Lord.

QUIA AMORE LANGUEO

In my side I have made her nest;
Look in, how wide a wound is here!
This is her chamber, here shall she rest,
That she and I may sleep in fere.* *together.
Here may she wash, if any filth were;
Here is socour for all her woe;
Come when she will, she shall have cheer,
Quia amore langueo.

I will abide till she be ready,
I will her sue if she say nay;
If she be retchless* I will be greedy,* *careless. *zealous.
If she be dangerous I will her pray;
If she weep, then bide* I nay; * beg.
Mine arms ben* spread to clip her me to. *are.
Cry once, 'I come!' now, soul, assay!
Quia amore langueo.

It is consummated

Jesus, therefore, when He had taken the vinegar, said:

"It is consummated."

SIXTH WORD

Jesus, therefore, when He had taken the vinegar, said: It is consummated.[1]

1. The Vision of the Dying Saviour

By this word, Christ announces His triumphant victory. He has been sent by His Father to save the world. At the first moment of His Incarnation He said: "Behold, I come to do Thy Will, O God." In the Temple of Jerusalem He declared to His parents that He had to be about His Father's business. During His public life He repeatedly stated that His food was to do the Will of Him who had sent Him. And now from the summit of the Cross He casts a retrospective glance over His whole life, the glance which dying men, we are told, are empowered to cast and which comprehends every thought, every word, every action in its minutest details. What a glorious vision unfolds itself before the eyes of the dying Saviour. He sees Nazareth where first He pitched His tent in our midst. He sees Bethlehem where He was born in extreme poverty and lowliness; and then Egypt where He had to fly from the anger of Herod; and, then, Nazareth again and the long, long years of submission, of toil, of concealment. He sees the synagogues, towns and villages through which He has passed preaching the Gospel and doing good to all. He sees the Supper Room, Gethsemane, and the road that leads from it to Calvary, with all its painful stations. And He cries: *Consummatum est*—"It is finished."

2. Christ's Work of Sanctification Begins

Looking at the whole of His past life Jesus has the clear consciousness that the Will of His Father has been His only guide. Everyone of His deeds, every word, and every throb of His Heart have been solely prompted by the desire of giving the greatest glory to His Father. He repeats then what He said the previous night in the Supper Room: "I have glorified Thee on earth: I have finished the work which Thou gavest Me to do." He has manifested His

1. John xix, 30.

Father's name to the men whom the Father has given Him. He has delivered His message, in obedience to the Father. He has sealed it with His Blood. He has drunk the Chalice which the Father has given Him. He has fulfilled all that had been foretold of Him by the Prophets. *Consummatum est.* His work is accomplished. He has overcome on the tree of the Cross him who had overcome man in the Garden of Eden. He has become the spring of eternal life to all those who would come and believe in Him. He has thrown open the gate to Heaven. And yet His work is not finished. Why, one would almost say that now it just begins. It is now for us, His members, to follow Him – to work, to suffer, and to die for Him. "Who now . . . . fill up those things, that are wanting of the sufferings of Christ in my flesh."[1] Only when the last of the Elect will, through suffering, enter with Christ into the glory of the Father, will the work of Christ be accomplished. Till then, Christ continues from the Cross to call men to Him that they may be purified in His Blood, and that dying to themselves they live in Him, with Him, and for Him.

SEVENTH WORD

And Jesus, crying with a loud voice, said: Father, into Thy hands I commend My spirit. And saying this He gave up the ghost.[2]

1. Christ's Cry of Boundless Confidence

After the reassuring glance which Christ has thrown on His past life there remains for Him but to turn to His Father and leave in His hands the life He has received from Him: "A body Thou hast fitted to Me." Accordingly, not with the gasping accents of a dying man, but with a loud voice, to prove that no man could take His life away from Him, but that He was laying it down of Himself, He cries, "Father, into Thy hands I commend My spirit;" to Thy Wisdom, i. e., that knows all things and to Thy Power that can do all

1. Coloss. i, 24. 2. Luke xxiii, 46.

things, I entrust My life that Thou mayest restore it to its full and to immortality.

Christ knows that immortality will be His, and that even His poor and mangled Body will soon rise full of glory. "Therefore doth the Father love Me; because I lay down My life that I may take it again."[1]

He prayed for His glorification, before He crossed the Cedron to begin His agonizing Passion in the Garden of Gethsemane. However, the pitiful scene we watched there; the abandonment, the sufferings, and the ignominy of the Divine Victim; and the cry we heard not long ago, may possibly have suggested the thought that either God had forsaken His Son, or, at least, that the Victim's confidence was shaken. This cry of Christ is one of boundless confidence and of triumphant hope. *Consummatum est.* Out of love for the Father "He humbled Himself by obedience unto death, yea, unto death upon a cross."[2] He may well then, say: "Father, into Thy hands I commend My spirit." The Father will exalt Him, and will give Him a name which is above all names, "that at the name of Jesus every knee should bend in Heaven, on earth and under the earth."

2. God our Loving Father

To glance at our past, alas, can only fill our hearts with fear and trembling. God's Will has not been the only rule of our life, nor, perhaps, the main rule. We have not always lived to promote the cause of Christ and to do good to His suffering members. God, however, is a tender and merciful Father, Who knows our poverty and our weakness. We may, then, turn to Him and, like the insolvent debtors and unfaithful servants that we are, throw ourselves on His Love and Mercy, and with the Church, often cry during life, but especially, at our last hour: "Into Thy hands I commend my spirit: Thou hast redeemed me, O Lord, the God of Truth;" or with St Stephen: "Lord Jesus, receive my spirit."

The last loud cry of the suffering Saviour seems to sum up the whole of His Message. However deaf to all our entreaties and almost austere and hard God may apparently seem, He is always our

1. John x, 17. 2. Phil ii, 8.

loving Father. Of us He only demands an absolute abandonment and a total resignation to His ever watchful Providence, in life and in death.

To end with a Colloquy to our Lady and Mother asking of her the grace that the last words of her dying Son and my Saviour may be deeply imprinted in my heart and be the light that guides all my steps.

QUIA AMORE LANGUEO

I sit on an hill for to see far,
I look to the valley, my spouse I see;
Now runneth she awayward, now cometh she near,
Yet from mine eye sight she may not be;
Some wait their prey, to make her flee,
I run tofore* to chastise her foo;† — * before † foe
Recover,* my soul, again to me, — * return
Quia amore langueo.

My sweet spouse will we go play?
Apples ben* ripe in my gardayne;† — * are † garden
I shall thee clothe in a new array,
Thy meat shall be milk, honey and wine.
Now, dear soul, let us go dine:
Thy sustenance is in my crippe,* lo! — * bag
Tarry thou not, my fair spouse mine,
Quia amore langueo.

If thou be foul, I shall make thee clean;
If thou be sick, I shall thee heal; — * anything
If thou mourn ought,* I shall thee mene;† — † care for
Why wilt thou not, fair love, with me deal?
Foundest thou ever love so leal?* — * loyal
What wilt thou, soul, that I shall do?
I may not unkindly thee appeal,
Quia amore langueo.

What shall I do now with my spouse
But abide* her of my gentleness, * endure
Till that she looked out of her house
Of fleshly affection? love mine she is;
Her bed is made, her bolster is bliss,
Her chamber is chosen; is there none mo.* * no more
Look out on me at the window of kindeness
Quia amore langueo.

Long and love thou never so high,
Yet is my love more than thine may be;
Thou gladdest, thou weepest, I sit thee by,
Yet wouldst thou once, love, look unto me!
Spouse, should I always feede thee
With children* meat? Nay, love, not so! * children's
I will prove thy love with adversitè,
Quia amore langueo.

My love is in her chamber, hold your peace!
Make ye no noise, but let her sleep;
My babe I would not were in disease,* * discomfort
I may not hear my dear child weep.
For with my pap I shall her keep;
Marvel ye not though I tend her to:
This wound in my side had ne'er be* so deep * been
But *Quia amore langueo.*

Wax not weary, mine own dear wife!
What mede* is aye to live in comfort? * reward
In tribulation I reign more rife* * largely
Ofter* times than in disport.† * oftener † pleasure
In weal and in woe I am aye to support:
Mine own wife, go not me fro!* * from
Thy mede is marked, when thou art mort,
In blysse; *Quia amore langueo.*

The King's Mother

O all ye that pass by the way, attend, and see if there be any sorrow like to my sorrow!

MATER DOLOROSA

THE KING'S MOTHER

The first Prelude is to call to mind how "there stood by the Cross of Jesus His Mother and His Mothers's sister, Mary of Cleophas, and Mary Magdalene;" and how after He had expired, Christ was taken down from the Cross by Joseph and Nicodemus, in the presence of His sorrowful Mother.

The second Prelude is to see with the eyes of the imagination Calvary and the Cross on the top of it.

The third Prelude is to ask sorrow with Mary, full of sorrow, anguish with Mary in anguish, tears and interior pain for the great pain that my Mother has suffered for me.

1. Our Love for the Sorrowful Mother

One of the characteristic features of Christianity—the characteristic which distinguishes it from all pagan religions—is the worship of sorrow.

The God we worship is a crucified God.

The Cross is our distinctive mark. It adorns our churches and our altars, even on the most solemn days. With it we sign ourselves so often during the day.

The Mass—the most solemn act of our religion—is the renewal of the awful sacrifice of Calvary.

Of all the members of Christ's mystical body we chiefly honour those who have shed their blood for Christ, the Martyrs; those who are most similar to Christ, who suffer and are poor. We know that there is but one road to Heaven, the road of the Cross. Hence it is that though we love to honour Mary in so many ways, and address her under so many titles, we feel specially attracted to her as she stands at the foot of the Cross.

2. Sufferings of Mary during Jesus' Life

Tota vita Mariae Crux fuit et Martyrium.

At the Annunciation Jesus entered into her life and with Jesus the Cross. The words of the Angel did not open to her the vision of a shining path strewn with roses, but a long road, ending with a Cross and followed by years of solitude *without Jesus.*

Simeon removed all doubt of it. Daily would the sword pierce deeper and deeper still into her heart. The flight into Egypt and the massacre of the Innocents would tell her what the Jews would do one day to her Son.

Hence her desolation when she lost Jesus, and the agony of her heart when Jesus left her to begin His public life. Hence her anxieties and motherly fears during those three years.

3. Sufferings of Mary during the Passion

But it was during our Lord's Passion that the sufferings of Mary became most heartrending.

We know how much the Saints felt the Passion of Christ. St Francis of Assisi would shed bitter tears at the thought of it. St Philip Neri could not even mention the word *Passion* without a pang. St Margaret Mary, during Holy Week especially, was in a constant agony of pain. The pain of these Saints was measured by their knowledge and love of Christ, and by their realization of Christ's sufferings. But what if they had been present at the Passion of their Lord? What if their knowledge and love, instead of being a little rivulet, had been an ocean?

Mary's love for Jesus is as boundless as the ocean. She loves Him as her Son, as her only Son, as her Benefactor, as her Saviour, and as her God. She has a clear perception of everyone of His sufferings. She penetrates deeply into His Heart—that infinite abyss of love and sorrow. By reason of her intimate union with Christ, all His sufferings find an echo in her heart, like the mother of the Machabees who, *quia amabat omnes, omnia ferebat in oculis quod in carne omnes.* And she has a clear perception of the indignity and the injustice of the treatment meted out to Christ. More painful still, she knows that for many the sufferings of Jesus will prove useless and but a cause of condemnation.

4. Jesus in Mary's Arms

At last the sacrifice is consummated and Jesus is laid down from the Cross and placed in the arms of His Mother.

Quis non posset contristari
Christi Matrem contemplari
Dolentem cum Filio?

She receives Him devoutly as she was accustomed to do when He was a little Child; but what a difference! She examines, one by one, the wounds of that precious Body and at the sight of each of them the sword pierces her immaculate heart anew. And raising her eyes, brimming not with tears but with infinite grief, she seems to tell us: "O all ye that pass by the way, attend, and see if there be any sorrow like to my sorrow."

No, O Virgin Mother, there is no grief like unto your grief. The death of God could be wept worthily only by God. However, God the Father being incapable of any suffering, not to let the death of His Son pass unwept, increased in your heart its capacity for suffering in a way we shall never understand, and poured into it all the grief that a pure creature could endure.

To end by asking my heavenly Mother to pour into my hard and pitiless heart a drop of that sea of grief that filled her maternal heart, that with her I may weep and grieve for my Crucified Master. Only thus may I hope to share in the glory of His Resurrection. *Si compatimur et conglorificemur.*

Juxta Crucem tecum stare,
Et me tibi sociare
In planctu desidero.

BEHOLD THY MOTHER!

Why was I crowned and made a Queen?
Why was I called of Mercy the well?
Why should an earthly woman been
So high in Heaven above Angel?
For thee, mankind, the truth I tell;
Thou ask me help and I shall do
That I was ordained, keep thee from Hell,
Quia amore langueo.

The Secret of the King

Behold this Heart which has loved men so much and which receives in return for the most part nothing but ingratitude, contempt, irreverence, and sacrilege!

THE SACRED HEART

THE SECRET OF THE KING

The first Prelude is to call to mind how one of the soldiers opened with a spear Christ's side, and immediatedly there came out blood and water; and the words of our Lord to St Margaret Mary: "Behold this Heart that has loved men so much and in return I receive from the greatest part only ingratitude."

The second Prelude is to see, with the eyes of the imagination, Mount Calvary.

The third Prelude is to ask light to know the infinite love of the Sacred Heart of our Lord and grace to love Him and to atone for my ingratitude and the ingratitude of others.

PART ONE

THE LOVE OF THE SACRED HEART

1. God's Love is Incomprehensible

There are two things which the human mind finds difficult to grasp: God's love for man and man's ingratitude towards God.

We may well conceive God as a solitary Being, happy in His own existence. But that He should lower Himself to think of abject persons like ourselves, to give us life, and carefully watch over us; that He should love us like a Father and even raise us to share His own life; that He should become like one of us, and for us die an ignominious death on the Cross, is something that altogether surpasses, our notion of what an infinite Being ought to be.

No wonder, therefore, if Christianity which teaches that God is our loving Father, that He became man and died for the salvation of the world, has appeared to many either a scandal or sheer madness. "We preach Christ crucified, to the Jews a stumbling-block, and to the Gentiles, foolishness."[1]

2. Difficulty of Believing God's Love

It is just the difficulty of believing this infinite condescension of God that constitutes the greatest stumbling-block to many generous

1. I Cor. i, 25.

souls of our day. They feel that the beauty, the virtues, and the life of Christ are above anything they have seen around them, or read of in history. But is He God? Could a truly Divine Person demean Himself for the love of men as Christ has done? Can the Child that is born in a stable, the Boy that sweats in a carpenter's shop, the Master that goes about with no place where to lay His head, the Man that dies a shamefull death cursed by the very people He has come to save—can He possibly be the Eternal, the All-wise, the All-powerful God? *Quomodo possunt haec fieri?* "How is this possible at all?" such doubting souls keep asking, and with them we who believe these mysteries and yet are staggered by the infinite love they imply, and sometimes even thrown on a stormy sea of doubts and uncertainties.

3. The Revelation of the Sacred Heart

The revelation of the Sacred Heart offers us the key to the mystery of God's condescension.

The revelation was first made on Calvary.

"But one of the soldiers with a spear opened His side, and immediately there came out blood and water. And he that saw it hath given testimony: and his testimony is true."[1]

For centuries souls had taken refuge in the open side of Jesus. Through it they had reached the Heart, and there they had been purified, sheltered and strengthened. They had been inflamed and transformed into the image of their Lord. But the devotion to the Sacred Heart had remained the privilege of a few chosen souls, till the moment came when God decreed to complete the revelation which He had already made on Calvary.

During the octave of Corpus Christi, in the year 1675, St Margaret Mary Alacoque, a nun of the Visitation Order of Paray-le-Monial, was kneeling before the Blessed Sacrament in humble and fervent adoration, when our Lord appeared to her, and disclosing His Heart, said: "Behold this Heart which has loved men so much!"

1. John xix, 34, 35.

4. Behold this Heart!

The veil is drawn aside to allow us a glimpse of God's inner chamber and to grasp the secret of His counsel.

"Behold this Heart!"

You marvel at God's mercy covering the whole earth like a boundless ocean. Behold its eternal and unfathomable spring! You wonder at His tenderness, penetrating with His Divine light the darkest corners of man's soul. Behold the sun that scatters its rays in all directions, "that enlighteneth every man that cometh into this world," "the Light that shineth in darkness and the darkness doth not comprehend it." You are astonished at God's love for even the most ungrateful sinner. Behold the ever burning-furnace of love, where sin is burned away and the little good there is in us is turned into gold of unparalleled beauty.

"Behold this Heart!"

The Apostle St John had already revealed to us that God is love. He had already directed us to look to God's love for the explanation of all the mysteries of our Faith. "And we have come to know and have believed the love which God hath in us."[1]

By showing us His Heart, Christ makes the revelation more clear and appealing. He materializes it, so to speak, through an organ that stands as the symbol and instrument of love.

"Behold this Heart!"—the Heart that has loved men so much! It may be difficult to accept this great fact—God's love for men—but once that is accepted everything else is explained.

5. Love's Marvellous Effects

We all know something of what human love can do: the love of a faithful wife, of a devoted father, of an affectionate child. If God is love, surely He will be driven by it to do things which to us, poor and ignorant beings, must look incomprehensible, if not foolish. A lover has but one desire: to give himself, to sacrifice himself, and to make the gift and the sacrifice of himself, if possible, eternal. God has fulfilled this law of love. He has given Himself in Bethlehem,

1. John iv, 16.

He has sacrificed Himself on Calvary, and He has made His gift and His sacrifice eternal on the Altar.

Why has God created the world? Why does He take care of the least of us? Why has He become man? Why does He die on the Cross? Why does He give His Body as our food, and His Blood as our drink? Because He has loved us. Because He loves us. Because He is Love.

"Behold this Heart!"

6. "We have Believed the Love which God Hath in Us"

When doubts and uncertainties occur to us, when, specially, crosses and tribulations fall upon us and we are inclined to lose faith and confidence, let us raise our eyes to the Divine Heart, listen to those words, "Behold the Heart!" and repeat with St John: "we have believed the charity which God hath in us."

We believe in the love of God. We believe that His plan is one of love, and that if sometimes He comes to us to lessen our joy, it is but on an errand of love. He wants to remove from us a few toys to give us gems of infinite price. He wants to gather the objects of our love near His Heart where, guarded by His love, we may find them one day, and be eternally happy with them.

PART TWO

MAN'S INGRATITUDE

1. God truly Feels our Ingratitude

Man's ingratitude towards God is the other point which our mind finds difficult to grasp.

We know, alas, that we frequently sin and that by sinning we rebel against God's Will and abuse His loving gifts. However, we find it hard to realize that sin is an act of ingratitude against God; still more, that God should be displeased with it, and feel something similar to what we feel when we are betrayed by a friend. We needed the Divine Heart to reveal it to us.

"Behold this Heart which has loved men so much and which receives in return for the most part nothing but ingratitude, contempt, irreverence, and sacrilege. I feel their ingratitude more than anything I felt in My Passion."

We thought that God had no heart like ours. At best we behaved towards Him and His wishes as we do towards a code of law. If we had treated the least of our friends, or even a simple acquaintance, as we have often treated Christ, we would never have forgiven ourselves. And still we went on without feelings of remorse, without desire to atone for our ingratitude. And yet we find it so difficult to forgive others even an imaginary offence, and we force our debtors to pay us back to the last farthing.

We thought God had no heart, that He would not feel man's ingratitude, while in reality He feels it infinitely more than anything He felt in His Passion.

2. Reparation and Atonement

Who will deliberately grieve the Sacred Heart any longer? Who will not try to atone for his past ingratitude and malice? And not only for his ingratitude and malice, but for that of others also.

Yes, it may seem strange that we who are so full of sins and who have a heavy debt to pay, should undertake to atone even for the sins of others.

Jesus demands it of us; He begs it.

Devotion to the Sacred Heart is a devotion of reparation and of atonement.

The Christian truly devoted to the Sacred Heart, sees our Lord so much neglected and despised, especially in the Blessed Sacrament, and is inflamed with a burning desire to do all he can to atone, to show that if many care not for Him, there are souls that love Him passionately.

3. Behold This Heart!

Let us behold the Heart of Christ when tempted to doubt about God's secret counsels and the dispositions of His Providence.

Let us behold that Heart when the idea of the infinite malice and ingratitude of sin tends to fade from our mind.

Let us behold that Heart so full of love, tenderness, and mercy for us, when we are drawn to sin.

Surely the dagger we may be about to plunge into that Heart will unconsciously fall from our hand, and our hearts will ever more throb with love for this infinitely loving God, and with sorrow for our great ingratitude and for the ingratitude of our fellowmen.

To end with a Colloquy to our Lord begging Him to reveal to me more and more the infinite love and the unsearchable riches of His Heart, that trusting in Him in all things and above all things, I may for ever abide therein.

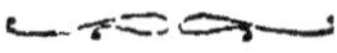

THE SAVIOUR'S LOVE

Man

Sweetest Saviour, if my soul
Were but worth the having,
Quickly should I then control
Any thought of waving.
But when all my cares and pains
Cannot give the name of gains
To Thy wretch so full of stains,
What delight or hope remains?

Saviour

What, child, is the balance thine,
Thine the poise and measure?
If I say, "Thou shalt be Mine,"
Finger not My treasure.
What the gains in having thee
Do amount to, onely He
Who for man was sold can see;
That transferr'd th' accounts to Me.

Man

But as I can see no merit
  Leading to this favour,
So the way to fit me for it
  Is beyond my savour.* *understanding
As the reason, then, is Thine,
So the way is none of mine:
I disclaim the whole designe;
Sinne disclaims and I resigne.

Saviour

That is all:—if that I could
  Get without repining;
And My clay, My creature, would
  Follow My resigning;
That as I did freely part
With My glory and desert,
Left all joys to feel all smart—.

Man

Ah, no more: Thou break'st my heart.

George Herbert.

The King in Glory

He is risen

THE RESURRECTION

THE KING IN GLORY

The first Prelude is to call to mind how, after expiring on the Cross, Christ our Lord descended into Hell to release the souls of the Just and then, coming to the Sepulchre, He rose from the dead and appeared to His Mother.

The second is to see the arrangement of the holy Sepulchre, and the place or house of our Lady, beholding its parts in particular, and likewise her chamber oratory, etc.

The third is to ask for grace to feel intense joy and gladness for the great glory and joy of Christ our Lord.

1. "He Descended into Hell"

It is a point of Catholic doctrine, handed down by Tradition, that the Soul of our Lord, on being separated from the Body, went into the hidden abode where the souls of the Just were detained—the bosom of Abraham, as our Lord Himself calls it.

No one was admitted to the beatific vision before our Lord's Passion. Though the souls in Limbo were purified from original and actual sin and had paid the debt of punishment due to the latter, they were not exempted, from the penalty of original sin, excluding them from the vision of God so long as the Redemption had not been accomplished. Something similar happens now when, though through Baptism we are set free from the guilt of original sin and of actual sins, and are no longer excluded from eternal glory, we have still to undergo the penalty of death.[1]

As He enters into Limbo, Christ sheds His light upon the souls that have so long waited for the day of their complete deliverance, and fills them with inconceivable joy. He is the victorious and triumphant King that acknowledges the merits of His faithful soldiers and liberally rewards them.

All who have passed away in God's grace, the Patriarchs, the Prophets, St Joachim, St Anne, St Zacharias, St Elizabeth, St Joseph and St John gather around Him—shortly after, the Good Thief

1. Cf. *Summa*, III, Q. 32, a. 5, ad 2.

too makes his appearance. The Saviour imparts to them the essential happiness of Heaven which consists in the vision of God, and thereby turns that lower region into Paradise. "Amen I say to thee, this day thou shalt be with Me in Paradise."[1] At the same time Christ asserts His supreme power over Hell. "At the name of Jesus every knee should bend in Heaven, on earth, and under the earth."[2] Satan and his satellites are made to understand that a stronger One than they has come to undermine the foundations of their kingdom.

2. "The Lord hath risen indeed"

Accompanied by myriads of Angels and by the souls which He has made partakers of His glory, Christ goes to the Sepulchre. First of all, He shows them His sacred Body and the marks of the terrible sufferings which He endured, and then, Soul and Body once more reunited, He stands before them in His glorified Humanity. The wounds in His hands and feet are shining stars; that of the side, a dazzling sun. His head is crowned with glory and honour, and His Heart throbs with unspeakable joy. "According to the multitude of my sorrows in my heart, Thy comforts have given joy to my soul."[3]

The first movement of His Heart is to burst forth in a hymn of love and praise to His Father for granting to Him the glory which He asked for in His prayer at the Last Supper. A voice is heard clearer than that which resounded on the banks of the Jordan and on the mountain of the Transfiguration: "Thou art My Son; this day have I begotten Thee."[4] No more poor and despised as one day in the stable of Bethlehem, but full of majesty and of glory; no more destined to lead a life of suffering and neglect, but to rule over all the nations. "Ask of Me and I shall give Thee the heathen for Thine inheritance, and the uttermost parts of the earth for Thy possession."[5] "And again, when He bringeth the First Born into the world, He saith: Let all the Angels of God worship Him."[6] The angelic choirs crowd around the risen Saviour, happy to render Him the homage which they did not refuse Him when Satan raised in Heaven the standard of rebellion. With the Angels the blessed Souls praise and adore their Liberator.

1. Luke xxiii, 43. 2. Phil. ii, 10. 3. Ps. xciii, 13. 4. Ps. ii, 7.
5. Ps. ii, 8. 6. Heb. i, 6

3. "This is the Day which the Lord hath Made: let us Rejoice and be Glad therein"

The love that caused us to grieve and suffer with Christ in His griefs and sufferings, should now prompt us to rejoice with Him in His joy, and to exult with Him in His glory. Does not a child delight in the happiness of his father, and does not a friend rejoice in the glory of his friend? Christ is our Father and our Friend. Though we are still in this vale of tears, weighed down by suffering and anguish, let us raise our eyes to Christ, and the sight of Him happy and glorious will fill our hearts with joy. On Holy Saturday, remembering the triumph of her Bridegroom, holy Church seems to fall in an ecstasy of love and joy.

"Let now the heavenly hosts of Angels rejoice: let the Divine mysteries be joyfully celebrated; and let a sacred trumpet proclaim the victory of so great a King. Let the earth also be filled with joy, being illuminated with such resplendent rays: and let it realize that the darkness, which overspread the whole world, is chased away by the splendour of our Eternal King. Let our Mother the Church also be glad, finding herself adorned with the rays of so great a light.... This is the Night, which now, all over the world, delivers those that believe in Christ from the vices of the world and the darkness of sin, restores them to grace and clothes them with sanctity. This is the Night in which Christ broke the chains of death and ascended conqueror from Hell... O! how admirable is Thy goodness towards us! O! how inestimable is Thy love. Thou hast delivered up Thy Son to redeem a slave...."

Such must be our feelings while looking on the risen Lord.

4. Jesus Appears to Mary

After His Father, Mary is first in Jesus' thoughts. Deep in grief, the Virgin has passed the night in prayer, waiting, with unshaken faith, for the Resurrection of her Son, when, suddenly her chamber becomes luminous with heavenly light and Jesus stands before her.

"O Mother!" "O my Son!", they cry out, and they are in each other's arms. No other words are spoken. They see each other's soul and read there thoughts and feelings which no human language can express. Our Lord feels happy in pouring abundantly into the soul of Mary that joy with which His Heart is overflowing, and Mary, like a true Mother, forgets herself and wholly rejoices in the joy and glory of her Son. All the while the choirs of Angels and the souls of the Just keep singing: *Regina Coeli laetare, Alleluia.*

"Oh that I had been there, and heard, O Jesus, Thy sweet words; that I had secretly stood near the window, and listened attentively, unseen by the eye of man, to every word which fell from the lips of my Lord Jesus Christ as He talked with His Mother about the joys of the citizens of Heaven. With what intense gladness would my heart have rejoiced in the Lord, could I, for my comfort in my earthly pilgrimage, so full of dangers as it is, have remembered even one or two words of that sacred converse! But perchance what passed was what man may not utter, which ought to be kept secret, which ought to be meditated upon in the joyous music of the heart alone. Blessed is he who knows that music, who by meditation rises above all earthly things, who is busy all day with Jesus and Mary, and neither cares nor thinks about what is going on in the world."[1]

O my Jesus give me grace to be intensely glad and to rejoice in your great glory and Your great joy! O that I may see how Your Divinity which, during Your Passion, seemed to hide Itself, now appears in Your most holy Resurrection, and now most miraculously shows Itself by Its true and most holy effects.

O my Jesus, give me to realize the tender office of Comforter which You exercise with Your friends—You the best and the most loving of friends!

O Jesus, fill my heart with joy and cheerfulness! make everything help me to rejoice in You, my Creator and Lord!

1. Kempis.

THE SIGNIFICANCE OF THE RESURRECTION

1. Christ's Reward

The Resurrection is the reward which God the Father bestows on Christ for the sufferings and humiliations of His Passion and Death.

"He humbled Himself by obedience unto death, yea unto death upon a cross. Wherefore God hath exalted Him, above the highest and hath bestowed on Him the name which is above every name, that at the name of Jesus every knee should bend in Heaven, on earth and under the earth ; and that every tongue should confess that Jesus Christ is Lord to the glory of God the Father."[1]

The Resurrection is the glorification of our Divine King. The King Who was born in poverty and humiliation at Bethlehem, Who lived in concealment and subjection at Nazareth, Who was despised and rejected by His people, Who was crowned with thorns and nailed to the Cross has become the Conqueror of death and Hell—the King of Kings, and the Lord of Lords.

"I am the First and the Last, and He who liveth ; I died, and behold, I am living for ever and ever ; and have the keys of death and of Hell."[2]

"Christ raised from the dead, dieth no more ; death no more hath power over Him. His death He died to sin, once and for all ; His life He liveth to God."[3]

2. The most solid Ground of our Faith

Often, during His public life, had our Lord told His disciples that He would suffer all indignities, and even death itself, at the hands of the Jews and of the Roman heathen, always, however, adding that the third day He would rise again. When challenged by His enemies to justify His extraordinary claims by working some feat in the heavens, He that could leave unheard no prayer for help, simply referred them to His Death and to the miracle of His

1. Phil. ii, 8-11. 2. Ap. i, 17, 18. 3. Rom. vi, 9, 10.

Resurrection. All were aware of such a prophecy, as appears from the request of the high priests to have guards at the Sepulchre. The Resurrection, then, is the test by which the claims of Christ are to stand or fall. And they do stand unshaken, for on the third day, Christ truly rose from the dead.

The Resurrection is, indeed, an indisputable fact. Its historicity does not depend exclusively on the Gospels, since it was accepted long before any of the Gospels had seen the light. The preaching of the Apostles, and specially of St Paul, such as is preserved for us in the Acts, is based on it. The three thousand Jews that embraced Christianity on Pentecost Day—barely fifty-two days after the Death of Christ—and the crowds that soon followed their example, were converted by the well-established belief that Christ had risen from the dead. Had the fact of the Resurrection not been solidly proved, the conversion of these first Jews, in Jerusalem itself, in the vicinity of Calvary where Christ had just died a blasphemer's death, and of the grave where His body should have been rottening, with the fear of imprisonment and even of death, would indeed be a mystery.

The Apostles, all along, professed themselves to be the witnesses of the Resurrection. They were conscious they had frequently seen the risen Christ, that they had conversed with Him, that they had touched Him, eaten and drunk with Him. The truth of the Resurrection is the central point of their preaching. When they are ordered not to speak about it, they simply answer: "We cannot but speak the things which we have heard." And when imprisoned and threatened again, they boldly answer: "The God of our Fathers hath raised up Jesus, Whom you put to death.... And we are witnesses of these things."

Barely twenty-five years after the event, St Paul writes about it to the Corinthians and gives the authority of many who had seen the Lord and were still alive.

All the Evangelists attest the Resurrection. They affirm that the tomb was found empty—unmistakably a fact which constitutes the simple test of the reality of the Resurrection and of the true belief in it. Christ's enemies themselves affirmed it and vainly tried to explain it away. The apparent discrepancies as to unimportant details, which we notice in the account which the Gospels give of our Lord's apparitions, seem to have been left providentially to prove that we are not in the presence of four versions of a concocted fact. The Resurrection of Christ is a true fact of history. But, then, if Christ be risen from the dead, His claims are true. He is God, and His teaching, His promises, the institutions are the teaching, the promises, the institutions of God Himself. There is but one thing for us to do—to fall down and adore Him.

3. An Earnest of our Resurrection

The Resurrection is not only the glorification of our King, but also of the whole of mankind. Christ enters into His Kingdom as the Leader of the army of God, to prepare a place for all who follow Him. He has scaled the battlements of the City of God, and from there He cheers on those who are still fighting in the plains below.

Still more. Christ takes possession of His glory as the Head of the mystical body of which we are the members. He has come on earth that we may be incorporated into Him, and be one with Him. Accordingly, He has associated us in His Death and in His triumphs as well. We die with Him to sin, to the old man—"We are buried therefore with Him"[1]—and forthwith we rise with Him to a new life. "Now if we have died with Christ, we believe that we shall also live with Him."[2] Christ's Death is our death to sin, and Christ's Resurrection is our resurrection to newness of life. Nay, God "raised us up and seated us together in Christ Jesus in the heavenly places."[3] This life is but a waiting for our future and complete resurrection. We daily wait for the day when our hearts will be eternally fixed on God, and for the day when our bodies will be vested with immortality. The seed of immortality and glory is already in us. It has but to grow under the influence of God's Sanctifying Spirit.

"Whereas our country is in the Heavens, whence we eagerly await as Saviour the Lord Jesus Christ, Who will transform the body of our lowliness, that it may be one with the body of His glory, by the force of that power whereby He is able to subject all things to Himself."[4]

1. Rom. vi, 4. 2. Rom. vi, 8. 3. Eph. ii, 6. 4. Phil. iii, 20, 21.

4. The Seal to Christ's Work and the Beginning of our Sanctification

By raising Christ to life, God the Father shows that He accepts the Sacrifice which the Son has offered on our behalf, and puts His seal on His redeeming work. Looking on our risen Lord standing at the right hand of the Father as a glorified Victim ever interceding for us, we know that we are no more children of wrath but sons of God, "and if children, heirs also: heirs of God, and joint-heirs with Christ."[1]

Once risen, Christ begins to apply His redeeming virtue to each individual soul.

"Christ's work of mercy," writes Card. Newman, "has two chief parts; what He did for all men, what He does for each; what He did once for all, what He does for one by one continually; what He did externally to us, what He does within us; what He did on earth, what He does in Heaven; what He did in His own person, what He does by His Spirit; His death, and the water and the blood after it; His meritorious sufferings and the various gifts thereby purchased of pardon, grace, reconciliation, renewal, holiness, spiritual communion; that is, His Atonement and our justification; He atones by the offering of Himself on the Cross, and... He justifies by the mission of His Spirit."[2]

Before the Resurrection Christ had undoubtedly the Spirit in the fullest measure. However, the Spirit dwelling in Him could not exert all His vivifying power. "He that believeth in Me, as the Scripture saith, out of his belly shall flow rivers of living water. Now this He said of the Spirit which they should receive who believed in Him: for as yet the Spirit was not given, because Jesus was not yet glorified."[3] Christ could not communicate to others the fullness of life, "But I tell you the truth: it is expedient to you that I go: for if I go not, the Paraclete will not come to you, but if I go, I will send Him to you."[4] It is when glorified that our Lord becomes for us an ever-flowing spring of grace and of life.

That is why His Resurrection is the cardinal point of Christian belief and of Christian life.

1. Rom. viii, 17.
2. Cardinal Newman, *Lectures on Justification*, ix, p. 24.
3. John vii, 38, 39.
4. John xvi, 7.

NOTES

1. The Order of events in the Resurrection

1) The Resurrection, the earthquake, the appearance of the Angel and the rolling of the stone.

2) The holy women go to the Sepulchre and enter it.

3) Mary Magdalene, under the impression that the Body has been stolen, leaves the Sepulchre and the other women, and runs to Peter and John.

4) The other women remain at the Sepulchre, and two Angels appear to them.

5) They leave the Sepulchre, and Jesus appears to them.

6) Meanwhile Peter and John go to the Sepulchre.

7) Mary, who had followed them, stands at the Sepulchre and weeps. Jesus appears to her.

2. Apparitions of our Lord

ON THE FIRST DAY

1) To the Women returning from the Sepulchre.

2) To Mary Magdalene at the Sepulchre.

3) To Peter.

4) To the two disciples going to Emmaus.

5) To the Apostles except Thomas.

ON THE OCATVE

To the Apostles and Thomas.

LATER ON

1) To seven Apostles on the Lake.

2) To the Eleven and five hundred disciples on a mountain of Galilee.

3) To James.

4) To the Eleven at Jerusalem, before the Ascension.

The Divine Consoler

And behold Jesus met them, saying, "All hail!"

But they came up, and took hold of His feet, and adored Him.

Then Jesus said to them: "Fear not, Go tell My brethren that they go into Galilee; there they shall see Me."

CHRIST APPEARS TO THE HOLY WOMEN

THE DIVINE CONSOLER

The first Prelude is to call to mind how the Women who had gone to the Sepulchre to anoint Jesus, saw, first, two Angels who announced to them the Resurrection, and, then, the Lord Himself.

The second Prelude is to see with the eyes of the imagination the road that leads from the city to the Sepulchre, and the Sepulchre itself.

The third Prelude is to ask light to know intimately the office of Consoler which Christ our Lord exercises with His friends and grace to rejoice at Hfs joy and glory.

1. On the Way to the Sepulchre

Though the Women who attended on Jesus, namely, Mary Magdalene, Mary the mother of James, Joanna, Salome and others, hardly think that He will soon rise to immortal life, they cling lovingly to Him in spite of the appalling tragedy of Calvary. Accordingly, their first thought, before the Sabbath rest begins, is to prepare spices and ointments to complete and perfect the work of Nicodemus and Joseph. In obedience to the Law, they rest on the Sabbath. But no sooner is this over than they rise and set out for the Sepulchre, undaunted by the dangers of the early hour and little thinking, at first, of the difficulties they may encounter. Truly "love feels no burden, thinks nothing of trouble, attempts what is above its strength, pleads no excuse of impossibility; for it thinks all lawful for itself and all things possible. It is therefore able to undertake all things, and it completes many things, and warrants them to take effect, where he who does not love, would faint and lie down."[1] And when, on the way to the Sepulchre, the difficulty of rolling away the heavy stone from the door of the Sepulchre first presents itself to these holy Women, they are not frightened by the apparent impossibility, but they proceed, sure that God will provide. They teach us to go on blindly and confidently along the way traced for us by Divine Providence in spite of difficulties. If we just keep straight on, they are solved for us at the critical moment by God's power.

1. *Imitation of Christ* iii, 5.

2. At the Sepulchre: a Vision of Angels

On arriving at the Sepulchre, the Women find the stone rolled away from it. The Lord has risen. Unaware of what has actually taken place, they are amazed. They enter the tomb and are greatly perplexed at not finding the Body of the Lord Jesus. The impulsive Magdalene can see but one thing: the Body of the Lord has been taken away. She immediately runs to the City to tell Peter and John about it, leaving her companions at the Sepulchre.

Soon after there appear to them two Angels in white garments. Full of fear the Women bow their faces to the earth. "Fear you not," said the Angels. "Ye seek Jesus of Nazareth, Who was crucified. He is risen, He is not here. Behold the place where they laid Him! But go, tell His disciples and Peter that He goeth before you into Galilee: there ye shall see Him, as He told you."[1]

The episode reveals to us the office of the Angels: they remind us of the words of our Lord, and they prepare us to understand His teaching and to receive His visit. They reprove us: "Why seek ye the living amongst the dead?" They are the first messengers of the Resurrection, as one of them was of the Incarnation. In the very act of announcing the triumph of Christ, they call Him "Jesus of Nazareth Who was crucified"—i. e., the Crucified One. And rightly so: it is Christ's supreme title to His glory and to our love.

"And they departed quickly from the Sepulchre with fear and great joy."[2]

How great is the simplicity and trust of these holy Women! Though, probably, they have never entertained a thought about the possibility of the Resurrection, they promptly believe the word of the Angels, and thereby make themselves worthy of a visit from Jesus Himself. Faith in His accredited messengers must ordinarily precede the vision of the Lord.

3. On the way to the City: the Appearance of Christ

"And, as they went to tell His disciples, behold, Jesus met them, saying, All hail. And they came and held Him by the feet

1. Mark xxi, 6, 7. 2. Matt. xxviii, 8.

and worshipped Him. Then said Jesus unto them: Be not afraid: go tell My brethren that they go into Galilee, and there shall they see Me."

The Divine King considers only what is good in the conduct of these Women. He remembers their love in the days of His public ministry, their sorrow during His Passion, and now their anxiety to embalm His Body. Not content with sending His Angels to announce to them His Resurrection, He Himself comes to meet them and allows them to kiss His holy feet. Now, as in His mortal life, His only desire is to show in eloquent deeds His merciful goodness and His infinite amiability. Could there be anything more loving and touching than the message which He sends to His disciples, whom He tenderly calls His brethren?

To end the contemplation by prostrating myself to the ground, and holding His sacred feet, lovingly worship our triumphant King. *Ave Rex noster!*

EASTER SONG

I got me flowers to straw Thy way,
I got me boughs off many a tree;
But Thou wast up by break of day,
And brought'st Thy sweets along with Thee.

The sunne arising in the East,
Though he give light, and th'East perfume,
If they should offer to contest
With Thy arising, they presume.

Can there be any day but this,
Though many sunnes to shine endeavour?
We count three hundred, but we misse:
There is but one, and that one ever.

George Herbert.

The Comforter of Sorrowful Hearts

Jesus saith to her: "Do not touch Me for I am not yet ascended to My Father: but go to My brethren, and say to them: I ascend to My Father and to your Father, to My God and your God."

CHRIST APPEARS TO MARY MAGDALENE AND TO PETER

THE COMFORTER OF SORROWFUL HEARTS

The first Prelude is to call to mind how our Lord appeared to Mary Magdalene and to Peter.

The second Prelude is to see with the eyes of the imagination the Sepulchre, the garden where the Sepulchre stood, and the dwelling of the Apostle Peter.

The third Prelude is to ask light to know intimately the office of Consoler which Christ our Lord exercises with His friends, and grace to feel intense joy and gladness for His great glory and joy.

PART ONE

CHRIST APPEARS TO MARY MAGDALENE

1. Mary Magdalene's Love

Mary Magdalene is a type of a soul that has fallen in love with Jesus. Though she hopes not to see Him again, her whole being is wrapped up in Him. She can only think and speak of Jesus: everything else has no existence for her. She has but one anxiety: what has become of the Body of her Master. She has but one fear: that it may be subjected to new ignominies.

Christ alone can console her and allay the anguish of her soul. She cares little for the Angels: they neither astonish nor frighten her, as they did the other women. She curtly answers their question, and immediately turns away without asking for further information. She sticks to her first idea, that which she has announced to the Apostles: "They have taken away the Lord from out of the Sepulchre, and we know not where they have laid Him." She is blind to everything else. Christ Himself appears to her, and yet she fails to recognize Him. He is the very last living person she expects to see, and her eyes are too dimmed with passionate tears to see the Face she loves so much. And thinking Him to be the man in charge of the place, she speaks words that only reveal the excess of her love.

"Sir, if you have taken Him hence, tell me where you have laid Him, and I will go and take Him away."

She addresses the gardener respectfully and yet she charges him with a crime. She merely alludes to the object of her love, as if the whole world knew about it, and she offers herself to do what was clearly beyond her strength. Truly the lover, and most of all the lover of God, is often beside himself.

2. "Mary!"

How infinitely good is our Divine Saviour! He appears to this poor woman out of whom He had expelled seven devils. He does not look at her past, nor at her lack of faith in His Resurrection. He only sees her love and her loyalty to Him.

One word is enough to recall Mary to the sense of the Reality before her, and to fill her heart with unspeakable joy—"Mary." It is the call of the Divine King—by each one's name.

And what a change does that simple word effect! Mary is in Heaven. How truly "if Jesus speaks but one word, we feel great consolation."[1] Mary throws herself at the feet of the Master—those feet so dear to her—and she clings passionately to them, afraid that Jesus may once more vanish from her.

"Cease touching Me," says the Master at last. "You will have other occasions to kiss My feet."

And, then, what a message to His Apostles!

"Go to My brethren and say to them: I go up to My Father and to your Father; to My God and to your God."

Such is the message He conveys to His cowardly and unfaithful Apostles, who deserted Him in the hour of danger, and even now are full of fear, despondency and unbelief.

Truly our Lord is all Love and Mercy.

PART TWO

CHRIST APPEARS TO PETER

1. Peter and John at the Sepulchre

At the voice of Mary Magdalene, Peter and John at once rush to the Sepulchre. Within the empty Sepulchre they find

1. *Imitation of Christ* ii, 8.

not the least trace of violence: the linen cloths in which the Body of the Master was wrapped, are there undisturbed, and the napkin that was about His head, lies folded apart. The Body, therefore, has not been stolen. At last the eyes of the two Apostles are opened: they believe that their Master has risen from the dead. They both return to their home, full of joy. It is just while Peter ponders in his heart over what has come to pass that Christ appears to him.

2. "Peace be to Thee!"

What a meeting this must have been, following as it did so closely on the other meeting, on Thursday night, in the palace of the high priest! Then, from the midst of His tormentors, Jesus had thrown a glance of infinite pity and compassionate love on the erring Apostle. Now, in the fulness of His glory, He comes to console him. The answer of the Apostle to that look of his Master had been a flood of tears that would never cease flowing. Now, again with tear-filled eyes, he throws himself at the feet of Jesus. He can utter no word. His heart is filled with shame, sweetened by love and confidence in Christ. To have denied Love—the Love that had chosen him, that had showered all gifts on him, that had forgiven him, and that now had come to him!

"Peace be to thee!" Jesus salutes Peter with the greeting He will address to the other Apostles this very day. No word of reproach; no remembrance of past guilt. The Saviour's only desire is that Peter understand the infinite love and mercy of His Heart, so that henceforth he may make it known to all men and none may despair, so that he may wholly distrust himself and place his confidence in Jesus alone.

3. "The Lord is risen indeed, and hath appeared to Simon"

The Lord has appeared to Simon—not to John who followed Him closely during the Passion, and stood with Mary at the foot of the Cross. And even today Christ is willing to reveal Himself to every strayed soul that seeks Him with contrition, with love, with confidence. The humble repentant and loving Apostle should be our model, as he is the rock on which we all, as members of the Church, are built.

A Colloquy of love and confidence at the feet of the risen King.

ON A DARK NIGHT

In a dark night,
With anxious love inflamed,
O, happy lot!
Forth unobserved I went,
My house being now at rest.

In darkness and in safety,
By the secret ladder, disguised,
O, happy lot!
In darkness and concealment,
My house being now at rest.

In that happy night,
In secret, seen of none,
Seeing nought myself,
Without other light or guide
Save that which in my heart was burning.

That light guided me
Most surely than the noonday sun
To the place were He was waiting for me,
Whom I knew well,
And where none appeared.

O, guiding night;
O, night more lovely than the dawn;
O, night that hast united
The lover with His beloved,
And changed her into her love.

On my flowery bosom,
Kept whole for Him alone,
There He reposed and slept;
And I caressed Him, and the waving
Of the cedars fanned Him.

As His hair floated in the breeze
That blew from the turret,
He struck me on the neck
With His gentle hand,
And all sensation left me,

I continued in oblivion lost,
My head was resting on my love;
Lost to all things and myself,
And, amid the lilies forgotten,
Threw all my cares away.

St John of the Cross.

The Good Shepherd

And it came to pass, whilst He was at table with them, He took bread, and blessed and brake, and gave to them. And their eyes were opened, and they knew Him: and He vanished out of their sight.

CHRIST APPEARS TO THE EMMAUS DISCIPLES

THE GOOD SHEPHERD

The first Prelude is to call to mind how our Lord "appeared in another shape" to two disciples, "as they were going into the country."

The second Prelude is to see with the eyes of the imagination the mountain road leading from Jerusalem to Emmaus, and the house where our Lord manifested Himself to the two disciples.

The third Prelude is to ask light to know intimately the office of Consoler which Christ our Lord exercises with His friends, and grace to feel intense joy and gladness for His great glory and joy.

1. THE UNBELIEF OF THE TWO DISCIPLES

Overcome with despondency and sadness, two of the disciples of Jesus, one of them Cleophas by name, leave the company of their friends and direct their steps towards Emmaus, a little village about eight miles from Jerusalem. The Passion and Death of their Master have dealt a blow to their faith in Him. They thought that He would redeem Israel from the foreign yoke and restore to it its ancient glory—and instead He Himself was ignominiously nailed to the Cross. And yet if their minds are bewildered, their hearts are still full of Christ. He was so great, so powerful, and so good! They cannot but talk of Him. They seem anxious to see if there is an explanation of the tragedy of Calvary, so that they may continue to cling to Him though dead.

Anyone could have left such disciples to their fate, but not so Jesus, the Good Shepherd. Faithful to His ordinary rule of revealing Himself to souls according to their dispositions, He makes Himself one of them, a traveller with travellers, and kindly questions them about the subject of their talk and the cause of their sadness. Eagerly do they give vent to their feelings of admiration for Jesus, mingled with sentiments of sorrow, bitter disappointment, and unbelief.

"And now besides all this, today is the third day since these things were done. Yea, and certain women also of our company affrighted us, who before it was light were at the Sepulchre. And, not finding His Body, came, saying that they had also seen a vision of Angels who say that He is alive. And some of our people went to the Sepulchre: and found it so as the women had said, but Him they found not."[1]

Such facts should have reminded them forcibly of what the Master had repeatedly told them about His Passion and Resurrection, but all is to no purpose. They have *their own plan* of salvation and they refuse to change it.

2. Christ's Reproach

Our Lord has spared the weakness of the holy Women and of Mary Magdalene, but He does not spare it in those who are to guide and teach others.

"O foolish and slow of heart to believe in all things which the Prophets have spoken. Ought not Christ to have suffered those things, and so to enter into His glory? And beginning at Moses and all the Prophets, He expounded to them in all the Scriptures the things that were concerning Him."[2]

The whole of the Old Testament is, then, truly full of Christ, and promises a Saviour Who will enter into His Kingdom by suffering and the Cross. It was the lesson which Christ had so often tried to impress, during His mortal life, on the minds of His disciples, and to which even now He returns. It is *the* lesson of Christianity; and fittingly does the Second Book of the *Imitation of Christ* end by saying: "So that when we have thoroughly read and searched all, let this be the final conclusion, 'That through many tribulations we must enter into the Kingdom of God.'"

3. Christ Manifests Himself

The two disciples have not yet recognized Christ in their fellow traveller, but they love Him as a dear consoling friend. And seeing that drawing near Emmaus, He makes as though He would go further, they entreat Him—they nearly force Him—to remain with them. They feel that they cannot part from Him—not as

1. Luke xxiv, 21-24. 2. Luke xxiv, 25-27.

yet. "Stay with us, because it is towards evening, and the day is now far spent. And He went in with them."

By doing good, their eyes are opened to see the Truth that all along the road, has been conversing with them.

They have invited Him to stay and break bread with them, and He gives them Himself, the Bread from Heaven, and turns their sadness into joy, and their despondency and lukewarmness into joyful confidence and fiery activity. What matters if the very moment they recognize Him and stretch out their arms towards Him, He vanishes out of sight? The Lord Whom they thought dead has risen indeed! And they too rise up in haste and hurry back to Jerusalem, eager to give the happy news to the friends they have left there full of sadness and fear.

"And they told what things were done in the way and how they knew Him in the breaking of bread."

A Colloquy of love and confidence at the feet of the risen King.

THEIR EYES ARE OPENED

The supper ended, comes a sudden change.
Rising majestic, solemnly He stands,
And with the light of Heaven in His eyes,
Takes bread into His venerable hands.—
Lo! In those hands uplifted now they see
The marks, where nails have pierced, like rubies glow;
That noble head had once been crowned with thorns
Their eyes are opened and the Master know.—
The Bread He blessed and brake; and at His feet
The two disciples kneel. Great their reward;
For stranger welcomed, joyful they receive
The Bread of Life, the Body of their Lord.—

The Good Shepherd

Jesus stood in the midst of them, and saith to them: "Peace be to you; it is I, fear not." But they being troubled and frighted, supposed that they saw a spirit.

And He said to them: "Why are you troubled, and why do thoughts arise in your hearts? See My hands and feet."

CHRIST APPEARS TO THE APOSTLES

THE GOOD SHEPHERD

The first Prelude is to call to mind how our Lord appeared to the Apostles assembled in the Supper Room, and how after reproving them for their unbelief, He gave them the Holy Spirit and power to remit sins.

The second Prelude is to see the Supper Room.

The third Prelude is to ask grace to rejoice with the Apostles at the sight of he risen Lord, and light to know intimately the office of Consoler which He exercises with His friends and with everyone of us.

1. The Fear of the Apostles

The Apostles hope no more, as they did on the occasion of Jesus solemn entry into Jerusalem, to see the kingdom of Israel restored. They are now full of fear and altogether dejected. They refuse to believe the testimony of the holy Women and of Mary Magdalene affirming that the Lord is risen, and the sweet messages which the Lord Himself conveys to them.

"And these (the women's) words seemed to them as idle talk and they believed them not."[1]

It seems as if the various reports of the Resurrection that reach them on this eventful day, only add to their fear and increase their bewilderment.

However, Christ has not prayed for them in vain. With the exception of Thomas, they all come together into the Supper Room to console and strengthen one another. The Good Shepherd has not lost time to gather the sheep that were momentarily dispersed. But what a difference between the band that stood around Him on Maundy Thursday, hearing the promise of the Kingdom—"And I dispose to you as My Father hath disposed to Me, a Kingdom"—and swearing fidelity to Him, and this group of terrified Galileans that bolt and bar the entrance door against any possible intruder, and tremble at the rustling of a leaf! Truly fear freezes man's heart, paralyzes his efforts, and creates out of darkness a host of terrifying dangers and obstacles.

---

1. Luke xxiv, 11.

2. "PEACE BE TO YOU!"

The first thought of the risen Christ is for His Mother; the second for His Apostles. All previous Apparitions recorded in the Gospel, were meant to prepare for this solemn Apparition to His Apostles. And though these have persistently refused to believe the Resurrection of their Master, before the day comes to an end, He appears in their midst and salutes them with His usual greeting: "Peace be unto you." And as they are troubled and frightened, thinking that they see a spirit, Christ says to them: "Why are you so troubled, and why do thoughts arise in your hearts? See My hands and feet, that it is I Myself; handle, and see, for a spirit hath not flesh and bones, as you see Me to have." And He shows them His hands and feet and His side.

Yes, it is truly their Master, and yet they seem reluctant to believe for very joy—it is so marvellous, so unexpected, and it means so much for them! Smiling on these little children of His, Christ says: "Have you here anything to eat? And they offered Him a piece of broiled fish and a honeycomb. And when He had eaten before them, taking the remains He gave to them."[1]

Who is not charmed by the infinite charity and condescension of Christ towards those who behaved in so cowardly a manner during His Passion? His Heart only remembers the love and attachment of the past years: He reads their souls through and through, and knows that they still love Him.

He gives them the most tangible proofs of His Resurrection so that no doubt should ever cross their minds, and the strength of their faith should become the strength of all future generations of Christians. "Him God raised up the third day, and gave Him to be made manifest, not to all the people, but to witnesses pre-ordained by God, even to us, who did eat and drink with Him after He arose again from the dead."[2]

At the same time He does not spare them, but "He reproved their want of faith and stubborness of heart, in that they had not believed those who had seen Him risen from the dead."[3]

1. Luke xxiv, 41-43. 2. Acts x, 40, 41. 3. Mark xvi, 14.

3. "As My Father hath Sent Me, I also Send You"

Having convinced the Apostles of the fact of the Resurrection and of the legitimacy of His claims, Christ hands over to them His Mission. "Peace be to you. As the Father hath sent Me, I also send you. When He had said this, He breathed on them; and He said to them, Receive ye the Holy Ghost: whose sins you shall forgive, they are forgiven them; and whose sins you shall retain, they are retained."

Christ will continue to live and work in His Apostles and in all their successors, in His Church, through the operation of His Spirit Whom He communicates to them. One of His main offices is to forgive sins. To all those who believe in the risen Lord, the Church will grant forgiveness of sin and impart a new life in Him.

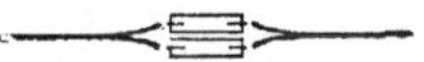

A Colloquy of joy and confidence with the risen Lord, thanking Him for the power of forgiving sins which He has granted to the Church and which will ever be a source of exceeding consolation to me, a poor sinner.

CHRIST IN HIS HOLY CHURCH

O blessed day of the Resurrection, which of old time was called the queen of Festivals, and raised among Christians an anxious, nay contentious diligence duly to honour it! Blessed day, once only passed in sorrow, when the Lord actually rose, and the Disciples believed not; but ever since a day of joy to the faith and love of the Church! In ancient times, Christians all over the world began it with a morning salutation. Each man said to his neighbour, "Christ is risen;" and his neighbour answered him, "Christ is risen indeed, and hath appeared to Simon!" To Simon Peter, the favoured Apostle on whom the Church is built, Christ has appeared. He has appeared to His Holy Church first of all, and in the Church He dispenses blessings, such as the world knows not of. Blessed are they if they knew their blessedness, who are allowed, as we are, week after week, and Festival after Festival, to seek and find in that Holy Church the Saviour of their souls!

Newman.

My Lord and my God

Thomas answered, and said to Him: "My Lord, and my God."
Jesus saith to him: "Because thou hast seen Me, Thomas, thou hast believed: blessed are they that have not seen, and have believed."

CHRIST APPEARS TO THOMAS

MY LORD, AND MY GOD

The first Prelude is to call to mind how the Apostle Thomas refused to believe that the Lord had risen, and how the Lord appeared to him and the other Apostles eight days after.

The second Prelude is to see the house were Thomas dwelt apart, and the Supper Room.

The third Prelude is to ask light to know intimately the infinite goodness of Christ, the Divine Consoler, and grace to believe and trust wholeheartedly in Him, our Lord and our God.

1. THOMAS' UNBELIEF

"Now Thomas, one of the Twelve, called Didymus was not with them (the Apostles) when Jesus came. The other disciples, therefore, said unto him, We have seen the Lord. But he said to them, Except I shall see in His hands the print of the nails, and put my finger into the place of the nails and put my hand into His side, I will not believe."[1]

All the Apostles refused, at first, to believe those who affirmed that they had seen the Lord. Thomas, however, goes to the extreme of unbelief, and combines it with the greatest obstinacy. In vain do his companions tell him that they have seen the Lord, and have fully tested the reality of His bodily Resurrection. He will not believe: he too must see; nay, he must put his finger into the place of the nails, and as if that were not enough, he must thrust his hand into the Lord's side. Not only does Thomas distrust the evidence of his companions, but like many other sceptics, he has come to disbelieve the testimony of his very eyes and ears.

Or was not, perhaps, the unbelief of the Apostle brought about by a secret grief that the Master had not appeared to him, who loved Him so much and had encouraged all the others to brave even death for Him? "Let us also go that we may die with

1. John xx, 24, 25.

Him," he had cried when Christ proposed to leave His safe shelter in Peraea to go to Bethany. Was not Thomas tormented by secret jealousy because his companions alone had been favoured? At any rate who can measure the grief and agony of Thomas during the week that followed the first Easter Sunday: hard and obstinate with his friends, but bleeding in anguish, in the secret of his soul. Did he think himself rejected by Christ? And yet he had but himself to blame for not having seen the Lord. He had not joined the company of his friends, preferring to brood all alone over the death of Christ and the end of his hopes.

2. Christ Appears to Thomas

"And after eight days, again His disciples were within, and Thomas with them. Jesus cometh, the doors being shut, and stood in the midst, and said: Peace be to you. Then He saith to Thomas: Put in thy finger hither and see My hands, and bring hither thy hand and put it unto My side; and be not faithless, but believing Thomas answered, and said to Him: My Lord, and my God."[1]

The Saviour displays once more His infinite love, tenderness and condescension. Far from abandoning Thomas to the fate which his obstinate unbelief deserves, He comes to his rescue and grants him the test which he has proudly asked for. No sooner has He saluted the Apostles than He turns to him. But Thomas needs no proofs now. In the presence of his risen Lord, he bursts out with an ardent cry of faith and of love: "My Lord and my God," and he prostrates himself at His feet.

3. "Blessed are they that have not seen, and have believed"

"Jesus saith to him: Because thou hast seen Me, Thomas, thou hast believed: blessed are they that have not seen, and have believed."[2]

Though Thomas' faith is great, since he only sees in Christ the visible Man and yet confesses the invisible God, Christ does not

1. John xx, 26-28. 2. John, xx, 29.

praise him for it. He has demanded too many proofs before believing. On the contrary, Christ says: "Blessed are they that have not seen and have believed."

It is the last of the Beatitudes proclaimed by Christ, and indeed the greatest, because it sums up all the others and is their well-grounded assurance.

We are those whom our Lord calls blessed. We do not see, nor have we any special revelation from on high, and yet we believe in Christ the Son of the Living God and in His true and abiding Presence in the Sacrament of Love and in His Church. We believe that in the Church and through the Church we can receive all the consolations granted by the risen Lord to His friends. Faith in the risen and immortal Lord and in His permanent work in the Church is the main grace we must ever ask.

A Colloquy asking our Lord, not to see or touch His wounds, but to grant me such faith that will make Him and His whole life a living reality to me.

CHRIST OUR LOVE

O Christ, the glorious Crown
Of virgins that are pure;
Who dost a love and thirst for Thee
Within their minds procure,
Thou art the spouse of those
That chaste and humble be,
The hope, the life, the only help
Of such as trust in Thee.
All charity of those
Whose souls Thy love doth warm;
All simple pleasures of such minds
As think no kind of harm;
All sweet delights wherewith
The patient hearts abound,
Do blaze Thy name, and with Thy praise
They make the world resound.

Venerable Philip Howard.

The Supreme Shepherd

When therefore they had dined, Jesus saith to Simon Peter: "Simon, son of John, lovest thou Me more than these?"

He saith to Him: "Yea, Lord, Thou knowest that I love Thee."

He saith to Him: "Feed My lambs." He saith to him again: "Simon, son of John, lovest thou Me?"

He saith to Him: "Yea, Lord, Thou knowest that I love Thee."

He saith to him: "Feed My lambs." He said to him the third time: "Simon, son of John, lovest thou Me?"

Peter was grieved, because He had said to him the third time, Lovest thou Me? And he said to Him: Lord, Thou knowest all things: Thou knowest that I love Thee."

He said to him: "Feed My sheep."

ÇHRIST APPEARS ON THE SHORE OF GENNESARET

THE SUPREME SHEPHERD

The first Prelude is to call to mind how our Lord appeared to seven of His Disciples on the shore of Gennesaret and entrusted His fold to the Apostle St Peter.

The second Prelude is to see the lake, and the shore on which Jesus stood.

The third Prelude is to ask light to know intimately the infinite goodness of Christ, the Divine Consoler, and grace to believe and trust wholeheartedly in Him, our Divine Shepherd, and in His Vicar, the shepherd whom He has appointed to take His place on earth.

1. The Miraculous Draught

"After this Jesus shewed Himself again to the disciples at the sea of Tiberias. And He shewed Himself after this manner. There were together Simon Peter, and Thomas who is called Didymus, and Nathanael who was of Cana in Galilee, and the sons of Zebedee and two others of His disciples. Simon Peter saith to them: I go a fishing. They say to him: We also come with thee. And they went forth and entered into the ship; and that night they caught nothing. But when the morning was come, Jesus stood on the shore; yet the disciples knew not that it was Jesus. Jesus therefore saith to them: Children, have you any meat? They answered Him: No. He saith to them: Cast the net on the right side; and you shall find. They cast, therefore, and now they were not able to draw it for the multitude of fishes."[1]

Without Jesus, our work is fruitless; but if Jesus is with us, though we may neither see nor feel Him, everything turns to our advantage: we catch a multitude of fishes in Peter's net, or, at least, those that come after us will do it and thus reap in joy the fruit of hard and unremitting labours.

"That disciple therefore whom Jesus loved, said to Peter: It is the Lord."[2]

---

1. John xxi, 1-6. 2. John xxi, 7.

"It is the Lord." It is the voice of the soul that lives in the light of Faith and sees the Master everywhere, and above all in His wonderful gifts. One feels in that cry the enthusiastic fervour of the lover in seeing his beloved, of the friend in seeing his dear friend.

"It is the Lord." In whatever guise He come to us and at whatever hour, in the light of day or in the shadow of night, we shall always try to see Him until the hour when, all veils having been drawn aside, He appears to welcome us home.

2. "Come and Dine"

"As soon as they come to land, they saw hot coals lying, and a fish laid thereon, and bread. Jesus saith to them: Bring hither of the fishes which you have now caught. Simon Peter went up, and drew the net to land, full of great fishes, one hundred and fifty three, And although there were so many the net was not broken. Jesus saith to them: Come, and dine. And none of them who were at meat, durst ask Him: Who art Thou? knowing that it was the Lord. And Jesus cometh and taketh bread, and giveth them, and fish in like manner." [1]

Could one find anything more enchanting than the partaking of that meal prepared by the Master, in the early morning on the shore of that lake so full of memories? The Apostles, full of love and awe look at the Master, and while they are hardlya ble to withdraw their eyes from Him for a single instant, they dare not speak a word. Jesus looks at them silently. Not even the Son of God can find words to convey the love with which His Heart is brimming for His disciples. It is a silent scene, but O how infinitely expressive! An image of Holy Communion and of the Eternal Banquet.

3. "Feed My Lambs: Feed My Sheep"

When therefore they had dined, Jesus saith to Simon Peter: Simon, son of John, lovest thou Me more than these? He saith to Him: Yea, Lord, Thou knowest that I love Thee. He saith to him: Feed My lambs. He saith to him again: Simon, son of John, lovest thou Me? He saith to Him: Yea, Lord, Thou knowest that I love

1. John xxi, 9-13.

Thee. He saith to him: Feed My lambs. He said to him the third time: Simon, son of John, lovest thou Me? Peter was grieved, because He had said to him the third time, Lovest thou Me? And he said to Him: Lord, Thou knowest all things: Thou knowest that I love Thee. He said to him: Feed My sheep."[1]

Suddenly the silenee is broken. The Master turning to Peter asks him: "Simon, son of John, lovest thou Me?" Three times the question is repeated, and three times the Apostle answers with words of ardent love and deep humility. The third answer is a cry that pierces the Heart of Christ far more than the repeated denials in the palace of Caiphas.

"Feed My lambs: feed My sheep." Once his mind is free from every thought of pride and superiority, and his heart only burns with love for his Lord, Peter is made the shepherd of his Lord's flock, His Vicar on earth, nay, in the beautiful expression of St Catherine, he becomes *Christ on earth*.

What a consolation for us!

Love is the only condition of the apostolate. The apostle must love Christ, and for Christ's sake he must love men and be ready to sacrifice his life for them.

The Primacy is, accordingly, the effect of love. Once more Christ lays down that charity is the fundamental law of His Church.

"Amen, amen, I say to thee, when thou wast younger thou didst gird thyself, and didst walk where thou wouldst. But when thou shalt be old, thou shalt stretch forth thy hands, and another shall gird thee, and lead thee whither thou wouldst not. And this He said signifying by what death he should glorify God."[2]

As a reward for a life of love and unremitting self-sacrifice, Christ promises to His Apostle what the Father gave Him—a cross.

4. Our Heavenly Meal

"When the morning was come, Jesus stood on the shore."

Even now He stands on our Altars and prepares there a heavenly meal for us. And when in obedience to His invitation, "Come

1. John xxi, 15-17. 2. John xxi, 18, 19.

and dine," we approach the Holy Table and receive the Lamb of God in silence and love, we too hear Jesus asking us: "Lovest thou Me?" "Yea, Lord, Thou knowest I love Thee," we shall answer with the loving and humble Apostle. And Jesus will say: "Feed My lambs," and perhaps, He will show to us the crosses which await us and which we must embrace with fervour and love.

To conclude the contemplation with a fervent Colloquy with my risen Lord and the Shepherd of my soul, protesting my sincere desire to love Him above all and my firm resolve to love, to work, and to sacrifice myself for the souls which He has entrusted to my care.

ON THE SHORE OF GENNESARET

The dimples of the sea of Galilee,
Its smiling face,
Where shadows dance,
Its rippling grace
Its sunny glance,
Enchant the heart with their hilarity:
Who goes a-fishing there finds ecstasy.

Enchantment dwelt there on that April morn:
The Sun arose:—
Who most adored
'Tis he first knows
"It is the Lord."
In Peter, who had wept with heart forlorn.
The faith that slept was there again reborn.

There with those childlike souls the Great Christ played;
The Son of Man
To fulness grown
Again began
To call His own;
His skill in fishing then once more displayed,
Though with Heaven's Glory He was now arrayed.

A picnic breakfast did His hands prepare;
    With them He sate
    Upon the shore;
    With them He ate
    Who evermore
Gives Bread of Angels, Bread beyond compare,
And feeds disciples with His Heavenly Fare.

With them He walks again upon the beach;
    Who thrice denied,
    With questions three
    He gently tried,
    "Lovest thou Me?"
Peter was grieved, but bravely answered each;
The Master by His gracious smile can teach.

We cannot catch the rapture of that morn,
    When nature laughed
    To see the Sun
    New risen, and quaffed
    Life's nectar, won
Through night of pain; but still in hearts forlorn
The joy of smiling Easter is reborn.

W. A. Wordsworth.

The King's Commission

And Jesus coming spoke to them, saying: "All power is given to Me in Heaven and in earth. Going therefore teach ye all nations: baptizing them in the name of the Father, and of the Son, and of the Holy Ghost. Teaching them to observe all things whatsoever I have commanded you."

CHRIST APPEARS ON THE MOUNTAIN OF GALILEE

THE KING'S COMMISSION

The first Prelude is to call to mind how our Lord appeared to the Eleven and commissioned them to go and preach His Gospel to all men.

The second Prelude is to see the mountain on which the Lord appeared.

The third Prelude is to ask light to know our Lord, His infinite love and His equally infinite power; and grace to rejoice at His glory, and to trust wholeheartedly in Him.

1. The Significance of this Apparition

On Easter Day our Lord had ordered His Apostles to go to Galilee. "Go tell My brethren that they go into Galilee, and there shall they see Me." At last He fulfils His promise. "And the eleven disciples went into Galilee, unto the mountain where Jesus had appointed them. And seeing Him they adored."[1]

This is the most public and most solemn of the apparitions of the risen Lord. On the Mountain of the Beatitudes He announced His Kingdom to His beloved Apostles and to the wondering crowd. Once more in the midst of His Apostles and surrounded by many of His former Galilean followers, He stands, perhaps on that very mountain, to deliver His last message—to hand over to His Apostles His authority and His power, and charge them with the task of spreading His Kingdom throughout the world. The Mountain of the Beatitudes, Calvary, and this mountain mark the highest points of ascent in our Lord's journey on earth: on the Mountain of the Beatitudes the Kingdom was proclaimed, and on Calvary it was established—*Regnavit a ligno Deus.* The apparition on this mountain proves that the Beatitudes and Calvary were no delusions, and encourages everyone of us to follow the King blindly along the path He has walked, that we may one day partake of His glory.

1. Matt. xxviii, 16, 17.

2. "ALL POWER IS GIVEN TO ME"

"And Jesus coming spoke to them saying: All power is given to Me in Heaven and on earth."[1]

The Divine King shines forth in the splendour and majesty of His glorified Humanity. All power is given to Him by God the Father. Though evil may seem to triumph for a while, we can rest assured that Christ is King not only of Heaven, but of the whole world—"King of kings and Lord of lords." That must be the solid ground on which to base our confidence, if it is to remain unshaken against the inroads of Satan, the threatening fury of men, and our weak and vacillating nature.

3. "TEACH YE ALL NATIONS"

"Going therefore teach ye all nations: baptizing them in the name of the Father, and of the Son, and of the Holy Ghost, teaching them to observe all things whatsoever I have commanded you."[2]

In virtue of His almighty power our Lord commands and commissions the Apostles and their successors to continue His triple saving mission throughout the centuries, all over the world. Accordingly they are, first, to re-echo the Voice of Christ—to repeat faithfully to the men of every age the truths which the only-begotten Son, Who is in the bosom of the Father, has declared to them.

Secondly, by means of the Sacraments instituted by Christ Himself, they are to give the Divine life to men, to restore and strengthen it in them.

Thirdly, by wise laws and directions they are to help men to walk safely along the path that leads to salvation.

4. "BEHOLD I AM WITH YOU"

"And behold I am with you all days, even to the consummation of the world."[3]

The Church, then, is nothing else but the Living and Eternal Christ, teaching, sanctifying, and guiding men through His Spirit and through the instrumentality of His ministers. In the Church men

1. Matt. xxviii, 18. 2. Matt. xxviii, 19-20. 3. Matt. xxviii, 20.

find Christ. Through the Church they are united with Him and partake of the graces and gifts which He has gained for them.

What a consolation for all obedient children of the Church! What a powerful motive for strengthening the bonds that unite us with this Mother! Christ with us all the days of our life, teaching us, sanctifying us, leading us to the pastures of eternal life by means of His appointed shepherds and of those interior graces which He continually pours into our souls. What need we fear? "Who then shall separate us from the love of Christ?" None but ourselves.

To end with the *Oblation* of the *Kingdom* and with a Colloquy of heartfelt thanksgiving to Christ for the gift of His Church, and of love, of obedience, and of loyalty to this dear Mother of ours.

FROM 'ST PATRICK'S HYMN'

Christ, as a light,
Illumine and guide me!
Christ, as a shield, o'ershadow and cover me!
Christ be under me! Christ be over me!
Christ be beside me
On left hand and right!
Christ be before me, behind me, about me!
Christ this day be within and without me!

Christ, the lowly and meek,
Christ, the All-powerful, be
In the heart of each to whom I speak,
In the mouth of each who speaks to me!
In all who draw near me,
Or see me or hear me!

THE FORTY DAYS AFTER THE RESURRECTION

The first Prelude is to call to mind how our Lord remained on earth forty days after His Resurrection and showed Himself many times to His disciples.

The second Prelude is to see with the eyes of the imagination the various places where our Lord showed Himself, and in particular the Cenacle.

The third Prelude is to ask grace to feel intense joy and gladness for the great glory and joy of Christ our Lord, and to trust wholeheartedly in Him, in the power of His Spirit, and in the Church established by Him.

1. With the Risen Lord

"To whom also He showed Himself alive after His Passion by many proofs, for forty days appearing to them, and speaking of the Kingdom of God."[1]

This statement of the Evangelist St Luke implies frequent interviews and communications of our Lord with His Apostles.

Our Lord had two objects in view in remaining so long on earth after His Resurrection. First, He wanted to give to the Apostles the most solid and convincing proofs of the fact of His Resurrection; and, secondly, He desired to put the finishing touches to the work for which He had come on earth, the establishment of the Kingdom of God. On the other hand, by showing Himself only now and then, He was preparing His Apostles for His final withdrawal from earth and for the invisible Mission of the Holy Spirit.

The fruit we must read from the contemplation of our Lord's glorious life must be, accordingly, a strong and lively faith in the Mystery of the Resurrection. Each one of us must be able to say; I believe that the very Jesus Whom I have seen laid in a manger, hidden in Nazareth, labouring, suffering and dying, is risen from the dead and lives an immortal life. With the Apostles we should announce the truth of the Resurrection and be ready to witness to it, even by the sacrifice of our life.

Another fruit which we must reap from such contemplations is a deeper knowledge and love of our Lord and of His Kingdom—the Kingdom which He announced to us in the first Exercise of the

1. Acts i, 3.

Second Week, which He promulgated by the example of His life and by His preaching, and which He established before ascending to His Father

To know Christ and His work better and better is the object of the Exercises of the Fourth Week.

2. The Work of the Holy Spirit

"And eating together with them, He commanded them that they should not depart from Jerusalem, but should wait for the promise of the Father, which you have heard (saith He) by My mouth; for John indeed baptized with water, but you shall be baptized with the Holy Ghost not many days hence."[1]

The Holy Spirit is to transform the Apostles and fill them with His gifts. He is to complete the work of Christ—the founding of the Church. He is to make the bodies of men His own temples and establish the Kingdom of God within their hearts.

During the Retreat, meditating on the teaching and the example of Christ, we conceive good desires, take strong resolutions and lay down a plan of life for the future. The Holy Spirit must come to complete the work, by further enlightening our intellect and strengthening our will for putting into practice what we have determined. Hence the necessity of prayer and self-recollection at the end of the Retreat, and after it even more than ever.

3. "You shall be Witnesses unto Me"

"They therefore who were come together, asked Him, saying: Lord, wilt Thou at this time restore again the Kingdom to Israel? But He said to them: It is not for you to know the times or moments which the Father hath put in His own power: but you shall receive the power of the Holy Ghost coming upon you and you shall be witnesses unto Me in Jerusalem, and in all Judea, and Samaria, and even to the uttermost part of the earth."[2]

We must leave to God to complete His own work, at the time and in the way which in His Providence He has decreed. Our only task is to pray, and prepare ourselves, for an ever increasing outpouring of the Holy Spirit to witness to Christ—to Christ's truth and to Christ's life—always and everywhere.

1. Acts I, 4, 5. 2. Acts, i, 6-8.

The Supreme Triumph of our King

And He led them out as far as Bethania ; and lifting up His hands He blessed them. And it came to pass, whilst He blessed them, He departed from them, and was carried up to Heaven.

THE ASCENSION

THE SUPREME TRIUMPH OF OUR KING

The first Prelude is to call to mind how Christ "was taken up into Heaven and took His seat at the right hand of God."

The second Prelude is to see Mount Olivet.

The third Prelude is to ask for grace to feel intense joy and gladness for the great joy and glorious triumph of Christ our Lord.

1. "He Ascended into Heaven"

Jesus led His Apostles in the direction of Bethany, to the Mount of Olives. He desired that His glorious Ascension should take place in the vicinity of the Garden where His Passion had begun, to impress once more on His Apostles that "it behoved Christ to suffer, and to rise again from the dead the third day."

"And lifting up His hand He blessed them. And it came to pass whilst He blessed them, He departed from them, and was carried up to Heaven."[1]

"And a cloud received Him out of their sight."[2]

"So the Lord Jesus . . . . was taken up into Heaven."[3]

The Divine King and Conqueror ascends into Heaven along with the souls which already partake of His Glory and with myriads of Angels who cry: "Lift up your gates, O ye princes, and be ye lifted up, O eternal gates, and the King of glory shall enter in."

If there is joy in Heaven over the conversion of one sinner, who can possibly realize the joy of the inhabitants of that Blessed Home at the glorious appearance of the Conqueror of sin and death? With jubilant joy the Church sings:

Ascending to the throne of might,
And seated at the Father's right,
All power in Heaven is Jesus' own
That here His manhood had not known.

---

1. Luke xxiv, 50, 51. 2. Acts i, 9. 3. Mark xvi, 19.

That so, in nature's triple frame,
Each heavenly and each earthly name,
And things in Hell's abyss abhorred,
May bend the knee and own Him Lord.
Yea, Angels tremble when they see
How changed is our humanity;
That flesh hath purged what flesh hath stained,
And God, the Flesh of God, hath reigned.

2. Jesus before the Father

At the Last Supper, Christ had asked to be glorified by the Father:

"Father, the hour is come, glorify Thy Son."

"And now glorify Thou Me, O Father."

The hour of Christ's eternal glorification has, indeed, come. Angels and Saints cry with one voice: "Worthy is the Lamb who was sacrificed to receive power and riches and wisdom and might and honour and glory and blessing!"[1]

And God the Father says to Christ:

"Thou art My Son, this day have I begotten Thee."[2]

He accepts and approves Christ's redeeming work, by making Him sit at His right hand as our Pontiff, our Victim, the Head of regenerated mankind, and the source and spring of Divine life.

"The Lord said to My Lord: Sit on My right hand."

3. Christ's Ascension is our Feast

"The Ascension of the Lord is our glorification," says St Leo. He offers to the Father the first fruits of our race and the Father places the oblation at His right hand. With Christ, our Leader and our Head, we acquire on Ascension Day a right to the possession of Heaven. It behoves us, then, to rejoice exceedingly—to rejoice for Christ on account of His joy and glory, and for our share in it.

Heaven is ours. We have but to go and take possession of it; and Christ Himself has shown to us the way to it.

1. Ap. v, 12. 2. Ps. ii, 7.

If we want to follow after Him we must tread our vices underfoot and turn them into stepping stones to Heaven.

4. The Final Message

" And while they were beholding Him going up to Heaven, behold two men stood by them in white garments. Who also said : Ye men of Galilee, why stand you looking up to Heaven? This Jesus Who is taken up from you into Heaven, shall so come, as you have seen Him going into Heaven. Then they returned to Jerusalem."[1]

While we also are looking up to Heaven and rejoicing with Christ for His glory and for ours also, the Angels warn us that henceforth our whole life must be spent in continuing the life and work of our Lord, and in watching for His coming. St John the Apostle, working and suffering for long, long years, and passionately longing for the coming of Jesus—"Come, O Lord Jesus!"—must be our model.

Prostrate before the throne of the Divine King, I shall conclude the contemplation by crying, along with the Angels and Saints of the heavenly court, "Worthy is the Lamb Who was sacrificed to receive power and riches and wisdom and might and honour and glory and blessing," and by renewing my promise of unswerving fidelity to Him.

THE GLORIOUS CONQUEROR

Rise—glorious Conqueror, rise
Into Thy native skies,—
    Assume Thy right:
And where in many a fold
The clouds are backward roll'd—
Pass through those gates of gold,
    And reign in light!

Enter—Incarnate God!
No feet, but Thine, have trod
    The serpent down:
Blow the full trumpets,—blow!
Wider yon portals throw!
Saviour—triumphant—go,
    And take Thy Crown!

1. Acts i, 10-12.

The King's Court

A great multitude, which no man could number, of all nations, and tribes, and peoples, and tongues, standing before the throne, and in the sight of the Lamb, clothed with white robes, and palms in their hands.

THE GLORY OF HEAVEN

THE KING'S COURT

The first Prelude is to lift up my face unto Heaven and behold how Christ and all His Saints with Him, who in this world had great conflicts, do now rejoice, are now comforted, now secure, and at rest, and shall remain with Him everlastingly in the Kingdom of His Father.

The second Prelude is to ask to know something of the joy that God has prepared for His Elect.

1. God's Eternal Garden

Heaven is the goal of our earthly pilgrimage. We naturally long for it more than "a servant longeth for the shade," or "the hireling looketh for the end of his work."[1] The vision of our eternal home, caught by the light of Faith, encourages us in our trials, strengthens us in our toilsome journey, and inspires us with ever higher and greater resolves, just as the sight of his native hills, seen now and then at the turning of the road, fills the weary traveller with new life.

Still better: Heaven is the lasting and consummate perfection of our being. It means untroubled peace and complete happiness, full and endless life.

As a matter of fact, what is Heaven? Till we enter it, we shall not know what Heaven truly is. "What eye hath not seen, what ear hath not heard—what hath not entered into heart of man—all these things God hath prepared for them that love Him."[2] We may, indeed, picture to ourselves Heaven as a most delightful place—God's eternal garden, as the Church calls it in her prayers for the commendation of a departing soul—where our eyes will rest on ever new scenes of everlasting beauty, our ears, delighted with the most mellifluous melodies, our imaginations, filled with noble and joy-giving images, and our bodies, agile, lightsome and wholly obedient to the soul, will fly unhampered across the immense universe. Heaven, after the final resurrection, will be all that, and exceedingly more and

1. Job. vii, 2. 2. Cor. ii, 9.

better than we can ever fancy. And what happiness will it mean for us when we remember that the sound of a violin string, touched by an Angel's hand, caused St Francis of Assisi, when racked by pain, to fall into an ecstasy of love.

And yet not in these delights does the happiness of Heaven consist.

2. The Vision of God

The happiness of Heaven is the outcome of the beatific vision, which is an uninterrupted gazing on God's infinite beauty. That vision will be eternal as God is eternal, and unchanging because it is, all at once, the totality of every good. It will be a participation in God's own eternity.

Heaven, we may say, is the complete and eternal realization of our end. The Blessed adore, love and praise God, the Principle and the End of their existence, in a new Heaven and a new earth, where every creature reflects the All-Good and contributes to increase the love and joy of the children of God. The memory will be full of His presence and of His favours; the intellect will enter into the powers of God and know Him as He is, face to face; the will will be transformed in God through love, and from this love there will flow a torrent of ineffable pleasure.

Though, on earth, we shall never grasp the nature of the beatific vision, in the light of Faith we can have some faint idea of it. For our benefit, our Lord deigned to reveal to His beloved Apostle, St John, what he keeps in store for His friends, by showing him the glory of the Blessed who already reign with Him.

The Apocalypse, as a matter of fact, is not only a prophetic revelation of the perpetual combat between Satan and Christ, but also a revelation of the glory and triumph which Christ has already achieved. It holds out the vision and promise of everlasting happiness with Christ, to the first Christians, all harassed by trials and persecutions, and some perhaps prone to compromise and even to backsliding. It describes the happiness of those who have passed away in the Lord and now rejoice with Him in the new Jerusalem. Instead of fanciful descriptions of Heaven, and of theological and philosophical disquisitions, which convey little to the mind of many, we had then better take up God's book, and consider what the beloved disciple wrote for our instruction at the command of his Master.

The Glory of Christ

Christ is the life, the spring and source of eternal life.

Accordingly, the first vision vouchsafed to the seer of Patmos is the vision of our Lord, the Son of God, God and Man, Redeemer and King. He is, like the Almighty God, Alpha and Omega, the Beginning and the End, the One that is living for ever and ever, and has the key of Death and of Hell. His dress marks Him as King and Priest; the sword issuing from His mouth, as Him Whose word is irresistible; the white head and hair symbolize His Divine eternity. One with the Father, He is the centre of all activity of the militant and of the heavenly Jerusalem: the spring of grace here below and of glory hereafter.

The vision of Christ, at the right hand of the Father, has been for millions of Christians a foretaste of Heaven and a mainstay in the midst of trials and sufferings. Each one of them would cry out with St Stephen: "Behold I see the Heavens opened, and the Son of Man sitting on the right hand of God,"[1] and make no account of the fury of the persecutors. It is this vision that should accompany us through life to brighten our path and strengthen our hearts. "Seek the things that are above, where Christ is seated on the right hand of God: mind the things that are above, not the things that are on the earth. For ye have died, and your life is hidden with Christ in God; when Christ, our life, shall appear, then also shall ye appear with Him in glory."[2] To be always with the Lord, to rejoice in His glory and to partake of it—that is Heaven. "Father, I will that where I am, they also whom Thou hast given Me may be with Me, that they may see Me in the glory which Thou hast given Me."[3]

4. Christ's Promise of Glory

In the seven letters to the Churches, Christ encourages His own to rise from tepidity and sin, to work and suffer for Him, with the

1. Acts vii, 55. 2. Col. iii, 1-4. 3. John xvii, 24.

thought of the heavenly glory, which He describes in ever more glowing terms.

(i)

Heaven is the public acknowledgment of the Blessed by Christ.

"I will confess his name before My Father and before His holy Angels."[1]

(ii)

Heaven is the sharing in the life of God.

"He that conquereth shall be clad thus in white garments."[2]

"To him that conquereth, I will give of the hidden manna."[3]

"To him that conquereth, I will give to eat of the tree of life, which is in the paradise of God."[4]

(iii)

Heaven is the Association and perfect union of each one of us with the triumphant Lord, with His life, His glory, and His kingly dignity – a union most intimate and most mysterious, felt but indescribable.

"And I will give him a white stone, and upon the stone a new name written, which no one knoweth except him that receiveth it"[5] – i. e., a most inward testimony that he is approved and eternally admitted into God's presence.

"As for him that conquereth and keepeth My works, till the end I will give power over the nations."[6]

"As for Him that conquereth, I will give him to sit *with Me upon My Throne* as I Myself have conquered, and sat down with My Father on His Throne."[7]

(iv)

Heaven is eternal life, with no fear of decay of death.

"He that conquereth shall not be harmed by the second death."[8]

"He that conquereth, I will make him a pillar in the sanctuary of My God, and never more shall he go out of it. And I will write upon him the name of My God, and the name of the city of My God, — the new Jerusalem, which cometh down out of Heaven from My God, — and My new name."[9] God takes him as His own; he becomes a perpetual citizen of Heaven, and one with Christ.

1. Ap. iii, 5. 2. Ap. iii, 5. 3. Ap. ii, 17. 4. Ap. ii, 7.
5. Ap. ii, 17. 6. Ap. ii, 26. 7. Ap. iii, 21. 8. Ap. ii, 11.
9. Ap. ii, 12.

(v)

Heaven is the soul seated along with Christ at the eternal banquet.

"Behold I stand at the gate and knock. If any man hear My voice, and open the door, I will come in to him, and I will sup with him, and he with Me."[1]

5. The Glory of the Blessed

As though to give more credit to such promises, Christ lifts for a moment, the veil that conceals Heaven from mortal eyes and reveals to His beloved disciple, the glory of the citzens of the heavenly Jerusalem, asking him to write down all that he sees. And what ineffable scenes unroll themselves before the ecstatic gaze of John!

(i)

The Blessed stand before the throne of God, and in the sight of the Lamb.[2]

They offer to God an incessant sacrifice.[3]

All their sufferings, physical and moral, are past.[4]

(ii)

The Lamb of God is their shepherd, and leads them to the mountains of the waters of life.[5]

They follow Him whithersoever He goeth.[6]

(iii)

The union of the Blessed with God is presented under the figure of a wedding,[7] and of a nuptial banquet.[8]

(iv)

The home of God and of the Blessed is described under the figure of a heavenly city, beautiful as a bride adorned for her husband.[9]

(v)

The life of the Blessed is the last vision vouchsafed to John. The tree of life is the Word made Flesh. It bears fruit throughout the year, i. e., for time and eternity, and that fruit is the life of the dwellers in the heavenly Jerusalem, while its leaves are

1. Ap. iii, 20.
2. Cf. Ap. vii, 9.
3. Cf. Ap. vii, 15
4. Cf. Ap. vii, 16, 17.
5. Cf. Ap. viii, 17.
6. Cf. Ap. xiv, 4.
7. Cf. Ap. xix, 7.
8. Cf. Ap. xix, 9.
9. Cf. Ap. xxi, 10-27.

for the healing of the Church militant. The Eucharistic Christ is our food; the glorified Christ, our reward. The "river of the water of life, clear as crystal, issuing forth from the throne of God and of the Lamb,"[1] is the Holy Ghost.

6. Longing for Heaven

"Come, Lord Jesus!" is the passionate cry with which St John ends his Apocalypse.

That should be the cry of every loving soul.

Our Lord Himself wants that we should be constantly watching for Him:

"Let your loins be girt, and lamps burning in your hands And you yourselves like to men who wait for their lord, when he shall return from the wedding, that when he cometh and knocketh, they may open to him immediately."[2]

Such is likewise the desire of the Church. Throughout her Liturgy she keeps Heaven before our eyes as our true home, the end of our journey, the real goal of our desires, so that "amidst the vanities and the varieties of our earthly existence, our hearts may be fixed there where are eternal joys."

Eternal life is essentially ours, even now, if we are in God's grace.

"He that eateth My Flesh and drinketh My Blood, *hath everlasting life.*"[3]

"As the living Father hath sent Me, and I live by the Father, so he that eateth Me, the same also shall live by Me."[4]

Death will but reveal the life of God that is already in us, consummate our union with Him, and seal it with immortality. Let us then live in Heaven, our true home and fatherland, and not only in expectation of it. But what will enable us to live such a heavenly life, if not the living companionship of our Eucharistic Lord?

Our churches are the counterpart of the heavenly Jerusalem.

The Altar is the throne of God and of the Lamb. At Mass Christ, the Divine Victim, is present and offered thereon, and we with Him.

1. Ap. xxii, 1. 2. Luke xii, 35, 36. 3. John vi, 55. 4. John vi, 58.

Holy Communion is the espousals of our soul with the Lamb.

The Liturgy reflects the splendours of the heavenly Court.

With Christ in our heart, we leave the church and go to work calmly, patiently, unsparingly for Him and His Kingdom, though the years of expectation may be long and painful like those of the beloved disciple. At the first glimpse we catch of our dear Lord's face, we shall forget all sufferings.

THE NEW JERUSALEM

Hierusalem, my happy home,
When shall I come to Thee?
When shall my sorrows have an end,
Thy joys when shall I see?

O happy harbour of the Saints!
O sweet and pleasant soil!
In Thee no sorrow may be found,
No grief, no care, no toil.

There lust and lucre cannot dwell.
There envy bears no sway;
There is no hunger, heat, nor cold,
But pleasure every way.

Our Lady sings *Magnificat*
With tones surpassing sweet;
And all the virgins bear their part,
Sitting about her feet.

Hierusalem, my happy home,
Would God I were in thee!
Would God my woes were at an end,
Thy joys that I might see.

Heaven Anticipated

Behold the tabernacle of God with men, and He will dwell with them.

CONTEMPLATION FOR OBTAINING LOVE

HEAVEN ANTICIPATED

[*The Spiritual Exercises*, pp. 118-26]

The Contemplation for obtaining love, though placed outside the Fourth Week, is the crowning point of the Spiritual Exercises.

Heaven is the home of love: of the Eternal Love that is God Himself, and of the created love poured by God into His creatures and requited by them to Him. Earthly life is a preparation for it, or, better, its beginning. That is why, throughout the Gospel, our Lord lays stress on the infinite love of God, our Father; and that is why, too, St. John, to whom heavenly secrets were primarily revealed, wrote that God is Love. To love God is the greatest and the first commandment: "Thou shalt love the Lord thy God, with thy whole heart, with thy whole soul, and with thy whole mind."[1]

The Contemplation for obtaining love gives us an idea of God's love, and teaches us how to return love for love. The subject-matter of its various points should be the constant food of our minds and of our hearts.

* * *

At the outset, St Ignatius calls attention to two things. "The first is that love ought to show itself in deeds rather than in words." It is an echo of the teaching of the Beloved Disciple: "My little children, let us not love in word nor in tongue, but in deed and in truth."[2] We are warned against hollow protestations of love, and even against sterile feelings. Though love is mainly an affair of the heart, we should distrust feelings that do not lead to work and to self-sacrifice.

"The second, that love consists in mutual intercharge of gifts, i. e., in the lover giving and communicating to the beloved that which he has or can give, and in like manner the beloved to the lover. So that if one has knowledge he gives it to him who has it not,

1. Matt. xxii, 37. 2. 1 John. iii, 18.

and likewise if he has honours and riches; and the other in turn does the same."

A true lover desires to give himself wholly to the beloved and be *one with him*. The gifts which he offers him are merely marks of such an ardent desire and a preparation for the moment of consummate union.

The first Prelude is to see how I stand before God our Lord, before the Angels and saints who are interceding for me.

The second Prelude is to ask for an interior knowledge of so many favours that I have received, so that acknowledging them to the full, I may be able to love and serve His Divine Majesty in everything.

FIRST POINT

1. Creation and Conservation

God is love. For God to love is infinitely more natural than it is for the bird to fly, the wind to blow, the sun to shine. As Love, God has wished to communicate Himself and His perfections to creatures, capable of knowing and of returning His love.

Through love He has created us. "Yea I have loved thee with an everlasting love, therefore have I drawn thee taking pity on thee."[1] Creation is but the overflowing of the life of God on to His creatures.

Through love he has created the beautiful world which we inhabit and the whole universe which gladdens our gaze. Everything proclaims loudly the love of our Creator: the smallest blade of grass whispers that it exists for us. Well did that Saint hear the voice of inanimate creation, who, walking through meadows, would gently touch the flowers and say: "I know, you tell me that God has made you for me, and that I must love Him with my whole heart."

It is God that supports us and prevents us from falling into nothingness. Like a tender mother He carries us in His Divine arms, shelters us from all danger, and showers His gifts profusely on and around us.

2. Redemption, Sanctification and Glorification

God is infinite love. The gift of life which He has made to us, and for our sake, to the material universe, could not satisfy

1. Jer. xxxi, 3.

His heart's desire. A lover longs to give himself to, and sacrifice himself for his beloved, and to make this gift and sacrifice an everlasting act. Bethlehem, Calvary, and the Altar show how God has fulfilled the law of love. In Bethlehem He gave Himself to us: "To you a Saviour is born." On Calvary He shed the very last drop of His Blood for us: "And walk in love, as Christ also hath loved you and delivered Himself up for us, an offering and a sacrifice of sweet savour to God."[1] On the Altar He gives and sacrifices Himself for each one of us, every minute of the day: "This is my Body which is given for you; do this for a commemoration of Me."[2]

In Christ and through Christ, God has made us the partakers of His very life. He has given us His grace and the host of gifts that go along with it: "By whom He hath given us most great and precious promises: that by these you may be made partakers of the Divine Nature."[3] Christ our Lord has established the Church to teach us infallibly His sacred doctrine, to sanctify and to guide us. He has left us seven channels through which the waters of grace flow from His Heart into our soul and body. From the Cross He gave us the sweetest gift of all—the gift of a mother—His Mother.

And what is God's purpose in showering so many gifts on us? Such gifts are but an earnest of the gift which God will make of Himself to the blessed soul, a beginning of that intimate union of God, the Infinite Lover, with the soul which He has drawn to Himself. God is, indeed, the heavenly Father Who, with outstretched arms calls to Himself the soul which He has created, along the path traced by His loving Providence and strewn with ever new flowers.

3. God's Gifts are Individual

But are not all such gifts—the creation of the universe and its preservation, man's Redemption and Sanctification—made indiscriminately to all men? Even if I had never existed, God would have created the world, and Christ would have died on the Cross. How then do such gifts argue God's love for me in particular?

1. Eph. v, 2. 2. Luke xxii, 19. 3. 2 Pet. i, 4.

And yet God's love in pouring out such gifts on each one of us could not be greater, were one alone the recipient of them. God loves us individually. For the least of us He would have created the world, He would have become man, and would have died on the Cross. "He loved *me*," St Paul would repeat, "and delivered Himself for *me*."

Moreover, is the benefit and the enjoyment which we derive from God's gifts, both natural and supernatural, less because we share them with others? "What does it matter," says St John Chrysostom, "that they are given to others, if what are given to you are as complete and perfect as if none of them were given to another than yourself?" Besides, is not companionship requisite to enjoy fully the good things of life? Is it not something mean and selfish to wish to have all things to oneself, with no one to share them?

4. Particular Gifts

Moreover, is not our whole life an uninterrupted series of gifts and favours received from God by each one of us in particular?

First, in the order of nature. God has given to each one of us a perfect, healthy body and the full use of our faculties, parents that care lovingly for us, the sweet companionship of brothers and sisters and friends, sufficiency, if not abundance, of temporal goods—joys, pleasures, amusements without number. From how many evils He has preserved us! How many dangers He has averted from us! With growing years, His gifts have also increased both in number and in magnitude, and if they be not unaccompanied with crosses, we know that, whatever the world and our weak nature may suggest to the contrary, the cross is the greatest gift of God to man.

Secondly, in the order of grace. Who can count or measure what God has done for each one of us in this order? The gift of Faith—how many favours it includes! And then our first Communion, our Christian education, and our state of life, lovingly chosen by God—it may be our call to a higher life in Religion, or to the Priesthood. How many sins He has forgiven us! How many warnings and inspirations He has sent us! How many prayers He has heard! How much light He has shed on our path! How many consolations He has poured into our hearts! Truly He has been all things to us.

Thirdly, in the order of glory. "I go to prepare a place for you." The Infinite Lover seems to be wholly occupied in preparing a throne and a crown of glory for the soul He loves. For every good deed of ours He adds a precious stone to our diadem. Every gift He lavishes on us is a mark of His desire to give Himself eternally to us and a means to draw us powerfully to His Heart. "In that day you shall know that I am in My Father, and you in Me, and I in you."

5. Sume et Suscipe

"What shall I render to the Lord for all that He hath given to me?"

First, a hymn of praise and thanksgiving. "It is truly meet and just, right and salutary that we should at all times and in all places give thanks to Thee, O holy Lord, Father Almighty, everlasting God."

Humble gratitude is the only attitude, which befits the soul in the presence of God's overwhelming benefits. "I am not worthy of the least of all Thy mercies, and of all the truth which Thou hast showed unto Thy servant."[1] To praise and give thanks is hard and galling to the proud man who boasts that he owes nothing either to his fellowmen or even to his Creator; but to good and noble men it is the sweetest of tasks. Gratitude opens more and more the hand that has given already. Gratitude to God is nothing else but the hymn of intelligent creatures, returning to Him all the rivulets of beauty, of wealth, and of grace that have flowed from that Primal Source; it is a joyful confession of our entire dependence on God's love and power.

Secondly, along with thanks, I must, with great reason and justice, give to His Majesty all that I have and all that I am. *Dilectus meus mihi et ego illi.*

"Take O Lord, and receive all my liberty, my memory, my understanding, and all my will, whatever I have and possess.

1. Gen. xxxii, 10.

Thou hast given me all these things; to Thee, O Lord I restore them; all are Thine, dispose of them entirely according to Thy Will. Give me Thy love and Thy grace, for these are enough for me."

Such an unreserved gift and absolute surrender to God, the Infinite Lover, on the part of the beloved soul is the best and surest expression of love, whether we consider what the beloved gives, or the extent of the gift, the manner in which the gift is made, or the motive that prompts it. Whoever makes such an oblation must neither do anything that he does not know to be God's Will, nor omit anything that he knows to be such. He must seek only God's pleasure in everything. The *Sume et Suscipe* realized in all the details of life, will make our life an uninterrupted act of love, free from illusions and self-deception.

A THANKSGIVING

Lord, in this dust Thy sovereign voice
First quicken'd love divine;
I am all Thine,—Thy care and choice,
My very praise is Thine.

I praise Thee, while Thy providence
In childhood frail I trace,
For blessings given, ere dawning sense
Could seek or scan Thy grace;

Blessings in boyhood's marvelling hour,
Bright dreams, and fancyings strange;
Blessings, when reason's awful power
Gave thought a bolder range.

Yet, Lord, in memory's fondest place
I shrine those seasons sad,
When, looking up, I saw Thy face
In kind austereness clad.

Newman.

SECOND POINT

1. In Search of God

The gifts of God are marks of His love, bouquets of flowers sent by the Infinite Lover to us, His beloved, darts sent by Him to wound our hearts. They are the wood whereby we kindle in us the fire of Divine love. The soul that sees itself to be an object of God's inexhaustible love, and feels inflamed with the desire of returning love for love, passionately longs for the presence of the Lover. Loaded with God's bounties, it cries with St John of the Cross:

Where hast Thou hidden Thyself,
And abandoned me in my groaning, O my Beloved?
Thou hast fled like the hart,
Having wounded me.
I ran after Thee, crying; but Thou wert gone.

O shepherds, you who go
Through the sheepcotes up the hill,
If you shall see Him
Whom I love the most,
Tell Him that I languish, suffer and die.

In search of my Love
I will go over mountains and strands;
I will gather no flowers,
I will fear no wild beasts:
And pass by the mighty and the frontiers.

In this second point of the Contemplation, St Ignatius teaches us how to seek and find God in all His creatures, and, most of all, within our own self. It is the great object of religion: "that they should seek God, if happily they may feel after Him or find Him, although He be not far from everyone of us: for in Him we live, and move and are."[1]

1. Acts xvii, 27, 28.

2. The Ever-Present Giver

God does not *send* His gifts like many other lovers, but He Himself graciously hands them to us. Everything which we use or enjoy, even the tiniest drop of water we swallow, may be looked upon as a kind of casket concealing the Infinite Lover. Though we do not see the Divine Hand, *we know* that we take it thence. Even more. God *is* in his gifts, and not merely hidden behind them. He is in the elements giving them being, in the plants giving them growth, in the animals giving them sensation, in men giving them understanding. He is in me giving me being, life, sensation, and causing me to understand. As when beholding a man's exterior, we pass on almost unconsciously, to regard the interior—the invisible soul which gives him being, life and motion—even so, beholding all creatures, we are to penetrate that which is within them, i. e., God, not indeed as their soul, but after another excellent manner by means of which He gives them being, and whatever they have.

Inexpressibly more wonderful is God's presence in His various supernatural gifts and communications. To impart Divine life to us the Son of God became man, and pitched His tent in our midst. He continues to live with us under the Sacramental Species. He Himself, present in His Church, teaches us the words of eternal life, gives us the waters of grace, and guides us heavenwards. Moreover, dwelling in us as in His mansion, He pours forth in our hearts the charity of God and all the gifts of the Holy Ghost.

In Heaven, the Divine Essence Itself is present in the mind of the Blessed as the mind's idea, i. e., as an intelligible to an intelligent thing.

3. Cor ad Cor

"What shall I return to the Lord for all He hath given me?"

We must seek God's presence in all things: "*videlicet in conversando cum aliquo, in ambulando, aspiciendo, gustando, audiendo . . . . in omnibus quae fecerimus,*" as St Ignatius says. We must try to know Him more and more intimately. To the feeling of humble and heartfelt gratitude with which our heart throbs at the sight of so many and so great benefits from God, must be added that of loving adoration and worship. We must give ourselves to God, the infinite Lover and the inexhaustible Giver, as to one, that dwells not beyond the clouds, but around us and in the very midst of our heart. We "are carried by His bowels and are borne up by His womb." God is a most tender mother. We must hold constant intercourse with Him, *cor ad Cor.* We must have recourse to Him throughout the day, in the midst of our work, our difficulties and our sufferings, as a child converses with and has recourse to its mother. Above all, we must make ourselves present to Him in our spiritual exercises. Our prayer should be an exchange of hearts, a requital of love.

THOU MUST SEEK MYSELF IN THEE

If by chance thou e'er shalt doubt
Where to turn in search of Me,
Seek not all the world about,
Only this can find Me out—
Thou must seek Myself in thee.

In the mansion of thy mind
Is my dwelling-place, and more
There I wander unconfined,
Knocking loud, if e'er I find
In thy heart a closèd door.

Search for Me without were vain,
Since when thou hast need of Me
Only call Me, and again
To My side I haste amain,
Thou must seek Myself in thee.

St Teresa.

THIRD POINT

1. The Indefatigable Lover

God, the All-Good and the Infinite Lover, is not content to manifest His love and His desire of ultimately giving Himself by showering gifts on us, while present to us more intimately than a mother is to her infant child. As a mother, with a deep and passionate love, prepares a cradle and linen for the child of her womb, so God has prepared and planned from all eternity for us, the children of His love, everyone of the creatures that contribute to our life and our delight. Even such an insignificant thing as the pen which I use, speaks to me of the infinite love of God ever thinking of me and ever working for me. That I may use it, God has made and preserved to this instant innumerable other things—the forces that produced the metal, the earth that kept it in its bowels, the men and the various instruments used to extract, to purify, to fashion and sell it, the means employed to convey it to me—all as messengers of a love whose only desire is to please me. It is God that, out of love, acts for me in all secondary causes; He enlightens and warms me in the sun, He gladdens my eye in the stars, He loves me in my relations and friends, He does me good in my benefactors, He instructs me in my teachers and directs me in my counsellors, He feeds me and slakes my thirst in the food and drink I take.

Reason, and still more, Faith, show us the Almighty as an *indefatigable lover*, constantly at work for us, solely prompted by love, and with but one end—a greater and more perfect communication of Himself to us.

In the natural world first of all.

"Are not five sparrows sold for two farthings, and not one of them is forgotten before God?

"Yea, the very hairs of your head are all numbered. Fear not therefore; you are of more value than many sparrows."[1]

Still more in the supernatural world—in the Church, which is but the body of Christ growing to its full maturity; in the soul of the just man, where the Three Divine Persons dwell as the living

1. Matt. x, 31.

fountain of charity; in heaven, where the Lord will gird Himself, and make His faithful friends sit down to meat, and passing, will minister to them.

2. Tecum in Laboribus

"What shall I return to the Lord for all that He hath given me?"

To the Infinite Lover, constantly active for me, I can but return a love that knows no rest. I must give myself to every duty of the moment, loving it as God's Holy Will, and doing it with all my heart, strength and mind. I must trust God's love wholly and blindly, receiving the sweet and the bitter as equally coming from His Heart. Out of love for Him, I must submit my will to the will of those who hold His place on earth; I must gladly spend myself and be spent on behalf of others.

THE WONDERFUL EFFECTS OF DIVINE LOVE

> Love is an excellent thing, a great good indeed which alone maketh light all that is burthensome, and beareth with even mind all that is unequal. For it carrieth a burthen without being burthened, and maketh all that is bitter, sweet and savoury. The love of Jesus is noble and it spurreth us on to do great things, and exciteth us to desire always that which is most perfect. Love wisheth to tend upwards, and is not to be detained by earthly things. Love will be at liberty and free from all worldly affection, lest its inner sight be hindered, lest it suffer itself to be entangled with any temporal interest or yield to difficulties. Nothing is sweeter than love, nothing stronger, nothing higher, nothing broader, nothing more pleasant, nothing more generous, nothing fuller or better in Heaven or earth; for love is born of God, and cannot rest but in God, above all things created. The lover flieth, runneth and rejoiceth, he is free and not held. He giveth all for all and hath all in all; because he resteth in one Sovereign Good above all, from Whom all good floweth and proceedeth.

Imitation of Christ.

FOURTH POINT

1. God in All

In the first point, St Ignatius has shown us the love of God communicating to us in His creatures all that He is and all that He has. In the second and third points, he has taught us to seek God in all His creatures, and to see Him unceasingly labouring for us in everyone of them. Briefly, the Saint has pointed out how we can make use of God's benefits to rise to the love that God displays in giving them. In the fourth point, he tells us to transcend God's benefits and to go straight to God, the infinite Goodness and Love.

The beloved, in his search after God, asks of all creatures planted by His loving hand, if He has passed through them:

O groves and thickets
Planted by the hand of the Beloved;
O verdant meads
Enamelled with flowers,
Tell me, has He passed by you?

And the creatures answer:

A thousand graces diffusing
He passed through the groves in haste,
And, merely regarding them
As He passed,
Clothed them with His beauty.

In St Ignatius' words we must look upon all things as the effects of God and the fruits of His love: "to see how all good things and gifts descend from above, as, for example, my limited power comes from the supreme and infinite Power on high, and in the same way, justice, pity, mercy, etc., just as the rays descend from the sun, and the waters from the spring."

By the very fact that God dwells and works in the creatures He so bountifully gives us, they are signs and reflections of Him, living images, however faint and imperfect, of His infinite perfections. They all bear in themselves His mark and impress. And if this is true of even the tiniest creature of God, much more is it so of man, made as he is in the image and likeness of his Creator, and inexpressibly more so of God's supernatural gifts.

2. DILECTUS MEUS MIHI ET EGO ILLI

"What shall I return to the Lord for all He hath given me?"

Every gift of God, as a mirror reflecting God's perfections and love, should contribute to increase my knowledge and my love of Him.

Accordingly, I must see God wherever I turn my eyes—in the order of the universe, in the beautiful things of nature and of art, in the discoveries of science, in my fellowmen, the special creatures of His love, in those that share His power and His authority, in the Church, the Bride of His love, and most of all in myself. "All things visible represent to me my Beloved," cries Blessed Ramon Lull. And again: "The lover regarded himself as a mirror in which he might see his Beloved."

I must love God in all things and all things in Him, on account of what they are in Him and have from Him, and even more, it the case of human beings, for what I hope they will eternally be. I may truly love all things lovable on earth and in Heaven, and not only God in them; but I must love them according to His Holy Will, i. e., according to the dictates of Reason and Revelation, because they are creatures of God, effects of His love, and subsist in images of Him. Created things are truly such; to consider them otherwise would be sheer idolatry. It is for us, however, to realize this fact more and more and make the sight of them, the use of them, or even the abstaining from any one of them, an act of Divine love and the means of approaching ever nearer to God, the infinite and inexhaustible Good.

And thus has St Ignatius shown us how we can make our life an uninterrupted vision and love of God, and how we can reach to the highest of God's love by thankfully praising Him, by reverently adoring Him, by working for Him, and by longing to be united with Him—always out of love and ever asking for a greater outpouring of it.

IMMOLATION

Dost thou believe in Me?
Yea, Lord, I do believe
Thou art Almighty God. What Thou dost give,
Or Death or Life, I equally receive.
Yet would I know Thee, Lord, whilst yet I live.

Dost thou love Me?
Yea, Lord, I love Thee well
Yet, if Love knew, Love could love better tell.

With thy whole Heart?
Yea, Lord, with all my heart,
For of Thy love my love is but a part.

With thy whole Soul?
Yea, Lord, with all my soul,
Yet doth the part still yearn to know the Whole.

With all thy Strength?
Yea, Lord, with all my might,
Yet should my Strength be stronger were there light.

With all thy Mind?
Yea, Lord,—but yet—but yet—
Forgive, Oh Lord, that chains their captives fret,
What doth avail Thy sunshine to the blind?
Dost thou not see how this poor little mind
Beats with vain hands against its prison bars?
See how they bleed! I hold to Thee the scars!
See how, with purblind eyes, more dim with tears,
It looks out through the unlifting mists of years.
May I not strive to see—not wish to know
And nearer to Thee by that knowledge grow
While yet I live?
All else, O Lord, I give. . . .

Give Me that too!
I will—*I do!*

H. W. Bliss.

APPENDICES

CONSIDERATIONS

A. OUR RELIGIOUS LIFE

I

OUR RELIGIOUS VOCATION.

I. Origin of our Vocation:—

1. God has called us.

> "You have not chosen Me, but I have chosen you."[1]

2. He has called us gratuitously.

> "Raising up the needy from the earth, and lifting up the poor out of the dung-hill: that He may place him with princes, with the princes of His people."[2]

Our heart must throb with feelings of humility, of confidence and joy, springing from the thought that He Who is infinite Goodness and Love has made us nothing in ourselves, that we may be everything in Him.

II. Object of our Vocation:—

1. *Amari et amare:*

The object of Religious Life is an ever closer communion of God with the soul and of the soul with God.

(1) Christ is the King that wants the religious soul to partake of His labours and of His glory; the Friend that wants to introduce it more and more into the secrets of His Heart; the Bridegroom that wants to give Himself wholly to it.

(2) The religious state, setting the soul free from all exterior cares, enables it to go straight to God; to offer to Him the greatest sacrifice, and constantly to practise the virtues that unite the creature with the Creator.

2. *Et laborare cum Christo:*—

The object of Religious Life is—through the mutual communion of God and the soul—to continue the life and mission of our Lord on earth.

> "And have appointed you, that you should go, and should bring forth fruit: and your fruit should remain."[3]

---

1. John xv, 16. 2. Ps. cxii, 7, 8. 3. John xv, 16.

(1) We must love souls as Christ loved them—in Christ Himself—and for Christ's sake give ourselves to them.

> "In this we have known the charity of God, because He hath laid down His life for us: and we ought to lay down our life for the brethren."[1]

(2) We must give Christ to souls by our prayers, by the example of a holy life, by our self-immolation, and by making use of all opportunities offered to us to turn souls to Him and to manifest His infinite goodness and beauty.

II
POVERTY

I. Excellence of Poverty:—

1. Poverty is freedom: the things of the earth are an obstacle to our progress towards Heaven; they cause cupidity, vainglory, excessive solicitude.

2. Poverty casts our soul on God; it enables us to be united with Him and to work with Him; it opens for us the gate of Heaven.

II. Our Lord's doctrine and example:—

> "Blessed are ye poor . . . . But woe to you that are rich."[2]
>
> "One thing is wanting unto thee: go, sell whatever thou hast and give it to the poor."[3]
>
> "So likewise everyone of you that doth not renounce all that he possesses, cannot be My disciple."[4]
>
> "The foxes have holes and the birds of the air nests: but the Son of Man hath not where to lay His head."[5]

III. The Virtue of Poverty:—

1. Our love for it:

We must love Poverty as a mother. Poverty is the basis of Religious Life; it feeds us materially and spiritually; it consoles us in life and death; it makes us heirs of the Kingdom of God.

2. Our practice of it:

We must love community life and dependence on our Superiors; dread exceptions and singularities; keep nothing superfluous, i. e., nothing that is not authorized by the practice of really good members of the community; be content with whatever is given us; and never complain of the effects of Poverty.

1. I John iii, 16. 2. Luke vi, 20-24. 3. Mark x, 21. 4. Luke xiv, 33. 5. Matt. viii, 20.

IV. The Vow of Poverty :—

1. Matter of the Vow :

Material things—not products of art or science—appreciable at a money value.

2. What is opposed to the Vow :

Animus domini, i. e., to possess or to use anything as one's own. Such disposition is shown by acting against the Superior's will.

Hence it is against the Vow of Poverty to accept, to keep, to use, to waste, to dispose in any way, of anything without the Superior's legitimate leave.

The permission may be express, tacit, or reasonably presumed, if the matter is urgent and one cannot go to the Superior.

3. Gravity of sins against the Vow of Poverty :

To sin grievously against the Vow of Poverty, the violation must concern things that, if stolen, would in all cases constitute a mortal sin ; or the act must be greatly opposed to the kind of Poverty professed by the Order. Beside sinning against the Vow, one may sin against justice if he appropriates to himself and disposes in any way of the goods of the community or of those to which the community was entitled.

When the thing is not alienated or consumed, but merely used, to measure the gravity of the sin, we must consider the value of the use and not the value of the thing itself.

III

CHASTITY

I. Nature of Religious Chastity :—

By the Vow of Chastity, a Religious sacrifices all carnal pleasures and marriage itself, a state that makes many of them lawful, that he may thereby secure greater union of his soul with God.

II. Excellence of Religious Chastity :—

It is the gauge of the union of the soul with Christ. Though every soul in God's grace is a spouse of Christ, the soul that has vowed chastity is pre-eminently so. Chastity in such a soul assumes the character of fidelity.

> "He that is unmarried hath a care for the things of the Lord, how he may please the Lord ; but he that is married hath a care for the things of the world, how he may please his wife and is drawn different ways, So also the un-

married woman and the virgin hath a care for the things of the Lord, that she may be holy both in body and soul."[1]

Chastity, with its attendant virtues of modesty, self-restraint, temperance, is the great antiseptic, the myrrh that embalms our carnal nature and keeps it pure till God touches it with new life and immortality. Talking in general, a Religious that keeps his chastity unspotted, is sure of maintaining himself in the friendship of God.

III. Fruits of Religious Chastity :—

1. Strength. Of every Religious it may be said as of Judith, "Thy heart has been strengthened because thou hast loved chastity."

2. Devotion. It is in a pure heart that there burns uninterruptedly the fire which Christ came to kindle on earth. The Religious finds in Christ's little ones, in His needy and suffering members father and mother and child, and spouse, and brethren, and pours out upon them and receives from them a hundredfold that affection which he might have had in the narrow sphere of a single household.

IV. Obligation of the Vow of Chastity :—

Any sin against chastity and any attempt to marry is a violation of the Vow and constitutes a sacrilege, or the taking away what was solemnly promised and dedicated to God. Sins *directly* against chastity are mortal if the two other conditions, i. e., knowledge and consent are verified. Sins *indirectly* against chastity such as immodesty, intemperance, etc., admit of parvity of matter.

IV

OBEDIENCE

I. Excellence of Obedience:—

1. Obedience is the greatest of moral virtues as it inclines man to yield up the stronghold of his individuality, i. e., his will and liberty. It is the substitution of God's Will at the centre of life instead of one's own.

2. Through Obedience a religious person becomes a perfect holocaust to His Divine Majesty. Obedience is, for a religious man, the cross of which our Lord spoke, when He said:

"If any man will come after Me, let him deny himself, and take up his cross and follow Me."[2]

1. Cor. vii, 32-34. 2. Matt. xvii, 24.

II. Advantages of Obedience :—

1. Obedience is the root of all virtues.

2. In particular, it implies a constant exercise of humility and charity.

3. It is a source of peace, of security, and of ever increasing merit.

III. The example of our Lord :—

"And was subject to them."[1]

"He humbled Himself, becoming obedient unto death, even to the death of the cross."[2]

IV. The virtue of Obedience :—

We must every day try to make our life a constant act of loving submission to God's Will and to the will of those that hold God's place.

1. Our Obedience, therefore, must be rendered to Christ and for the love of Christ, acknowledging Christ alone in the Superior, whoever he be, and his voice as the voice of Christ.

2. It must be full of trust and confidence in Christ's infinite love and providence.

3. It must be perfect, doing whatever the Superior wills and as he wills it, and conforming our will and judgement to his.

V. The Vow of Obedience :—

By virtue of the Vow, a religious person is bound to obey under mortal sin whenever the Superior commands according to the Rule provided the thing commanded is of moment and the order is given in virtue of holy Obedience.

V

OBSERVANCE OF THE RULE

I. Aim of Rules :—

The special object of each Religious Congregation and it characteristic traits are embodied in its Constitutions, its Rules, and its manner of life.

Our Rules, therefore, are helps to observe the Religious Vows and practise all other virtues, i. e., to keep the law of charity and attain perfection, according to the spirit of our Institute.

II. Excellence of our Rules :—

1. They are the expression of God's Holy will and of the will of Holy Mother the Church which has approved them.

1. Luke ii, 52. 2. Phil. ii, 8.

2. To observe them is to preserve oneself from all evil: they are a hedge round about the garden of our soul, the outworks of the interior citadel.

3. They are the surest and shortest ways to perfection, as the life of St John Berchmans well shows it.

4. They are the source of peace, of charity, of fruitful work.

III. How the Rules ought to be observed:—

1. Faithfully and diligently.

2. Out of love for our Lord to Whom the Rules unite us; out of love for our Vocation, perseverance in which is bound up with observance of the Rules, and for our religious perfection.

3. We must, above all, detest the *habit* of breaking any of our Rules.

IV. Obligation of the Rules:—

Though, ordinarily, Rules do not bind under sin, it is rare for one to violate a Rule without committing, at least, some venial sin, prompted as he usually is, in his acting against the Rules, by some ill-regulated motive.

VI

MENTAL PRAYER

I. Object of Prayer:—

The object of prayer is to fix our soul in a state of habitual union with Christ our Lord. Through prayer Christ becomes the atmosphere in which we live, the sun in which we bask, the life which we live. Prayer makes us fit instruments in the hands of God for the salvation of souls. If we do not pray, we are cut off from the source of grace. The souls that come to us feel that we are not in touch with God. The busier we are, the greater our need of prayer.

II. What our Prayer should not be:—

1. It should not be a kind of spiritual reading or a light consideration.

2. It should not be an examination of conscience. Nothing dries up more quickly the springs of spiritual life than the constant thinking of ourselves, even of our defects.

3. It should not be an isolated item of our daily life, but it must rather be extended throughout the day. However busy, we must be able always to converse with God with peace, with joy, and with fervour.

4. Above all it should not be looked upon as a heavy, unpleasant duty, but as the hour of loving intercourse with God, "the hour in which the soul lives: that is, lives its true life and rehearses for the life of eternity ..... when the heart speaks to God, and—what is of infinitely greater moment—when God speaks to the heart."

III. Characteristics of our Prayer:—

1. It must have its fixed time, fixed subject matter, fixed method, to be varied, as far as lies with us, according to our needs and dispositions.

2. It should be a mutual intercourse of heart to heart. Though the exercise of the other faculties is necessary—the truth or fact we contemplate must be thoroughly grasped and made part and parcel of our being—prayer must be chiefly a work of the heart.

3. We must constantly ask our Lord to teach us to pray and make daily efforts to progress in this Divine art.

IV. Main subject matter of our prayer:—

1. The words and deeds of our Lord and, above all, His sacred Person as revealed to us in Holy Scripture and especially in the New Testament.

2. The prayers of the Church, and especially the Psalms, the Ordinary and the Proper of the Mass.

3. The various Mysteries, Feasts and Sacred Seasons which month after month, our holy Mother the Church places before our eyes.

VII
FRATERNAL CHARITY

I. Excellence of Charity:—

The love of our neighbour is both the mark and the measure of our love for God.

II. Characteristics of true Charity:—

St. Paul has given them in his first letter to the Corinthians, Chapter XIII:

> "Charity is patient, is kind; charity envieth not, dealeth not perversely; is not puffed up; is not ambitious, seeketh not her own, is not provoked to anger, thinketh no evil; rejoiceth not in iniquity, but rejoiceth with the truth; beareth all things, hopeth all things, endureth all things."

Our fraternal charity must be —

1. Supernatural, prompted by grace and based mainly on Divine motives. "I and thou and between us Jesus," gives the note of true friendship.

2. Considerate, i. e., particular and individual.

3. Kind: "Nothing draws us nearer to God than the effort of the heart to trample on self, and this effort of unselfishness is rarely more effectively made than when we strive to be kind to others."

4. Patient and forgiving.

5. Sympathetic: "Rejoice with them that rejoice, weep with them that weep."[1] In dealing with others, nothing helps one so much as to have a tender and sympathetic heart.

We must abstain from anything that can hurt the feelings, especially of the sensitive and of the suffering: reduce our self-assertion to the lowest possible figure, and mortify our aggressiveness in matter of rights, claims, credit, place, gratification; and try to please others, i. e., to find out what will help and recreate others, make a morose man smile, rest one overworked, draw out of himself an anxious one, promote general cheerfulness.

III. Sources of Charity:—

1. The Sacred Heart of Jesus. In Him alone shall we find light and strength to love our brethren as He loves them.

2. A constant effort to divest oneself of one's self-love, self-will, self-interest.

VIII

"GO AND TEACH"

I. Greatness of the Christian Teacher:—

> "Is there anything greater than to discipline souls and mould the ways of the young? I certainly consider the person that knows how to mould the souls of the young far superior to any sculptor and to any painter."[2]

The Christian Teacher is God's helper in the development of souls; the channel through which God's grace flows into them. This is particularly true in the case of little children, the choicest of flowers in Christ's garden.

II. Object of Christian Education:—

The symmetrical development of body and soul, mind, heart and will, i. e., of the whole personality, according to the nature and

1. Rom. xii, 15. 2. St John Chrysostom.

dignity of a being created in the image and likeness of his Creator and redeemed by Christ our Lord.

III. Nature of Christian Education :—

1. It must, first of all, be directed solidly to form the Christian character of our pupils and to give them a thorough grasp of the Faith.

2. It must be Christian throughout, whatever be the subject we teach.

3. It must be truly educative, not loading the memories of our pupils with facts, but gradually training them to see, to think, and to reason for themselves.

4. It must be individual, i. e., we must identify ourselves with each one of our pupils, we must know his needs, his difficulties and the way to help him.

In particular, we should look after the most refractory of our pupils and after those who have qualities that make for leadership.

IV. What a Christian Teacher should be :—

1. He must sacrifice himself without limit and without reserve : Christian teaching must be *the* work of one's life — a vocation and not a profession.

2. He himself must, first, be formed after Christ, the Divine Model, and live by His life, for the teacher *is* the school.

3. He must have a high esteem and love of his work and of his pupils, trying to gain their love and their confidence.

4. He must never give way to discouragement. The teacher, especially, "beareth all things, hopeth all things, endureth all things."

5. He must seek constantly to improve himself.

6. He must pray : and what better prayer can he daily offer to God for his pupils than the following prayer of St Peter Canisius :

> O Lord Jesus, Who for these children did not hesitate to die a most bitter death, Who look upon them as exceedingly dear to You, Who commanded them to be brought to You, Who deem whatever is done to them as done to Yourself, I pray and entreat You to keep them in Your Name. Yours they are, and to me You have given them. Place Your words in my mouth : open their hearts, that they may learn to love You and to fear You. Turn away Your face from my sins, so that nothing in me may stand in the way of Your goodness. Grant that the task You have imposed upon me of instructing these children, I may fulfil wisely, holily, firmly, for Your glory which alone I have in view in this work. Amen.

B. THE SOUL, GOD'S INNER SHRINE

I

"YOU ARE THE TEMPLE OF GOD"

1.

A Soul in grace is God's shrine :—

> "Know you not that you are the temple of God, and that the Spirit of God dwelleth in you ?"[1]

> "Or know you not that your members are the temple of the Holy Ghost, Who is in you, Whom you have from God and you are not your own ?"[2]

> "And what agreement hath the temple of God with idols? For you are the temple of the living God."[3]

> "If anyone love Me, he will keep My word, and My Father will love him and We will come to him, and will make our abode with him."[4]

Christ dwells in it :—

1) As the principle of supernatural life.

> "I am the vine ; you the branches : he that abideth in Me and I in him, the same beareth much fruit, for without Me you can do nothing."[5]

2) As a fountain of living water springing up into eternal life.

> "He that believeth in Me, as the Scripture saith, Out of his belly shall flow rivers of living water."[6]

3) As the head of the body of which each one of us is a member.

> "Now you are the body of Christ, and members of member."[7]

2.

The end of the Retreat is to purify, to restore, and to beautify the temple of God in the soul : "that Christ may dwell by faith in your hearts."[8]

3.

The Railings of the Temple :—

1) Modesty, especially of the eyes.
2) Silence :—
   a) the Great Silence ;
   b) Silence during the day ;
   c) the Silence of Charity and of Humility.

---

1. I Cor. iii, 16. 2. I Cor. vi, 19. 3. II Cor. vi, 16. 4. John xiv, 23.
5. John xv, 5. 6. John vii, 38. 7. I Cor. xii, 27. 8. Eph. iii, 17.

3) Recollectedness:—
   a) Mind your own business;
   b) Control of one's imagination and heart;
   c) Union with God.

II

THE PURIFICATION OF THE TEMPLE

"All the army assembled together, and they went up into mount Sion. And they saw the Sanctuary desolate, and the gates burnt, and shrubs growing up in the courts as in a forest or on the mountains, and the chambers joining to the temple thrown down. And they rent their garments, and made great lamentation, and put ashes on their heads."[1]

1. Things that must be removed

1) Impure animals that profane and desecrate the temple of God in our soul: mortal sins.

2) Idols that must be pulled down and cut to pieces, daily: the evil inclinations of our mind and heart, especially egotism with its two main branches, love of independence and love of comforts.

3) Dirt and stains that must be constantly removed: venial sins, deliberate and half-deliberate; slothfulness.

2. Means

1) Examination of Conscience: foresee occasions of failures and take precautions;

2) Confession;

3) Particular Examination;

4) Renewal of spirit from time to time;

5) Self-denial: never yield to thyself.

"There is one thing which keeps many back from spiritual progress and fervent amendment, and that is the dread of difficulty, or the labour of the conflict And they indeed advance most above all others in virtue, who strive manfully to overcome those things which they find more grievous or contrary. For there a man makes greater progress and merits greater grace, where he overcomes himself more and mortifies himself in spirit."

1. I Mac. iv, 37-39.

III

THE FOUNDATIONS OF GOD'S TEMPLE

"And the rain fell, and the floods came, and the winds blew, and they beat upon that house, and it fell not, for it was founded on a rock."[1]

Deep and heartfelt humility constitutes the foundations of the temple of God in our soul.

"When thou art invited to a wedding......sit down in the lowest place."[2]

"Dost thou plan to raise a big spiritual edifice? See first of all to the foundation of humility......The greater the edifice, the deeper does one dig the foundation."[3]

1.

Negative Side

1) Drive away:
   i) thoughts of self-complacency;
   ii) desires of praise;
   iii) unkind thoughts of others.
2) Carefully avoid:
   i) speaking of yourself and setting yourself up as a model;
   ii) sticking obstinately to your views;
   iii) talking unkindly of others and of their work;
   iv) criticizing superiors.
3) Conquer, or at least keep under control:
   i) feelings of anger, of resentment, and of impatience;
   ii) any sulkiness;
   iii) feelings of discouragement.

2.

Positive Side

1) Always cultivate in your heart an abiding sorrow for your sins.

2) Look upon your companions as the chosen friends of Christ and consider yourself unworthy to serve them. "Sit down in the lowest place."

3) Whenever anything hard and humiliating befalls you, say promptly: "It serves thee right."

1. Matt. vii, 25. 2. Luke xiv, 8-10. 3. St Augustine.

IV

THE STRUCTURE OF GOD'S TEMPLE

1) The floor of God's temple:

Obedience and subjection for the love of Christ.

"And He was subject to them."[1]

2) The Golden walls of God's temple:

True evangelical Poverty.

"The Son of man hath not where to lay His head."[2]

3) The crystal windows of God's temple:

Chastity of mind and body.

"Blessed are the pure of heart for they shall see God."[3]

4) Its green and azure roof:

And boundless confidence in God.

"The Lord ruleth me, and I shall want nothing."[4]

V

THE WOOD FOR THE SACRIFICE

The daily cross of our self-immolation and self-abnegation:—

1) The crosses which God Himself sends us either directly or indirectly through His creatures: petty pains and discomforts; troubles, annoyances, and disappointments, misunderstandings and contradictions; neglect and ingratitude.

"The sacrament of suffering is the sacrament that God administers through every creature and the most difficult to receive with the proper dispositions."

2) The crosses inseparable from our state of life and our temperament: the daily round of irritating concerns and duties, the special difficulties due to our own temperament, likings and dislikings—the climate—our state of health.

3) The crosses which we must freely embrace: "Let each be convinced that he will make progress in all spiritual matters in proportion as he shall have divested himself of his self-love, self-will, and self-interest." "If any man will come after Me, let him deny himself and take up his cross."

4) The point which will be in particular the object of constant abnegation and mortification: the subject matter of our Particular Examen.

1. Luke ii, 57. 2. Luke ix, 58. 3. Matt. v, 8. 4. Ps. xxii, 1.

VI

THE INCENSE OF PRAYER

"Let my prayer, O Lord, ascend like incense in Thy sight."

Prayer must be the life of our soul, and the busier the life is, the more intense should the prayer be.

Characteristic notes of our exercises of piety:

1) they must stand first;

2) all the prescribed time must be given to them;

3) they must be diligently performed, driving away all wilful distraction and drowsiness;

4) they must be sustained by the habit of frequent and fervent ejaculatory prayers.

VII

THE GROUNDS

The choicest flowers should grow in them to delight and charm the eyes of even casual passers-by. Our aim should be to draw souls to us by the charm of our ways, and the sweetness of our virtues, and then lead them to our Lord, the perennial spring of our whole life.

1. Charity :—
    1) Supernatural: "I and thou and Jesus between."
    2) Devoted: "meet in all good things the wishes of others." (St Anselm).

       Forget thyself to please and help others.
    3) Considerate: each soul is a little world, and not a clod of earth.
2. Meekness and Patience:

   Yield to others: don't be fighting, grasping, aggressive, self-asserting.
3. Kindness:

   Never say anything that may offend or wound.
4. Politeness and Gentleness.
5. Always cheerful.
6. Sympathetic:

   Throw yourself out of yourself. Try to please others: try to find out what will help and recreate others, make a morose person smile etc.

VIII

THE DEDICATION OF THE TEMPLE

The Enthronement of the Sacred Heart in the Shrine of our own heart and our absolute and irrevocable consecration to Him: *Sume et dispone.*

Our Lord takes possession of the temple of our heart and in it, as on a throne of love, He sacrifices Himself continually for the glory of the Father and for the salvation of mankind; and we with Him and for Him. He becomes the heart of our heart, the life of our life, the spring of all our activity. We may consider Him as a furnace of love: as a sun that enlightens and warms: as an ocean of water watering the flowers of our garden. "A river of water of life clear as crystal, from the throne of God and of the Lamb."[1] — As an abyss of all grace and virtue where we may plunge all our miseries and imperfections and sins and be clothed with the infinite treasures of the Divine Heart.[2] — We must often enter into this Divine Temple, shut ourselves in with the key of loving confidence and remain there as long as we can. Our faculties must be the ministering Angels: the memory will be filled with our Lord, the intellect, busy in knowing Him more and more and the will, in loving Him passionately. Here we retire in time of prayer and silence. Here we come with the wood of our mortifications to keep the fire burning, and to burn our incense. The zeal of the love of the Sacred Heart will punish by means of some penance any profanation that may have been committed.

Mary the Custodian of God's Temple

Mary's Rôle:—

All comes through Mary: Jesus and with Jesus everything else.

We chiefly need humility and confidence: the devotion to Mary maintains these virtues in our heart.

Mary is the model all virtues.

Practices in her Honour:—

Constant recourse to her; imitation of her virtues; Rosary; Angelus; visits to her altars and shrines; the keeping of her Novenas and Feasts.

Our Heavenly Helpers

St. Joseph; our Guardian Angel.

1. Ap. xxii, 1. 2. Cf. The abysses of the Sacred Heart in St Margaret Mary's writings.

C. PRIESTLY REFORMS

I

THE PURIFICATION OF A PRIEST'S HEART

ACCORDING TO THE TRIPLE COLLOQUY OF THE THIRD EXERCISE OF THE FIRST WEEK

1. "That I may feel an interior knowledge of my sins and an abhorrence of them."
   (1) Habitual sins;
   (2) Besetting sin;
   (3) Proximate occasions of sin.

2. "That I may feel the disorder of my actions in order that, abhorring it, I may amend and order myself rightly."
   (1) Lack of right and pure intention;
   (2) Lack of regularity;
   (3) Sluggishness.

3. "That I may know the world, in order that abhorring it, I may put away from myself worldly and vain things."
   (1) Natural principles and motives of life;
   (2) Pride and insubordination;
   (3) Love of money and comforts.

II

THE PRAYER OF A PRIEST

The Mass: the Priest lives by the Mass and for the Mass.

Preparation:—

(1) Remote: the whole day;

(2) Proximate: meditation.

Subject matter of meditation: Missal, Breviary, Scripture, especially the New Testament.

Celebration:—

(1) Careful as to ceremonies;

(2) Devout.

Thanksgiving:

Never to be omitted—at least for a few minutes; continued throughout the day by frequent and fervent visits to the Blessed Sacrament: a few such visits should be fixed.

The Breviary: "Let nothing be placed before the Divine Office."

(1) Constant attention;

(2) Slowly: "Haste is the ruin of devotion." (St Francis of Sales);

(3) Best time, place, posture.

Administration of Sacraments: especially Eucharist and Penance; and Divine Services:

(1) Careful observance of ceremonies;

(2) Piety visible to all.

Preaching:

Serious preparation: "Let us work on our knees." Our preaching must be the voice of the Divine Master prolonged in all its majestic simplicity.

God's House:

"Dilexi decorem Domus Tuae."

Spiritual Reading:

Scripture and lives of Saints: knowledge of spiritual life.

Night Examination of Conscience:

Special attention on a few fixed points.

Confession:

"A thing forcibly brought home to me by experience is the capital importance to a Priest of weekly Confession. Every serious prevarication goes with a neglect of Confession" (Fr Rickaby).

Throughout the Day:

Union and familiar intercourse with our Lord.

III

THE SANCTIFICATION OF A PRIEST'S ACTIVITIES

The Church and Christ's Vicar: loving attachment.

The Bishop: obedience and loyalty: "Omnes Episcopo obtemperate ut Jesus Christus Patri" (St Ignatius, M.).

Other Ecclesiastical Superiors: respect, obedience, subordination.

Brothers in the Priesthood: respect; *never* say anything disparaging; help, spiritually by brotherly correction, in the ministry, and materially.

Helpers in the Ministry: confidence and sympathy.

Souls entrusted to his care:—

knowledge of them in particular;
instruction: catechism in church and school; and privately;
the sick;
children;
boys: vocations;
young men;
pious souls: direction;
nuns: respect them—help them—use them—direct them;
slack and bad Catholics: win their heart and confidence;
non-Catholics: don't miss opportunities to instruct them and promote lay apostolate.

Civil Authorities: respect and obedience in their sphere; win their respect and confidence.

Visits: complimentary, if at all, few and short.

Invitation to meals, etc.: a Priest usually gains by declining them: sobriety and edification in our talk.

Casual Companions, v. g.,: travelling: "*bonus odor Christi.*"

Money affairs, suits, fees, etc.: always *ut alter Christus.* We must safeguard the rights of the Church, but woe to a Priest if people think that he is attached to money.
Accounts always in order.

Family Relations: "*In iis quae Patris Mei sunt oportet Me esse.*

IV

A PRIEST'S IMMOLATIONS

1. Chastity.
2. Duties: unpleasant—insignificant—monotonous, to be diligently performed.
3. Weaknesses: natural likings and dislikings, to be constantly controlled and overcome.
4. Sufferings: contradictions—failures—lack of encouragement—disapproval—lack of means—sickness, all to be borne for the sake of Christ.

5. Mortification of
   i) imagination : restraint on idle thoughts ; the sternest discipline as to bad thoughts ; self-denial as to reading, pictures, etc.;
   ii) will : repress the least sign of revolt, of wilfulness, and of sulkiness ;
   iii) intellect : avoid being cocksure ;
   iv) eyes : modesty, even with ourselves ;
   v) tongue : always speak the truth ; keep secrets, never speak ill of others ; no grumblings ; be polite and clean in every word ; no jokes about holy things.
   vi) touch.
6. Mortification of Body, as regards food and drink ; smoking ; sleep ; amusements ; corporal chastisement.

Christo Confixus sum Cruci in laboribus in vigiliis, in jejuniis.

V

A PRIEST'S REFORM

Cf. page 135.

D. SACRIFICIA A SACERDOTE OFFERENDA

I

SACRIFICIUM LABIORUM

The Duty of Praise :—

The whole universe should be a hymn of praise to God, our Creator and Lord.

Inanimate creatures blindly obey the Creator's laws and thus praise Him: *Caeli enarrant gloriam Dei.* Still, they are dumb: "they speak by silences."

Man is the conductor of the choir formed of all material creatures: he is their mind and heart. He must praise God for himself and he must praise Him in their name, for His infinite greatness and for His inexhaustible goodness toward all.

The love of God truly appears infinite in His gifts when we consider:

> *quis dat—cui dat—quot et quanta dat—quo amore et desiderio dat.*

Man's only possible attitude in the presence of God is one of praise and of thanksgiving of the heart and the lips.

> *Te Deum laudamus.*
> *Agimus Tibi gratias, omnipotens Deus.*
> *Gloria Patri et Filio et Spiritui Sancto.*

So did all the Saints.

But many men are ungrateful, and many more forget what they owe to God.

Hence a man is set apart—the Priest—to offer a continuous sacrifice of praise to God, in the name of all, and in union with Christ: *in unione illius divinae intentionis qua ipse in terris laudes Deo persolvisti.*

An instrument is given to him on which to play an ever new symphony to the Lord—the Breviary.

The beauties of the Breviary :—

1) It is the prayer of Christ and of Christ's mystical Body, the Church.

2) The Psalms, in particular, are *voces Spiritus Sancti, vox Ecclesiae,* the voice of Christ.

"Every emotion of man, pure and noble, has been set to words in the Psalms."

3) The Breviary gives us the best parts of Holy Scripture; the words and the works of the Saints; the best hymns in honour of God, and the best prayers we can offer to Him.

4) The Breviary furnishes us with continual food for prayer, for meditation and for spiritual reading, whatever be our dispositions and the time of the year.

Requisites to say the Breviary properly :—

1) Constant attention;
2) Slowly and distinctly;
3) The choice of the most appropriate time, place and posture.

II
SACRIFICIUM CORDIS

In spiritu humilitatis et in animo contrito suscipiamur a Te, Domine.

Christianity has brought to us the consciousness of our sins and of our sinfulness.

Such consciousness is the most essential thing in spiritual life: the least trace of self-complacency and self-approval and of disparagement of others is an abomination before God.

Interior humility implies :—

1) An abiding consciousness of our misery, and sorrow for our sins and ingratitude;
2) Fear and distrust of self;
3) Sincere esteem of others.

It is fostered by :—

1) Daily examination of conscience;
2) Frequent Confession;
3) The love of *ama nesciri et pro nihilo reputari.*

In case of failures, of snubs, of contradictions, we must raise our heart to our Crucified King and thank Him, though in the midst of tears.

Exterior humility implies :—

1) Care of the good name of others: we must beware of running down or even belittling others, and of destructive and uncharitable criticism.

2) A constant watch against worldliness, by cultivating ;
   i) the spirit of penance and mortification ;
   ii) the hatred of all unnecessary show ;
   iii) the spirit of obedience and submission.

III
SACRIFICIUM CORPORIS

Excellence of Purity :—

The body is the instrument of the soul: the senses are the windows through which the soul looks at the outer world.

Through the senses the soul gets in touch with material creation ; it uses it for the development of the whole man ; it raises it and spiritualizes it.

Danger of the soul being unduly attracted by creatures; of being immersed in them.

Purity is the divine purifier of our knowledge and love of creatures; it is a divine antiseptic; the myrrh that preserves our bodies from corruption.

Our Lord's doctrine: "Blessed are the pure."

St Paul's doctrine: I Cor. vii, 32 ff.

What Purity is to a Priest :—

1. The strength of his interior life.

Interior life is the heart turned Godwards: it is living in a Divine atmosphere, in touch with the Divine realities, with Christ. Purity gives to the whole man an affinity with God: it makes him a fit member of Christ's Body and the temple of the Holy Ghost.

2. The strength of his apostolic life.

Purity gives love to the heart, freedom and energy to the will, youth and strength to the body.

3. The gauge of his consecration and dedication to Christ, the bond of union with Him.

4. Purity is indispensable: without it the life of a Priest is a continuous sacrilege.

How to keep pure :—

It is not very difficult to be perfectly chaste: it is indeed very difficult to be just pure enough to avoid serious sins.

1) We must watch over :—

i) our eyes,

ii) our reading,

iii) our thoughts and imagination,

iv) our body,

v) our heart,

vi) our dealings with others.

2) We must fill our minds and hearts with the thought and love of Jesus and Mary and with the most touching scenes of their life. We must humbly and trustfully pray to them.

3) We must love the Cross :—

i) work hard;

ii) be temperate;

iii) practise some mortfication.

4) We should never deceive ourselves, but declare war *a outrance* to anything that stains: it is the ruin of soul, of our work, of God's work.

IV
SACRIFICIUM CHRISTI

Christ the High Priest :—

Christ as God is the centre of the whole universe: *Primogenitus omnis creaturae*; *Omnia per Ipsum.*

As Man, Christ is the Restorer of creation, the New Adam, the Head and Heart of regenerated mankind: *Oportet Illum regnare ... ut sit Deus omnia in omnibus.*

From the beginning Christ was the Priest and the Victim: *Agnus occisus a constitutione mundi.*

All other victims were symbols and types of Christ, and acceptable to God in Christ.

Becoming Man, Christ was Victim—at His Incarnation: *Hostiam et oblationem noluisti, corpus autem aptasti mihi;*

during His whole life;

during His Passion.

On the Cross He laid down His life; He poured out His life-blood in sacrifice of sweetness to the Father.

The Mass :—

The Mass is the Sacrifice of Christ made over by Him to His Church; it is the representation of the Sacrifice of Calvary and the means whereby we come in contact with its saving power.

The Priest is Christ's minister, His organ and co-operator. With Christ, he should offer the sacrifice of himself, i. e., his adorations, his thanksgiving, his atonement and his supplications: *adimpleo ea quae desunt passioni Christi.*

Sanctity which the Mass demands in the Priest :—

He must live for the Mass and by it.

How to celebrate Mass devoutly :—

Before Mass: remote preparation—purity of conscience; immediate preparation—prayer, meditation.

During Mass: perfect observance of rubrics; especially, distinct pronunciation of all the words, and dignity in all movements;

"Qui Missam praecipitat in infernum praecipitat."

After Mass: thanksgiving.

V

OPUS CHRISTI

The Priest is Christ's apostle :—

The Priest is not only a victim that offers *sacrificium labiorum, cordis, et corporis;* not only the visible Priest that offers Christ's Sacrifice; not only the dispenser of God's grace; and the ambassador of Christ: *legatione pro Christo fungimur;*

with Christ he lives *ut testimonium perhibeat veritati.*
and with Christ he must say: *manifestavi Nomen Tuum hominibus.*

This is especially true of Missionary Priests—God's fighters in the war zone.

Motives for zeal :—

1) The dignity of the work: *divinorum divinissimum.*

2) Christ's wish: *Sitio.*

3) Our duty.

Foundations of our zeal :—

1) *Deus vult omnes homines salvos fieri:* every soul we chance to meet.

2) He wants to save them through men.

3) The conversion of a soul is God's work, but I may turn it towards the Light; I may reflect to it the Light, and I must seek how to do it effectively in each particular case.

General means :—

1. I must have the conquering spirit; be truly *procurator Christi*;

2. Seek all ways to bring souls to Him;

3. Make use of all opportunities afforded to me.

4. In trying to bring to Christ persons who are not of the Faith or do not belong to the true Church, I must imitate our Lord: get something, if I cannot get all: raise them a little higher; draw them a little nearer to Him.

In every case I must do *my utmost*, and not only *my bit*.

In particular :—

1. Living apologetics: I must announce the Gospel by speaking deeds; by being an incarnation of the Gospel.

2. Prayer: votive Masses for the Propagation of the Faith; for schismatics.

3. Penance.

4. I must prepare apostles amongst Catholics: instruct all well in the Faith, but a select few, in a particular way;

Promote zeal, and Vocations—even lay-Vocations, amongst women especially;

Make the best use of nuns and other religious in the parish.

5. I must daily fit myself better for my work by studying more and more our Catholic Doctrine and how to present it, the mentality, the customs of persons I want to reach, their language, and anything that can raise me in the eyes of non-Christians and make me more useful to them.

6. I must have an entry-book of losses and gains; now and then have an eye on the losses—

careless Catholics, bad Catholics, lapsed Catholics, ought-to-be Catholics—

and *every day try* to do *something*.

How is it that just in the same circumstances some Priests make always converts, and some Priests none?

E. A PROGRAMME OF LIFE FOR YOUNG PEOPLE

I

KNOWLEDGE AND LOVE OF CHRIST

Christianity is nothing else but Christ — the knowledge of Christ and the love of Christ and of everybody else in Him. Christ alone is the Truth. "He that believeth in the Son hath life everlasting." Christ is our Way to the Father, our Model and Pattern. "If any one will come after Me, let him deny himself, and take up his cross, and follow Me." Through Him is the Divine Life communicated to us. By abiding in His love we become one with Him and one with all His brothers.

1.

Has the knowledge of our Lord Jesus Christ struck deep root within me?

Have I ever carefully read His Gospel? Am I imbued with His principles of life? Am I conversant with the truths He has revealed to us? Do.I thoroughly know the catechism?

2.

What restraint does the thought of Jesus Christ exercise on me?

Do I realize that sin is not merely a foible or a shortcoming, but a deliberate offence against Jesus Christ, a wound inflicted on His Heart, a deliberate attempt to turn Him out of the temple of my soul?

3.

What is our Lord to me?

Is He a living Friend, to Whom I turn in my trials, in my needs, with Whom I love to share my joys and my sorrows — or is He only a shadowy being Whom we still happen to worship in our churches? Did I ever shed a tear for the anguished Sufferer of Gethsemane? What consolation did I seek from Him in my sorrows? Did His triumphs ever interest me? Do I desire that He should be known and loved by all men?

II

CHRIST LIVING IN THE BLESSED EUCHARIST AND IN THE CHURCH

Christ is the Life of our life. We long to see Him, to feel Him, and to converse with Him. In His infinite love for us, He has fully satisfied these desires of our heart. He is truly Emmanuel, that is, God with us. He has pitched His Tabernacle of love in our midst. He is with us every day, till the end of time.

1.

"My delights are to be with the children of men."

In every Tabernacle of our churches there dwells under the Sacramental species the same Christ Who lived, wrought miracles, suffered and died for us, and Who now sits at the right hand of the Father. On our Altars there is daily renewed the Sacrifice of Calvary. In our Communions we receive the Body and the Blood of Christ, and become one with Him.

Have these ineffable truths ever sunk deeply into my heart? Do I ever think of my lonely Friend in the Tabernacle? Do I love to visit Jesus and talk with Him of my needs and my difficulties? Do I feel sick for a sight of the Tabernacle, whenever forced to live away from the church? Do I prepare myself for Communion by keeping my body and mind free from every stain of impurity, and my heart and tongue from every uncharitable thought and word? Do I try, at least on my Communion days, to make Christ live in me, in my mind, in my speech, in my whole behaviour? Do I try as often as it lies in me to begin the day with the Mass? And while at Mass, do I try to stand as Mary stood at the foot of the Cross?

2.

"Behold I am with you all days, even to the consummation of the world."

Christ lives in, and continues His saving mission through His Church — His Vicar on earth, His Bishops, His Priests. Through them He teaches us, sanctifies us, He guides us.

Do I see Christ alone in my Ecclesiastical Superiors? Am I obedient to them as to Christ, or do I resist and criticize them instead of laying the matter, if need be, before higher Superiors? Do I love and trust the Church as my Mother? Am I a loyal Catholic defending all that the Church defends, and condemning what she condemns? Do I realize that disloyalty to the Church is disloyalty to Christ? "Whoever heareth you, heareth Me, and whoever despiseth you, despiseth Me."

III
CHRISTIAN LIFE

Its splendour: Truth of Faith, of Life, of Speech

All life manifests itself by acts. We live by Christ, if our life is like His. He is Light and Truth. Our soul, then, must be a palace of light with no dark corners or screens in it.

1.

"Walk as children of the light."

Our Faith is a mine of inexhaustible riches. It is a lamp to guide our steps; a torch to dispel the darkness that lies in the souls of our fellowmen.

Am I deeply attached to my Catholic Faith? Do I esteem it above all earthly treasures? Do I keep it secure from the doubts and dangers of unbelief and impiety? What means do I use to increase my knowledge of it? Do I seek to impart it to others?

2.

"That doing the truth in charity we may in all things grow up in Him Who is the head, Christ."

Our life must be expression of our Faith. We must all be martyrs, witnesses for Christ. Every moment of our life we are, as it were, in the witness-box, with the world around us. Every word, every deed of ours is a piece of evidence for or against Christ.

Am I straight and sincere with God, without mental subterfuge and deceit? Do I try to justify actions that are in His eyes unjustifiable? Do I seek to appear in the eyes of my neighbour other, or better, than I am? Am I true to the tenets of my Faith and to my duties as a Catholic? Do I seek to make Catholic ideals and principles supreme in my life? Am I faithful to my particular duties, in spite of temptations and the bad example of others? Am I obedient to God's voice and inspirations?

3.

"Let your speech be yea, yea; no, no."

The Church teaches us that God's highest perfection is His Truth, because truth is the basis of all goodness. Our Lord speaks of the devil as "the father of lies," for untruth is the basis and ground of all wickedness.

Am I, out of fear of man, afraid of acknowledging what I really believe or what I have actually done? Do I ever state as true what I know is not so? Do I, in my speech, indulge in deliberate exaggerations and untruths, especially concerning others? Without saying what is clearly untrue, am I not perhaps, fond of crooked ways of speech, which I know will produce false impressions, and which are the worst kind of lie?

IV
CHRISTIAN LIFE

Its Beauty: Chastity

Purity is youth's peculiar virtue. It is the rock that supports the edifice of a young man's physical, intellectual and moral life.

1.

Excellence of Purity :—

1) Purity makes us dear to Christ and to our Lady.

2) Our body is sacred, being temple of the Holy Spirit, a member of Christ, and often the living tabernacle of Christ's immaculate Body.

3) Purity gives light to our mind, love to our heart, strength to our will and imparts freshness and beauty to our very body.

Do I greatly esteem this beautiful virtue? Do I look upon it as the great preservative of my whole life? Do I really and seriously take every care to keep it intact?

2.

Means to keep our purity untarnished :—

1) Correct ideas.

Chastity before marriage, during married life, when circumstances demand it, or even throughout one's life, if called to it, is a matter of will. Difficulties are brought about not by any need of nature, but by morbid thinking, bad reading, and unclean environment. On the other hand, to be pure does not mean to be free from temptations, but to control oneself in such a way as to avoid deliberately doing, desiring, or approving anything that is unlawful, or anything that tends to excite to what is unlawful.

2) Self-control.

Constant watch over our senses and especially our eyes, our thoughts and our imagination, our manners in dealing with others and with ourselves.

Careful avoidance of any reading that stains the mind or rouses passion; of any bad companion, of any improper or dangerous amusement.

3) Prompt and uncompromising resistance to the first prompting of the flesh, of bad companions, of Satan.

4) Prayer, and especially, prompt recourse to our Lady;
Frequent Communion;
Hard work and the practice of little acts of mortification for the love of Jesus.

Am I fully convinced that, with God's help, I can be pure in body and mind? Do I fight immediately and uncompromisingly against temptations? Do I mortify my senses, especially the eyes, thus to cut off the occasion of many an evil thought? Do I carefully avoid as poison bad books, bad companions, bad talk?

"Blessed are the pure for they shall see God."

V

CHRISTIAN LIFE

Its Distinctive Mark: Charity

"By this shall all men know that you are my disciples, if you have love one for another."[1] This love is shown in gratitude, kindness and sympathy.

1.

Excellence of Gratitude:—

"Ungrateful" is the bitterest taunt to a man of honour. But gratitude in a Christian rises higher: we read of Christ as often *giving thanks.*

We must be grateful to our benefactors: a hearty 'thank you,' even for the least favour; to our teachers and superiors: we must second their efforts to better us; above all, to our parents: by openness and dutiful love.

Am I mindful of the favours done to me? or do I return evil for good? Do I speak ill of my superiors and teachers and rise against their authority instead of co-operating with them? Am I

1. John xiii, 35.

frank with my parents? Do I obey and study hard, to please them now and be able one day, if need be, to support them?

2.

Kindness distinguishes the true Christian :—

We must bear with one another; for who is free from faults and defects? As all need help, we must not grudge it to others. But true union of mind and heart marks the followers of Him Who prayed "that they all may be as one, as Thou, Father, in Me and I in Thee ... that the world may believe that Thou hast sent Me."

We must be kind to all—friends and enemies, sinners and unbelievers too, for they are, or are to be, the children of God, the brothers of Christ, and co-heirs to Heaven.

Do I treat all as my brethren? Am I on good terms with all? Is my heart free from jealousy, hatred and revenge? Does my tongue speak well or ill of others; abstain from abuse and slander? Do I lend a helping hand to others, or do I fight, and cause pain? Am I a sower of discord or a maker of peace?

3.

Sympathy is the flower of Charity :—

Sympathy with those in sorrow or suffering proves that mankind is one family. If any one part of our body is hurt, all the others feel for it and hasten to its aid. But we are all members of Christ.

Works of mercy not merely characterized the Heart of Christ, but He makes them the standard at the Last Judgement. "Amen I say to you, as long as you did it to one of these My least brethren, you did it to Me." No wonder the Saints looked upon it as a favour to be able to relieve others.

Do I feel and show sympathy to those in pain or poverty? Or do I meanly rejoice in their woe? Do I see Christ in my suffering brethren, and seek to relieve them, as best I can?

F. HEAVENWARDS

I

THE ORIENTATION OF THE SOUL

—TAKE TO THE RIGHT—

We are constantly moving towards eternity, and we must make sure of the right way.

The right way to God :—

"*Keep the commandments;*" i. e., Obedience to

1) the Commandments of God ;
2) the Precepts of Holy Church ;
3) the orders of our Parents and Superiors ;
4) the duties of our state of life.

Means to walk constantly on the right road to God :—

Conquer thyself, i. e., deny thyself by constantly

1) performing diligently your duties ;
2) obeying your Superiors ;
3) being kind and considerate ;
4) conquering your whims and passions.

"Enter ye at the narrow gate, for wide is the gate and broad is the way that leadeth to destruction and many there are who go in thereat. How narrow is the gate that leadeth to life : and few there are that find it."[1]

II

THE ORIENTATION OF THE SOUL

—KEEP STRAIGHT ON—

There is but one real evil : sin, i. e., disobedience to God's Holy Will and to the will of those that hold His place, misuse of our senses and of our faculties and of other created things.

Wrong attitudes, i. e., attitudes that will gradually lead us to offend God grievously :—

1) to seek what pleases, forgetful of God or even in defiance of His law, and with no consideration for others ;

1. Matt. vii, 13, 14.

2) to be habitually lazy and easy-going;
3) to shirk unpleasant duties and shrink from hard tbings;
4) to follow one's caprices and one's independent notions as to what is right or wrong.

How to fight them :—

1) Be on your guard against your peculiar wrong attitude;
2) don't yield to it: "that way lies Hell;"
3) drive, rather, to the opposite way.

III

THE SOUL'S LIFE

I. Purity :—

1) Purity of eyes, refusing to look at or read deliberately anything improper;
2) Purity of body, observing modesty of look and touch even with oneself;
3) Purity of mind and imagination, banishing promptly any evil thought;
4) Purity of heart, allowing no improper affection to ente into it;
5) Purity of manners, as behoves a son of the Immaculate Mother of God.

II. Truthfulness :—

1) Truthfulness of speech:
   no lies, no half-truths, no exaggerations;
   open and straight with all: neither shy nor sly.
2) Truthfulness of behaviour:
   no hypocrisy;
   no human respect.
3) Truthfulness of life:
   be true to one's conscience, one's duties, one's vocation, one's Faith.

III. Love :—

1) Be patient and kind, giving way to neither jealousy nor anger; nor brooding over wrongs;
2) Think and speak well of others;
3) Be sympathetic and self-sacrificing;
4) Be zealous for the welfare of souls redeemed by Christ.

SCHEMES FOR RETREATS

SCHEMES FOR AN EIGHT DAYS' RETREAT

I

EVE OF THE RETREAT

THE DAY OF PREPARATION

Patron Saint . . . . *St. Ignatius.*

Maxim . . . . "*I will lure her into the wilderness and I will speak to her heart.*"

Ejaculatory Prayer—"*Here am I: for Thou didst call me.*"

Consideration: Introduction, pp. 1-6.

Spiritual Reading —*The Spiritual Exercises*, General Aim and Structure pp. 1-10.
Annotations i, iii, v, xi-xiii, x, pp. 11-32.
Imitation of Christ, i, 20; ii, 2.

FIRST DAY

THE DAY OF SELF-ORIENTING

Patron Saint . . . . *St. Francis Xavier.*

Maxim . . . . "*What doth it profit a man, if he gain the whole world and suffer the loss of his own soul?*"

Ejaculatory Prayer—"*Good Master, what shall I do that I may receive life everlasting?*"

First Exercise: Godwards, or the End of Man, pp. 7-11.

Second Exercise: Self-control, or the End of Creatures, pp. 12-7.

Consideration: Our Religious Vocation, pp. 363-4.

Third Exercise: The Three Sins, pp. 18-24.

Spiritual Reading —*The Spiritual Exercises*, Principle and Foundation, pp. 34-8.
The Additions, pp. 58-65.
Imitation of Christ, iii, 9, 10.

SECOND DAY

The Day of Compunction

Patron Saint . . . . *St Peter.*

Maxim . . . . *What have I done for Christ? What am I doing for Christ? What ought I to do for Christ?*

Ejaculatory Prayer—"*O God, be merciful to me a sinner.*"

First Exercise: Our Sins, pp. 25-9.

Second Exercise: Repetition of I and II Exercises with Triple Colloquy, pp. 30-5.

Consideration: Poverty, pp. 364-5.

Third Exercise: Hell, pp. 36-43.

Spiritual Reading —*The Spiritual Exercises*, Object of the First Week, pp. 47-8.
Examens of Conscience, pp. 39-46.
Imitation of Christ, i, 22; iii, 14.

THIRD DAY

The Day of Conversion

Patron Saint . . . . *St Augustine.*

Maxim . . . . "*Be mindful..... from whence thou art fallen: and do penance.... or else I come to thee and I will move thy candlestick out of its place.*"

Ejaculatory Prayer —"*Father, I have sinned.*"

First Exercise: Venial Sin, pp. 44-7.

Second Exercise: Death and Judgement, pp. 52-6.

Consideration: Chastity, pp. 365-6.

Third Exercise: The Prodigal, pp. 57-63.

Spiritual Reading —*The Spiritual Exercises*, Rules for the discernment of spirits, pp. 157-69.
Imitation of Christ, iii, 52; i, 25.

FOURTH DAY

The Day of Fervour

Patron Saint . . . . *St Paul.*

Maxim . . . . "*He must reign, until He hath put all His enemies under His feet.*"

Ejaculatory Prayers—"*My Lord and my God.*"
"*I will follow Thee whithersoever Thou goest.*"

First Exercise: The Kingdom of Christ, pp. 65-76.
Second Exercise: The Incarnation, pp. 79-84.
Consideration: Obedience and observance of the Rule, pp. 366-8.
Third Exercise: The Nativity, pp. 87-90.

Spiritual Reading —*The Spiritual Exercises*, The Mysteries of the Life of Christ our Lord, pp. 136-56.
Imitation of Christ, ii, 1, 7, 8.

FIFTH DAY

The Day of Generosity

Patron Saint . . . . *St Ignatius.*

Maxim . . . "*If any man will come after Me, let him deny himself, and take up his cross daily, and follow Me.*"

Ejaculatory Prayers—"*To suffer and be despised with Thee!*"
"*I desire and choose poverty with Christ poor, rather than riches; reproaches with Christ laden therewith, rather than honours.*"

First Exercise: Two Standards, pp. 116-23.
Second Exercise: Three Classes, pp. 125-9.
Consideration: Three Modes of Humility, pp. 130-3.
Third Exercise: Reform, pp. 134-6.

Spiritual Reading —*The Spiritual Exercises*, The Election and Reform, pp. 96-101.
Imitation of Christ, iii, 12, 54.

SIXTH DAY

THE DAY OF LOVING COMPANIONSHIP

Patron Saint . . . . *St. John the Evangelist.*
Maxim . . . . *"Come after Me."*
Ejaculatory Prayer — *"Lord, to whom shall we go? Thou hast the words of eternal life."*

First Exercise: Vocation of the Apostles, pp. 155-8.
Second Exercise: The Sermon on the Mount, pp. 161-8.
Consideration: Mental Prayer, pp. 368-9.
Third Exercise: Christ upon the Waters, pp. 171-5.
Spiritual Reading: — *The Spiritual Exercises,* Three Modes of Prayer, pp. 127-35.
Imitation of Christ, ii, 8; iii, 4.

SEVENTH DAY

THE DAY OF LOVING COMPASSION

Patron Saint . . . . *St. Francis of Assisi.*
Maxims . . . . *"He loved me and delivered Himself for me."*
"With Christ I am nailed to the cross; it is no longer I that live, but Christ that liveth in me."
Ejaculatory Prayer — *Fac ut portem Christi mortem,*
Passionis fac consortem,
Et plagas recolere.

First Exercise: In the Cenacle, pp. 201-15.
Second Exercise: In the Garden of Gethsemane, pp. 217-22.
Consideration: Fraternal Charity, pp. 369-70.
Third Exercise: The King on His Throne, pp. 251-8.
Spiritual Reading: — *The Spiritual Exercises*, Rules for ordering oneself in the matter of food, pp. 110-2.
Fruit of the Third Week, pp. 102-6.
Imitation of Christ, ii, 11, 12.

EIGHTH DAY

THE DAY OF JOYFUL UNION

Patron Saint . . . . *St. Joseph.*

Maxim . . . . "*Remain in Me and I in You.*"

Ejaculatory prayer —"*Yea, Lord, Thou knowest that I love Thee.*"

First Exercise: The Resurrection, pp. 291-9.

Second Exercise: On the Shore of Gennesaret, pp. 323-6.

Consideration: "Go and teach," pp. 370-1.

Third Exercise: Contemplation for obtaining love, pp. 347-59.

Spiritual Reading —*The Spiritual Exercises*, Rules for thinking with the Church, pp. 174-82.

Imitation of Christ, iii, 5, 6, 31.

II

EVE OF THE RETREAT

THE DAY OF PREPARATION

Patron Saint . . . . *St Margaret Mary.*

Maxims . . . . "*I will lure her into the wilderness and I will speak to her heart.*"

"*Shut the door upon thyself, and call to thee Jesus thy beloved. Stay with Him in thy cell, for thou shalt not find so great peace anywhere else.*"

Ejaculatory Prayer—"*Here am I: for Thou didst call me.*"

Consideration: Introduction, pp. 1-6.

Spiritual Reading —*The Spiritual Exercises*, General Aim and Structure of the Spiritual Exercises, pp. 1-10.

Annotations i, iii, v, xi-xiii, x, pp. 11-32d.

Imitation of Christ, i, 20; ii, 22; iii, 2.

FIRST DAY

THE DAY OF SELF-ORIENTING

Patron Saint . . . . *St Francis Xavier.*

Maxim . . . . "*What doth it profit a man, if he gain the whole world and suffer the loss of his own soul?*"

Ejaculatory Prayer—"*Good Master, what shall I do that I may receive life everlasting?*"

First Exercise: Godwards, or the End of Man, pp. 7-11.

Second Exercise: Self-control, or the End of Creatures, pp. 12-17.

Consideration: "You are the Temple of God." pp. 372-3.

Third Exercise: The Three Sins, pp. 18-24.

Spiritual Reading —*The Spiritual Exercises*, Principle and Foundation, pp. 34-8.

The Additions, pp. 58-65.

Imitation of Christ, iii, 9, 33.

SECOND DAY

The Day of Compunction

Patron Saint . . . . *St Mary Magdalene.*

Maxim . . . . *What have I done for Christ? What am I doing for Christ? What ought I to do for Christ?*

Ejaculatory Prayer —" *O God, be merciful to me a sinner.*"

First Exercise: Our Sins, pp. 25-9.
Second Exercise: Hell, pp. 36-43.
Consideration: The Purification of the Temple, p. 373.
Third Exercise: Tepidity, pp. 48-51.

Spiritual Reading —*The Spiritual Exercises*, Object of the First Week, pp. 47-8.
Examens of Conscience, pp. 39-46.
Imitation of Christ, i, 22, 111, 4.

THIRD DAY

The Day of Conversion

Patron Saint . . . . *St Teresa.*

Maxim . . . . "*I know thy works, that thou art neither cold nor hot. I would thou wert cold, or hot. But because thou art lukewarm, and neither cold nor hot, I will begin to vomit thee out of My mouth.*"

Ejaculatory Prayer — "*Lord, if Thou wilt, Thou canst make me clean.*"

First Exercise: Death and Judgement pp. 52-6.
Second Exercise: The Prodigal son, pp. 57 63.
Consideration: The Foundations of God's Temple, p. 374.
Third Exercise: The Kingdom of Christ, pp. 65-76.

Spiritual Reading —*The Spiritual Exercises*, Rules for the discernment of spirits, pp. 157-69.
Imitation of Christ, iii, 52.

FOURTH DAY

A Day at Nazareth

Patron Saint . . . . *St Joseph.*

Maxims . . . . "*My food is to do the will of Him that sent Me.*"

"*He is truly great who is great in charity.*"

"*And he is truly learned who doeth the Will of God, and renounceth his own will.*"

Ejaculatory Prayer—"*Jesus, Mary and Joseph.*"

First Exercise: Nazareth, Interior Life, pp. 105-9.
Second Exercise: Nazareth, Life of Love, pp. 109-11.
Consideration: The Structure of God's Temple, p. 375.
Third Exercise: Nazareth, Life of Hardship, pp. 112-4.

Spiritual Reading — *The Spiritual Exercises*, The Mysteries of the Life of Christ our Lord, pp. 136-56.

Imitation of Christ, ii, 1, 7, 8.

FIFTH DAY

The Day of Generosity

Patron Saint . . . . *St Ignatius.*

Maxim . . . . "*If any man will come after Me, let him deny himself, and take up his cross daily, and follow Me.*"

Ejaculatory Prayers — "*To suffer and be despised with Thee.*"

"*I will follow Thee withersoever Thou goest.*"

First Exercise: Two Standards, pp. 116-23.
Second Exercise: Three Classes, pp. 125-9.
Consideration: Three Modes of Humility, pp. 130-3.
Third Exercise: Reform pp. 134-6.

Spiritual Reading —*The Spiritual Exercises*, The Election and Reform, pp. 96-101.

Imitation of Christ, iii, 12, 54.

SIXTH AND SEVENTH DAYS

WITH OUR SUFFERING LORD

Patron Saint . . . . *St John the Evangelist.*

Maxim . . . . "*He loved me and delivered Himself for me.*"

Ejaculatory Prayers—Versicles from the *Anima Christi*, or the *Stabat Mater.*

SIXTH DAY

First Exercise: In the Cenacle, pp. 201-15.

Second Exercise: In the Garden of Gethsemane, 217-22.

Consideration: The Wood for the Sacrifice and the Incense of Prayer, pp. 375-6.

Third Exercise: The King betrayed and deserted, pp. 225-30.

SEVENTH DAY

First Exercise: King and Victim, pp. 239-49.

Second Exercise: The King on His Throne, pp. 251-8.

Consideration: The Grounds, p. 376.

Third Exercise: The Sermon on the Cross, pp. 261-76.

Spiritual Reading —*The Spiritual Exercises*, Rules for ordering oneself in the matter of food, pp. 110-2. Three Modes of Prayer, pp. 127-35.
Imitation of Christ, ii, 11, 12; iv, 1-4.

EIGHTH DAY

THE DAY OF JOYFUL UNION

Patron Saint . . . . *St Therese of the Infant Jesus.*

Maxim . . . . "*Thou shalt love the Lord thy God with thy whole heart and with thy whole soul and with thy whole mind. This is the greatest and first commandment.*"

Ejaculatory Prayer —"*Give me Thy love and grace, for this is enough for me.*"

First Exercise: The Resurrection, pp. 291-9.

Second Exercise: Contemplation for obtaining love, pp. 347-52.

Consideration: The Dedication of the Temple, p. 377.

Third Exercise: Contemplation for obtaining love, pp. 353-9.

Spiritual Reading —*The Spiritual Exercises*, Rules for thinking with the Church, pp. 174-82.
Imitation of Christ, iii, 5, 6, 22.

SCHEMES FOR A FIVE DAYS' RETREAT

I

EVE OF THE RETREAT

The Day of Preparation

Patron Saint . . . . *St Ignatius.*

Maxim . . . . "*Come apart into a desert place, and rest a little.*"

Ejaculatory Prayer —"*Here am I: for Thou didst call me.*"

Consideration: Introduction, pp. 1-6.

Spiritual Reading —*The Spiritual Exercises*, General Aim and Structure of the Spiritual Exercises, pp. 1-10.
Annotations i, iii, v, xi-xiii, x, pp. 11-32.
Imitation of Christ, i, 20.

FIRST DAY

The Day of Self-orienting

Patron Saint . . . . *St Francis Xavier.*

Maxim . . . . "*What doth it profit a man, if he gain the whole world and suffer the loss of his own soul?*"

Ejaculatory Prayer —"*Good Master, what shall I do that I may receive life everlasting?*"

First Exercise: Godwards, or the End of Man, pp. 7-11.

Second Exercise: Self-control, or the End of Creatures, pp. 12-7.

Consideration: The purification of a Priest's heart, p. 378.

Third Exercise: The Three Sins, pp. 18-24.

Spiritual Reading —*The Spiritual Exercises*, Principle and Foundation, pp. 34-8.
The Additions, pp, 58-65.
Imitation of Christ, iii, 9.

SECOND DAY

THE DAY OF COMPUNCTION

Patron Saint . . . . *St Peter.*

Maxim . . . . *What have I done for Christ? What am I doing for Christ? What ought I to do for Christ?*

Ejaculatory Prayer—"*O God, be merciful to me a sinner.*"

First Exercise: Our Sins, pp. 25-9.

Second Exercise: Repetition of I and II Exercises with Triple Colloquy, pp. 30-5.

Consideration: The prayer of a Priest, pp. 378-9.

Third Exercise: Hell, pp. 36-43.

Spiritual Reading:—*The Spiritual Exercises,* Object of the First Week pp. 47-8.
Examens of Conscience, pp. 39-46.
Imitation of Christ, i, 22.

THIRD DAY

THE DAY OF CONVERSION

Patron Saint . . . . *St Augustine.*

Maxim . . . . "*Be mindful...from whence thou art fallen: and do penance...or else I come to thee and I will move thy candlestick out of its place.*"

Ejaculatory Prayers—"*Father, I have sinned.*"
"*Have mercy on me, O God, according to Thy great mercy.*"

First Exercise: Venial Sin, pp. 44-7.

Second Exercise: Death and Judgement, pp. 52-6.

Consideration: The sanctification of a Priest's activities, pp. 379-80.

Third Exercise: The Prodigal, pp. 57-63.

Spiritual Reading:—*The Spiritual Exercises,* Rules for discernment of spirits, pp. 157-69.

FOURTH DAY

The Day of Fervour

Patron Saint . . . . *St Paul.*

Maxims . . . . *"Remain in Me and I in you."*

"As the branch cannot bear fruit of itself, unless it abide in the vine, so neither can you, unless you abide in Me."

Ejaculatory Prayer—*"My Lord and my God."*

First Exercise: The Kingdom of Christ, pp. 65-76.
Second Exercise: The Incarnation, pp. 79-84.
Consideration: A Priest's immolations, pp. 380-1.
Third Exercise: Nazareth, pp. 105-14.

Spiritual Reading: —*The Spiritual Exercises*, Exercises of the Fourth Day of the Second Week, pp. 77-95.

Imitation of Christ, ii, I.

FIFTH DAY

The Day of Love

Patron Saint . . . . *St Francis of Assisi.*

Maxim . . . . *Christus Crucifixus liber vitae et solutio omnium difficultatum.*

Ejaculatory Prayers—Versicles from the *Anima Christi* or the *Stabat Mater.*

First Exercise: In the Cenacle, pp. 201-15.
Second Exercise: The King on His Throne, pp. 251-8.
Consideration: Reform, pp. 134-6.
Third Exercise: The Resurrection, pp. 291-9.

Spiritual Reading: —*The Spiritual Exercises*, Three Modes of Prayer, pp. 127-35.

Rules for thinking with the Church, pp. 174-82.

Imitation of Christ, ii, 12.

II

EVE OF THE RETREAT

THE DAY OF PREPARATION

Patron Saint . . . . *St Ignatius.*

Maxims . . . . *"Come apart into a desert place, and rest a little."*

"O taste and see that the Lord is sweet."

Ejaculatory Prayer - *"Here am I, for Thou did'st call me."*

Consideration : Introduction, pp. 1-6.

Spiritual Reading —*The Spiritual Exercises,* General Aim and Structure of the Spiritual Exercises, pp. 1-10.

Annotations i, iii, v, xi-xiii, x, pp. 11-32.

Imitation of Christ, i, 20.

FIRST DAY

THE DAY OF SELF-ORIENTING

Patron Saint . . . . *St Francis Xavier.*

Maxim . . . . *"What doth it profit a man, if he gain the whole world and suffer the loss of his own soul?"*

Ejaculatory Prayer —*Good Master, what shall I do that I may receive life everlasting?*

First Exercise : Godwards, or the End of Man, pp. 7-11.

Second Exercise : Self-control, or the End of Creatures, pp. 12-7.

Consideration : Sacrificium labiorum, pp. 382-3.

Third Exercise : Three Sins, pp. 18-24.

Spiritual Reading —*The Spiritual Exercises,* Principle and Foundation, pp. 34-48.

The Additions, pp. 58-65.

Imitation of Christ, iii, 9.

SECOND DAY

THE DAY OF COMPUNCTION

Patron Saint . . . . *St Peter.*

Maxim . . . . *What have I done for Christ? What am I doing for Christ? What ought I to do for Christ?*

Ejaculatory Prayer – "*O God, be merciful to me a sinner.*"

First Exercise: Our Sins, pp. 25-9.
Second Exercise: Repetition of I and II Exercises with Triple Colloquy, pp. 30-5.
Consideration: Sacrificium cordis et corporis, pp. 383-5.
Third Exercise: Hell, pp. 36-43.

Spiritual Reading: —*The Spiritual Exercises*, Object of the First Week, pp. 47-8.
Examens of Conscience, pp. 39-46.
Imitation of Christ, i, 22.

THIRD DAY

THE DAY OF CONVERSION

Patron Saint . . . . *St Augustine.*

Maxim . . . . "*Be mindful ... from whence thou art fallen: and do penance ... or else I come to thee and I will move thy candlestick out of its place.*"

Ejaculatory Prayers — "*Father, I have sinned.*"
"*Create a clean heart in me, O God: and renew a right spirit within my bowels.*"

First Exercise: Venial Sin, pp. 44-7.
Second Exercise: Death and Judgement pp. 52-6.
Consideration: Sacrificium Christi, pp. 385-6.
Third Exercise: The Kingdom of Christ, pp. 65-76.

Spiritual Reading: —*The Spiritual Exercises*, Rules for discernment of spirits, pp. 157-69.

FOURTH DAY

THE DAY OF FERVOUR

Patron Saint . . . . *St Paul.*

Maxim . . . . "*Remain in me and I in you.*"

Ejaculatory Prayer —"*My Lord and my God.*"

First Exercise: The Nativity, pp. 87-90

Second Exercise: Nazareth, pp. 105-14.

Consideration: Opus Christi, pp. 386-7.

Third Exercise: The Sermon on the Mount, pp. 161-168.

Spiritual Reading —*The Spiritual Exercises*, Exercises of the Fourth Day of the Second Week, pp. 77-95,

Imitation of Christ, ii, 1.

FIFTH DAY

THE DAY OF LOVE

Patron Saint . . . . *St Francis of Assisi.*

Maxim . . . . *Christus Crucifixus liber vitae et solutio omnium difficultatum.*

Ejaculatory Prayers—Versicles from the *Anima Christi*, or the *Stabat Mater.*

First Exercise: In the Cenacle, 201-15.

Second Exercise: The Crucifixion, pp. 251-8.

Consideration: Reform, pp. 134-6.

Third Exercise: On the Mount of Galilee, pp. 328-31.

Spiritual Reading —*The Spiritual Exercises*, Three Modes of Prayer, pp. 127-35.

Rules for thinking with the Church, pp. 174-82.

Imitation of Christ, ii, 12.

SCHEMES FOR A THREE DAYS' RETREAT

I

EVE OF THE RETREAT

THE DAY OF PREPARATION

Patron Saint . . . . *St Therese of the Infant Jesus.*

Maxims . . . . *"O taste and see that the Lord is sweet."*

"Work while it is day; for the night cometh when no man can work."

Ejaculatory Prayer — *"Here am I, for Thou didst call me."*

"Speak, O Lord, for Thy servant heareth."

Consideration: Introduction, pp. 1-6.

Spiritual Reading — *Imitation of Christ*, i, 20.

FIRST DAY

THE ORIENTING OF THE SOUL

Patron Saint . . . . *St Stanislaus Kostka.*

Maxims . . . . *"I was not born for the things of this world, but for those of eternity."*

"What doth it profit a man, if he gain the whole world and suffer the loss of his own soul?

Ejaculatory Prayer — *"Not what I will, but what Thou wilt."*

First Exercise: Godwards, or the End of Man, pp. 7-11.

Second Exercise: Self-control, or the End of Creatures, pp. 12-7.

Consideration: Christian Life: its splendour, pp. 390-1.

Third Exercise: The Three Sins, pp. 18-24.

Spiritual Reading —*Imitation of Christ*, i, 1.

SECOND DAY

The Purification of the Soul

Patron Saint . . . . *St Aloysius Gonzaga.*

Maxims . . . . *"Every mortal sin crucifies Christ again."*

"There are three depths which no human mind can sound: the depth of our sinfulness, the depth of our unworthiness, the depth of our nothingness."

Ejaculatory Prayer —*"Lord, be merciful to me a sinner."*

First Exercise: Hell, pp. 36-43.
Second Exercise: Death and Judgement, pp. 52-6.
Consideration: Christian Life: its Beauty, pp. 391-2.
Third Exercise: The Prodigal, pp. 57-63.

Spiritual Reading: *Imitation of Christ*, i, 23.

THIRD DAY

The Life of the Soul

Patron Saint . . . . *St John Berchmans.*

Maxim . . . . *"I am the Way, the Truth and the Life."*

Ejaculatory Prayer —*"Lord, to whom shall we go? Thou hast the words of eternal life."*

First Exercise: The Kingdom of Christ, pp. 65-76.
Second Exercise: Nazareth, pp. 105-14.
Consideration: Christian Life: its distinctive mark, pp. 392-3.
Third Exercise: The King on His Throne, pp. 251-8.

Spiritual Reading: —*Imitation of Christ* i, 8.

II

EVE OF THE RETREAT

The Day of Preparation

Patron Saint . . . . *St Therese of the Infant Jesus.*

Maxims . . . . *"O taste and see that the Lord is sweet."*

"I walked down the valley of silence,
Down the deep, silent valley alone,
And I heard the sound of no footsteps
Around me, save God's and my own."

Ejaculatory Prayer—*"Here am I, for Thou didst call me."*

Consideration: Introduction, pp. 1-6.

Spiritual Reading:—*Imitation of Christ*, i, 20.

FIRST DAY

The Orienting of the Soul

Patron Saint . . . . *St Agnes.*

Maxims . . . . *"Beware! In the heyday of youth one is as our first parents in Paradise, moving in a world of beauty and goodness, but within easy reach of the forbidden fruit."*

"The service of God is the touchstone of genuine piety."

Ejaculatory Prayer —*"Not what I will, but what Thou wilt."*

First Exercise: Godwards, or the End of Man, pp. 7-11.

Second Exercise: Self-control, or the End of Creatures, pp. 12-17.

Consideration: "Take to the right," p. 394.

Third Exercise: The Three Sins, pp. 18-24.

Spiritual Reading —*Imitation of Christ*, i, 1.

SECOND DAY

The Orienting of the Soul

Patron Saint . . . . *St Mary Magdalene.*

Maxim . . . . *"Behold the Heart which has loved men so much and which receives in return for the most part nothing but ingratitude."*

Ejaculatory Prayer —*"My Jesus, mercy!"*

First Exercise: Hell, pp. 36-43.
Second Exercise: Venial Sin, pp. 44-47.
Consideration: "Keep straight on," pp. 394-5.
Third Exercise: Death and Judgement, pp. 52-6.

Spiritual Reading —*Imitation of Christ*, iii, 52.

THIRD DAY

The Life of the Soul

Patron Saint . . . . *St Therese of the Infant Jesus.*

Maxim . . . . *"I can only scatter flowers, eagerly catching at any slight sacrifice in word or look, doing for Thy sake even the very least things."* (The Little Flower to our Lord).

Ejaculatory Prayer —*"Jesus, meek and humble of heart, make my heart like unto Thine."*

First Exercise: The Kingdom of Christ, pp. 65-76.
Second Exercise: Nazareth, pp. 105-114.
Consideration: The manifestations of life, p. 395.
Third Exercise: The King on His Throne, pp. 251-8.

Spiritual Reading: —*Imitation of Christ*, i, 8.

A SELECT LIST OF BOOKS FOR RETREAT TIME

First Week

Man	Fr N. J. Scott, S. J.	Sands & Co.
Earth to Heaven	Bishop Vaughan	Sands & Co.
Sin and its Consequences	Card. Manning	B. O. & W.
Venial Sin	Bishop Vaughan	B. O. & W.
Our Failings	Fr S. Von Oer, O. S. B.	Herder.

Second, Third and Fourth Weeks in general

The Christ, the Son of God	Abbé Fouard	Longmans.
Life of Christ	Fr Meschler, S. J.	Herder.
Life of Christ	G. Papini	Hod. & Stou.
The.Personality of Christ	Abbot Vonier, O. S. B.	Longmans.
Hail! Full of Grace	Mother M. Loyola	
Our Divine Saviour	Bishop Hedley	B. O. & W.

Second Week

The Soldier of Christ	Mother M. Loyola	B. O. & W.
The Mystery of the Incarnation	Fr E. Hugon, O. P.	The Faith Press.
The Prince of Peace	Archbp. Goodier	B. O. & W.

Third Week

Our Lord's Last Discourses (John xiii-xviii)	Abbé Nouvelle	B. O. & W.
The History of the Sacred Passion	Fr Luis de la Palma, S. J.	B. O. & W.
The Watches of the Sacred Passion	Fr Gallwey, S. J.	Art. & Book Co.
The Crown of Sorrow	Archbp. Goodier	B. O. & W.
The Man of Sorrow	Fr R. Eaton	Sands & Co.

Fourth Week

The Forty Days	Fr R. Eaton	B. O. & W.
The Risen Jesus	Archbp. Goodier	
The Life of the World to come	Abbot Vonier, O. S. B.	B. O. & W.
Life Everlasting	Bishop Vaughan	B. O. & W.

Life Everlasting	Bishop Vaughan	B. O. & W.

Contemplation for obtaining love

The Ladder of Ascent to God	Blessed Bellarmine	B. O. & W.
Living with God	Fr R. Plus, S. J.	B. O. & W.
Life of Union with our Lord	Abbé Maucourant	B. O. & W.
The Forgotten Paraclete	Bishop Landrieux	B. O. & W.
Way of Interior Peace	Fr De Lehen, S. J.	Benziger.

General Spiritual Reading—

A) For Religious Persons

Waters that Go Softly	Fr Jos. Rickaby, S. J.	B. O. & W.
Three Fundamental Principles	Fr Meschler, S. J.	Herder.
The Grace of Interior Prayer	Fr Poulain, S. J.	Kegan.
Some Principles & Practices of the Spiritual Life	Fr Maturin	Longmans.
Self-knowledge and Self-discipline	Fr Maturin	Longmans.
The Science of the Spiritual Life	Fr Clare, S. J.	Manresa Press.
Holy Wisdom	Fr A. Baker, O. S. B.	B. O. & W.
Religio Religiosi	Card. Gasquet, O. S. B.	B. O. & W.
Spiritual Treatises	Venerable de Blois	B. O. & W.
Sponsa Christi	Mother St Paul	Longmans.
Delight in the Lord	Fr Considine, S. J.	B. O. & W.
Autobiography	St Teresa	Paulist Press.
The Ascent of Mount Carmel	St John of the Cross	Benziger.

B) For Priests and Ecclesiastical Students

The Eternal Priesthood	Card. Manning	B. O. & W.
Jesus living in the Priest	Fr Millet, S. J.	Benziger.
The true Apostolate	Abbot Chautard	Herder.
Ecclesiastical Training	Card. Bourne	B. O. & W.
The Young Apostle	Fr Godfrey	B. O. & W.
Lex Levitarum	Bishop Hedley	B. O. & W.
Manuale Cursus Ascetici	Fr Aurelian, O. C. D.	Puth. Seminary.
The Mirror of Priests	Fr Aurelian, O. C. D.	Puth. Seminary.

C) For Young People

Jesus of Nazareth	Mother M. Loyola	B. O. & W.
The Soldier of Christ	Mother M. Loyola	B. O. & W.
Home for good (for girls)	Mother M. Loyola	B. O. & W.
Heavenwards	Mother M. Loyola	B. O. & W.
Facing Life	Fr R. Plus, S. J.	B. O. & W.
Living Temples	Fr Jarrett, O. P.	B. O. & W.
Ye are Christ's	Fr Jos. Rickaby, S. J.	B. O. & W.
Parting of the Ways	Fr Lucas, S. J.	Sands & Co
In the Morning of Life	Fr Lucas S. J.	B. O. & W.
Home truths for Mary's Children (for girls)	Mother M. Cecilia	B. O. & W.
More Home truths for Mary's Children	Mother M. Cecilia	B. O. & W.
Shall I be a Priest ?	Fr William Doyle, S. J.	Irish Messenger.
The Way of Youth (for young men)	Fr Alexander, O. F. M.	B. O. & W.
Talks to Boys	Fr Conroy, S. J.	Benziger.

REFECTORY READINGS

From *The Imitation of the Sacred Heart* by Fr Arnold, S. J.

I Day—Bk. I. Chaps. 1-4.
II Day—Bk. I. Chaps. 6-9, 25.
III Day—Bk. I. Chaps. 10, 12, 23, 24.
IV Day—Bk. II. Chaps. 2-8.
V Day—Bk. II. Chaps. 11-14.
VI Day—Bk. II. Chaps. 15-17, 19-21.
VII Day—Bk. III. Chaps. 3, 5, 6, 9, 13, 19-21.
VIII Day—Bk. III. Chap. 26.
Bk. II. Chaps. 22-26.

From *The Practice of Christian and Religious Perfection*
by Fr Alphonsus Rodriguez, S. J.

I Day—Religious Perfection: Vol. I, Treat. I, Chaps. 1, 2, 6, 9, 15.
II Day—Humility: Vol. II, Treat. III, Chaps. 1, 2, 5, 6, 7.
III Day—Mortification: Vol. II, Treat. I, Chaps. 2, 4, 5, 6, 7, 12.
IV Day—Prayer: Vol. I, Treat. V, Chaps. 2, 8, 9, 21, 25, 28.
V Day—Silence: Vol. II, Treat. II Chaps. 4, 5, 6, 7, 8.
VI Day—Temptations: Vol. II, Treat. IV, Chaps. 1, 6, 10, 18.
VII Day—Passion of Christ: Vol. II, Treat. VII, Chaps. 1, 2, 3, 4, 8.
VIII Day Charity: Vol. I, Treat. IV, Chaps. 1, 2, 5, 6, 7, 8, 9.

From *Manual for Interior Souls* by Fr Grou, S. J.

		CHAP.
Eve of Retreat:	Fly, keep silence, rest	18
I Day:	God is all, creatures nothing	13
	Employment of time	15
	Dignity of man	25
	Price of a Soul	35
II Day:	Fear of God	10
	Weakness and corruption of the human heart	17
	The human 'I'	29
	Faithfulness in little things	19
	The thought of eternity	40

		CHAP.
III Day:	The world	24
	The thought of death	39
	Peace of the soul	47
	Profit from our faults	20
	Trust in God	43
IV Day:	Jesus Christ	55
	Continual prayer	42
	Humility	33
	Generosity	31
	The Crib of Bethlehem	54
V Day:	Obedience	32
	Fundamental truths of interior life	48
	The interior of Jesus Christ	56
	Holiness	11
	Martha and Mary	37
VI Day:	Temptations	27
	Our conduct in temptation	28
	Spirit of Faith	22
	True virtue	2
VII Day:	The Holy Eucharist and the Cross	58
	Annihilation	30
	The Crucifix	59
VIII Day;	The love of God	44
	The love of our neighbour	23
	Purity of intention	36
	Simplicity	41
	Spiritual childhood	50
	God alone	38
	Trust in God	43
	The intention of Mary	53

From *Christ, the Life of the Soul* by Abbot Marmion

I Day—	Baptism, the Sacrament of Divine adoption	p. 152
II Day—	*Delicta quis intelligit?*	p. 169
III Day—	The Sacrament and virtue of Penance	p. 187
IV Day—	Our supernatural growth in Christ	p. 228
V Day—	*Panis vitae*	p. 279
VI Day—	Prayer.	p. 325
VII Day—	Love one another.	p. 351
VIII Day—	The mother of the Incarnate Word	p. 368

From *Growth in Holiness* by Fr Faber

I Day—Ruling Passion	Chap. 7.
II Day—Abiding Sorrow for Sin	Chap. 19.
III Day—Lukewarmness	Chap. 25.
IV Day—Prayer	Chap. 15.
V Day—Human Respect	Chap. 10.
VI Day—Temptation	Chap. 16.
VII Day—Mortification	Chap. 26.
VIII Day—Fervour	Chap. 31.

CPSIA information can be obtained
at www.ICGtesting.com
Printed in the USA
BVHW011401210319
543347BV00004B/98/P